# NEW WASICHU,

# CROSSING

Shires Press

# SHIRES✿PRESS

4869 Main Street
P.O. Box 2200
Manchester Center, VT 05255
www.northshire.com

New Wasichu, Crossing: Our Story Is Just Beginning
ḥ2014 by Gary Lindorff

ISBN: 9781605712048

***Building Community, One Book at a Time***
*A family-owned, independent bookstore in*
*Manchester Ctr., VT, since 1976 and Saratoga Springs, NY since 2013.*
*We are committed to excellence in bookselling.*
*The Northshire Bookstore's mission is to serve as a resource for*
*information, ideas, and entertainment while honoring the needs*
*of customers, staff, and community.*

Artwork and cover design by Evan Lindorff-Ellery (lindorffellery.wordpress.com)
Layout assistance by Liz Cook (liz-cook.com)

*Printed in the United States of America*

# NEW WASICHU, CROSSING:

# OUR STORY

# IS JUST BEGINNING

## Gary Lindorff

*Dedicated to my father, who planted within me the courage to trust what I know.*

These are the days of miracle and wonder, and don't cry baby, don't cry, don't cry.

—Paul Simon
"The Boy in the Bubble"

# Contents

### Part I

♦ This writing arises out of the urgency to speak truth to my tribe, the Wasichu: Earth requires our protection. We need to cross.

♦ The doppelganger, our soulful double, is returning via dreams, art, real-life encounters. It replenishes the self's memory through deep resonant self-recognition.

### Part II

♦ Crossing is a form of death; consciousness is traded for spiritual survival, but what are we crossing to?

♦ Nature responds to our remembering what it means to be a spiritual being.

♦ In an early dream I was told by a voice to become a human bridge.

♦ Who were the ancient Celts and the druids?  What do the great stone circles tells us about the people who created them?

♦ Celtic identity doesn't have to be genetically established to be embraced by a culture.

♦ Black Elk's vision is central to the rainbow warrior mentality.

# Chapter three:   Poor Wasichu

♦ A ritual that heals is a working mystery.

♦ Lack of openness to the spiritual dimensions of an illness is an illness in itself.

♦ We can cross to the energetically expressive side of things but severing the elastic bond that keeps snapping us back to the materialistic Weltanschauung is a problem.

# Chapter four:   Closing the Power Gap

♦ In the sixties we struggled with a generation gap; what stands in our way now is a power gap.

♦ To answer, *Who are we really?* it behooves us to dig deeper into the archetype of the doppelganger.

♦ What is my path as a New Wasichu?

# Chapter five:   Crossing Alive / Crossing Dead

♦ Dreams are holographic snapshots of the whole picture. Wallace Black Elk: "One little part of you is sacred." In that little part is everything.

♦ What does it mean to be in partnership with nature?

♦ Spontaneous remissions are preceded by a shift in awareness. Shifts in awareness are quantum events.

♦ The more territory one's mind stakes out in life the more one has to lose to death, the great crossing.

# Chapter six:   Dreaming and Firewalking   81

♦ I am a Wasichu trying to wake up, trying to take my power.

♦ A strong rapport with the spirit world requires utter humility and utter confidence.

♦ If life is a competition, what if nature is the loser?

♦ We all have it in us to be magical.

# Chapter seven:   Morning Star   89

♦ Jung's principle of synchronicity applies to any form of serious divination.

♦ During the firewalk we were contained by an archetypal field, in fact more than one.

♦ The attack on the World Trade Center challenges us to conduct ourselves as initiates of a new time, to cross with courage but there has to be a new thing in our cosmology that holds space and calls to us from a great distance because we aren't there yet.

# Chapter eight:   Ethos of the Road   95

♦ In shamanic healing ritual the ego has to be silenced so the spirit can do its work.

♦ Crossing the black path is part of the medicine way for the New Wasichu.

♦ There are two kinds of "mind".

♦ We might compare the duality perspective to a powerful program.

♦ Pre-historically, the psyche was Earth-centered.

♦ We will have to overhaul our relationship to power, knowledge and matter.

♦ How Native peoples kept clear of falling into duality is tricky – hence the red path.

## Chapter twelve:  End to the Blind March    147

♦ In a big dream I find myself stuck on a cliff face and discover a cluster of crystals.

♦ Healing with crystals is old and new: new to me and our culture. Shamans today are (Cynthia Bend) "remembering and reviving the ancient skills."

♦ Don Alverto Taxo (Master Shaman of Equador) explains that the time has come for the eagle to fly with the condor.

## Chapter thirteen: Like Grass in a Burned-out Forest  159

♦ The ancestral spirits would keep tabs on us but we have "divorced" our ancestors; we are spiritual orphans.

♦ Who we are at our core abides much deeper than personal or familial memory.

♦ Today's shamans are the purveyors of the cultures that need to sprout up, of which they are the harbingers.

♦ We are literally Mother Earth's (Gaia's) children; we must let our imaginations expand to embrace what this means.

## Chapter fourteen:  Believe It    173

♦ Chakras are energy fields, subtle "wheels of light"; as such they conduct cosmic and geo-energy through all the layers of the aura toward specific regions of the physical body.

♦ Earth has its own chakras.

♦ Facing death often breaks down the structures of our disbelief in alternative approaches to healing.

♦ We aren't necessarily responsible for the environment, only for ourselves.

♦ Seeing Earth as a body, both in the physical and energetic sense, is an evolution of our awareness of Earth as Mother.

## Chapter fifteen:  Going Deeper

♦ What has been happening on the stage of the middle world has been building for a long time. As the damage goes deeper, we are called to go deeper into Earth's wound, through our own wounding.

♦ Whatever needs healing becomes the pathway *to* healing.

♦ What does Jung mean by the collective unconscious and the archetype of totality, the Self?


## Chapter sixteen:  The Root Chakra

♦ The root chakra reminds us that we're here because creation wants us here. First we find grounding in place and tribe, then we focus on the life that we want.

♦ All of our chakras helped our ancestors survive, each holding its own formula for maintaining the vitality necessary for the continuation of life.

♦ Earth's Dreaming is on the line as well as Earth's ability to Dream.

♦ The middle world is little more than the dressing of a void that is trying to decide whether it wants to collapse in on itself or become real.


## Chapter seventeen:  Now Our Story is Beginning

♦ In Black Elk's great vision he is shown what is possible. The great tree centers the hoop of all the nations of the two-leggeds and all living things.

♦ He is told that he will walk both the red road and the black road of power. The tree of life is rooted right at the point where these two roads cross.

## Chapter eighteen: Nuts and Bolts and Three Fish

♦ The popularity of blogging is an example of how the world is changing.

♦ We are being challenged to reinvent ourselves and poets are helping us do that.

♦ Rumi tells a story of three fish, representing aspects of ourselves and of the human race.

♦ We, the New Wasichu, *become our walk* as we learn to let the red and black paths move through us.

# Foreword

*W*asichu, Lakota for *those who take the fat,* for me evokes the ones who are closed to seeing spirits, who don't experience all things as related and fail to comprehend how magical thinking can be normal. More literally, it refers to those who slaughtered the buffalo nation, brought alcohol and disease to the Native peoples, and took possession of Turtle Island by deceit and force.

Clearly, it is a challenge to look at ourselves as a people or a culture with such a sordid past, but it is even more challenging to see ourselves as deserving of a guilt-free future. We are such a large country and such a diverse population racially, spiritually, politically, and socially that it is easy to duck any label that carries a negative charge by adopting the attitude, *mistakes were made, get over it, let's move on.* And maybe on some extraverted level this works for us but then why is it so hard to move forward? It is not my intent to hang "Wasichu" around our collective neck like the albatross (in Coleridge's epic poem, "The Ancient Mariner"). Nor do I see any intrinsic value in simply drawing attention to our dark side. *Wasichu* does come with a long collective shadow, the assimilation of any portion of which is healing work, not only for the country but for the land. But it also comes with powerful medicine. Using the dismemberment metaphor that crops up frequently in this book in various contexts, let us break down the old and realign our essence around a new prospect, a new set of possibilities, a new collective vision. We will be stronger and happier for it. We will be the New Wasichu.

There is a spirit or an ethos to our past that transcends book history. It is *our* story, it is a story that has a life of its own, that whispers to our conscience and watches us sleep and dream. Depending on how we agree to tell it, it is our living story and a seamless story, a story for the ages that can still end well. But not so fast! There has been no resolution for the Native Americans. That the nearly total displacement of the Native inhabitants of Turtle Island and the seizure of their lands took almost 500 years and involved different European powers doesn't mitigate the inhumanity and calculated nature of the crime. We tend to think that we can buy our way or legislate or rationalize or even pray our way out of guilt or complicity, but there is really only one way off of this karmic wheel: Heal this place, and maybe the place will heal us. We must sit with the land and love it and listen to it. The land is truly our Mother.

Pressing on—as a country, as Americans, and as Wasichu—we cannot completely disassociate ourselves from the crimes of our forefathers any more than we can wash our hands of the crimes of our own generations. We are not, and never were, the victims of a few bad people. All of us are capable of the lowest and the highest acts, but hiding in the middle, in the middle world, where we can make all the rules and control everything, is no longer an option; it really never was. Like the New Hampshire state motto, emblazoned proudly on license plates, says, "Live free or die." Who or what will kill us if we don't "live free" or break free of the old Weltanschauung? We are extremely vulnerable right now whether we know it or not.

*This is a good day to die,* and there are countless ways to go.

The problem is not on Spirit's side, that Spirit won't work with the Wasichu or that it can't understand a nonnative language—albeit Wallace Black Elk identifies English as a "dangerous language" replete with words that "weaken your mind" (1). The problem is that the Wasichu don't see the sacred in things or nature.

Wallace Black Elk's hope for the future included the White, the Red, the Yellow, and the Black Nations (2). The New Wasichu are no particular color, but we are the *karmic* descendants of the Wasichu. What we must ask ourselves is this: If there were still 50 million buffalo on the Great Plains (3), if Turtle Island was still covered with old-growth forests, if all the lakes were clear and deep and all the rivers ran pure, prairie grasses to the horizon, the running of the salmon unobstructed, would we know any better than our forefathers how to live here? The New Wasichu would answer, *yes.*

I apologize for the predominate usage of the masculine pronoun throughout the text. My story, one of the main threads that weaves in and out of this work, is a man's story; gender bias, both conscious and unconscious, is therefore unavoidable. At times I have tried to use that to advantage. For example, in speaking critically of the patriarchy, I pull no punches; I am qualified to criticize the male mindset or psychology from inside out. Unfortunately, I must suffer the blind spots of gender, which manifest as extreme impatience with the stupidity of other men, as well as my own forays into cluelessness. When possible I have tried to broaden the perspective, always striving for a more holistic, human point of view.

The term *Weltanschauung* crops up throughout the narrative. In the official English translations of the *Collected Works of C. G. Jung* (Adler and Hull), this word is left in the German. A literal translation of Weltanschauung is world vision or world view, but the German language makes it a compound word, *worldvision,* and capitalizes it, as it does all nouns. But for a proper translation, I think the English equivalent ought also to be capitalized. It means the whole of how we view the world, not consciously but reflexively, folding in the myriad causal and acausal factors that contribute to who we are, living in this time and space. I am somewhat in awe of this word and therefore will stick to the German most of the time except to give the word a break by substituting *Worldview.*

The italicized passages indicate where the story dips into the personal dimension, whether dream, memory, poetry, or dramatic moments. Every effort has been made to include only those narrative elements (metaphors, whole poems, asides) that amplify the permutations of the thesis. Often an author of nonfiction sows his/her personal story between the lines of the text or conceals his feelings in the language without realizing that he is broadcasting his psychology. In this writing, subjective and objective work together as equals, symbiotically (one opening into the other), all in service of unpacking the larger story of how one might approach a life in these uniquely challenging times.

A note on the frequent use of parentheses throughout the text: Going against recommendations, I find them indispensable. I only hope that the reader agrees that they add to rather than detract from the narrative.

Finally, I would like to comment on the word *shaman*. Joan Halifax (Zen Buddhist Roshi, anthropologist, author of several books on shamanism) informs us that *shaman* harks back to the Vedic *sram*, meaning "to heat oneself or practice austerities" (4). We also have (Ph. D., author, shaman) Barbara Tedlock's claim that the term originates from the Siberian Evenki language meaning "the one who knows". (5) These intriguingly complementary insights into the origins of "shaman" only add to the mystique of a word that has come into popular usage over the last thirty years largely to convenience Western culture's need for definition. Now that a significant literature has grown up around it, a lot of backpedaling would be required to replace it with a better term, if indeed that were possible. As usual, when English adopts a word for popular consumption, the word adapts to what the people require of it. Now that the word *shaman* has taken on a life of its own, we have no choice but to work with it. Speaking for myself, I am grateful that we have a word. The shaman, so to speak, is out of the bottle.

What is a shaman? A shaman is one who dies to him- / herself through rigorous initiation or who, having survived some life-changing experience (essentially a rebirth), proceeds to live in two worlds—the middle world and the sacred—between which he/she travels at will.

Relatively few people have encountered a shaman in his/her teaching environment of choice—nature—because it is easier to engage with the shaman indoors, where one does not have to deal with insects, mud, dust, smoke, animals and weather. In an urban environment, where nature comes in the form of a park, there are many distractions and little privacy. In any case, the number of people who have engaged shamans in a workshop setting—whether park, retreat, convention center, backyard or living room—is quite impressive. At least for now, the workshop is the shaman's classroom.

# 1

## Doppelganger: Our Soulful Double

### I

I begin this writing out of a sense of urgency to speak some truth to my tribe, the Wasichu. The earth, our mother, requires something of us now, something that we haven't been able to provide until now: protection. We must prove that we love her by protecting her. This statement would be understood by my father, David (Sr.), an intelligent and wise man, but it would not have made sense to his father or his father before. Our tribe is just barely emerging from a very dark time. We aren't clear yet.

*We need to cross.*

My father, age 88, needs to cross—I mean, *before* he dies! He needs to know *how* to cross. And I need to cross. His life, by his own reckoning, is ending, whereas mine will most likely continue for a while, but we have this much in common: We can't see or feel or dream what we need to do on this side. This side is ending. It's breaking into tiny pieces. For the most part, our dreams, as Wasichu, reflect that confusion. I push a little deeper. But this is my initial statement, my ticket in. The parameters are these few questions (Would that I could boil them down even further!): *Who am I? Why am I here? Where am I going?* (These are similar to the three questions that a person seeking healing must be able to answer, or so a medicine man informed Lewis Mehl-Madrona [M.D. Ph. D., author of *Coyote Medicine*] [1].)

*Oh, to recover my essence, to consolidate my essential identity . . . to dissolve the caste system, to embrace the least and the best of me! Otherwise, how to carry on to a ripe old age with friends who want to be around me . . . with family, loving and understanding and defending me and wanting to be around me. I want to be loved for who I am, not because I am related.*

My father (Jungian analyst and author of *Pauli and Jung: The Meeting of Two Great Minds*) is of sound mind, but my mother . . . What happens to love when someone you love slips into Alzheimer's? You love them because you love them, because of who they are relative to you and because they reciprocate on some level. Your essence responds to their essence. And then, as their essence dissipates, love struggles for a new port, a place to be received. As the heart of the object of love fails to recognize the love coming in, love founders. The heart is so used to protecting itself from rejection; unconditional love is required. We talk about loving our kids unconditionally, but how often is that truly the case? Let us hope that it's not that rare, but loving oneself unconditionally might not even seem possible.

*How can one love oneself thoroughly and unconditionally if one doesn't know who or what one is loving?*

I have a friend, Frank, who sees a virtual therapist, Dr. Morgan. He walks down the beach that morphs into New York City, arrives at Dr. Morgan's address, a brownstone, climbs three stories, enters a waiting room, and waits to be ushered into the office. It's a real place with *expensive* modern paintings on the walls and a couple of Chinese porcelain dogs. Last time he went, the doctor had him repeat some phrase like a mantra, and eventually someone entered from an interior door—another Frank, except this Frank was a contented, happy man. His contentment was written all over him.

Welsh poet, novelist, and editor Grahame Davies recently shared a poem that was based on a dream in which his double showed up: a naked double. Davies was walking along a seaside cliff when this double appeared, running full speed, clutching a framed portrait of his family. He ran straight for the cliff, disappearing over the edge. Convinced that this character must be shattered at the bottom on the rocks, Davies left the scene but returned a few months later (in the same dream) on a lower path with access to the cliff base, where he expected to find the remains of the naked man decomposing among the rocks. Instead there was his double, hunched within the concavity of the vertical embankment, still clutching the family portrait to his chest. What happens next is, Davies flees like the protagonist in the epilogue of Ray Bradbury's *The Illustrated Man* and, as in the 1969 film based on the book, his doppelganger ineluctably follows.

The doppelganger came up in the Victorian-era gothic stories by Edgar Allan Poe, Nathaniel Hawthorne, E.T.A. Hoffman and in the writings of the Romanticists Johann Tieck, Jean Paul, Albert Von Chamisso, and Heinrich Heine. It also appears in the works of Fyodor Dostoevsky, Oscar Wilde, Stefan George, and later, Franz Werfel and Hermann Hesse (2) as well as in the writings of Rudolf Steiner (founder of anthroposophy). It's not really the shadow we are dealing with here however, as was the situation in the literature of the second half of the nineteenth century going into the early twentieth; the doppelganger of the twenty-first century would seem to revealing itself as an archetype in its own right, free of shadow qualities. Regardless, there is something ominous (on the side of propitious), something inevitable about confronting one's double.

We can't live all of our selves (much less all of our soul), and sometimes the best splits off to live a separate life, in our dreaming perhaps—but why not also literally? If the double embodies the vitality and an indispensable portion of one's essence, then its reality—in an intuitively logical and, certainly, a psycho- and mythological sense— validates, one might say *qualifies,* the ego's very existence. As the ego's credibility wanes, it might send out little SOS signals at a frequency that only the doppelganger receives, wherever he or she is dwelling.

A fascinating case in point is to be found in Wes Moore's memoir, *The Other Wes Moore,* except the author, a successful businessman and Rhodes scholar, is the soulful double who hears the SOS of his existentially suffering counterpart. He happened to be reading an article in the *Baltimore Sun* about a jewelry store holdup involving a fatal shooting. One of the apprehended men, now serving a life sentence, was also known as Wes Moore, one year younger, raised in the same neighborhood where the author grew up. The author became obsessed with learning everything he could about his namesake. He reflects: "I was surprised to find just how much we did have in common . . . how much our narratives intersected before they fatefully diverged . . . there were nights when I'd wake up in the small hours and find myself thinking of the other Wes Moore, conjuring his image as best I could. . . . Sometimes his face was mine" (3).

*My doppelganger was my* Life *magazine twin. I must have been around eight when he made a brief appearance in a black and white photo in an issue of* Life *that looked more like me than I, and then disappeared, taking my smiling eyes, freckled cheeks, and crooked smile with him—a smile that I imagine he never lost, that was his ticket into a world of love and friendship and fulfillment. (So unforgettable is the moment my mother showed me this photo that I remember exactly what I was doing leading up to it.)*

The doppelganger can find us via a photo or, as in the following example, a painting. There is an amusing story behind Picasso's famous portrait of Gertrude Stein. When he first showed the finished work to her, she complained that it didn't look like her, to which he replied, "It will." I have contemplated this anecdote for years. Although it is impossible to ever know what Picasso really meant, my initial assumption—that he was depicting her future self—now seems less likely than the notion that he was painting her doppelganger; when he looked at her, that is what he saw. We should all be so sagaciously rendered.

In Cesar Calvo's, *The Three Halves of Ino Moxo*, the magical semi-autobiographical narrative of a quest to find an elusive shaman in the heart of Amazonia, Calvo's doppelganger materializes as a fictional cousin, Cesar Soriano. This Soriano not only shares Calvo's obsession, traveling with the author to interview Ino Moxo, but he is the one who narrates the story.

When and if the doppelganger returns would seem to be a matter of destiny. In the event that it does show up, whether from within (for example, in our dreams) or without (in objective form), we might characterize it as the mirror image without the mirror. In a sense, the mirror has become a doorway or *nierika* to a viable parallel dimension of original self-awareness through which the self or ego comes face to face with the "other me." Neither reflection nor projection, the doppelganger's overarching purpose is to "go" (or travel) with the individuating self as helpmate or alter self for as long as the self needs to be reminded of its twin status. (What is being offered here is an ideal definition to be applied where useful or discarded as experience dictates.)

Obviously, the doppelganger means different things to different people, depending on the needs of the self or how one relates on a deep level to this volatile collective work in progress sometimes referred to as *consensus reality* or, shamanically speaking, the *middle world*. For some, this man-made reality is more than upsetting; it is disheveling or even ruinous. For these folk, the appearance of the doppelganger signifies an opportunity for the self to repair itself.

Rupert Sheldrake (author and former director of studies in biochemistry and cell biology at Cambridge University) advances the process of *morphic resonance* to explain how memory works in a simple organism. Instead of theorizing that memory is stored somewhere in its primitive nervous system (for example, to account for the incredibly intricate and versatile building skills of the mud wasp, *Paralastor*), Sheldrake proposes a much simpler explanation based on self-recognition or *self-resonance*. (Morphic resonance is based on the idea of *morphogenic fields*, a term that biologists coined in the 1920s to apply the field theory of the new physics to a new biology. Morphogenetic fields were conceived as "Invisible regions of influence . . . existing within and around organisms . . . with inherently holistic properties" [4]). Even though humans are, arguably, the most complex organism on Earth, sometimes simple explanations are the most helpful: When the self is at risk of losing the ability to recognize itself, the doppelganger returns with the morphic self-field or template—not the memory of the formative self from childhood, but the essential self-image, or *self-imago*. So the effect is homeopathic. Sheldrake: "This self-resonance helps maintain an organism's form in spite of the continuous turnover of its material constituents." He continues, "It involves an effect of like on like" (5). In other words, if we can imagine the human being as a damaged snowflake, then the doppelganger is the snowflake that, against all odds, duplicates the crystalline structure of its disheveled twin, in effect replenishing the memory of its mate through the agency of deep resonant self-recognition.

How this works is perhaps less mysterious than it sounds when we consider how it plays out in a controlled research setting: Phantom limb pain (affecting two-thirds of those who have lost a limb), is often experienced by the recovering patient as spasms or chronic clenching of the phantom limb even though it no longer exists. In *The Tell-Tale Brain*, Vilayanur Ramachandran (neuroscientist, professor at the University of California, San Diego) proposes that the source of this affliction lies in the brain rather than, as convention dictated, in the peripheral nerves because, even though the limb is no longer physically there, it continues to exist for the brain in a (virtual) traumatized state. Rather than deny the brain's *proof*, Ramachandran's approach is to blindfold the subject while a mirror is positioned in such a way that it reflects the healthy (opposite) limb, creating the illusion that the phantom limb is visible. The patient, the blindfold now removed, is then instructed to move the healthy limb while remaining focused on the "restored" limb. They discovered that the illusion that the phantom limb is no longer paralyzed not only convinces the brain, but it trips a healing response in the brain. The reflection provides a three-dimensional template that the conventionally underutilized brain seizes upon to revision or, in essence, *remap* the phantom limb, but really what it is doing is repairing *itself* (through the agency of *mirror neurons*). This is precisely the effect that the appearance of the doppelganger constellates in the self when its scaffolding is in need of repair. The idea that pain originates in the brain led Ramachandran to the realization that the patient's brain can *unlearn the pain* associated with a phantom limb. (6) This needs to happen to clear the way for the recuperative powers of the whole-body field to continue the process of regeneration.

In yet another illustration of the presumably endless ways the doppelganger manifests, the double, appearing this time in a dream, initiates a greeting, evincing an outgoing congeniality as it approaches the dreamer for the first time. The dreamer (age 33) is in his apartment. He is about to exit into a hallway that leads outside, to the back of the complex, but also down to the basement. He is heading for the basement.

> As I opened the back door I could feel something behind me. Literally right behind me . . . I could not fully look behind me for some reason. I could however make out another me. The me in back was blurry and much like a shadow. I knew it was me, but I couldn't make myself out fully. I opened the back

door in the apartment and went into the hallway. I then proceeded to go down to the basement. Just before opening the basement door, the door opened, and there was another me standing in front of me. I could see my third self clearly, and I was face to face with him. The third self raised his hand in a gesture of hello. He then said, "Hey!" and smiled. I like this and so I too raised my hand in greeting and said, "Hey!" back and also smiled. Upon doing this, the shadow me disappeared and the dream ended.

In this dream, the "me" that was blurry, on or above ground level, is the dreamer's shadow: a *shadow self*. The shadow is, by definition, unconscious, so it makes sense that it remains elusive in the ego's realm—which, in this dream, consists of the apartment and the "back of the complex." When the dreamer goes down into the basement, he is descending below the threshold of ego conscious, where the reality of the unspoiled or shadow-free self becomes full blown and autonomous. Now it can approach the dreamer "face to face," initiating contact as the doppelganger.

We need not be surprised by the appearance of the doppelganger in these men's dreams and fantasies. One might expect all manner of challenging self-encounters to pepper the lives of such talented and introspective individuals. Furthermore, if the human race is worth its salt, then this would be the time for people to experience every kind of jolting and extraordinary encounter. The hourglass has run out of sand for this age of "man." Sometimes I see tragic implications in this sentiment, other times incredible humor and endless irony. I am reading books written in the 1980s and 1990s that broadcast warning after dire warning that we are crossing the line of no return. Lines are always being drawn in the sand and redrawn or forgotten. For example, (author, educator, activist, some might say environmental prophet) Bill McKibben's 350.org has drawn a line with that number (the safe upper limit of carbon dioxide in the atmosphere), which we have far exceeded. If we can't get back to that number, we won't survive—or at least, he cautions, nature, as we know it, won't.

There is a spirit of helplessness afoot, and the stage has been set for the likes of mystical scholar, Andrew Harvey to enter dramatically with his *sacred activism* and tell us what to do. He is right, of course. Patriarchy is in its last throws, done, kaput! It has mined the world and tried to burn everything down in its last act, to take down nature with it: mountains, rainforests, whole ecosystems, the weather, even messing with the moon. But instead of succeeding in destroying the earth, patriarchy has just succeeded in pissing off the Great Mother.

The Great Mother wants us to be whole, to invite our better parts back. I was going to say, our *exiled parts,* but who exiled whom and which self is more real? Am I not creating a venue for the homecoming of my soul? I look outside and see a magical setting exuding power and presence, but no one is out there. I'm in here looking out!

*I planted another standing stone on the left side of the arch (facing the field), opposite the one that's been holding space on the right, by the tree. Taking advantage of the first snowfall of the year, it still required all of my strength to pull this stone up from the lower pasture on the orange sled. The old rope lead broke under the strain at the start, as I knew it would.*

*Ever since our trip to Brittany, I have been mesmerized by what happens to a large elongated stone when it is planted and allowed to stand upright. It shape-shifts into a completely reconstituted entity. It wakes up, so to speak. As soon as the job was done—the tools and wheelbarrow removed from the immediate area, the ground packed and cleaned up, and I took a few steps back—it was easy to imagine the two stones tuning to each other and the whole place adapting to the presence of, and welcoming, the new stone.*

*I visited Diane to check out her medicine circle. It is divided into four sections with paths opening from the outside, gated at the four directions, with a tall post in the center decorated with ribbons at the top. I was curious to see how she incorporates the plant people into the design. There was a large aster in the south quadrant and golden rod in the north, and plenty of other varieties of herbs and perennials asleep under the snow. In each of the quadrants was a larger stone representing a different member of her family: mother, father, son, daughter. We could easily have gone on talking about this creation of hers but we both had things to attend to.*

*Ah, writing . . . It's like budging that sled from a standstill. The old inertia! The old rope handle breaks, but I have another length of better rope in my pocket. How many times have I engaged in this unnatural process? If I didn't cherish the fruit, I would not bother. But there is a good reason for the effort. I must persevere. I must believe that some chemist, some capitalist, some machine, some laborer, some distributor, wholesaler, retailer contributed to the moment of this pen winding up in this hand, writing these words for a reason that points beyond me; I'm not a fool, and I have no desire to waste ink, or time, or life.*

*Diane's medicine circle represents family: her own, the family of stones, the family of plants. It is family size, not scaled for large gatherings. It is full, like a full heart. Most likely, she prays there a lot, or, even more likely, it is a prayer, the materialization of a prayer.*

*When I read ecstatic poems in public, I create a living room in the middle of the venue with overstuffed chairs, standing lamps, warm, ornate carpets, and candles, and around this, on three sides, I set up semicircular rows of chairs for the audience. The house lights are turned off so that all the light is concentrated on the living room set, except for the ambient candles. People are invited to make themselves comfortable in the living room, where I will be reading. The purpose for all this is to offer a welcoming space for the poems, creating a venue for the homecoming of the soul. Poets are often shy people, but no shyer than many in the audience. The illusion of the living room soothes this shyness, clearing the way for the poem to come into its own.*

*I am co-hosting a poetry reading at a local college. We are assembling as many poets as we can to read to and about Mother Earth: poems that have been written in despair and from a place of celebration, out of respect for Her situation, for communion and healing—a marathon reading where there is no list of readers but poets can come up in the order that feels right and speak or read their own words or the words of a fellow poet for as long as they want and be heard and held by a room full of their peers and elders. The stage will be modestly and respectfully prepared to evoke the natural world with branches, some candles, sage. And there will be an opening and closing ceremony to speak to the directions, to bring in the ancestors as well as to thank and release them. And lastly, there will be a collective statement, oath, promise that the poets will compose during the reading that will circulate—a statement of hope and commitment to peace and reciprocity and coexistence and brother- and sisterhood and whatever else seems timely, which will be posted and published, bearing the signatures of the writers who participated. Maybe we will call this evening of poetry, "Cry to Earth" . . .*

Right in the middle of this sentence, I interrupted my own thought to write:

### Crossing the Black Path

It is the end of the day.

The trouble is we are dying . . .
Nobody talks like that,
But surely the setting sun understands this language.
But the wind,
If you want the wind to hear now, you shout.
The wind is busy mocking the weather report.
There is a turbine on the ridge that needs to turn,
A roof to blow off,
A flower to stir,
A prayer to deliver,
An old eagle to loft. . .

Shout: The trouble is we care!

*Did somebody say something?*

The clouds travel over us
And sometimes look down!

*Don't let us be road kill!*

We are crossing now,
Almost to the double line now.
There is a roaring in our ears;
We are just like turtle, moving from swamp to pond,
Deer in search of cover,
Making a dash for it,
Mouse racing the juggernaut!

Eagle is scanning in our direction,
But not for us, my sister,
And not for the tear in which
Our fear is reflected, my brother.

How can anything be understood

Amidst this cacophony of prayer?
All this *crazy* praying
For all the things
That were once given . . .

Because we are crossing now
We are praying.
Our fear is praying for us!
So small, so small in time and space.
Is this really all we are?

Is this really our day to die?
Our warm bodies full of blood and breakable . . .
Fathers and mothers and children crossing.
Naked, anxious,
Leaving one side to cross to the other.

This black path
We are crossing . . .
With respect, we pray,

*Let us cross !*

## II

In "Crossing the Black Path," the middle is the double yellow line that must be crossed if life is to continue. It is a numinous boundary. As long as we are on *this* side, where we can no longer stay, we are not safe, but crossing calls up all our fears of the unknown.

*Will we die? And if so, what is death? If we make it, will we all be together?*

Crossing is a form of death regardless of what one thinks. Consciousness is traded for spiritual survival. We are being pushed and pulled. Some people seem to be on the far side waiting. Imagine the herd crossing one deer at a time.

I sent "Crossing the Black Path" out to my father, Tom Cowan, Grahame Davies, and poets/writers Timothy Flynn and Jefferson

Ackor. Cowan responded with a poem about falling into a deep winter sleep in the middle of a prayer:

> Deep snow
> now across the prayer
> I went to sleep with,
> saying, sliding into sleep.
> I never finished it.
> But the dream!
> Oh, how I found my way home
> and the cat too, / lost in the dreaming,
> somehow
> knew where to go.

Perhaps we should just follow the animals' lead and take our chances!

I asked my father if he thought "Crossing" was a dark poem. He replied:

> "Crossing the Black Path" invokes fears. I have just now been looking at my dreams from 2001 with great interest. Many I had forgotten, and there were large gaps of no dreams. We are both moving into new territory and rightly have fears. I look at Jung in *The Red Book* and see the fears he had. His fears of dying to the old fear of going mad. I don't know what my fears are, but I see them lurking in the dark. I see from the dreams how I have been engaging the unconscious, and it me, and with no real confrontation. My work with Jennifer (his yoga teacher) could be my last chance (to cross the dark road). During my last session . . . it was like she was calling me back from the dead. We had been doing an exercise with chakras, in which I saw a gigantic tree trunk that had grown through the house. I went down to the ground level to see its roots, and I saw what looked like a door in the tree. I knew I should go in, but I didn't. Old story!

That *is* an old story: the story of resisting, hanging back.

*My real work is to heal a little bit of the earth, the land. I am looking outside into the back of our property and here is what I see: the original break in the rock wall opening onto the pasture, the double arch of woven saplings, medicine wheel, standing stones . . . This is my practice: healing the land, so the land knows that we want to be here. There is the arch and the stones that guard the arch, a threshold. I respect that more than I can say. I honor it, and I stand in awe of it. On this side, I struggle to work. On that side, I do ritual, I struggle to pray.*

When we act alone, out of synch with nature, out of intimate contact with the elements, we are like a cancer cell running amuck. Henry Beston, author of *The Outermost House*, offered this diagnostic monition: "The world today is sick to its thin blood for lack of elemental things. . . (7)" When we vision quest, do a sweat lodge, commune with the seasons out on the dunes or just sit quietly in the woods for awhile, being present, then we are behaving like a normal cell in a healthy body, the body of Earth, and the earth begins to recover its health. The trick is finding a way to adapt to the earth's needs and to be of service on this level through ritual or ceremony that makes sense to us as individuals. First, because of what we must surrender (i.e., control), this work is humbling, but if we persevere, a point is reached or a threshold crossed as we witness nature responding to our remembering what it means to be a human being. Then the work begins to magnify, to take on greater significance and become ecstatic. This is one way of looking at the learning curve of becoming spiritual beings. (What I am saying about ritual is also true of a life-style that incorporates ritual.)

Of my poem, "Crossing the Black Path," Seattle poet, J. van den Ackor wrote: "The imagery, the suspense and the noise; I had to read it several times before it stopped making me tense. The feeling of exposure and peril, of not knowing the path to safety, but being compelled to keep moving is quite powerful. To my thinking, the final four lines nicely contain the entire poem, but honestly I prefer the whole story for its incredible sense of foreboding and determination."

*This black path*
*We are crossing . . .*
*With respect, we pray*

*Let us cross!*

The Native people of Turtle Island speak of the red road or the pollen path. Our black path is the antithesis of that: It cuts across the red path at right angles. Our black path leads us everywhere except to the place of wisdom, growth, knowledge, relationship, reciprocity. But this black path is more than a symbol of the Wasichu's road to nowhere. It might be the symbol of death in life, the living death. For those of us who have chosen to side with nature, our dash is a dash for reclamation of our soul's re-memberment. The terror is the terror of leaving our old, albeit dysfunctional, structures; of choosing to dis-identify ourselves from our own doomed culture, the juggernaut that just might not let us cross.

Again, the question arises: *What are we crossing to?* Didn't the pioneers ask themselves this very thing at every ford? Is our crossing any less epic and historic than their transcontinental trek?

*I once had a dream where the road I was traveling, hitching at first and then driving, eventually became a path along which many were walking, like a column of ants. This procession was not a forced march, either. It felt voluntary. People were stepping out of line to sightsee, and yet it was a procession. When the road narrowed to a path, we were passing down a brick corridor through a nineteenth-century-vintage industrial district. And shortly the path opened to a sweeping view of a valley with a gigantic smelting furnace presiding over the far end, which held my attention at first, but as the path descended the left-hand sweep of the valley, I became more interested in these (also quite large) identical stone or brick sets of towers that were connected at the top like the towers that are used to support suspension bridges, minus the spans. And after passing these, the path began to ascend a hill, leaving the valley, and we were all still proceeding in line as if we had a sense of where we were going, and there was almost a lightness of mood, certainly nothing foreboding. . .*

In this dream, we are climbing out of the valley of the bridge towers and the smelting furnace, leaving the nineteenth-century industrial district far behind. Sometimes in dreams, distance may be equated with the passage of time. This dream, which starts with a personal journey and ends with a collective trek, might represent the crossing to a new era or age.

In his *Shamans, Healers, and Medicine Men*, ethnopsychologist, cultural anthropologist Holger Kalweit outlines the four ages of Earth or man as told by a Nepalese Magar: The first age is the golden age, distinguished by no problems, no disease. In the second age, "sacrifices and rituals developed." In the third age, people argued and fought about the right way to *do* the sacrifices and rituals, "resulting in the appearance of passions and illness." In the fourth age, "death, danger, war, pain and material craving dominated humanity." But, according to this history, this was when the first shaman, Rama Puran Tsan, appeared (8).

The Hopis of northern Arizona also trace creation's (as well as their own tribal) history through four successive worlds (or ages) and four transcontinental migrations encompassing the four directions, an odyssey of almost unimaginable scope in terms of both real time and geographical space.

In extending the chronology of ages (which is just a way of charting the progress of civilizations or of Earth's story relative to humanity or a specific branch of humanity), we might agree that the status of the *New Age*, whatever form that might assume, is "future" in the sense of "imminent," but that its dawning is contingent on many factors. Our interpretation of the above dream suggests that the new age is close, but we have to get there on our own power by climbing out of the "old" valley, as opposed to just sitting tight and waiting for the new age to come to us!

When you look at our cities, you can tell they are made exclusively by "man"; there is no trace of the influence or hand of the gods. At least now, heading into the second decade of the twenty-first century, we are witnessing a groundswell of awareness of the shortsightedness of filling in a swamp or an estuary to make way for urban sprawl, even if the debate still favors sprawl over preservation of what little remains of the natural world. The hubris of the phenomenon of the *overnight city* is captured in a photograph in a 1970 *National Geographic* article about the new Yugoslavia, in which the caption says it all: "A swamp once oozed where the modern complex of New Belgrade blooms on the outskirts of Yugoslavia's capital. (9)"

In the old days, the gods provided the blueprint for civilizations. Even Rome had their blessing. (The mythical founders of Rome, Romulus and Remus, were the twin sons of the Vestal Virgin Rhea Silvia, fathered by Mars, the god of war.) Today it seems that all roads lead away from the gods. Now—at the very point when the fourth age is waning and about to end and the earth can barely stand another rape, murder, oil spill, offshore drilling, landfill, clear-cut, sapped aquifer, human bomb, species extinction, or nuclear accident, and the gravity of her biospiritual integrity is growing weaker—something noble and aboriginal in the human race is stirring, but first it has to fall out of love with godless power that has held sway for millennia. It has to be able to look at wealth and tall buildings and say, like somebody with a hangover, *What did I ever see in that?*

The nascent return to this long-lost *god sense* might first manifest as the outrage that crops up in a poem by Friedrich Hölderlin that he penned in 1798:

> . . . you don't believe
> In Helios, nor the sea being, nor the thunder being,
> And the earth is a corpse, so why thank her? (10)

The fourth age may be ending, but what is rolling in?

In my father's father's time, everything was held together by a strong glue of belief, ideas, facts, assumptions, attitudes, maps, templates, and language. One doesn't question gravity; the stuff that holds one's time together is similar. Everything in a Weltanschauung mutually attracts and coheres. Even dissent and revolution are sucked into the field of a Weltanschauung. We can't know what a new way would look like because it requires a crossing from what we know and have accepted, and that acceptance is embedded in the matrix of our being, down to the cellular level. The epoxy that holds a Weltanschauung together is stronger than the things that form the conglomerate. Major pieces can break off, and it's still there: patriarchal monotheism, anthropocentrism, duality, class consciousness, the "just" war, hierarchical thinking, environmentalism, midlife crisis, how we relate to food and starvation, how resources are managed, how language is managed, how wars are fought, how peace is understood, gender bias, how we experience time and energy, how we approach a mountain, what we mean by literacy, what constitutes a good education—none of these pieces is critical to the longevity of a Weltanschauung. It's much more mysterious than that. It is something that Carl Jung, founder of Analytical Psychology, called the Zeitgeist (spirit of the times), which holds everything together like epoxy—but when we're in it, it's more like an existential fog that we accept, even when we're suffocating, because we're afraid of what we'll see when our confusion lifts. Or, to be even more graphic and borrow from a Vedic metaphor, we are the "frog in the rock" (11) who isn't aware of its imprisonment until the *hammer of fortune* releases it.

Like Rumi (thirteenth century Persian poet) we might mutter: *If I could taste one sip of an answer, / I could break out of this prison for drunks* (12).

The solvent is a new spirit or zeitgeist—a spirit that begins as nothing more than a vibration, a spot of color in a drab vista or a new feeling about life, an excitement that begins to spread. At first it produces nothing; at least, nobody notices what it is up to. Eventually, though, as it begins to dissolve the conglomerate of the old Weltanschauung, people feel free to act differently, dress differently, dance and sing differently, write differently, and treat each other differently.

It is much easier to see how the dawning of a new Weltanschauung looks in retrospect: sweeping in on the world stage, taking down edifices that used to mean something, smoking out all the old assumptions from ground up, as if Maya (the great Hindu deity in charge of weaving and unweaving the illusory underpinning of the phenomenal universe) had stepped in to work her magic. Everyone is affected: Some of us are hurt or confused, some of us are sacrificed, some are justified, and some are redeemed. But until Rumi's *prison for drunks* cracks open, and some drunks turn out to be savants (!), we might begin to look around for our doppelganger.

*When the Berlin Wall came down (in 1989), my doppelganger was there. In real life, I was still waiting for the hammer of fate to strike the stone of my imprisonment! I was about to travel there with my father to witness its demolition. We had booked our flight to Berlin, and were all packed and ready to leave when my father happened to slip on some ice and injured his back. We never went, but my inner eye became the screen for an ecstatic projection of myself moving along with a boisterous crowd representing all nations led by Germans of all ages, from West and East, surging into the breach from both sides of the shattered wall. No question, a part of me took part in that epic event that cleared the way for a united Europe and the dissolution of the Soviet Union.*

In our time, our soulful double needs to remember her/his hurting, confused, or unredeemed twin who joined the marines or who works for General Electric in a cubicle or as a CEO or who manages a franchise or who started out as a housepainter and now owns a contracting business but has painted himself into a corner of the proverbial maze.

*I once worked for a good man who was stuck like that. He had one false tooth in the front. At parties he would remove the tooth, tie on a bandana, and become a pirate. (His beard was so thick, by the end of the day he always appeared unshaven!) He morphed into someone who was entertaining, irreverent, and endearing. He was so close to his doppelganger that all he needed was a few props.*

Not surprisingly, there is a mythic or archetypal precedent for this bifurcation of the self. For example, it crops up in this explanation for why certain shamans are not able to journey or fly: Apparently, there were two brothers who were the first shamans. Both descended from heaven. Both wanted to be "reborn through a woman" but for that to happen, they had to each find a woman that had nothing dark about her—no shadow. Both succeeded in locating such a "gleaming woman," but the first to be reborn is "able to fly through the air in his séances." The second brother suffers from amnesia and forgets that he is a twin. He is "unable to fly through the air but he consults the spirits through the use of amulets and a spirit wand" (13). In the Upanishads (in the later texts, according to Maureen Lockhart), we learn how something similar happens when the *prana* (or the individual soul) wants to enter the body. For example, the Maitrayani Upanishad (propounded by Sage Maitreya) explains, "the Self becomes twofold in order that it may 'experience the illusion of a life in the world as well as eternal reality'" (14).

(Incidentally, we are the descendants of that shaman brother who relies on amulets and wand. The *spirit wand* is the prototype of any tool or gismo that channels energy to manipulate or control our environment: microwave, laser, jackhammer, CAT scan, x-ray, telescope, remote control, ballpoint pen, Taser, a dentist's high-speed drill, digital scanner, joystick, computer, iPod—all manner of tools or techno-wizardry without which we lose our effectiveness.)

This reminds me of the folk tale of the two brothers who start off together to seek their fortune. Coming to a fork in the road, they reluctantly agree to split up, but realizing that they will want to meet up again after their adventures, or just in case they might need each other some day, they break a forked stick in two and each takes a piece, so the stick serves as their magical link. Because it is a fairy tale, it is easy to overlook the profundity of the forking of the way, but the harsh truth is that a fork in the road, for two travelers bent on seeking their fortunes, might presage a permanent separation. The doppelganger is the one who holds the more complete piece of the stick, representing a bit of the original path that led to the forking of the ways; he is the one who retains the clearest memory of the epic bifurcation.

What it really comes down to is a remote, mutual re-membering, a homing instinct that can potentially bring these two selves together again. But on one side, the ego side, the remembering assumes the form of a semiconscious distress call, and on the doppelganger's side, it assumes the form of a homesickness of the soulful self for the worldly self—all trending toward a kind of holographic reunion in which each recognizes within itself the germ of the other as it begins to agitate for a reunion of the whole.

Deepak Chopra (physician and author specializing in Ayurveda and the mind-body connection) quotes a Upanishad that beautifully captures the artless serendipity that characterizes the homing of the two selves when the time is ripe: "A man (a whole man) is like two doves sitting in a cherry tree. One bird is eating of the fruit while the other silently looks on" (14).

In our collective story that original fork in the path came up a long time ago in our DNA. And where is that magical stick? We are deep into this Weltanschauung that precludes our claim to destiny. Unless the doppelganger returns in one form or another, individuation reaches an impasse and grinds to a halt.

*In a recent dream: There were four very large wings, not necessarily sets, that I have arranged by size, in descending scale. I am getting ready to mount them onto an ornate backing like something that would go over a door or lintel.*

Whether we paint houses for a living or work for General Electric—whatever we do—many of us have hung up our wings.

*Not long ago, Neva, an extraordinary woman who helps souls cross, presented me with a healing medicine object of power: a magnificent hawk feather with the Welsh dragon beaded onto the quill. This feather, so I was informed, comes with a Native American spirit, a scout of consummate skill. Learning how to work with this feather has been a struggle, but I credit this woman with healing my amnesia.*

*Many years ago, I used to be able to "fly"—that is, journey—but have forgotten how. In the above dream, I am struck by the detail of how the wings are not paired; they are single wings. In a dream, an object can carry the charge of the whole archetypal field of what the dream is trying to communicate, and what that might be depends on the dreamer's personal associations as well as the archetypal message. In this dream, the wings are being displayed, ornamentally, from large to smaller. If we take large to mean larger than life, or larger than everyday scale, then here we see a downscaling of the archetype to a more familiar or personal dimension. So the installation of all the wings over the interior lintel signifies an effort on the part of the conscious self to prepare for the arrival of something from the sky realm, but also from the archetypal realm. Consequently, the wings become heraldic; the door, a portal.*

# 2

## Bridging

*The dragon/hawk feather, as a powerful bridging symbol, has been working on me at a deep level.*

*When, at the age of 18, I went out to the Navaho reservation with a friend as a volunteer tutor at Navaho Community College, I was not avoiding the draft. I was (albeit I would have used different words then) questing for what the Lakota mean by "Mitakuye Oyasin" (or We are all related). What I found was a damaged sanctuary, a demilitarized zone—the Navaho middle world.*

*Even though the wide-open wilderness of the desert was very good at concealing, from a young man trying to mind his own business, the bitter intratribal debates that dominated reservation news, there were plenty of signs that the tribal circle was in shambles: semiwild dogs carving out the carcasses of free range horses hit by pickups; Indian elders hanging out drunk at trading posts, hawking the family silver, pawning exquisitely woven rugs. As far as I could tell, the young (male) students at NCC were half-baked crew-cut cowboys, cheering for the cowboys on TV. The only activist we met was a young longhair Apache; he had just gotten his two front teeth knocked out and was seeking asylum in our apartment out of sheer desperation.*

In 1973, three years after I left the reservation (a century after Black Elk's vision), Black Elk's tribe, the Oglala Sioux, engaged in an armed standoff with federal agents on the Pine Ridge Reservation in South Dakota that escalated into the now legendary Wounded Knee Incident. What renders this event so extraordinary in the history of Indian/Wasichu affairs is that public opinion sided with the Native American cause over the federal government's decision to intervene in tribal affairs. The Native people were apparently repairing their tribal circle and they didn't need any help.

It wasn't until five years later, in 1978, that Congress passed the Indian Religious Freedom Act. But when Nicholas Black Elk had his vision in or around 1873 and, incredibly, until 1978, it was against the law of the land to engage in traditional Indian spiritual practices. No wonder he kept his vision to himself for seven years.

Black Elk's great vision celebrates two circles: the tribal circle and the larger, more inclusive hoop of *Mitakuye Oyasin*, the family of all creation.

*I went out there to think, to sojourn with the desert and to write my manifesto, "Man Behind the Waterfall," which opens with the sentence: "Nineteen is not such a bad age to decide to breathe your own air." After my return home from the reservation, my CO (conscientious objector) deferment in my wallet, I traveled to Europe, again, to think. I kept a journal dedicated to "my dragon"; I called myself Nogard, "dragon" backward. The name was my way of honoring, while concealing, my relationship with the dragon, which I tended to associate with the East. I saw the dragon as mythical guardian of the treasure, which, later, I understood to be the Self, the priceless pearl that it is, classically depicted as, holding in its mouth. The name Nogard was the perfect cover for a young man who was always reflecting. It was my ability to reflect that had protected me from the draft's imperious middle world authority, but this ability was far from an invisibility cloak. In fact, as I made my way through the land of the Wasichu, I found that reflection offered "no guard" or protection for the heart, the conscience, or the soul. I was forced to choose between playing by the rules of the middle world and playing badly, or, like Lewis Carroll's Alice, journeying much deeper into my own reflection for affirmation and self-preservation.*

*Luckily, the desert had helped me clarify my priorities. Almost overnight, I had become an outsider in my own country out of necessity, an introverted young warrior of sorts. And when my spiritual life began, with a vision here, big dream there, a consciousness-altering experience here and there, even though I was precocious in that vein, most of me couldn't keep up. Thankfully, my poetry never lost a beat and was able to hold space for me as I struggled to pull the pieces together. The universe was letting me know that it wasn't going to let me off easy; there was a destiny card to play. (For example, my first love was the daughter of a man who was very high up in the Department of Defense.) Anyway, back then things were happening so fast and furiously that I was only able to follow one thread, and that was the thread that led me to Jung and shadow work. I suppose Spirit knew that if this thread were lost, I simply wouldn't make it. Dream work and Jung became the sacred, alchemical container for this numinous opus called my life.*

*Very early on in my life, I was sick fairly often. We played in a stream of untreated sewage from the university. Every time I had a high fever, I hallucinated terrifying waking dreams of alien visitations and world's end, tapping into, probably channeling, the collective psyche of the late fifties, which was hopelessly mired in a Cold War psychosis.*

*In one of these dreams, I was alone on a beach. There was a huge steel bridge that dead-ended in the sea. A voice commanded me to stretch across the Atlantic Ocean from North America to Europe, forming a human bridge. I was only about 6 at the time, no more than 3½ feet tall. The effect of this on my psyche was absolute terror, which took years to dissipate. I had no means of comprehending what the voice was asking of me. As it turned out, that comprehension wouldn't happen for more than 50 years!*

What about the Welsh dragon on the handle of the medicine feather? What does it mean as a symbol by itself, *and what does it mean to me?* It occurs to me that if this remarkable gift had not come into my life, literally placed into my hand, I might never have suspected that this dragon and hawk could share a common thread.

In *The Mabinogi* (a collection of stories culled from Medieval Welsh manuscripts whose title alludes to *Mabon,* a mythic wonder boy), the story "Lludd and Llefelys" introduces an epic battle between an indigenous red dragon and an invading white dragon. The agonized shrieks of the former, recurring every May Day eve, cause women to miscarry, forests to wither, and animals to become sterile. The wise Llefelys, king of France, advises his brother Lludd, king of Britain, to dig a pit in the center of Britain, fill it with mead, and cover it with a silken cloth. The dragons consume the mead and fall asleep. Lludd imprisons them in a stone chest, still wrapped in their cloth, in *Dinas Emrys,* a precipitous stronghold of rock in Snowdonia in present-day northern Wales.

The dragons remain at Dinas Emrys for centuries until King Vortigern (self-exiled monarch of post-Roman Britannia) tries to raise a strong tower on the summit. But no sooner are the building materials assembled than they disappear overnight, as if swallowed up by the hill—not just once, but three times. Vortigern consults his wizards, who advise him to seek out a child who has no father, sacrifice him, and sprinkle the foundations with his blood. The child turns out to be none other than Myrddin or Merlin. This wonder boy sidesteps the traditional practice of foundation sacrifice by announcing the real cause of the problem: Apparently the weight of the building materials, added to the pressure of the existing foundations, was distressing the dragons in their inebriated subterranean slumber. Vortigern, following Merlin's instructions, frees the dragons, who continue their fight where they left off. The red dragon finally defeats the white dragon. Merlin explains to Vortigern that the white dragon symbolizes the Saxons; the triumphant red dragon is Vortigern's dragon and the dragon of "our people (who) will arise and will valiantly throw the English people across the sea" (1).

The dragon on the Welsh flag is emblematic of the warrior spirit of the Welsh people, who—whether literal descendants of Vortigern's people—are, in a sense, the people of the red dragon who "threw" the Saxons out of Britain. The dragon celebrates their mythic origins, as well as their chi or life force, which can be suppressed or drugged but will not be vanquished.

While Native North Americans are famously warrior-like, epic survivalists, they were so relentlessly harassed and exploited that their hoop (as I personally witnessed) was damaged almost beyond repair. With apologies to any tribal Worldviews that disagree with this portrayal, Native American spirituality is based on a great vision of two circles or hoops: an inner hoop, what the Sioux call *Tiyospaye*, the circle of the extended or tribal family, which is centered within the great hoop of universal relatedness of creation that keeps us together as a great family (stones, trees, clouds, rivers, everything). Now this hoop is in grave danger of being obliterated. If that happens, the human race will step thousands of years backward.

*The medicine gift of the dragon/hawk feather is the first time the dragon and the hawk (or eagle) have joined forces for me. (Martín Prechtel [shaman, author, and master storyteller] explained to me once that the bobcat is the servant of the mountain lion, so it may be said the hawk prefigures the eagle.) The feather represents the energy of the winds and the sky realm, and behind the feather, as I said, and as I was told, stands a paragon of an Indian, a native spirit guide.*

*Where does this leave me?*

In the backyard is a medicine path, made of flat fieldstones, that I use when I am heading down to the medicine wheel. One morning, I spotted a strange stone right on one of the steps of the path, which I had neglected to pick up the first time I saw it, perhaps sensing its power. When I brought it inside to look it over, my eyes were immediately drawn to the image of an old eagle in the grain (head and neck). I received this as a welcome sign, but I sensed that the stone had more to reveal, so I kept it with me, in my coat pocket, in the car. Sure enough, two days later I was studying the texture of the stone, and there, on the opposite side from the eagle, was the unmistakable likeness of a dragon (in 3-D). By holding the stone sideways, one can plainly see that the same arch of the grain that forms the eagle's feathered neck also defines the dragon's muscular neck. The eagle is a wise old specimen, whereas the dragon looks younger. The stone brings together these two aspects of a great archetypal spirit.

There is another interesting piece to this puzzle that I cannot ignore. (And I might add that sometimes it is by seeing life as a jigsaw puzzle that comes together piecemeal that we are able to step out of a linear mindset that would have us view our life path as one dimensional!) The red slate that used to be quarried in this area (Poultney and Fair Haven, Vermont), of which there is precious little left, is the color of the red path, which has long symbolized, for me (as well as many others in the land of the black road) the path of the sacred/intentional life. It happens that red slate is also quarried in Northern Wales. (The Welsh immigrated here in the nineteenth century to work these slate quarries.) I have heard it suggested that Wales and Vermont share the same vein, which makes perfect sense when we consider that 250 million years ago, all of the continents were joined together like pieces of a giant puzzle into one landmass that we now refer to as Pangaea.

Red slate, for me, is (to borrow T. S. Eliot's phrase) the "objective correlative" of a profound connectedness—not just emotional, but geographical. Perhaps because the land was once all one place, as we learn how to live on the land in a sacred manner and as we learn to dream with the land, we might feel compelled to cross the great water to join our medicines, our chi, our redness, our grief, our karmas, our stories with the medicines of people whose land literally continues where ours leaves off, vein for vein, mountain range for mountain range.

*When Neva was trying to envision what to bead into the handle of the feather, she was looking up and saw a cloud with the head of a red dragon on one side and its tail on the other. This is meaningful on several levels: The cloud represents the mystery, Wakan Tanka, and it is eagle's realm, but I can't help but think that the head and tail on either side of the cloud points to another, tantalizing mystery.*

Lewis and Clark documented several accounts of rumors of Native encounters with a light-skinned, blue-eyed tribe that spoke with a lilting/brogue accent. They were on the lookout for this tribe but never made contact with them, so these rumors faded into the stuff of legend. The most tantalizing comes up in this Whitehouse (expedition journalist) entry, of Wednesday, April 2nd, 1806:

> Our guide also mentioned that he had seen one of the Indians of the Clar-a-mus Nation, & that this Indian was almost white, & that he mentioned they had fire Arms among them. From the above information received from our guide, I am of opinion, that if any Welch nation of Indians are in existence, it must be . . . those Indians, & not the flatt head Nation, as before mentioned; this I believe, from their Colour, numbers of Towns, & fire arms among them, which I flatter myself will be confirmed, whenever the River Mult-no-mack is fully explored. (2)

George Catlin, painter, traveler and astute observer in his own right, inspired by the journals of Lewis and Clark, set out to study the customs and histories of certain Indian tribes "before it was too late". (3) He became obsessed with the Mandan tribe and has the distinction of becoming, according to William Traxel, "one of the last White men to have close contact" with the Mandans, of whom Catlin wrote that "they must have sprung from some other origin than that of other North American tribes, or they are an amalgam of natives and some civilized race." (4) Their eyes were typically gray, hazel colored or blue; the hair of the women, blond or reddish-drown. He observed that their river-side villages were walled and fortified, their fishing boats, of stretched skin, were round like coracles. (A relative contemporary of Catlin, La Chapelle, observed the Mandans playing a ceremonial instrument resembling a harp.)

Perhaps the strongest living proof of Celtic migrations to North America, the Mandans disappeared around a hundred and fifty years ago (just as Catlin predicted, even as he was writing about them), but archeological evidence of a prehistoric, precontact Celtic presence is easy to find. According to Traxel, 275 structures, including megaliths, underground buildings, dolmans and mysteriously incised stones dot the eastern United States (5). Many of these sites are so similar to the ancient stones and cairns found all over Cornwall, Wales, Ireland, Brittany, and Scotland, it is only natural to speculate that they were left behind by the same mysterious people or a remarkably similar culture. One of the best known examples of an ancient site that unfailingly inspires both wonder and unbridled speculation in its visitors, is America's Stonehenge, in Salem New Hampshire, an extensive complex of stone chambers and ceremonial spaces said to date back to 2,000 B.C. Nobody knows who built it, much less to what purpose. (Thomas Cahill identifies the Iberian Celts as the great sea-farers of their time and therefore the most likely to have visited and settled in present day New Hampshire, but if the prehistoric dating of America's Stonehenge is accurate, its builders would have to have been predecessors of the Celts who at the time of its creation were just beginning to spread into western Europe.)

*Just last year, a group of eight friends and I sat inside a hollow mound near South Woodstock, Vermont, a stone chamber about the size of a small living room, located on private land recently designated Celtic Hill. The ceiling was formed from several massive slabs of rock. This was no root cellar. The space exudes the passage of centuries. The experience was very disorienting, as I could easily have been back in Ireland. (There was even a standing stone within about a hundred yards of the entrance that had earlier sent my L-shaped dowsing rods spinning in my fists.) Harvard professor Barry Fell dismisses any possible confusion of this chamber with a humble root cellar, identifying it as a megalithic "temple" whose lintel bears dedications to Bel, the sun god (6).*

*Let us hope that we are becoming a people who are much less sure of ourselves!*

What we call history might just be regarded as the left brain's attempt to spin out a chronological *non-fictional* story (with a formal beginning minus most of the classic story-telling elements) that conforms to the Weltanschauung of those who are telling it. In spite of these efforts to tell a non-fictional story, any history, dry or bursting with metaphor, is a powerful form of story-telling or myth-weaving. If we accept this or that would-be history as fact, our knowledge turns out to be nothing but a rug with certain patterns that will inevitably be pulled out from under us. We tumble and everything goes flying and when we catch our balance we find ourselves on a different rug with a different pattern, and someone is trying to convince us that *that* is the non-story that we ought to swallow. The history that I learned in school was nothing but the carpet I was standing on at the time. Once one has lived through such a tumble one begins to approach life more fluidly or acrobatically, no longer the student after a degree but more like an auditor, sitting in on the class of Life and drawing one's own conclusions. (Having grown up in the sixties, and contributed my own two-bits to its history, I have often found myself bemusedly shaking my head at how it is taught in schools.)

The old story of Columbus discovering a so-called New World, thus paving the way for European expansion and inevitable domination (which functioned as a teachable history until around 1950), no longer holds water. We now know that Columbus's preformulated designs on the people he "discovered," coupled with his western European prejudices, blinded him to alternate outcomes in his encounters with the trusting, curious people that he summarily enslaved and exploited. These people—who were, by anyone's standards, very sophisticated traders—were already benefiting from a thriving economy based on the rules of barter and cross-cultural coexistence.

The new stories that need to be told to fill the vacuum left by the deflation of the bogus histories that my generation was raised on are available in books like Barry Fell's *America B.C.: Ancient Settlers in the New World,* Robert Cahill's *New England's Ancient Mysteries,* and Traxel's *Footprints of the Welsh Indians.* Readers of every ilk, justifiably starved for these more intellectually titillating, less ostrich-like narratives, will continue to be treated to revisionist histories until truth, common sense, and poetic justice sort things out.

Once we begin our own investigations, sit with the evidence, visit some of these megalithic sites with an open mind, the dots begin to connect themselves in fascinating ways. There is enough evidence out there to support any number of theories and timelines. Truly we are living in a watershed moment, not just for the writers of the new histories that will have to account for the authentication of Celtic or druidic temples in our midst but, for those of us who, as children, swallowed the Columbus myth, this new openness to interpreting or reinterpreting the accumulating evidence feels like the high that attends the breaking of a long difficult fast. The Celts were here; a few years ago I would not have credited that claim. Now I long to know who were these people who left their writing, known as *Ogham*, on the stones of Turtle Island.

Our imaginations seem bent on associating the ancient Celts, and more particularly, the druids, with stone formations on the British Isles and the European continent that pre-date their appearance. The fact is, the Celts, relative to pre-historic and Neolithic time-lines, were the new-comers: a linguistically homogeneous, Indo-European culture of loosely linked chiefdoms comprised of warriors, farmers, artisans and a learned caste (druids) whose migrations have been traced to present day Turkey, the Russian Steppes, northern Italy, the Alps, and Austria and Germany, as well as parts of what is now Spain. (7) We know that their ancestors started moving from the Russian Steppes into Central Europe around 3000 BC. (It was around this time that Stonehenge and Newgrange were being created two thousand miles distant to the west!) Prior to this period (pre-Bronze Age / late Neolithic) facts are sketchy, but most scholars agree that there was a (pre-Celtic) proto-Indo-European language spoken at least a thousand years before divergence began. Traces of this ancestral tongue remain in many modern European languages as well as in Sanskrit, Gaelic and Latin.

What was this Indo-European or proto-Celtic culture like? Wisdom back then would have been synonymous with survival. But Peter Berresford Ellis (historian, literary biographer, novelist) wants us to understand that "the Druid caste had its roots in the 'food-gathering age'". (8) The druids, these walking libraries of bardic memory, with their *oak-knowledge*, their working knowledge of the land and the weather, the cosmic cycles and the telluric cycles, would have been the Brahmins of their people. The primeval forests were vast and impenetrable, teaming with predators and spirits and incredible bounty, if one knew one's place. As Celtic culture took shape from these early beginnings, let us imagine this proto-Indo-European culture was essentially a forest-culture, that these pre-Celts came *with* the forest, and with *oak knowledge* (9) in their blood.

With the dawning of the Bronze Age, the forest-centered or oak-centered culture transformed into a metal-centric culture. (An oak-centric culture would have been based on a unique magical relationship with the oak as benefactor and teacher[1] with the druids fulfilling the role of oak-priests or shamans whereas a metal-based culture was oriented toward worldly engagement and questing beyond a village-centric Weltanschauung.) Religious veneration of, not just the oak, but other tree-beings, as sacred teachers and providers, was gradually formalized through the subtle agency of acculturation into a forest-centered *cult* and eventually the mysteries of oak-knowledge were tamed and diluted. The oak (as well as other sacred trees), though not forgotten, were demoted from source, or god or godlike, to cult-status.

As they moved westward, through Asia Minor, these Bronze people with oak-knowledge slowly evolved into the people we know as the Celts; by 2000 B.C. they were a distinct ethnic group.

Ellis explains what happened this way: "By the start of the first millennium B.C., when the Celts began their expansion, all learned men and women in their society were designated as having oak-knowledge." (11) In short, the druids had forfeited their Brahmin-status.

It was when the Celts entered the great theater of Western history (the Danube and Rhine River basins) that the prestige of the warrior class started waxing, along with the importance of the artisan caste. In other words, as the need for *oak-knowledge* receded, in deference to trade-savvy and battle prowess, so did the influence of the druid-caste wane. (The bards, a variously skilled poet-class whose status and social function served a wide range of functions from minstrel to seer, with the "erosion" of druidism. . . . "subsumed many druidic and vadic skills". [12] This helps to explain why people today confuse bards

---

[1] Cowan points out the relationship between "door" and "oak" in both Sanskrit and Gaelic. (10)

with druids, but it was not the job of the druid to immortalize the insatiable egos of chiefs and warriors or to celebrate great battles in poetry and song.)

Around 500 B.C. the Greeks began documenting encounters with the Celts and relatively soon after that the Celts became major players in the saga of Roman expansion.

Once the Romans had succeeded in colonizing most of the continent, their goal became that of marginalizing the Celts by driving them deep into Britain where they were able to organize sporadically around strong leaders in remote locations. But what really saved the Celts from being wiped out or assimilated was the collapse of the Roman State, and the eventual total withdrawal of the Roman legions from the coast.

This relatively violent period of Celtic retreat, ending in a fortuitous reprieve from confronting the Roman juggernaut, amounted to nothing less than a brief golden era for the druids, who for centuries had been experiencing marginalization within their own culture, not to mention outright persecution under varying degrees of Roman domination. At the same time that the Celtic tribes were being beaten seaward or into the wilderness by the Romans, the druids were rediscovering their primordial roots! All over the British Isles and Gaul (western France) there were world-class ritual centers such as Carnac (Brittany), Newgrange, Rathcroghan (Ireland), Avebury and Stonehenge (England) that were already nearly 2000 years old by the time the Celts laid eyes on them. (Many of the [originally 3,000] standing stones at Carnac are believed to be significantly older.) It is reasonable to assume that the druids would have recognized these places for what they were -- the prehistoric equivalent of the great pyramids. (The outer bank of Stonehenge is 320 feet across and at Avebury the two inner circles are each 340 feet in diameter. As with the pyramids, there is a correspondingly immense intelligence about these places that seems to have less to do with their age, their scale and that they are precisely aligned with the heavens and more to do with the feeling of awe they inspire in us.)

One might argue that it was iron technology that ushered the ancient Celts into history, and into direct confrontation with Rome, but surely it was coming to the British Isles (and Brittany) that restored the druids to their former rank as the Brahmins of the Celts, at least for a little while.

Even today the stone circles, standing stones and earthworks, that covered the landscapes that we now identify with remote Gaelic ancestry, a mere fraction of which survive today, exude a permanence that seamlessly complements the natural land features they now resemble. One senses that the people who were responsible for the creation of these monumental places enjoyed both a grounded as well as cosmic relationship with the Earth and, more incredibly, like the Egyptians, they found a way to express this relationship for all time. Clearly they were not planning on going anywhere. If the stones reflect anything about the character of their builders, it is that they were completely in tune with where they were.

However, when it comes to the Celts, we have a people who awaken some wild desire in us to *be* or *experience* Celtic, whatever we mean by that, and thus begins the quest to find out. One can picture the Celts looking out at the watery horizon of the Atlantic and dreaming about what might lie beyond the limits of sight. Why *would* such a people stop at the western fringe of the continental land-mass, especially in view of the fact that, as the Romans learned firsthand, their ships were larger, stronger and more sea-worthy than the Roman galleons, though not as maneuverable in battle. The horizon for the Celt, at least the near-horizon, was viewed as a magical threshold. Where the heavens met the earth was a *place* in a very real sense, and as such, it beckoned. It is their legacy, as a (generally) westward moving people, in touch with their own mystically charged sense of destiny, that lures us to strike out on our own wanderings and voyages of spiritual discovery, trusting the beckoning horizon to be good to us.

Some scholars are not convinced that the druids were with the Celts from the beginning. This confusion is justified by the fact that they, the druids, left no written record, or specifically "druidic" artifacts. It is only natural however, to question the accuracy of classical (Greek and Roman) writers whose observations on the Gaulish druids were colored by their assumed superiority to the Celts. In the case of Strabo, Diodorus Siculus and Julius Caesar, their source has been lost to time. Unfortunately much of how we picture the druids has been influenced by the writings of Posidonius Caesar and Julius Caesar whose reputation in Rome was at least partly based on how he dealt with the Celtic threat on the battlefield. He wrote his *Commentarii de Bello Gallico*, (*Commentaries on the Gallic War*) around 50 BC, where he argued that the druids originated in Britain.

Ellis neatly cuts through this debate over where the druids came from by evoking mythic sources. Writing in the present tense of eternal mythic time, he apprises: "In the earliest reference we hear that the children of (the goddess) Danu come to Ireland from four fabulous cities. In each city they have been taught by Druids. . . . So the gods, too, had to learn their wisdom at the hands of mystical Druids." He continues, "The Druids of the Dé Danaan conjured storms in an attempt to drive away the invading Milesians (the first wave of the Celts) . . . (while) It was a Milesian druid, Caicher, who prophesied the victory of his people over the Dé Danaan" (13). The point is that there were already druids in Ireland of mythic origin, unrelated to the Celts, who strove to repel the Celts and overpower their own druids. (Ellis is distinguishing between these Druids [capital 'D'] of the Dé Danaans, who tutored the children of Danu, and the druids [small 'd'] of the Milesians, the new comers, who's powers and wisdom are, at this stage, a wild card.)

One version of this mythic history of Ireland, as retold by Lady Gregory in *Gods and Fighting Men*, tells what happens when a fleet of Milesian warriors, under the leadership of (high druid) Amergin, journeys to Ireland to avenge the death of Ith, one of their own, who had quested there previously. The Tuatha De Dannan (spelling varies) resent the presence of the Milesians, but by their own candid admission, their warriors, whom they claim to be superior to the Milesians, are not ready to engage in battle. (In mythic time, that could mean a hundred years not ready!) So Amergin comes up with an intriguing proposal.

> Amergin bade the men that were with him to go back to Inver Sceine, and to hurry again into their ships with the rest of the

Sons of the Gael, and to go out the length of nine waves from the shore. And then he made his offer to the Tuatha de Danaan, that if they could hinder his men from landing on their island, he and all his ships would go back again to their own country, and would never make any attempt to come again; but that if the Sons of the Gael could land on the coast in spite of them, then the Tuatha de Danaan should give up the kingship and be under their sway.

According to Caitlin and John Matthews, nine waves is the "traditional distance of exile from the land," the ultimate magical watery threshold (15). By bidding his fellows retreat by nine waves, Amergin is respecting the Tuatha De Dannan's sovereignty, including their right to defend themselves, by granting them space to summon their full power as the current inhabits of a sacred land. So the Tuatha De Dannan's druids conjure storms and wind, and the Gaels suffer hugely: Ships are scattered and sink, men and women drown, and Amergin loses his brother and, by some accounts, his wife. Finally, Amergin, stirred by the desperation of his comrades, steps into his power and, with humility, simultaneously unleashes his own enchantments while eloquently expressing his intentions and hopes for his people and future generations, soothing the elements with gentle words of praise for the bounty of the land: "That they may find a place upon its plains, its mountains, and its valleys; in its forests that are full of nuts and of all fruits; on its rivers and its streams, on its lakes and its great waters". His words summon the Celtic spirit, successfully establishing their sovereign right to settle there, with the land's blessing.

Only when he steps ashore does he surrender to the ecstasy of arrival and belonging or homecoming with these famous words:

> I am the wind on the sea;
> I am the wave of the sea;
> I am the bull of seven battles;
> I am the eagle on the rock;
> I am a flash from the sun;
> I am the most beautiful of plants;
> I am a strong wild boar;
> I am a salmon in the water;

> I am a lake in the plain;
> I am the word of knowledge;
> I am the head of the spear in battle;
> I am the god that puts fire in the head;
> Who spreads light in the gathering on the hills?
> Who can tell the ages of the moon?
> Who can tell the place where the sun rests? (16)

Jason Kirkey, in *The Salmon in the Spring*, evokes a "druidic archetype" (17). Because of its psychic nature, an archetype is not time bound, nor is it geographically restricted. And yet, undeniably, such an archetype draws power and authenticity from the land of its origin. The mystique of the landscape—the bogs, fens, sea caves, waterfalls, forest glens, mist-shrouded drumlins concealing lakes of black depths, prehistoric faerie mounds, menhirs, grassed-over ring-forts and stone circles holding space in cow pastures, ancient cairn-studded summits of strangely solemn mountains—remain powerful purveyors of the ancient druidic and, by association, Celtic legacy.

Utilizing magnetic imaging (the same technology that detects submarine shipwrecks), archeologists are able to visualize and map what has remained concealed underfoot for millennia. After all the geophysical data have been amassed and interpreted, Conor Newman, archeologist, admits "from an archeological point of view we find ourselves reaching a point very rapidly where we run out of things to say that are descriptive . . . When it comes to the nub of the question, What is it? Why was it built?, archeology, in fact, at that point, has to embrace things like mythology, social anthropology, cultural anthropology, to find out what is going on" (18). It seems inevitable that not just archeologists but all scientists who interact with the natural world will want to follow the lead of those pioneers in the scientific community who have allowed themselves to be exposed to what Hank Wesselman calls the *informational fields* that characterize certain wild places or risk being overwhelmed by all sorts of, well, information that cannot be quantified or adequately evaluated by conventional means.

We might experience such informational fields ourselves when we visit historic sacred destinations: shrines, cathedrals or world-class ritual sites such as Newgrange, or awe-inspiring places in nature. That is, we might begin to sense a potency that is original to the place itself, which we might ascribe to its primordial Dreaming.

There is a mythic history that archeology can't or won't touch, and it is all in the land's dreaming, as well as in the unmolested faerie mounds.

My wife and I participated in a walking tour of the Burren (*Boireann* = a stony place), a windswept landscape of karstic limestone on Galway Bay in County Clare. At one point, our guide gathered our little group between two grassed-over mounds and told us the story of the closest one, based on what the archeologists had learned by extracting everything that was of value to them, leaving an uneven pile of dirt. *What about the other mound?* someone asked. Apparently the archeologists cut a deal with the locals and/or the authorities, leaving the second mound untouched, but our guide was tight-lipped about that one, as one often finds among those who ramble the cherished land—they don't reveal everything they know.

Every era has its hierarchy of *knowledges*, as well as what we, as consumers (used to instant gratification, poised at the receiving end), are more interested in—technologies, or the fruits thereof. Michel Foucault identifies so-called subjugated knowledges as "those knowledges that have been disqualified as inadequate to their task . . . naïve knowledges, beneath the required level of cognition or scientificity"(19). Lynne Hume, in discussing Foucault's writing, says something that brings us right back to these two mounds in the Burren:

> Foucault supports a resuscitation of subjugated knowledges and suggests that it is through the reappearance of local popular knowledges, "disqualified knowledges," that criticism performs its work (20).

The *private, inherited, or local* narrative (story as memory) or knowledge (lore) feeds something in us that wants and deserves to be more respected! Slipping scraps to the dog under the table may no longer suffice, especially as it occurs to us that the dog may be a lion. (The internal monologue goes something like this: *Really? The remains of so many royal bodies were unearthed, way out here; layers and comingling layers of the remains of princes, chiefs, and influential souls, along with their gold and jewels and weapons? Staggering. You don't say! But . . . have you ever heard the faeries sing? That's what I really want to know!)* That's what the lion under the table wants to ask. The dog doesn't care; he is happy with his gristle bone . . . with his gold torque under glass!)

Visions and stories definitely have their place in this epic, romantic, half-invented, some would say *resuscitated* chronicle of a people who have, for hundreds of years, captured our collective imagination, whether we be scholars, poets, artists, therapists, historians, scientists, Christians, neopagans, writers, spiritually oriented folk, or simply lovers of a good tale. While archeological evidence is seductively surfacing on both sides of the Atlantic and ancient history is being recooked, and before another official recipe is force-fed or programmed into our fact-hungry brains, let us simply acknowledge that what attracts us to the Celts most of all is their mystery!

Celtic identity or heritage doesn't have to be archeologically or genetically established to be embraced by a culture or incorporated into the identity and Worldview of a people. It can be based on other markers: for example, language, music, geographical orientation, toponymy, and mythic resonance. The ancient stories percolate just beneath, and sometimes through, the historic narrative and the Christian rhetoric.

It may be helpful to imagine any long-standing affinity with the Celtic soul or spirit as a unique alloy created from the melding of certain components: linguistic, aesthetic, historic, quasi- or mythic-historic, geographical, narrative, emotional, psychic (dreaming), and ancestral.

Michael Dames points out that the Old English word for foreigner, *wealh*, is the origin of *Wales*, whereas in Welsh, Wales is called *Cymru*, which derives from the older Celtic word *combrogi*, meaning *compatriot* or *one of us* (21).

I see a rough parallel between the Welsh relationship to the ancient Celts and the New Wasichu (us) and the Native Americans. Let me suggest that the old Wasichu are the *wealh* or foreigners, whereas the

New Wasichu are *combrogi* or compatriots of the people who lived here before us.

Thousands of years from now, if people are still living on Earth and there are still forests and fish in the sea, birds in the sky, worms in the earth and four-leggeds roaming around, it will likely be because we came to our senses in the first half of the twenty-first century, maybe because we were moved by the calamitous pitch of circumstances to do what was best for the planet. Time was about to run out. We were madly consuming everything and killing each other off when something remarkable happened. *What happened?* How did we know what to do? What would this future accounting of ancient events look like? Easy to see how the history of such a critical timeline as the one we are presently navigating would be subject to imaginative interpretation. With precious few objective facts to draw on, a baffling collection of random artifacts to decipher, and overwhelming evidence of a seemingly totally avoidable all-out war against the environment to riddle out, combined with a paucity of firsthand accounts from which to extrapolate, how could such a future history not incorporate elements of myth? For example, what wonderful tale will our future historians invent to explain the, by then, uniform admixture of microscopic polymers found in all of the planet's oceans and seas, and how will they ever explain our mining of the moon?

There is a movement afoot among Native Americans that embraces the rainbow spirit of the new age and promotes the idea that it is time to pass along the Native wisdom. I think Nicholas Black Elk's vision, which he essentially bequeathed to the Wasichu, is central to the rainbow warrior mentality. Mending the two great hoops, healing the tree of life, the world tree, cannot be accomplished by any one people. In giving John Neihardt the medicine name *Flaming Rainbow* (Pta Wigmunke), Black Elk was acknowledging his heroism, for he was not only Black Elk's translator, but also his champion, considering what was at stake (22).

# 3

## Poor Wasichu

$A$nyone who has tried knows that it is almost impossible to create a communally meaningful ritual from scratch because, as Kalweit reminds us, "Ceremonies work through symbols" (1). Symbols are not mere inventions of the mind; they are neither fictions nor metaphors. Our associations to symbols may be personal, but a true symbol always points beyond what is known. Cultures that still rely on ritual-ceremony to access healing are honoring the mystery surrounding life and death and existence itself. They are secure in their not-knowing because ceremony vouchsafes their special relationship to mystery and has for untold generations. In indigenous ceremony, when no Wasichu are present, the *symbolic meaning* or *value* of ritual is simply bypassed. What is being experienced is wholly engrossing. Its effect on consciousness does not suffer the split between observer and observed or experiencer and experience.

The ability to stand back from experience, which might once have served an evolutionary purpose, has morphed into the super-pandemic of our times. A ritual fully experienced is a *healing* or a dance or something else that is not exterior to the self or to the group. To the indigenous (or initiated) participants, it is a journey that floods the senses, completely erasing the need to understand, interpret, express, judge, anguish, or hold back. This is why it is risky business to invite an outsider to the ceremony, because then it *is* a ceremony versus a working mystery. It is common practice during the *Yuwipi* ceremony for the shaman or medicine man to unceremoniously evict *anyone* with impure or negative thoughts before anything begins.

Kalweit has this to say about the classic Western approach to illness:

> Our spiritual horizon ends where the actual causes of illness begin. Western symptom therapy is actually a bastion of discrimination against the shamanic way of healing. Our

deficiency is our narrow etiological understanding, the reduction
of the illness . . . to its material, physical manifestation (2).

Lack of openness to the spiritual dimensions of an illness
constitutes a serious illness in itself, one that might best be treated
outside of its domain of influence. Isolated from its institutions and
protocols, it (our unhealthy materialistic Worldview) can be treated as a
constriction of vision that generates a narrowing of options for both
doctor and patient. But when a healing depends upon contact with
spirits, such semiblindness becomes an impediment to ritual protocol in
the sense that without the good will and credulity of all present,
nothing can even get started!

I hope that Spirit takes pity on us as our suffering surfaces and that
we will be pardoned last minute. The 1999 film *The Matrix* (brain child
of the Wachowski brothers) comes to mind. No matter how the world,
our world, may appear to us, in fact we are on death row ordering our
last meal. The word *psychosomatic* is descriptive of where we stand frozen
in place, or where the medical community stands: straddling the
emotional and the physical, but no closer to dissolving the split or
warming up to a new paradigm of health that incorporates the full
spectrum of intuitive or energetic or soul-centered approaches to
healing, such as dreamwork (in groups and 1:1), lucid dreaming,
dowsing, fasting, cleansing, prayer, chanting, meditating, ritual sweats,
yoga, feng shui, sound and color therapy, acupuncture, crystal therapy,
plant spirit medicine, ayurvedic medicine, biodynamic massage, flower
essences, naturopathy, shamanic healing (extraction and soul retrieval),
and Chinese herbalism.

If the time comes for a dying patient in intensive care to be placed
in hospice care, the patient is—mercifully, and perhaps for the first
time—allowed to relax into the illness and into the experience of dying.
The person's condition is allowed to take its course, but more than
that, his/her destiny is back in his own hands. Energetically speaking,
the person's condition diffuses into the "context of (their) entire life"
(3), and beyond that, the *cosmic surround* (4), and everyone breathes a
sigh of relief as he, even on the verge of passing, morphs into a whole
person.

Healing favors a space where illness (or injury) is being approached as a situation or an environment and, above all, a relationship. When we talk about illness as a *condition* we are getting closer to being able to enter into a relationship with it. When we look closely at a health condition, we likely discover what Ayurveda teaches: that, in the words of Chopra, "many different conditions interact to create disease—the disease organism plays one part, aided by the patient's immune resistance, age, habits, time of year, and many other factors" (5). By treating an injury as an "accident" or disease as symptoms or toxins or something attacking the body or something of the body that is attacking itself, this, although demonstrable on one level (biochemically, biologically, diagnostically, by the book), crudely denies the full reality of illness. It reduces our ability to enter into relationship with the illness and obviates any possibility to fully commune with its nature, character, or point of view.

How space is conceived and used is critical to the treatment of illness. In the altered space of ritual, the materialization of disease—which is, in fact, quite often provisional and profoundly unstable—is altered. That is to say, as consciousness is altered, as space/time is altered, so is the whole context of how we experience disease or injury.

Disease is not a *thing*, although we may not become aware of it until it manifests in the thing-realm, as cholera or tuberculosis or the common cold. Modern medicine cannot effectively treat a malaise without knowing what it is in the finite universe. But it is only a thing (that can be boiled down to processes with material properties and treatable symptoms and causes) if we treat it as such or wait too long to interact with it on common ground. When someone is sick one of the primary goals of the healer should be to make sure the person doesn't become one with the illness which can easily happen as the symptoms of the illness or injury displace the patient's sense of self-identity. Gordon Wasson (famed ethnomicologist and the first Westerner to participate in a Mazatec mushroom ritual) recorded an all-night healing-séance conducted by curandero Maria Sabina in the course of which she learned that her patient, a seventeen-year-old boy, was going to die. A puma had (irretrievably) devoured his *nagual* (his animal-spirit double). Sensing the severity of his plight, he asked Sabina, "Am I all right?". She answered, "Your spirit is all right. I am with you, . .but you are in a tough spot. (6)"

Initially, and depending on how we choose to approach it, illness can be treated as an energetic reflection of our relationship to the universe, which is itself primarily a reflection of relationships, *all* our relationships, most of which we aren't aware of! (Even our *innocent* exposure to pathogens or to toxic chemicals is not innocent in the sense of happening in a void, out of context with our life story.) Not to see this is to live in hell, if, citing its etymology² we conceive of *hell* as synonymous with the concealment or total eclipse of spirit by matter. In the world of healing, hell would be treating a patient as a body quickened by chemistry in a spiritless material universe. The antidote to hell, then, is the Weltanschauung that recognizes the true power of ritual to heal, by salvaging our relationship to *matter* as (Latin) *mater*, our mother. Would our mother want us spending even one minute in hell?

Perhaps we place too high a premium on health or the idea of health. Sometimes we need to get sick to remember that we have a body, that we are embodied beings, but when we get really sick or "terminally" ill we need to remember that our bodies are impermanent, even ephemeral. With the ingestion of ayahuasca (alias, *Mother of All Plants, Vine of the Soul* [7]) it is normal, depending on the dose, to pass through a purging, a ritualized evacuation which the body, one might say, ecstatically submits to. Sometimes illness is like that – a wise, powerful teacher who is there to walk us through something. Suffering being unavoidable, perhaps we ought to commit ourselves to learning what we can from the highs and lows of embodiment. As long as we are on Earth, or *of* Earth we can't *not* be related but *how* we are related can sometimes sicken or even kill us.

Looking at disease as a breakdown or reshuffling of relationship on the micro as well as the macro level opens the door to expanding our definition of disease to include war-waging, racism, and bigotry. (The pandemic eruption of the Spanish flu during the last days of World War

---

² Middle English, from Old English, akin to Old High German *helan* to conceal or hide (8).

I, killing more soldiers in two years than the war itself, is a horrific reminder of how war and disease are two faces of the same plague.) How we relate to ourselves, each other, our neighbors, other races, other nations, nature, the world, microbes and matter, outer space, inner space and even other realities is a good indicator of how well we are in general.

As a Vietnam peace veteran (card-carrying CO), I have often entertained the thought that our age-old addiction to waging war (cold or hot) to solve problems (a disease that directly or indirectly affects every-body on Earth) would diminish if our warriors, at the threshold of discharge from active duty, were required to share their unabridged stories (stories of heartbreak, terror, sacrifice, boredom, trauma, mistakes that cost lives, shame, loyalty to a questionable cause and real heroism) to a council of compassionate elders (old soldiers and civilians), who would ritually honor their stories, absolve them of all guilt (unless a crime was committed), acknowledge their agonizing struggles to come to terms with whatever they experienced, debrief them, and reassure them that they won't be marginalized but assisted every step of the way in their return to civilian life, and then ritually see them across a threshold back into meaningful relationship. For this to happen, there will need to be sympathetic communities to return to! First truth, then sympathy; watered with truth, sympathetic communities will spring up and the idea of war will wither on the vine.

Many of us were impressed and, frankly, stunned by the news of South Africa's post-apartheid creation of the Truth and Reconciliation Commission, which invited both the perpetrators and the victims of the old hellish system of apartheid to engage in a communal (publicly attended and broadcasted) ritual of truth telling. The focus of these hearings was on healing the individual and the community at the same time. Of course, the healing didn't stop there, but radiated outward to the wider community: the watching (or listening) world.

As we begin to be open to this way of experiencing and treating disease, we might watch for theories of disease that treat the whole person as somebody connected in myriad ways, theories that view illness as an ethos, a condition of relationships that shade into our waltz with life, death, and the universe. It's all energy, a living field. A healer's or practitioner's reliance on ritual (large or small) as a way to synchronize soul with spirit, community, and world is energetically based.

By contrast, many of our best allopathic doctors are specialists, which means that they preside over small kingdoms of the human body. They have backed themselves into corners and even stake claims over certain diseases that tend to manifest in their areas of expertise. They defer to each other's territoriality like certain fish who defend arbitrary boundaries that are invisible to all but their immediate neighbors. The curandero, or energy healer, knows that the body is not a jigsaw puzzle of real estate. It is more cosmic than that. If a puzzle, then it is a puzzle where the spaces between the pieces (pieces being nerves, bones, tissues, cells, organs, veins, hormones, membranes) are more critical than the pieces.

The Shipibo (an indigenous people from Peru), for example, use icaros or sacred songs to affect the diseased body at the quantum level. José Stevens (Ph.D., president/cofounder of Power Path Seminars) explains what is happening this way:

> Inside the human body are vast reaches of space—just as in outer space. Shamans say that these spaces are not empty but are filled with patterns like radio waves. This is not in contradiction to the understanding of quantum physicists and neurobiologists who are beginning to uncover how empty the human body is at the subatomic levels (9).

In essence, these shamans (working with the plant spirits) affect changes in the energy patterns of the body by "singing their intent into the 'now point,' or what quantum physicists call the quantum field" (10).

Andrew Harvey announces, "It's time we realize that we have crossed the energy Rubicon. This new world of ours needs to be seen and understood and interacted with as an energetic system of power" (11). Yes, more and more of us are able to cross to the energetically expressive side of things; but severing the elastic bond that keeps snapping us back to the materialistic Weltanschauung is a problem.

Chopra likens our situation to knowing that we are under a powerful spell but not being able to break out of it, somewhat like being trapped in a lucid dream.

I have read my poetry to rapt audiences and, afterwards (*after words*) promptly collapsed in on myself like an ancient cat in a dark corner of the temple.

> *Look over there—*
> *That's where I should be!*
> *Look in here at this great empty hall!*
>       — From author's poem, "My Goddess"

# 4

## Closing the Power Gap

In the 1960s, we struggled with a generation gap. Now what stands in our way is a *power gap* between what we know and feel and what we do with what we know and feel—between who we *think* we are and who we are, between where we are and where we could be. After we close the book, leave the workshop, return home from a vacation or retreat that awakened something in our soul, finish the movie, exit the theater or the rock concert or the sermon, finish an inspiring article that moved us to reshuffle our thinking, emerge from a mutually engrossing conversation, or from a dream that refuses to fade, how do we keep from collapsing in on ourselves? We are reminded of what we are really capable of feeling, sensing, or grasping. What then?

We have unfinished business in the material or middle world, karmic obligations that summon us at precisely the moment when we are feeling most centered. Sometimes it is simply because we are strong that there is work to do. But what is our work?

*It is the job of the sick to get well. It is the job of the well to go deep.*

At internationally respected teacher, author, and lecturer Tom Cowan's workshop on Celtic spirituality, there was an exercise that caught me off guard and took me somewhere unexpected. We were instructed to journey to a goddess of battle and ask to "learn more about the sins of the warrior."

*I fell asleep to the drumming almost immediately. When the call back sounded, I found myself in the court yard of an oriental god of war. I had already passed through the front gate, past a fountain of blood, and was standing inside the outer sanctum of the temple, a low building of dark glazed brick, searching for where the god might be keeping himself. I was poised and ready for anything.*

Given that I am a pacifist, I woke from this journey full of wonder. What was my business with this god of war?

At such a workshop, one feels empowered to do the work that one is here to do, or at least to find out what that work is. Nobody deigns to judge. Everyone feels empowered by a palpable sense of common purpose; there is synergy. How many people would have to be missing for the synergy to begin breaking down?

*When we go home, people will try and stay in touch, but for now, we bask in the power of the circle. The circle will follow us home: a magical protection, a portable temenos, a safe spot. The feeling that lingers is one of strong solidarity, of knowing who is with you, beside you to left and right, and across from you. A strong circle is a circle in which everyone can see everyone else. But our houses are rectangular and winter is long, our lives demanding.*

*The wood stove is cranking, but it's no match for the elements. As winter seeps into the house, I realize that my mind has wandered.*

*Red-tailed hawk was in the tree in the center of the field until just a moment ago. His cloud-colored breast was catching and reflecting the sun; no way could I have missed him! I continue to watch as he flies to some trees at the foot of the field; his red-brown fantail flashes and that's it—he melts into the forest.*

Black Elk explains the medicine of *wochangi*, which Joseph Epes Brown translates as "influence." Sometimes I see a hawk and it means next to nothing, whereas this time, its appearance grabs my full attention and buoys my spirits, letting me know that I am not alone. Black Elk might say that its *wochangi* is strong (1).

*This hawk wants me to close the gap, the space between here and there, between where I am and where I should be, between head and heart, heart and soul.*

Kalweit tells the story of a Dutchman, Peter Hurkos, born shaman, turned housepainter: Hurkos was born with his head in a caul that had to be surgically removed or he would have suffocated. In other words, Hurkos was born, then his head was delivered from its own womb, a kind of hood (2), or, to borrow Aniele Jaffe's phrase, "supernatural uterus" (3). I thought this might be the precursor of the hood that Cowan has written about that monks wear and that some of his magical Celtic heroes wore as a kind of prophylactic covering for the head, which the ancient Celts understood to be the seat of the soul. (Cowan himself wears a hooded cloak during the Wild Hunt as a shamanic covering that allows him to move around incognito and semi-invisibly.) He suggests that the conical wizard's and witch's hat is an exaggerated hood, the hood being pointed. But the mystique of the hood is that it conceals, protects, shrouds, and contains the head and the face while allowing one to see where one is going. He writes: "The term 'hood' in American English still refers to someone who operates outside the law, a criminal who conceals his identity, a denizen of the nether regions of society . . ." (4). So Hurkos was not able to fully live out his destiny. He should have gone around in a hood to protect his extraordinary mind. Instead, he disguised himself as a housepainter. I can't help wondering how things might have gone differently for him if he had been raised as a Celt!

The place of the head in Celtic traditions is magical. In Celtic heroic tales, the head of a charismatic leader could magically continue without the body, dispensing wisdom and advice (5). In our culture, the head's autonomy, its self-appointed mandate to dictate and manipulate, has nothing to do with magic or charisma or the mystical relationship between the head and language. It has to do with how, a long time ago, the Wasichu opted to side with one half of the brain. The left brain became the all-powerful gatekeeper, even, unfortunately, in sleep. How many times have I heard people say, "I don't dream" or "I don't remember my dreams"? That's the head talking. If the head doesn't understand something, or doesn't want to, it writes it off to imagination or relegates it to the unconscious, or worse: the void of forgetfulness.

In Wallace Black Elk's story, Spirit approached him from behind and announced its approach with four hoots. This was when Wallace was nine years old. He writes:

> Then he hooted four times and I felt a finger poking me in the top of my back . . . and this voice said, "I am here, I am here." "Hoo. Hoo." Is what I heard on the inside . . . It felt like someone comforting me by putting his hand on my head. Then he came around and stood in front of me and sat down (6).

This was very clever of Spirit, to approach nine-year-old Wallace from the back because, from a distance, Spirit's power was colossal. It felt to Wallace that a whole mountain was coming, and he was terrified. So Spirit sneaks up, making itself as small as it can. "Hoot Hoot/Hoot Hoot/Hoot Hoot/Hoot Hoot." Mountain-owl-loving-fatherly, Spirit does not hide its power, nor its mystery, and yet, ultimately it/he is comforting like a father, laying his hand gently on Wallace's head, only then stepping around, effectively closing the power gap. After Spirit leaves, Wallace discovers that he can talk to animals. His personal power has been activated, his gifts can begin to flow. The ancient Celts would have no trouble appreciating the magical dimensions of this encounter, nor would it elude them that Spirit's laying a hand on Wallace's head is key.

*When I was around 19 or 20, I saw my old soul in the mirror, through the reflection of my own face looking back at me. This affected me in a strange way: It bestowed upon me the ability to reflect. So I am able to write poetry from a place of relative objectivity. I am able to write and reflect on the voice in my writing simultaneously, and legitimately, because it's not exactly me who is speaking through my poetry, it is me plus this wise reflection. Nor is it automatic writing or channeling, because I am in it in the same way that the reflection of that wise face in the mirror found me via my reflection. It's a riddle worthy of a lifetime of pondering. And I am that riddle or paradox. I am two in one or one in two. Obviously, I can't be that one I saw in the mirror, but neither is it accurate to say that I am just myself. And now, at this late stage in my life, I am not really sure who I am.*

Our heads are truly magical. If we gaze long enough into our own visage, we might discover that we are not who we think we are. Irish poet and scholar John O' Donohue describes the face as the "icon of creation . . . In the human face, the anonymity of the universe becomes intimate" (7). As New Wasichu, we owe it to ourselves to study where this face has been.

Today I tore a page out of *National Geographic* from my dentist's waiting room: an article about the "Hidden Yosemite." I simply could not close the magazine on this true story of how James Savage, operator of three trading posts, led a band of militia to deal with the Indians, then residents of the valley we now call Yosemite.

When they arrive, the *Ahwahneechee* are all gone except for one old woman who explains that she is "too old to climb the rocks." They waste no time in laying waste to the village, no doubt rounding up or slaughtering the few who stayed behind. Yosemite (probably a corruption of *yo'hem-iteh*), roughly translated, means "they are killers" (8). This is our heritage. It took men like Savage to clear the way for the miners and traders who were the first wave of *us*.

This glossy scrap of our shadow history is another kind of mirror or a piece of the honest looking glass that fell off the wall of our ancestral home.

*Who are we? Do we want to know?*

The answer might be, *No, we don't want to know.* But if we want to take our power, we may have to learn who we are!

We seem quite harmless in our big heated boxes of goods, furniture, piped-in water, and food. But we are anything but harmless. The good red path crosses the double-lined road that holds Turtle Island and her dreaming hostage in a monstrous web.

*Beyond a doubt, the moment I studied that black and white photo of my* Life *magazine twin, I began walking the black road into the middle world, while my smiling twin continued on the red road without me. It was as if my soul twin was saying, "Look at me. We are going our separate ways now, but you must not forget me as long as you live. Look at my face. I am you." To this day, I can see that photo with my inner eye, just as clearly as I saw it then.*

*Now, finally, in my sixth decade, I can proclaim that the red path is my path. I choose it. I remember it! It has always been my path in principle; now there is no question where my loyalties lie. And I will gladly die crossing if that is my destiny, for then at least I will not die a traitor to my real people, my ancestors: the stone people, the tree people, the winged ones, the cloud people, the insect nation, the turtle and snake people, the four winds, the grasses, and the mountains, whom I love as much as I love my wife and son, my stepdaughters, my mother and father, only somehow with even greater tenderness as some kind of profoundly involuntary compensation for how we have made them suffer.*

When the reality that we have both inherited and created thins sufficiently to reveal the existence of another path that tempts us to abandon the path we have always traveled, it behooves us to delve deeper into the archetype of the doppelganger.

Wallace Black Elk and Nicholas Black Elk are spiritual doubles. The parallels are so conspicuous that I would wager many who have read *Black Elk Speaks* assume that *Black Elk: The Sacred Ways of a Lakota* is another of John Neihardt's books. All the evidence for this is in the preface by Wallace Black Elk's translator, William Lyon. (In fact, Lyon believes that Wallace Black Elk's life work continued where Nicholas Black Elk's work left off. Wallace was the great-nephew of Nicholas.) Nicholas was not prepared for his tremendous vision at age nine, and he kept it to himself for seven years, which must have felt to him like a second lifetime. Most shamans are not initiated until puberty, albeit they may be called by the spirits at any age. At 16, the dam of resistance broke, and Nicholas was able to share his vision. Wallace's story was almost the opposite in terms of owning his destiny. He was groomed to be a shaman/medicine man beginning at the age of five. "His introduction occurred around 1926, a period in which the elders were certainly very much in fear of losing their shamanic lineages. From their perspective, the ability of their shamans to tap into the sacred mystery powers was their most valued knowledge. To lose their shamanic powers was surely seen as tantamount to the death of the 'old ways'" (9). And that, Wallace clarifies, would be "real death" where "spirit is gone forever" (10).

Wallace "had so many grandfathers" involved in teaching him the way of the red road. Eleven of them, to be precise, assisted in his early training, "the goal of which was to educate him to the point where the spirits could take over" (11).

According to Lyon, "Both (Black Elks) spell their Lakota name the same—Hehake sapa. Hehake = male elk, sapa = black. . . . Wallace has said his name refers to a black elk as seen in silhouette at early sunrise or late sunset as opposed to black in color. . . . They both first encountered spirits at the age of five and they both had their first visionary experience at the age of nine. On that level they are very much related . . . so much so that Wallace will say they speak to one another . . ." (12).

So, here we have these two Black Elks. One is the color black, and the other is silhouetted black against dawn or dusk. Which is it? The ancient Celts believed that day begins at dusk, when the sun goes down. Life germinates in the darkness of the womb. The sun doesn't go away; it returns to the womb of the Great Mother to be reborn and renewed. How else could it manage to rise 1.5 quintillion times and always appear fresh and strong and filled with enough energy to give away to Earth and sister Moon?

As contemporary humans we might easily identify with Wallace's position of not knowing how he stands in relationship to his time. Is it the end of the day or just the beginning of a new day? Or do we stand simultaneously at the threshold of both dawn and dusk?

The shaman is no stranger to paradox.

*Yesterday, I experienced two appearances of hawk. The first time it showed itself, it was perching in the middle of the field. The second time it crossed the road as I was driving, again flashing its red tail fan just when I turned my head to watch it swoop across the field. Later in the day, I decided to take the bold (or foolish) step of removing the hawk/dragon feather from its box. I decided to expose the feather to the elements, judging that it was becoming too precious to me, that I was placing it on a pedestal. I performed a simple ritual in the medicine circle, tying it to a branch in the little oak that grows in the east quadrant, calling hawk "brother"!*

That night I had two dreams. The first dream:

*I am driving with my sister and I catch sight of a beautiful young hawk flying parallel to us. I stick my hand out the window, hoping to attract its attention, and it lands on my hand for a second, then flies off; it comes back again, responding to my coaxing. But instead of letting it make up its own mind, I lose patience and try to grab it, first by its fee. When it slips my grasp, I close my hands around its neck and manage to bring it into the car.*

This is so against my conscience and my inborn heart wisdom that I initially overlooked the violence of my dream behavior, choosing to focus on the epiphany of the hawk coming to me at all. It actually lands on my hand more than once, as if testing my intentions. By grabbing it and forcing it into the car, I have abused its trust. In the dream, I interpret the spots of blood on its neck as evidence of a previous injury and—incredible as this sounds—instead of admitting that I might have harmed the bird, I jump to the absurd conclusion that its injury was what motivated it to come to me in the first place.

What does a man moving along the black path to nowhere look like to a red-tailed hawk hunting high above the boundary of the road? A lost, desperately driven creature . . . a homeless, self-imprisoned victim of some kind of linear trance . . . *And yet it comes to me.*

The second dream:

*I am standing in an open vehicle parked on the side of the road with a student I was tutoring (in another dream), and I am eating an asphalt sandwich: a sandwich made from the surface of the road. And on the sandwich there is a coating of some grayish granular stuff that is used to treat the road and it has a slightly sweet taste. I am trying to get my student friend to try it, which he does reluctantly, letting me know that it doesn't appeal to him. I keep taking more bites out of the sandwich when I come to a stick embedded in the middle. Only then do I toss the sandwich onto the shoulder of the road.*

*No wonder I have felt listless and heavy.*

These dreams show me exactly where I am in relationship to the black path and to hawk. By grabbing hawk, I am attempting to assimilate the red path without leaving the black, without even slowing down! My poems have been calling me out, but I haven't been up to it. I am consuming the road for sustenance, but there is nothing healthy in it. Finally, when I come to the embedded stick, I am repulsed. These dreams are two ways of looking at the same crisis: Grabbing hawk from the car *is* eating the road. In this dream I am perilously close to identifying with the black road. Far from an act of power, this is an act of impotence. The stick snaps me out of this weird uroboric loop that has me compulsively consuming the all-consuming path.

To this road, with Walt Whitman, I say: "You road . . . I believe you are not all that is here,/ I believe that much unseen is also here . . ."

And I say, "I am not afraid to leave you . . ."

And I say, "The east and the west are mine, and the north and the south are mine. I am larger, better than I thought . . ."

And I say, "From this hour I ordain myself loos'd of limits and imaginary lines" (13).

*Out of respect for the path I have chosen to walk (the red path), I can no longer seek asylum in the false security of taking sides. Things are not black or white, good or bad, alive or dead, and we are neither conscious nor unconscious, awake or asleep. When I am dreaming I am awake. But I have not been dreaming regularly for a long time; I have been walking around with my eyes open, but I have been asleep. These distinctions are no longer helpful. I must take responsibility for my life as one seamless experience, one stretched-out moment of possibility, where choice of focus is all-important and "real and unreal are not differences in kind but of degree" (14).*

*In my dream, hawk risked his life to teach me something.*

What is trustworthiness? We have burned so many bridges! Acting like Saint Francis is not going to convince the birds of our sincerity. Animals too look for signs! When Francis returned from the crusades, they no doubt watched him with interest; they saw how different he was from the others; how ecstatic and dedicated to his visions this crazy barefoot monk was. They watched him distance himself from his family. They watched him step outside the rigid hoop of his upbringing and education into the wider hoop of his calling.

Sicangu's (Lakota medicine woman), Yellow Bird Woman's dream, that she had before the Sun Dance, is about entering into this new/age-old relationship with the sacred, a relationship based on a two-way trust that is unshakeable and nonnegotiable—one might say contractual. It is about seeing and being seen:

> In this dream I was at a Sun Dance and there were all women dancing (dressed the old-fashioned way like her grandmother) . . . they're in a circle in the Sun Dance ground, and they all have an eagle on top of their heads . . . I was in the middle. It was still sitting on my shoulder . . . (Then) all these women were old-time dancing . . . Those eagles flew up above them flying in a clockwise circle. They were all looking at me, and I was looking at

them, and their eyes were yellow. They were scary, and I looked up and my eagle didn't even look at me; he was looking way over there (15).

# 5

## Crossing Alive/Crossing Dead

Dreams are holographic if we let them be. They are snapshots of the whole picture. Wallace Black Elk says, "One little part of you is sacred" (1). But in that little part is everything. That's how it is possible for life to replay in seconds when one is on the verge of cashing in one's chips. But it's not just at the moment of passing. All of life is contained and reflected in every single moment.

*(This would be the time for a reality check!)*

*The phone rings:*
Me: *Hello?*
Voice: *Good morning Mr. Lindorff. (pause) Are you a home owner?*
Me: *Yes.*
Voice: *Does your home have a septic system?*
Me: *No.* (I am lying and hang up.)

If *all of life is contained and reflected in every single moment,* and we are not just talking metaphorically here, then how does this apply when one's attention is interrupted by a telemarketer? There are several ways to approach this question. If Spirit or the Self is calling through the telemarketer, then the marketer's pitch becomes symbolically charged or numinous, and not just the question but the precise words and life itself assume the character of a great dream. The numinous question is:

*Are you a home owner?*

I have a home, but I have been away for a month and a half; my wife and I just returned the day before yesterday. But do I "own" my home? The whole question of ownership taps right into a core issue of my life: the morality of owning a piece of a rapidly shrinking planet. Owning land legally only sets the stage for a deeper, tacit covenant expressive of a sacred indebtedness to the spirit of a place that we can choose to honor or not. If we do, we become full partners with the land, participating in its renewal. Ownership expands beyond the idea of possession to the idea of being allowed into the land's dreaming— essentially being possessed by the land in the sense of being chosen by the land *to* possess it.

Children must be taught to become territorial.

*Even when I was very young, most likely trying to make sense of our family's move from an apartment to a new house on three acres, I remember wondering how far down in the earth we owned. 150 feet, the depth of our well? A mile? All the way to the center of the earth? Nobody could tell me. But even before the morality of land ownership came up, I was instinctively worried about the legitimacy of it. Owning a three-dimensional piece of a round planet seemed ridiculous; would it not have to taper toward the center like a piece of pie? For someone obsessed with digging to China, such questions were bound to arise. (How would I know when I had dug beyond our wedge of Earth?) And property lines seemed extremely sketchy. I was always being admonished not to play on the boundary where our neighbor's property started in the middle of the field, but when it came to who owned what plant or stone, where was the line? How could a line be drawn across a clump of moss or a log or a rabbit's nest?*

It is apt to speak in terms of the "footprint" of a building, which refers to the area of the foundation. I live in an intentional community made up of a handful of families who, originally, pooled resources to purchase land on which to raise and homeschool their kids. Most of the land is common land, and yet my wife and I have been dedicating a portion of this land to the cultivation of ritual and ceremonial space. At the same time, the land has cultivated, in us, a new sense of home that reflects our soulful interaction with, not just the immediate environment, but the world.

Not everyone can be a homeowner, but everyone can be at home in a place where, in Kirkey's words, "the place and the person are extensions of one another, mutually co-arising" (2). Something in me winces at being tagged a homeowner, simply because such an appellation reminds me of my privileged status, but I am pleased to say that I live in a place that I love, that I call *home*. "Ecology is the study of the household." Furthermore, Kirkey reminds us, the word *ecology* comes from the Greek word for house, *oikus*. Therefore, becoming ecological beings means that the land is our house. If there is any question as to how literally to take this, we have Gary Snyder, who takes his metaphors *very* seriously, to reify the connections: "If you've learned about the kitchen and the dining room, you've learned about the household. If you know about the household you know about the watershed" (3).

*I watched our modest two-story Cape go up in the middle of a field, from excavation to finishing touches during the summer of '55 and was privy to every step of its construction. I remember the pungent earthy smell of the clay slurry that came up during the drilling of the well, the sodden chalky smell of wet cement and plaster and the resinous smell of the 2 x 4s of the framing, the woody perfume of sawdust mingling with the faint vapors of turpentine and paint, mingling with the sounds of hammering and sawing, the rich odors of disturbed earth and the tar they applied to the foundation. There were pieces of building materials everywhere: bits of colorful tile, nails, solder, linoleum, odd sections of copper pipe, silver washers, wood, and insulation. The whole building site was literally alive for me, and part of that aliveness had to do with my childish participation and my witnessing how the house began as a hole in the ground and how it came together from materials that I could feel and smell and hold in my hand. Later, exploring outward from the house, as I grew up, I became intimately familiar with every single inch of the land. When I left that place as an adult, for a good twenty years my dreams always brought me back there and there was a part of me that never left. I have since learned that some of the plants and animals I befriended there will never abandon me in this lifetime: white pine, golden rod, elm (where the oriole wove its nest of milkweed silk), butternut, shagbark hickory, apple tree, praying mantis, writing spider, skating spider, green snake, damsel fly, oriole, thistle, milkweed, dandelion and skunk cabbage, to name a few. Even today, I depend on all of these to remind me of who I really am.*

As to the septic system reference, it happens that in last night's dream I was cleaning a wound on my leg and flushing the infection down the drain of the kitchen sink. In the dream I am not in my own house but am visiting the home of a good friend who is absent. So, this annoying and seemingly random phone call, which I might easily have ignored in favor of pursuing my train of thought, is not what it appears, but it reveals itself to be a powerful attractor of associations, which begin to crystallize around the lattice of my life.

Psychologist/philosopher Ken Wilber uses the term *holarchy* to describe the way in which reality is organized as independent wholes that make up larger wholes, which are, in turn, part of a larger whole, ad infinitum. The attractive units of this holarchy he calls *holons*. (*Holon* was coined by Arthur Koestler.) You can observe this *holarchy* everywhere in all kinds of life situations and contexts (physical, biological, or mental), not just in the showstopping synchronistic episodes that occasionally punctuate our days (4).

We think it's a lot, the journey from birth to death, but it only seems like a lot when it isn't connected.

It's like toning, the ancient practice of vocalizing a continuous chain of sustained phonemes. The more voices you have, each humming whatever note comes out, the better it sounds. Every note belongs, and it comes out as perfect. So it is with a life.

When we don't feel connected, we are only hearing one or a few notes at a time. When we make foolish and hurtful mistakes, that's the note we make, but as long as we remain connected, somehow it tends to come together harmoniously in the end. Sadly, connection is not for everyone. Some lives are train wrecks. Where is the beauty or poetry in a train wreck? Sometimes it doesn't connect, and it winds up being a hodgepodge. . .So the question is, beautiful to whom? The greatest art, if it is truly great, reveals something beyond beautiful or ugly for that matter. But life offers exactly that: the opportunity to stop and study ourselves, in any given moment, as masterpieces. Certainly our lives are worthy of the same contemplation with which we honor masterworks, and, as with viewing any masterpiece, we must be prepared for something magnificent or sacred to shine through the weave of all the drama and stuff (the paint) of our lives.

*How do we maintain this awe of self?*

*Here is what came to me this morning when I was feeding my cat, Olive: She is on her table behind the sofa waiting patiently for breakfast. The bag of food is right next to her, but she needs me to open it. If she were starving, she would still need me to open the bag. Her brain can't tell her how to do it; it doesn't have the key, and the instructions are not part of her cat program. So she is dependent on me to oblige, and this keeps her dependent. That is how it is with me. Spirit is in the bag, a paper or two thicknesses away, and I can't open the bag! It's beyond me. I mean, I can't access Spirit on a regular basis to take care of my spiritual needs. To become this supercat, I need to shift out of my dependent personality into a more capable self.*

Wallace Black Elk says you always have to have a spirit guide. When you "go there," for example, "when you have the fire and the stone-people (referring to the sweat lodge), you offer a little green (cedar) and water to them. . . . Then somebody is watching you. When you go there you have courage, patience, endurance, and alertness. If you are missing one of them, that's your weak spot" (5). (This bit about *somebody is watching you* reminds me of a little boy at bat! The adults on the sidelines are the spirits cheering for his success.)

I have to think about this. When I go into the woods to a power spot, I am firing on more cylinders, and when I bring in the seven directions (north, south, east, west, sky, earth, and within) and begin speaking out loud, things start humming. I can open the bag and feed myself. Using Wallace's model, when I do this work, I am operating on those four cylinders: *courage, patience, endurance, and alertness.*

*One time, years ago, I was sitting in just such a power spot, on a favorite sun-warmed boulder just off an old overgrown logging road, sections of which had long eroded down to bare ledge. I was in the middle of a peaceful meditation, breathing in the incense of balsam and white pine, when my concentration was shattered by the strangest commotion. Some young men were trying to muscle their car through the forest on the logging road, which I knew to be impassable except by foot. Even though I could not see them through the dense foliage, I could easily picture exactly what they were doing, given their excitement and expressions of frustration and occasional barbed commentary on each other's ineptness. Their girlfriends were with them, tactfully maintaining a very low profile. The forest soon absorbed the din, and I was able to enjoy about a half an hour of relative calm before they were backing the car up the same path and the whole bizarre circus repeated in reverse, receding whence it came. As I struggled to return to my meditation, I began to sense that I was being observed by another man who was meditating deeper in the woods—a man who looked like me.*

Here is an instance when the road came to me; it found me in deep retreat where there should have been no road. This is one way of looking at our precarious situation as we try to make a place in our lives for the practice of retreat from the proverbial rat race.

The problem is that the middle world pursues us and, if we're not careful, eats us alive. It starts nibbling at the edges, going after our sweetness, our essence. It's ongoing and relentless and affects us both psychically and physically. Wallace Black Elk refers to the body as a robe. If you take care of the robe, it can last a long time, and it looks pretty good, a good fit. As it starts to fail, we begin to realize it's just a package, and we begin to move into the mind, which is somewhat less tied to the middle world, depending on how we use it.

*In my case, my mind is probably intact, but my brain and my body have been compromised. (The latest research indicates that our brain's functions start to decline around age 45.) When my mind is engaged, it holds my brain like an orange floating in a pond. When the brain is left to its own devices, courage and alertness soften and lose their edge. Everything is tentative—memory, facts.*

This relates to what Deepak Chopra writes about. Understanding mind or intelligence as *field*, or higher self as field, explains a lot and takes pressure off the brain—which we associate with neural synapses and electrical impulses—to provide answers. But that is a different model than Wallace Black Elk's because Wallace is talking about spirits who exist outside of mind. Deep down, I prefer Wallace's explanation. (It speaks to 99% of the million-year-old biography of the human experience.) Unfortunately, the model that comes closest to my middle-worldly experience is Chopra's. Why unfortunately? Because it takes a book—a very fine book, but a book nonetheless—to explain how mind "can go deep enough to change the very patterns that design the body" (6). When the mind accomplishes things that spirits have always done in the body, bending the rules of science, that happens in the quantum realm, outside of time and space. According to Chopra, in cases of spontaneous remission, research has shown "that just before the cure appears, almost every patient experiences a dramatic shift in awareness. He knows that he will be healed, and he feels that the force responsible is inside himself but not limited to him—it extends beyond his personal boundaries, throughout all of nature" (7).

Chopra's *quantum healing* is based on the ancient principles of Ayurveda. As he explains, in rural India, where a stripped-down version of Ayurveda is still practiced, even though the *spiritual ancestry* that Ayurveda taps into is being eroded by the institution of modern medicine, one finds that the holistic "intricate rules for daily life" that Ayurveda prescribes are "in the air" (8). This is a good way to describe a holistic medicine: that it views healing as a real possibility that is everywhere—in the body, in the mind, and in the universe, that is, the quantum body.

Wholeness has to include the quantum body, which is infinite, but that means we can't circumscribe what it is about holistic medicine that heals. Neither can we isolate what part of a spontaneous remission was spontaneous other than to observe that *shift in awareness* (or acknowledge that there was a shift in awareness) preceding the cure. Chopra chooses to represent a quantum event with a "?" situated beneath (or beyond) a line, the line representing the threshold of the phenomenal world of the senses.

A shift in awareness is a quantum event.

It's like the Hubble telescope's deceptively miniscule straw-sized opening onto the universe that reveals galaxies beyond galaxies. It's holographic—one little bit of infinity is infinite!

But the infinite is not outside of us. What am I getting at? Without a personal experience of *Wakan Tanka* or *Tunkashila*, we will never find ourselves and will always be writing books about the "?" all the way to the bitter end. Being a Wasichu, I understand Chopra and I understand Jung. Being a New Wasichu, I must be critical of any language that distances the self from Spirit or abstracts the face of the infinite.

What about Jung? He had no qualms about referring to *spirits* to explain certain psychic phenomena, bemoaning the "terminological crudities of science" in its refusal to *go there* (9). He was, apparently, able to differentiate between psychology as a science and psychology as a "technique." Although he himself was comfortable changing hats and shifting orientation from analyst to alchemist, this versatility of mind could easily be interpreted by his critics as straddling. But Jung understood the nature of the psyche better than anyone in his time and was comfortable with the relativity of consciousness to the unconscious. What becomes problematic for those of us who have tried to follow Jung's lead is that he never quite figured out what to do with the ego. (Maybe that is the job of religion.) The Jungian conundrum can be summarized as follows: We need an ego, or our *ego-complex*, to individuate, to interact with and assimilate psychic contents, but nobody ever fully individuates, so we are stuck with the ego—the questionable centerpiece of modern civilization—for the duration. Unless the ego learns to submit to the forces of initiation it will become more *complex* than ego, lost in a privatized world of its own projections and transformation will keep eluding us.

Jung did not consider himself a Jungian. As a psychologist, he was an incomparable empirical scientist, but as a practitioner, he was an old-time alchemist at heart. (He claimed the great physician and alchemist Paracelsus as a blood ancestor.) But because of his protean stance to theory and practice, he could never make everyone happy. (Anecdotally revealing was Jung's conspicuous absence from Martin Buber's lecture at the Psychological Club [precursor of the Jungian Institute] because "Buber had criticized his . . . focus on the Self rather than others, his 'I and Me' rather than the 'I and Thou'" [10]. Whether Buber fully understood Jung at the time is questionable, because Jung consistently defined the collective unconscious, the archetypes and the psyche as transpersonal, on the order of a Thou; apparently Buber was not convinced.)

At any rate, the Jungian shadow is the expanding intellect, and Jung must bear the responsibility for this blind spot that amounts to a golden carrot: *The one who has studied the most mythologies and symbolic systems, cosmologies, and religions is the best Jungian.* True enough, to become fluent in the archetypal language of dreams calls for a higher and deeper understanding of symbols that amounts to a "cogitation aurea, a 'golden' understanding"; and, simply stated in an alchemical text, "those with symbolic understanding have easy passage" (11). How tempting to imagine that anyone who managed to become fully individuated would be seeing the world through golden spectacles, the elusive *vitrum aure* of the alchemists (12). But let us not confuse *symbolic understanding*, which is analogical and essentially intuitive, with *acquired knowledge*, which is counterintuitive. Using a Vermont metaphor, intuitive knowledge is distilled knowledge—it's the syrup to the sap, and I wouldn't be surprised if the ratio is the same: 1:40.

Individuation is never easy, and knowledge is the least of it! As Jung himself reminds us: "It is what you *are* that heals, not what you know" (13). But what we *are* is not static. It has a history, it will be tested, it matures and, as it passes through the stages of life, it evolves. After Jung's example, anyone who chooses to become a Jungian analyst must undergo extensive analysis as a core requirement of their training. In other words, every practicing analyst must have, to some extent, individuated. The trouble crops up with the certification-process that formalizes one's readiness to practice. I have worked with seven Jungian analysts in the past (a couple of them quite renown), and the one that seemed gifted with this *cogitation aurea* was a young man whose application to the Zurich Jungian Institute was rejected, so he just hung out there and took courses until his dreams let him know it was time to hang up his shingle. One time I looked up during one of our sessions, and his gold-rim glasses had formed little shining orbs around his eyes. He was the real McCoy.

(There is a difference between having knowledge and *knowing*. Knowledge has already been experienced and is capable of being taught or assimilated, but it is not fresh. Knowing or coming to know carries the sense of direct perception or personal experience. Sometimes knowing opens to us from deep inside as we mature, like seeds or doors or vistas.)

Wallace Black Elk cuts through our overemphasis on acquired knowledge and certification with his story of how Spirit approached him as a mountain, as four sets of hoots, closing the gap, and then a *tap, tap, tap*—only then stepping around to his front. This is a story that works for me, and I can't help but think it could work for many of us. (Even if it doesn't happen, we owe it to ourselves to prepare for when it might!) Wallace was just a child when Spirit approached him, but I think there's a universal lesson here: that Spirit sees us all as children. And if we could swallow our pride and admit that we don't know anything, there is always the possibility that Spirit will approach us just this way—with a few hoots and a gentle tap on the back.

*This is what I am waiting for and hoping for because I can't warm up to the* "?". What is the "?"? It is a threshold, the line over which we can't follow because nothing is the same on the other side. It's when matter and energy do this little dance and become something different than we could ever imagine. And that's the point: It can't be imagined! It has to be experienced! Until something is experienced, we can *pretend* to understand it or we can write books about understanding it, but we have no connection with it; we are doomed to be bystanders of the mystery, settling for numinous question marks.

Take water. Water is water, right? No—water is *life*. Wallace Black Elk gives us the Lakota word *mni* for water, which translates into m + ni, *breath of life*. He says, "Water is *a living*" (14) (my italics); that is a verb-noun. He could have said it's *alive*. It could just be a typo, but *a living* comes closer to the point; it's not a living "thing" because a *thing* (in the Wasichu's camp) is not alive. Water likes to move and change form, and its medicine is life, so it's a living mystery. (In fact, as theoretical physicist F. David Peat points out in *Blackfoot Physics*, chemists have yet to agree on how the molecules of $H_2O$, the building blocks of water, are arranged. If, as some molecular chemists suggest, water consists "of a subtle but complex arrangement of a vast number of molecules, this means that information could indeed be 'written into' water by very slightly changing the nature of this arrangement" [15].)

Joseph Bruchac (Abenaki writer and storyteller) tells a humorous (Watala) story that illustrates this primal shape-shifting spirit of *mni*:

> Three men were ready to do a sweat together. They made their sweat lodge by the lake and built their fire. Now the stones were heated and ready to be taken into the lodge, but they discovered that they had forgotten one thing. None of the men had brought a bucket to carry the water into the lodge and the lake was some distance away from their houses. By the time someone went to get a bucket, the rocks would be too cool.
>
> "I will use my power," the first man said.

> He went down to the lake and found a fish carrying basket.
> . . . When he dipped the basket in the water and carried it back
> to the sweat lodge, not a drop of water leaked out. He put the
> basket by the door of the lodge . . .
>
> "That is good," said the second man. "Now let me see what
> I can do with my power."
>
> He, too, went down to the lake and found there a drip net.
> He put the drip net into the lake and it came up filled. He
> carried it back to the sweat lodge and the net did not leak when
> he placed it beside the first man's basket . . .
>
> "I, too, will bring back some water," said the third man,
> who had remained silent until then.
>
> He walked down to the lake, knelt, put his hands into the
> water and moved them in a circle. When he stood up, he was
> holding a ball of water. . . . He carried it back to the lodge and
> placed it on the ground next to the basket and the net. When he
> poked his finger into it, the water ran out.
>
> "This may not be good enough," the third man said. "It
> leaks too easily."
>
> The other men said nothing, but when they went into the
> lodge, the third man was the one who led the sweat (16).

In other words, you can take the most common element, water, and
we don't know what it is. So how are we going to approach the
quantum universe? Everything over the *?* *line* is beyond us, which is
pretty much 99% of the universe.

We're very smug about how we classify and divide, but when you
take away our words, we know absolutely nothing about reality. We
don't see the mystery in anything—how everything in it is *a living.*

*That means we're done, finished.*

We think we're ready to graduate, but we're tied up and blindfolded, lying on our faces, and the universe is wondering if we really want to be here. It's walking around us, wondering if it would be unkind to wake us up and untie us, our consciousness is so fragile. We should probably be eased into reality little by little. For example, here is *mni*—we call it "water."

This kind of re-education is not about learning a new language, it is about forgetting everything we learned in school and starting over with fresh introductions. It is about inviting the mind to simultaneously expand and ease ever deeper into experience. (Experience first, language will follow.) This goes against the grain of contemporary Western society, which "increasingly filters its selection and interpretation of the world environment" (17). The Australian Aborigines avoided this pitfall by, over the ages, "rigorously connecting language and thought to careful perception of the natural world. . . . As the Aboriginal mind matures it is initiatically introduced to revealed knowledge in stages. . . .With each initiation comes a new vocabulary or language that enables them to comprehend these mysteries. (With them) these timeless revelatory languages are always connected to the tangibility of Earth's topography" (18). In other words, as the Aboriginal mind matures, there is an initiatory language waiting for it that will illuminate the new topography.

This is not true of the English language. Marie-Louise von Franz (who worked closely with Jung) points out that "our language (by which she means German, but her critique applies equally to English) is completely causally structured, entirely oriented toward cause and effect. We are so bound to the idea of a cause and its effect that linguistically and intellectually, we cannot get away from it" (19). For the inmate of the English language, neither is there any way out of a linear relationship to time. Present, past, and future are hardwired into the grammatical structure of our every expression, making it difficult if not impossible to verbalize any kind of spiritual or transcendent experience, where the subject (I) is secondary or nonexistent and time is completely relative to one's state of consciousness. One might say that the only initiation that the English language anticipates is the initiation into an increasingly industrial (production and consumption oriented) and technological mindset.

When it comes to spiritual or transcendent subjects, English is a borrowing or assimilative language. Narratives that introduce new (to the culture) concepts or new categories of experience expressive of alternate, parallel, or transcendent realities, for the most part, have to redefine terms that already mean something. (Advertisers are very good at this.) Writer, historian, philosopher Mircea Eliade did this for *ecstasy* when he defined shamans as *technicians of ecstasy*. In the 1960s, when there was so much experimentation with mind-expanding drugs, English failed miserably to rise to the occasion, retaining no hint of a psychic or spiritual revolution, but leaving us with such words and phrases as *freak out, drop out, tune out, blow your mind, space out, vibes, bad trip,* and *good trip.*

Carlos Castaneda's books came close to pushing the envelope of language for talking about new kinds of experience, infatuating readers with Don Juan's explanations of the *nagual* and *tonal* and the *first, second,* and *third* attention. (Only one of his books was actually published in the sixties [in hardcover], launching the tale of his apprenticeship to the enigmatic Yaqui sorcerer, but I think we can all agree that Castaneda's convoluted journey through *nonordinary reality* is organically rooted in the spirit of the sixties, a zeitgeist that specifically encouraged such adventures.) Another high point in the literature, Alan Watt's *The Joyous Cosmology: Adventures in the Chemistry of Consciousness,* almost did justice to the new mind-blowing psychedelic landscape. And I will never forget the excitement of studying D. T. Suzuki's *An Introduction to Zen Buddhism,* not just for the refreshing esoteric concepts but for the language of Zen. For example, the words *koan and satori* were English and yet not English, but I was determined to make plenty of room in my brain to let it *be* English—it was my hurting native language itself that was pushing to be initiated beyond the old too-familiar categories! Watt's had plenty of faith in the ability of English to communicate new kinds of experience, which he was anxious to introduce with *The Way of Zen* (in 1957), where he was quick to point out that understanding the principles of Tao and Zen would call for the scrambling of current (Western) thought-patterns. (20) (The word "psychedelic" [*mind or psyche-opening* ], perhaps the most association-rich word to come out of the 60s [but one that has since lost much of its original storied meaning], was actually coined in 1957 by Osmond Humphry, a British psychiatrist doing LDS research in Canada. For me that word even has a smell—that of sandlewood and a pungent, perfumy East Indian incense that they would burn in the head shops where I went to buy my bell-bottoms.)

The roots of English go deep, but popular usage is incredibly shallow and subject to programming. (George Orwell, author of *1984*, discusses the systemic manipulation of language in his essay, "Politics and Language.") Indigenous languages are dying at an accelerating rate, but so are modern languages. Manipulation and dumbing down of language by the media (news packagers), lawyers, politicians, preachers, teachers, and marketers has become the norm. We expect to be seduced and lied to, exaggerated to, and flattered by remote strangers (trying to get us to spend money on ourselves), but we ought to consider how the long-term programming of language affects our basic trust in words, even the words that come from our own mouths. When we lose touch with the expressive potential of language, we forfeit the power to be believed, or worse, the capacity to believe ourselves.

Clearly, English-speaking peoples have not been around long enough to initiate each other—or, perhaps more to the point, they have been too busy touting their own version of reality to taste and smell and see and feel and dream into what lies beyond their mean. For the Australian Aborigine, language and experience have never been exclusive. By their paradigm for living, education never stops; consequently, age is not the main factor in determining an individual's stage of maturity, rather whether one has been initiated. (An uninitiated adolescent cannot be expected to understand what an initiated young man understands, even if the young man is his chronological peer, and so on through the various stages of maturity in both men and women.) When a preacher told some elders, "You, too, should learn like the children," they replied, "An abundance of different knowledge is ours—we already have our fill" (21).

We are also full, but our situation is the opposite of these elders. We *are* like children in that we have a lot to learn, but first we have to empty. Peat relates, "A Blackfoot Elder said that the white race is the youngest race. It has energy and potential, but, for the past few thousand years it has been playing like a child, while it is watched by the black, yellow, and red peoples. Now the time has come for the white race to . . . assume its responsibilities along with the three other colors in the world" (22).

For our graduation, maybe we will be introduced to the sacred spirit we call *bear*, known to many Native American tribes as ancestor, spirit guide, helping spirit, guardian, lover, dream keeper, and medicine doctor.

> Owl, your call paints you exquisitely
> On the perch of my owl-loneliness!
> —— From author's poem, "Oh Stone"

Here is a medicine story about the *red path* that teaches about the color *red* first; then it shows how powerful that is when it takes you somewhere. This is not a meandering path like the Zen way. It's direct and unambiguous. It gets you across whatever you need to cross; then maybe you can get back to the Zen path, if that's your way. Wallace Black Elk says:

> When we come to this lodge (the stone people lodge) we come here to paint those stone people red. We say it that way in our language. We don't say that we come here to heat up the rocks. There's also a powdered paint we use to paint them when a person goes on a vision quest or there is a healing ceremony (paint from the Bad Lands). . . . Now, like I prayed when my dad was sick. So the spirit came in, and I prayed with those powdered paints. Then the spirit took those powdered paints and said, "This is sacred." Then he drew a line over and across that rock pit in the lodge. So from there I walk across it, and my dad crossed it, and came out alive. (23)

There is much left to the imagination in this passage; the mystery is being respected. Does "he" (who drew the red line) refer to Wallace's father or the spirit? As we learn to let go of our outmoded either-or assumptions about reality and begin to trust our perceptions to guide us deeper, we might find that we are well equipped to enter any kind of reality, even a reality in which Spirit acts through one or all of us in ritual. There is a refreshing literalness, a just-so-ness, a celebration of tangibility to this anecdote that may be hard for our brains to digest. The challenge, of course, is to accept the gift without question.

And this is a powerful gift from Spirit. The *red path* is literally a red path that begins in the lodge, transecting the fire pit, pointing straight out of the womb (tezi) (*Tunkan tipi* = birth-age shelter). The stone people lodge is the womb where the fire is returned to the stone people, and in turn they rekindle the fire in our souls. We rededicate ourselves, and ideally, we walk from lodge to lodge. ("You go from here for two or three months, then stop at that lodge" [24]). Then Wallace has something to say about how to walk.

> The most simple way is the best. So every step you walk to the lodge is a prayer. From there you walk off, and every step you take is a prayer. . . . So the right step is from this lodge. . . . So it's best to lift this foot and place it in the stone people lodge. . . From then you go on for another two or three months. (25)

Again, this is not *just* a metaphor. He is teaching us how to walk, how to rededicate ourselves to our Earth-walk, maybe even how to be reborn. It's not a head game. *How you pray is how you walk, and how you walk is how you pray.* Life is a big medicine walk.

If we don't realize that, we are cheating ourselves of a birthright.

This may sound extreme to those of us who don't pray, but this approach to praying is not about religion or morality or even language; it is about moving in a sacred way through life by relinquishing some control over where our next step will land us. As we get older this becomes easier, but humility can be practiced at any age.

Praying, as a practice, comes with being human. Sometimes it helps to have a template but it's not rocket science. When I was a child I learned the Lord's Prayer, the prayer that stands as Jesus's example of how to pray. . .like this: "Our Father who art in heaven. . ." When we walk prayerfully we might see it as a form of praying to our Mother: "Our Mother who art beneath us. . ." First, we are barefoot. Each time we step we leave a sorrow or a pain behind to be absorbed by the earth or sand or concrete we are walking on. Our first steps in the meditation may be heavy but as we go we lighten up and each step gradually becomes a royal step or Buddha-step or a warrior step or the kind of step you take when you are around someone who needs their sleep.

One of the most familiar or common forms of prayer is about *asking* (akin to Sanskrit *prach, to ask*) for something that is needed (for oneself or another) such as health. Prayerful walking can be about continuing along as who we are, through thick and thin, without abandoning the attitude of prayer. What I am describing is as much metaphor as physical movement, so anyone can do it. It is not tied to a specific practice but if we think about those different times in our lives when we have walked (or if wheelchair-bound, rolled) mindfully, that is what is called for here.

Walking from (stone) lodge to lodge is a uniquely Native American tradition that the Wasichu may experience if they don't mind going a little out of their way, but I think we can all identify with the need to build in rituals that keep us focused and honest as we progress through life one step at a time. And yet, how many of us live this way? If we did, I can imagine that death would be a very natural step, something like continuing to the next stone lodge.

The more territory one's mind stakes out in life, the more one has to lose to death: the great crossing. Holger Kalweit goes into this. "Among the Siberian Buryat the soul, after having roamed around its former dwelling place for three days, must step into the ashes of the fireplace; if it leaves no trace there, it becomes aware of its new state and sets out for the land of the dead" (26). Complications arise as consciousness sheds its layers. "The Ojibway believe that on its way to the world of shadows the soul will encounter an obstacle for every transgression in its former life" (27). Another cross-cultural archetypal feature of the journey of the soul of the deceased is having to cross a barrier or series of barriers—a river or a ravine or a mountain—that separate the living from the ultimate destination of the dead. He explains that the soul's progress depends upon its own spiritual readiness to leave the ego behind, Wallace Black Elk's "robe" of the soul.

According to the California Chumash Indians, the soul must be encouraged to leave and will only head for *Similaqsa* after the property of the deceased has been ritually destroyed (28). Eventually there is a bridge that the soul must cross. As it crosses the bridge, two huge monsters rise from the water. However, the soul of anyone who has regularly attended the traditional *toloache* (leaves from the ritual plant) rituals has nothing to fear and may pass over the bridge safely.

The Australian Aborigines will use special songs to assist an erratic spirit to its resting place (29).

The Sioux speak of the soul traveling along a southward spirit path until it arrives at a fork where the ancient grandmother, Maya Owichapaha, is waiting to judge the readiness of the soul to continue on to Wakan Tanka, to the right. *Maya Owichapatha* means "she who pushes them over the bank," which is where the unprepared soul must quarter (30).

The Tibetan and Egyptian Book(s) of the Dead instruct the deceased to "calm down, dissociate himself from his earthly life, attune himself to the new situation, and in particular, learn to confront his expectation and conceptions in a detached manner" (31). The so-called Egyptian *Book of the Dead* actually refers to a miscellany of spells and incantations or *orations* that were originally referred to as "Spells of Emerging in Daytime." James Allen, curator in the department of Egyptian art at the Metropolitan Museum of Art, goes on to explain that these texts "are not about death but about life: specifically, eternal life as a spirit" (32).

If one is adept at letting go in life, he or she will presumably have an easier time consummating their crossing at death. "The Zen monk allows the (archetypal) images (generated by fear of letting go) to come and go; they pass his all-pervasive wakefulness without leaving emotional traces in his consciousness" (33). These emotional "traces" are apparently very substantial and very real in the no-man's-land between the reality of the living and whatever awaits the soul on the far side. Kalweit goes as far as to submit that "It . . . depends on the psychic maturity attained during one's lifetime whether the entry into the Beyond causes us pain or transforms us into a blissful state" (34).

For some people, the river that needs to be crossed is a turbulent, raging torrent, whereas for others, it is a narrow brook. In one Ojibway narrative of the journey of the soul, there is a river that must be crossed on a fallen tree. As the soul approaches, the tree itself transforms into a serpent. If the soul remembers what words to recite, everything goes smoothly—otherwise not (35).

In *Monty Python and the Holy Grail* (1975), there is a scene in which the knights are stopped at the entrance to the Bridge of Death that spans a bottomless precipice that is blocking their quest. (Even though this is not a soul crossing, the lesson is instructive.) The gatekeeper asks Sir Galahad three questions. He answers the first two correctly. The third question is "What is your favorite color?" Much relieved and almost glibly, he answers "blue". He tries to change it to yellow but too late, he is launched into the precipice. Apparently he didn't know his favorite color. The teaching here is don't underestimate the value of simple proofs of self-knowledge; they may come in handy in the end.

# 6

---

## Dreaming and Firewalking

*You want to know what nuclear is? They think they have the power. . .
Grandfather is wisdom, Grandmother is knowledge . . . When they come
together that's power.*
> — Wallace Black Elk (from *The Sacred Ways of a*
> Lakota)

I am writing now because I am a Wasichu trying to wake up, trying to
take my power.

*I was dreaming all night but I don't remember anything, and this fundamental
apathy has found its way into my holographic self-snapshot. Not lazy, but tired, not
tired, but sad, not sad, but indifferent, not but, but and . . .*

Last evening, two friends were talking about their cell phones,
about the amazing abilities of these little handheld computers.

*It can do this . . .* and *Oh, listen to this, you won't believe this!*

*One said he can take a walk in the woods on Mt. Killington and his phone will
track him and map his way back, topographically and all . . . Oh, and the two of
them were at a concert and one dropped his cell under the seat and was able to use
his friend's cell as a light to find it. It's also a flashlight! What's wrong with this
picture is how the whole conversation was about the wonders of these wee computers,
and if you own one then you have access to powers and resources that are just short of
miraculous. We happened to be inside a church where my wife had just delivered her
sermon about the birth of Christ, announced by a heavenly star, about how back
then there was an openness to revelation or to the influx of miracles and the
fulfillment of prophecy. I guess that was because the old dream was all played out.
Maybe there was a vacuum in the holographic snapshot.*

In our age, we know how to make a hole in the sky, but we lack the
eyes to see beyond. In indigenous cultures, the sky and the earth,
though distinct realms, are creatively and spiritually connected.

According to Holger Kalweit, a shaman of the Tsimshian people of the Canadian northwest begins his soul journey through a hole in the sky (1). The Huichol creation story unfolds when the Sun asks the Deer Spirit, Kauyumari, to find a nierika or portal through which Grandfather Fire (Tatewari) leads the sky gods to Earth. The Wasichu have a strange relationship with the sky. On a clear night, at least in the country, we can see just how many satellites crisscross the heavens. We are always sending rockets into space and gazing at the stars, but to what purpose? Technology has given us a chance to be greater than we are, to see and imagine far beyond ourselves, but our science is stuck in the flypaper of seeking what it wants to find, tiptoeing around the mystery. Hubble, with its farseeing eye, and Kepler, are the exceptions, but for the most part the international space program has divided the pie of space into thirds: one for pure research, one for military opportunism, and one for commercial exploitation (tourism and future mining). Little has changed in the last 600 years in terms of how we approach frontiers. Our vision lags far behind our worldly ambitions.

Let's face it, we are ready for any kind of technological breakthrough, but if a spirit came in and sat down across from us, we would not know how to respond without instructions.

*When I was very young (nine or ten), when my brother and I shared a large room upstairs with a partition between us that didn't quite reach to the ceiling, allowing us to converse through the wall, he and I used to talk until one of us fell asleep into the gaps between utterances. Our conversations consisted mostly of me asking him questions and him answering with oracular authority.*

*My brother was deeply into science and science fiction at the time and was well versed in the jargon of the brand-new science of space exploration. So one of these evenings we were both lying in our beds, staring at the ceiling, lulled into a kind of soporific hypnosis by the pulsing drone of the insects, and I asked him to explain infinity. I forget exactly what he said, but my mind started picturing a giant tube filling all known space, something like a giant intestine leading off as far as I could imagine and looping back on itself in an impossibly intricate mass, except there was no symmetry or pattern involved. It was just all there was filling the interstellar vacuum. His words had somehow kicked out the floor, walls, and ceiling of my room to the infinite, and the endless tube was my way of keeping this inconceivable vastness at bay. Then I imagined these people walking through this tube in one direction from the beginning of time, never getting anywhere, just trekking generation after generation, following the pitch-black opening. The image is reminiscent of Plato's cave, except there are no silhouettes or shadows of caravans, nor reflection of light . . . nothing but the meaningless progression. I was able to hold this vision as long as I was an observer, but then I stepped into the body of one of these tube people, and something unexpected happened. We came to a dead end, but without any light, it was absolutely real, and it was the antithesis of everything we had ever experienced as a race. The opposite of birthing—an end to our epic trek. And then something even more unpredictable occurred: The black wall began to disintegrate visually into a kind of colorless field of nothing and everything. It was indescribable and infinite! (It was what I would now describe as the vacuum plenum.)*

*I got my experience of infinity, but I was too young to absorb the lesson that with infinity comes infinite possibilities, an "infinite ocean of energy in potential" (2) or, from a journeyer's point of view, a jumping-off place, a nierika. At that moment in my life, my only choice was to either go mad or return to my adolescent reality. It was almost impossible to reestablish my own dimensions; I had to wake up my brother and beg him to talk me down and back to my room and my body, my self-field. I doubt he would remember this, but for me it was huge, and like the dream of the voice telling me to span the ocean, it added to my blueprint for a cosmology that stretched my imagination way beyond its childish limits, pushing me to the extreme edge of sanity. What was sanity in the 1950s but the surface tension of a watery abyss with no bottom? I was just trying to stay afloat, and, in retrospect, I see that my only hope of surviving my childhood, without the guidance of a wise elder, was to figure out how to survive my own visions and nightmares.*

There is trouble in the tent of the Wasichu, trouble in the Western world, trouble in the global world. I wish I could say that I'm not contributing to this trouble, like Black Elk, who can simply state: *It's not me.* "I'm just a little prayer tie." But the spirits come in and ask, "What do you want? Why did you call?" And he tells them, and they say what they see and fix it. They accept the offerings and leave.

In the Wasichu's world, almost everyone is essentially helpless. Nobody has a ritual that powerful. And where is the individual who enjoys that quality of rapport with the spirit world? Very few individuals function on that level because it combines utter *humility* and utter *confidence* (3) -- the humility of praying, the confidence that one's prayer will be received. I guess those would be the fruits of wisdom and knowledge. If you harbor any doubt, nothing happens. So if you don't think anything is going to happen, you're probably right. That's why, in the *Yiwipi* ceremony, they cover every single source, every place where light can enter before spirit can be summoned. We have to blindfold our source of doubt, which is our ego consciousness, because our ego plays by a whole different set of rules, and we know every game has its rules. That's one way of looking at the trouble in the Wasichu's tent. If you're playing Monopoly, you can't win with a *full house*. The rules apply only to the game that we're playing, which is why nothing was accomplished at the 2009 Climate Summit in Copenhagen and exasperatingly little was accomplished at the 2011 Summit in Durban or in Rio in 2012 or in Warsaw in 2013, and why it is so rare for anything to be accomplished at such a plenary meeting of nations. One of the unspoken ground rules seems to be: *There can never be consensus on anything of importance for the welfare of the planet.*

At a candlelight vigil, everybody knows what needs to be done! It's simple, it's elegant, it's revolutionary, it's local and expansive and visionary, it's the answer. But to someone driving by who doesn't agree, we are only nine people standing in the cold, holding signs and cupping candles. The fact is, there aren't that many people out there *not* playing Monopoly. They're getting kicked around by the winners, and they keep landing on the wrong squares and paying through the nose, losing everything, slipping into bankruptcy or getting lucky and putting the screws to their neighbors, but as long as they're playing by the rules and playing the game, there is no other option; the rewards and penalties are all in the rules.

My own mother, whose father was a coach, taught me to "be a good loser." After all, in Monopoly someone always wins and someone always loses. This was great advice for surviving high school and the working world, but Vietnam and the Cold War with its arms race to doomsday (and Erich Neumann's *Depth Psychology and a New Ethic*) challenged my mother's wisdom. If life is a competition, what if nature is the loser? Or common sense? Or compassion? Or the Maldives? Or what if the monarch butterfly or the great blue whale is the loser? Is that permissible, or should we simply refuse to play?

Banish the thought that our self-destruction is by consent! Banish the thought that we could play a different game. Banish the thought that we could summon Spirit on a collective scale and that the same thing that happens in the stone people's lodge might just happen in the Wasichu's tent. Spirit might show up and ask what we want, and if what we want is all for the good and the healing of the planet, it might just say, "Fine, I'll fix it." But we would have to be humble and confident and set things up by Spirit's rules, and we'd have to sit down and be courageous and patient, alert and enduring (resilient). And if there is anyone who doesn't believe that it's going to work, kick them out. Maybe there's a party down the street where they'll fit in. Show them the door.

*What composes effective ritual? What game are we playing, and what are the rules? There is a lot at stake here—too much. And I don't make light of it. There are close to two billion Christians and a like number of Muslims out there who aren't going to sanction changing the way things are done. Period. The world is in a state of religious lockdown.*

Last night I went for my biweekly acupuncture treatment. This one was for stimulating my dreaming. For the last third of the session, I was lying on my stomach with needles flanking my vertebrae, and I must have dozed off. With a few minutes left in the session, I woke to the following dream:

*There is a small black and white tiger on me. He isn't dead, but he is flat out on my back. He seems to have given me the gift of all his vitality. He has no energy left. I gently lift him off my own back.*

And the night before last, this dream:

*There are some spirits in a cave waiting. I see them with my dreaming eyes. They are standing by the cave entrance, luminous, glowing like an old watercolor. They are waiting for my father, I guess. Maybe he is coming or maybe they will emerge from the cave soon and greet him. These are good people, kind spirits, ancestors perhaps. They are dressed in medieval garb: tunics, robes with sashes. They are colorful like fruits bathed by candlelight.*

A few nights ago we participated in a firewalk on New Year's Eve. Leading up to the ceremony, for several hours we circled up in a large yurt under (I will call her) Teresa's leadership, 30 of us, getting to know each other, drumming, taking turns looking into each other's faces. Halfway through the evening, we broke circle to build the fire, selecting logs from a pile and ritually placing them at right angles to the grid of logs that had already been laid out by the fire tender, and with each log, another prayer, another intention was added to the pyre. When the square pile reached chest high, we were instructed to stuff wads of newspaper, our "old stories," between the logs. Next, we poured on used cooking oil—the oil of anything left that was holding us back. Last, we ignited our torches of rolled newspaper smeared with oil from the primed pyre and collectively lit the great bonfire whose sacred purpose was to reduce every last bit of wood to a wide path of glowing embers that would entice, tease, test, and ultimately surprise the soles of our feet. For me, just then, the firewalk was the mother of crossings. I could not see anything threatening in it. It was simply something I needed to do. The only hurtle for me was my personal lack of preparedness, which must be normal. How can you breathe until you breathe, fly until you fly, walk on red-hot embers until you walk on red-hot embers? The way I saw it is, we have latent hungers and desires that rise spontaneously out of our deepest nature, as well as the abilities to respond to those desires.

We all have it in us to be magical, and every cell in our body ecstatically knows this. Every cell lives to further the whole holographic wonder we call *life*. Otherwise, how could the hair growing out of my earlobe be collaborating with the nail of my big toe?

Chopra's example of what happens in the body when we think "I am happy" is particularly illuminating of this beautiful two-way flow of ecstatic information—a kind of four-dimensional poetics of manifestation that we are capable of tapping. In his words, "a chemical messenger translates (our) emotion . . . into a bit of matter so perfectly attuned to (our) desire that literally every cell in (our) body joins in. The fact that (we) can instantly talk to 50 trillion cells in their own language is just as inexplicable as the moment when nature created the first photon out of empty space" (4).

Maybe it was my feet that needed to do this firewalk and were taking charge. So in a sense, my holograph reflected this foot-dreaming-medicine power. Every trace of me was communicating with the ecstatic response of my feet to an overwhelming summons. (In some indigenous cultures where black magic or sorcery is a real problem, sorcerers take full advantage of the resilient holographic field of what constitutes a human being; by doing violence to a trace part of their victim, they manage to inflict harm on the rest. "Pieces or parts of a human body [hair, urine, spittle, nails] are causally connected to the person in such a way that action [heating, singing or piercing] on the trace image or part would affect that person" [5]).

*I saw a black snake raise its head in the orange-glowing window of the woodstove in the yurt, its muscular body pressed against the glass. I watched its head rise higher against the underworldly surges of heat as if trying to get a look at us before receding into its fiery home.*

Each exercise took us deeper, and most of the group were good sports and serious initiates. A few couldn't hold the space, but everyone eventually rose to the occasion, thanks to the arrow breaking and the rebar bending.

*At the firewalk, the moon came out to watch. I was drawn to be the first to cross, waving my arms in slow motion in honor of hawk. I tried to convey hawk's nobility and fierce grace by not hurrying. This was a symbolic act, an archetypal drama I needed to stage and needed the group to witness. If I had been alone I would have taken more time to prepare emotionally, mentally and physically. As it was I was a little concerned about appearing indulgent. . .Everyone who was walking crossed a number of times.*

Our instructor was brilliant, in her role as teacher and master of ceremony, at encouraging risk taking relative to each person's unique journey while fostering an atmosphere of celebration around New Year's. She shared some of her story of how she came to facilitate firewalks. Years ago, she had been diagnosed with multiple sclerosis and was wheelchair bound when she heard of firewalking. She told her story as a medicine or teaching story, as proof that we can change our biology. It is one thing to read about such spontaneous remissions, but working with someone who has walked that path of power is quite another thing. One's soul responds with a knowing nod or a leap or by ruffling its feathers, and the clouds part and the vista opens and you begin to wonder if anything is really impossible or is *impossible* just a tape that we switch on because we're terrified of being powerful, because *then what?*

The other side of the argument provides the subtext for our lemminglike march toward oblivion—that the tape has brainwashed us into accepting that *nothing is possible.* The *matrix* has infiltrated our psyches and changed us into prophets of pessimism and impenetrable skepticism; even our cells have been altered to reproduce our entrenched lethargy and craziness or worse, and so the loop reminds us *ad infinitum* that we have drifted too far to find our way back.

> . . . *drifted too far, too far.*

Seth (self-described *energy personality essence,* speaking through author Jane Roberts) says the rational mind is very comfortable with insoluble problems because they keep it busy. In fact it *creates* insoluble problems just to justify its existence. He says the self, which he refers to as multi-dimensional. . . "creates varieties of conditions in which to operate, and sets itself challenges, some doomed to failure, . . .at least initially, because it must first create the conditions which will bring new creations about" (6). We are living in a time when doom and creation are vying for the stage.

When you have miracles, the rational mind has to sit down and shut up for a change. The deadening loop fades into the background, and suddenly no problem is insoluble. I wish it wasn't either/or, but it looks like the rational mind will have to take a step back in a fully functional world and be willing to serve as adjunct to the comprehensive wisdom of the mind, the heart, and the soul.

*In the morning when we were leaving, we stopped so I could retrieve a piece of charcoal from the fire bed. I stooped, selected a chunk, offered my breath, and, only when I stood to head back to the car, did I realize that the still smoldering coals had been raked into the form of a great heart. Since I hadn't noticed the heart at all when I knelt, it was as if the fire was spontaneously communicating its love to me and that it saw my struggles.*

# 7

## Morning Star

In Jung's Foreword to the Wilhelm/Baynes translation of the *I Ching*, the ancient Chinese *Book of Changes*, he introduces the "curious principle" of synchronicity as:

> . . . a concept that formulates a point of view diametrically opposed to that of causality. Since the latter is merely a statistical truth and not absolute, it is a sort of working hypothesis of how events evolve one out of another, whereas synchronicity takes the coincidence of events in space and time (in this case the throwing of coins or the counting of forty-nine yarrow sticks) as meaning something more than mere chance, namely a peculiar interdependence of objective events among themselves as well as with the subjective (psychic) states of the observer or observers (1).

This brief description of how synchronicity works applies to any form of serious divination. Elsewhere Jung explained the working of synchronicity in terms of the constellation or activation of the archetype, an "ordering principle" that extends energetically across time and space. Synchronicity effectively "brings a reordering of the pattern of things within which situations and conditions are contained" (2). Before Jung's wholehearted, public embrace of the *I Ching*, divination, at least for the Western world, was never taken seriously by the intellectual community but was regarded at best as an old-world entertainment. Jung, in a sense, was laying down the gauntlet to his peers; he knew that the time was right for casting these pearls. Across cultures, there have always been those who have used divination as a way to hear from the divine or the other side, going back many thousands of years, and the ritual protocols for reading signs, events, and omens are myriad. In a way, what seems to matter more than the ritual form of a divination is the attitude of respect and awe of the querent for the divine grounding of the process.

There is a scene in the book *The Reindeer People* in which the author is sitting beside Kesha, a traditional Eveny herdsman. It is late and, as they are the only ones awake in the yurt, Kesha feels free to reveal some of his hunting secrets to the author, who has won his confidence and friendship. He demonstrates how it is possible to practice divination by cooking the shoulder blade of a reindeer over the coals of a flameless fire. The fine cracks that appear are graphically interpreted as the landscape where the hunting is best. Kesha expresses dismay that the young men would often return from a hunt empty-handed only because they were closed to the old tried and true ways of seeking information. (3)

*I didn't want to be like one of those young hunters, behaving as if I were the first to do something that wise people have been practicing for centuries.*

For how many centuries have people walked on fire?

Going back to Jung: It is hard to identify the archetype that was containing me (or my wife, Shirley, and me) in the aftermath of the firewalk or to describe my subjective state relative to the reordering of "the pattern of things" within which we or our situation were contained. What is clear is that the firewalk, as a powerful archetypal event, was not something to file away. Rather, it was something to marvel at and ponder.

The day after the firewalk, a good friend stayed with us while she and my wife cofacilitated a women's retreat at a local venue. She brought with her a deck of cards she consults, and that morning, with the firewalk so fresh in our thoughts, we three took turns picking a card randomly from her deck, asking what it all means for the new year. After choosing a card from her Motherpeace Goddess deck, I brought out the Tantric Dakini Oracle cards, and we each randomly selected one of those.

Here is what came up:

First drawing (Motherpeace deck): *The Nine of Cups.* This is the wishing card. Priestesses have come with offerings to the sacred wishing well where a statue of the Goddess presides. They drink of the spring and become ecstatic, "energized by the love of the Mother." The book says: "This is a visionary card. The priestesses open themselves to the inner ability to envision future events. . . . Because they are open . . . they are able to wish for what they want without doubts. . . . Optimism and trust in the future . . . a time for wishing for whatever one wants and trusting that one deserves to get it" (4).

Second drawing (Tantric Dakini deck): *Number 19, Phoenix.* According to the authors, 19 "signifies the ultimate mystical attainment, combining the number of unity, '1', with the number of completion, '9.' This card corresponds to the sun of the traditional Tarot. From an alchemical fire of transformation, there rises up an eternal flame burning up the past and all illusion. From the flame a Cosmic Couple is born in divine union, the celestial Buddha . . . and his consort. They are colored blue, symbolizing the complementary aspects of the celestial voidness as wisdom and means. . . .They also represent the Philosopher's stone. . . . Feed the bird and it will move in the nest and then rise up like a star in the firmament" (5).

What is so interesting in these two readings is how the archetypal field of 9 spans the two decks—interesting but not, numerically speaking, out of character. Jung was keen to point out in his essay on synchronicity (1952) that natural numbers have performed a key role throughout the history of divination. Furthermore, von Franz, who carried forward Jung's research on the acausal principle of synchronicity and the archetypal roots of math and number, informs us that "when numbers are used as instruments of divination, they do not have their quantitative aspect . . . which is their chief characteristic in the Western theory of number . . . but *they have a field aspect of—rather, their series appears as—a continuum*" (my italics) (6). So, here we see that the Tantric Dakini reading enhances the power of the 9. In the Motherpeace deck, there is a celebratory sense of arrival for the priestesses at the Eden-like wishing spring presided over by the moon goddess. The Tantric Dakini card turns up the heat on the 9 so that now, instead of just arriving at the moon spring—where renewal and hope always return as promised, in cyclical fashion, conveying both an air of relief as well as ecstatic inevitability—now the Moon Goddess is marrying the masculine Sun in its fiery aspect.

The Motherpeace card is the 9 of the Moon Goddess, whereas the 9 of the Tantric Dakini card is the 9 of the sun, but by adding the 1, something mystical, transformative, and transcendent happens. The negative influences of the past are incinerated. Out of their celestial union emerges the red star: neither moon nor sun but something new and unique that carries a little of the energy of both. This is the new phoenix.

The text for the Tantric Dakini (19, Phoenix) states that "fire levels all things, reducing all structures of mankind to ashes. . . . Out of the ashes of the fire of passion there arises the capacity for selfless love. (7)" It is noteworthy that the pyre for the firewalk was structured as a giant cube (half a cord) of logs. This could represent the structures of humankind. Out of the ashes, the morning after the walk, there appeared this beautiful heart. But the structure was needed for the creation of the rectangular bed of ashes. Without the imposing structure of specially stacked logs, the flame would not have been able to consume so many logs in such a short time (a mere two hours), but the symbolic dimension was just as vital: The cube was symbolic of our structures, just as the newspapers that we wadded up were our old story. We built a structure out of our intentions and poured on the old oil of our insoluble impurities that float upon the waters of the deep unconscious.

*But can a whole civilization do this ritually? Do we perform this ritual so the whole civilization doesn't have to burn down the structures that it has identified with?*

When the twin towers of the World Trade Center came down, mine was a dual response. On the day of this epic disaster and for several days after, the skies were immaculate blue—even the weather was waiting to see what would happen next. I was heartbroken over the devastating loss of human life, but at the same time, at that still place, at the bottom, I was not surprised. A month after the debacle, when I visited Ground Zero with my father, noxious fumes still hung in the air.

*What came down that day? What is the lesson? How have we grown?*

While they were still sifting through the toxic ashes, the public was invited to submit ideas for a memorial. My concept was to send up a satellite with a powerful lens focused on the stars above Manhattan, and there would be a dome below to provide an enormous concave screen for a live projection of the heavens so that visitors could enter a peaceful twilight sanctuary: a garden dome, perhaps with aerial gardens, mossy stones, and whispering fountains, random niches buffered from the sounds of commerce. In grief, I treated myself to the thought, as with Chernobyl: *This is enough, this will catalyze a shift in our trajectory.*

Not so.

So the structure goes up in flames, burns, is reduced to embers. We, the initiates of a new time, cross, learn a little bit, a little more, about selfless love and courage, and the earth reciprocates with a heart, composed of ashes. What could be more beautiful, more grounding, saner than that?

There *has* to be a new *thing* in our cosmology, something outside of the familiar solar system that holds space and calls to us from an immeasurable distance because we aren't there yet, and it behooves us to journey—not only to journey, but to watch for other journeyers who are just returning.

The power of wishing is (etymologically) related to the love goddess Venus and to desire. Wishing signals, if only momentarily, to the cosmos, that one wants to be related, to be seen, to be approached, to close the gulf, to be loved.

*One of my favorite songs from childhood, and one that my mother used to sing to us when we were growing up, was that sweet song that Jiminy Cricket sang in Disney's* Pinocchio, *"When you wish upon a star". The song says that wishing on a star can make your dreams a reality, regardless of who you are. Presumably from the star's perspective we are all the same. As long as our hearts are in our dreaming the star will not judge whether our wish is reasonable or over the top.*

Every morning Wallace Back Elk's grandfather would pray to *anpo wie*, the morning star. He would sit there by a little fire that Wallace would prepare. There would be a little bucket of fresh water, and he would "hold up his arms and pray. It was beautiful. That star would dim and brighten, like in a fog. Then it would swirl back down or go sideways, stop and shoot back up. Oh, it was so beautiful! So every day we would greet the morning star that way. My grandfather told me that when you hold your arms up to pray there, it was like touching the face of *Tunkashila*" (8).

The Australian Aborigines have different names for the sun, depending on whether it is rising, shining full, or setting. In a single day, the sun can be male or female. They tell a story about Mother Sun who lived inside a cave on the *Nullarbor Plain* until the Great Father Spirit woke her up. Until then, the earth was barren, because all life forms were not ready and were fast asleep in time. As Mother Sun journeyed across the sky, everything became charged with life and began to move and blossom and flourish and reproduce. Mother Sun gave birth to Morning Star, whose wife is the Moon. Their children are the ancestors of the Aborigines. (9) To us, the stars seem far away, but to the Aborigines, they couldn't be closer. They are family.

When Wallace Black Elk was locked up in the loony bin, a spirit unlocked the door of his padded cell. The spirit pushed the doors wide open and invited him to walk outside.

> So when we got out there, there was a man coming down from the clouds . . . and those two met and started talking. So I was standing there and looking around. It was really good to take a breath and see all that *Tunkashila* had created and what Grandmother had given me. So this other spirit came from the morning star (10).

# 8

## Ethos of the Road

*The faraway line of the freeway faint murmur of motors, the slow steady
semis and the darting little
cars; two twin towers with faint lights high up blinking; and we turn on the
raised dirt road
between two flooded fallow ricefields -- wind brings more roar of cars.*

*Hundreds of white-fronted geese
from nowhere
spill the wind from their wings
wobbling and sideslipping down*
                —— Gary Snyder, "Spilling the Wind"

In the Lakota/Sioux *Yuwipi* ceremony, the medicine man is tied up in a blanket by his assistant. All the lights are doused. The spirits enter, and animals and little lights fly around. When it's over, the lights come back on, and there is the medicine man sitting with the rest of the people. The blanket is neatly folded. That's how it is to a greater or lesser degree with any shamanic healing ritual. The ego has to be bound and gagged or silenced somehow or other so that Spirit can move in and do its work.

Although the charade persists, medical doctors know that they don't heal anyone. Sometimes the medicine, the science works. People are kept alive on a daily basis by the pills they take or the treatments they receive. (This morning my nasal decongestant made the difference between hours of wiping my eyes and blowing my nose and making myself useful and being good company.) But half the time something in the patient is triggered by the placebo effect, and the doctor goes with the flow. George Thomas (Ph. D., M.D.), writing for his blog, *Medicine: Facts and Fiction*, states unabashedly: "not everyone is cured of strep throat by penicillin, and some people with strep throat recover without any antibiotic at all. If I were responsible for the treatment of 1,000,000 patients, I would have no hesitation in making certain recommendations, but if I am recommending treatment for just one person, I am never 100% certain if the treatment (a) will work, and (b) is necessary" (1). The treatment, although statistically effective, is extremely impersonal. What he is saying here is that he would treat the individual the same as he would treat many individuals with the same diagnosis, only with less confidence, because chances are a large proportion of the many will respond to the medication while, with an individual, improvement is less certain. This conclusion is based on hard data. This approach is the exact opposite of the indigenous approach to plant healing described by Stephen Buhner in *Sacred Plant Medicine*, which presumes that "no two diseases or people are identical." The same may be said of the *spiritual identities* of the plants, which helps explain why "every medicine that is prepared is unique" (2).

By contrast, some allopaths (allopathic physicians) have no qualms about prescribing powerful drugs the way high-tech weapons are used on the battlefield. These doctors are less healers than strategists, or— Buhner's term—*disease technicians* (3). (To be fair, taking our cue from the definitions of the word in question, we might divide allopaths into two camps: the first camp would be those who practice allopathy based on a "system of medical practice that aims to combat disease by use of remedies producing effects different from those produced by the special disease treated" and by following a certain protocol of treatments, and the second camp would be those who adopt "a system of medical practice making use of *all* measures that have proved of value in treatment of disease" [4], which might include unconventional treatments.)

Western medicine seems to have reached a crossroad some twenty or thirty years ago. Politics of health care aside, the whole approach to modern medicine has increasingly been streaming in two almost opposite directions as certain physicians, one by one, begin to step away from the lab-coat persona to explore what it means to be a modern healer.

Almost daily advances in medical technology, along with diagnostic breakthroughs, are beyond impressive, but what are the chances of the average person benefiting from this science if society can't evolve out of a market culture? Perhaps what's needed is a whole new algorithm for walking us around our old approach to health care, shifting our focus from how to provide affordable health care to *how we approach health itself.* The fact is that people who choose to embrace a holistic lifestyle rarely, if ever, set foot in a hospital or a clinic. Medicine that depends on technology will never be affordable to the world until the word "affordable" is obsolete. Perhaps access to technology should be considered a human right. In the meantime, low- or no-tech medicine is effective, available, and affordable.

Shirley is incredibly open to holistic treatments and remedies. She is open to any modality if she approves of the healer/practitioner. I love her attitude, but it bothers me that health is so elusive. Something is often missing. There is plenty of good medicine out there, but good healers who know how to use the medicine are rare. This includes allopaths. It is common knowledge that many of the drugs that conventional medicine depends on are derived from plants, but all medicines come from the earth, so even the most synthetic drugs can be administered shamanically with respect for the spirits of the chemistry. According to vegetalista/curandero Don José Campos (whose grandfather was a curandero and whose father was a conventional doctor), "the thing with pharmaceuticals is, you also have to know to ask for the relief to bring that other experience in . . . to invoke spirits when you work with pharmaceuticals and that adds something else to it" (5). Even as the number of shamans in the world is shrinking, the number of shamans who are also MDs and the number of MDs who have undergone shamanic training is on the rise. But, for the most part, traditional shamans are immersed in a very ancient calling.

Lyon writes in his preface to Wallace Black Elk's *Black Elk: the Sacred Ways of a Lakota*, "We should protect these elusive and shy professionals (shamans) as we do our most endangered species. They are the guardians of a rare, but once powerful, force in human-kind" (6). *Shy? Elusive?* The proper training or initiation of a healer guarantees that the healer will not identify with the medicine but will work with the spirit of the medicine as channel, interpreter, or partner. One Apache shaman, whom Lewis Mehl-Madrona revered, told him that he (the shaman) was as "powerful as a dead chicken". When pressed, he broke down the credit for healing accordingly: 70 percent goes to the patient, 20 percent to Creator and 10 percent to the healer. (7) Shamans and healers know their place, which is one reason they generally keep a low profile.

Our firewalk instructor and I engaged in a little correspondence about the firewalk and I was surprised to learn that she felt she had failed us, that her facilitation / instruction had "fallen short". She was even contemplating sending out an apology to the group. Then I realized that I had caught a glimpse of this angst or doubt in her eyes and had dismissed it because I thought things had been going fairly well and told her so. But according to her she was really struggling to do her job, to get out of her own way and was entertaining doubts that we were going to be ready; everything was moving too quickly.

I wrote back that everybody even remotely involved with this kind of work can't help but sense that time is accelerating but, having said that, it is also true that in ritual space, time slows down. Eliade distinguished between profane or *homogeneous* time and sacred time which he understood as *heterogeneous*. Probably at no other period in history have these two dimensions of time been so interpenetrating and so at odds. One reason for this is, we are starving for meaningful ritual and we do ritual so seldom that there is a lot of pressure, pressure on ourselves as participants to rise to the occasion or get something out of it. There is a tendency to be over-anxious. From the ritual leader's point of view it is hard to tell who is in and who is only half in. Ritual leaders do what they can to "hold space" but ultimately everyone in a ritual is held by invisible hands. If profane or homogeneous time and heterogeneous or sacred time are at odds there is a problem, the space is compromised, and there is only so much that the ritual leader (no matter how gifted and experienced), or even the invisible hands, can do for us.

Certainly Teresa's statement that we can "change our biology" is revolutionary to many of us and hugely inspiring but where do we start? Often the ego is identified with what needs to change in our biology! The ego is a problem; fear is a problem; the space that we inhabit when we go home is often a problem as well as our relationship to time. All of this is brought into the compass of ritual.

*I am reminded of how a client's illness, or shadows of his illness, cropped up in certain of his dreams. In one, as a kind of phantom, he revisited a house that he associated with his past, passing through rooms where people were going about their lives. They didn't see him or sense his presence. Next he was caught up in a vortex in the sky above the house, and this powerful, unfamiliar woman appeared in the whirlwind hissing angrily, "You shouldn't be here!" This woman's salient warning was only the icing of proof that he was in grave danger. Was the vortex his illness or his fear? Or both? The vortex has the power to carry one over the rainbow, but if one is unprepared for the journey, one may lose one's ticket back.*

I want to believe that Spirit is just waiting for us to learn our lessons so it can point out the next step, but it might be that in our zeal to evolve, we have plunged recklessly ahead of ourselves, we have missed a few red flags along the way and suddenly we are standing on the edge of a precipice.

One of the hazards of living on the cusp of a new age is that we might outpace ourselves! There are no substitutes for *the work*, and, in terms of the large picture, there are no shortcuts.

It might feel like cramming for an exam in a dream in which everything is weighted against our passing the test (so familiar to many of us). Is the test legitimate or bogus? Should we step back and grant ourselves more time to prepare, or *go for it?* These days, when so much depends on our seizing the moment, *passing the test* could mean the difference between graduating to a more mature or soulful level of understanding or spending another year in the dream classroom, which may strike us as a living death. Yet if the prerequisite for learning what we need to know is a turning from the precepts that guided our every thought and action before, this can take time. Like any radical retraining, the lesson might even require us to fail so that we come back more focused!

This raises the question: *When is fear of—or anxiety associated with— pressing forward, a hindrance, and when is it legitimate?*

*Shirley gave me a large glossy picture of the face of a green-eyed white tiger. She came home from her retreat with it. Yesterday I taped this tiger up and looked deeply into its eyes for a good half hour. Suddenly I began to sense that it was looking back at me with ten times my focus, scanning me. Is Spirit scanning me and not finding what it is looking for? Is my higher self trying to find something that's been missing?*

"Don't let us be roadkill!" I shout in my poem. "Let us cross!"

Up to now, I have been picturing the red road as crossing the black path, the asphalt. Now I flashed on this image of the red path *incorporating* the asphalt road as threshold. It's just part of the red path. You can't avoid it. It's there because of who we are and where we've been, and crossing it is just part of the sacred medicine path. It's our destiny as the New Wasichu, and for each one of us it means something different. As we cross the black segment of the red, we will be scanned by Spirit at the double line, just like travelers are scanned by those full-body scanners at airports. If Spirit sees we're not ready, we have to come clean and try again. We have to submit to this Spirit scanning because we are contaminated; we might be wired and could do a lot of damage.

Wallace Black Elk wrote there was a prophecy from the spirits that was broadcast nineteen, now twenty, generations ago. Periodically since then, every time his people came together they spoke more languages. Even so, they are still the Earth People, the Lakota, because they speak the same *mind* (8). I suppose the big question is: *Is this mind available to the Wasichu?*

To avoid falling prey to the ambiguities within our own language, we will distinguish between two kinds of "mind," which we will identify as *mind* and mind. The etymological roots of *mind* have to do with memory (Old High German *gimunt*) and the verb form *to remember*. This would be the *mind* of the shared or universal language that the Lakota speak by virtue of their *remembering* who they are: the Earth People. (When a people are "of the same *mind*," maybe they don't *need* to talk; they can communicate very simply and elegantly with their eyes or expressions or gestures. They know the routines, rituals, when and why things are done and in what particular order.) The second mind refers to the "sum total of the individual's adaptive activity considered as an organized whole though also capable of being split into dissociated parts", also "one's available stock of mental and adaptive responses"

(9). This mind amounts to a kind of mental self. It is more than a faculty, but it is an abstraction; still, we need it to keep evolving inasmuch as the world we have created is shored up by mental constructs and deals in abstractions. This mind is independent of memory; it is rational and adaptive.

When the Indian Claims Commission offered the Seminoles a token settlement for 30 million acres of the Everglades in 1976, some eventually accepted the offer and some refused it. This contributed to a profound split within Native communities and led to the formation of the Independent Traditional Seminole Nation and the Seminole Tribe of Florida, Inc. In this standoff between these two Seminole "minds" in the Everglades, we see, in microcosm, what we all face as a world of nation states and *tribes*: the recurrent pattern of a sovereign people opting to live in two different worlds.

Lyon writes that there are "things I now know about shamanism that shall never be put into writing." My guess is he is referring to realities about shamanism that have no mental (intellectual) correlative, so they cannot be adequately described. As long as we are identified with our mental self, we are on the other side of the track from the kind of shamanism he is talking about. And he also says, by way of helping us understand the *mind* of the Earth People, "it turns out there is only one side; it is our perspective on things that makes it appear as a duality" (10). To appreciate where Lyon is coming from here (in suggesting that the *one side* that he is referring to is not one-sided), it helps to consider that the original meaning of the word *side* was predualistic. It comes from the Old English *sawan*, to sow, and *sid*, meaning large, low, wide (11). So, it may be that the idea of taking sides goes back to the ancient scenario of two planters deciding to establish a line between their furrows; henceforth the word *side* implied this arbitrary territorial demarcation, rather than evoking the verb (and the image of) sowing the wide furrow.

In his ballad, "Tangled up in Blue", Bob Dylan sings to this (Lyon's) divisive *perspective on things* that may or may not reveal itself to a Wasichu as he or she journeys down the road of life. The song tells his story in terms of entanglements from which he extricates himself. In the process he realizes that "all the people we used to know", whether "mathematicians" or "carpenter's wives", have become an illusion to him, "tangled up in" the blue of different points of view. The problem isn't that we feel any differently about things; in fact our feelings are the same. (Maybe he is even saying that our feelings are what draw us together.) The problem is that we start from different "points of view". He, the wandering minstrel, compares himself to a road, moving ever on from "joint" to joint or from point to point.

Dylan is such a prolific and playful lyricist, it is easy to overlook the profoundly philosophical underpinning of his seemingly random, eclectic metaphors. The blue that "we" are all *tangled up in* could be the blue of the illusion of duality that functions much like the blue screen (or green used in filming movies and weather reports) upon which is projected the backdrop for all kinds of special effects or meteorological maps.

As related in his *Chronicles, Volume One*, during a recording session in New Orleans, Dylan was troubled by the last line of his song "Ring Them Bells," wishing he could replace the word *and* in the phrase "breaking down the distance between right and wrong" with *or* or *from*. But it is too late in the session for editing. He concludes, "The concept of being morally right or morally wrong seems to be wired to the wrong frequency. Things that aren't in the script happen every day" (12). Dylan lived much of his life off script, which is why or *how* he was able to see the entanglement of life as the stuff of illusion.

Outside the script, things might be right *and* wrong, or the distance between right *or* wrong might collapse. When life is scripted, our choices are limited. We each walk out into the same street and are hailed by different special effects and mental maps as our mind's perspective plays across the blue screen of our reality. We don't all see or think the same thing, but we are all tuned to the same wavelength. It is a little like being in a play in which all the actors are working from slightly different scripts. The slightly different scripts are our subjectivity, our point of view; the stage set is the middle world. So, when Paul Simon quips in his song "Gumboots," "I was walking down the street when I thought I heard this voice say: 'Say, ain't we walking down the same street together on the very same day?'", the most honest response would be *more or less*.

Our entanglement in the blue of duality is our fate to the extent that we spend most or all of our time on script. A classic example would be working for a company that provides what we need until it dissolves or we get laid off and we realize our well-being was an illusion. We choose or settle for a certain way of life until that way of life no longer sustains us, at which point we are confronted by a different set of choices, and so forth. Or, another example: We are healthy for most of our lives, and suddenly we come down with a serious illness that changes our perspective on life. Then we are temporarily off script. Dylan became a free-spirited folk icon overnight with his ballad, "Don't Think Twice, It's All Right" where he is ". . .walkin' down that long, lonesome road, babe. Where I'm bound, I can't tell." *Don't think twice* is excellent advice for anyone who wants to escape the entrapment of duality.

Let us dwell on that word *duality*. No one would deny that duality is "real"—as real as a hammer and nail or fire and ice, right? Well, yes, but it's not the only reality. You can lay a hammer and nail on the ground together, and where is the duality? It's in our perspective, but it's also in our application of the hammer and the nail. Once you pick up the hammer and drive the nail into a piece of wood, you have changed reality to suit your perspective. Or, say, you want to create a space for trapping heat against the cold: more duality. Wallace Black Elk says, "My people never discovered anything because we are part of the fire and we're part of the rock. . . We are still connected to our roots" (13).

Lyon notes, "They do not question the existence of power, only its application" (14). The Hopis always knew about the uranium at Four Corners, and they always knew to leave it alone. Their prophecy told them that once it was disturbed, all hell would break loose. So the Earth People were/are not inventors and builders and explorers; they are people of place and keepers of a living knowledge that is mindful and intuitive, neither abstract nor practical. Their knowledge belongs to them, but only because they themselves belong to the land whence the knowledge arose.

Now let us return to this question of perspective: The duality perspective seems to function as birth certificate and passport for the self-centered mindset. Without it, the justification for human autonomy evaporates. With this proof of legitimacy, the conscious self begins to make choices based on the illusion of autonomy. We might compare the duality perspective with a powerful program. But the history of Western consciousness reveals that the psyche was not always self-serving and self-centered, but Earth-centered and mother-/goddess-oriented. The matriarchal age, often depicted in mythical cycles as a golden age, was followed by the patriarchal age, heralding the autonomy of ego consciousness with its double-edged sword of duality, severing self from soul and soul from world. But now that we are on the verge of destroying the planet as we know it, it makes sense to personalize what is happening, even reducing it to something as intimate and immediate as an argument between ourselves and our beloved consciousness. If this is a relationship worth salvaging, then we will have to completely overhaul our relationship to power and knowledge and matter—not next week but *now*, if possible, before the next sunrise—ideally, yesterday.

*Spirit, it seems, is always willing to fix things if you know how to ask.*

Perhaps the hardest part for us is to admit that something in us or between us—each other, nature and our world—is broken. The oneness of our all sharing the same hoop, the *same-sidedness*, or the possibility of sowing the *ample* or wide furrow, is broken. We know all about stress, but an admission of brokenness is foreign to our culture. After all, it is in our nature to believe that we can fix anything once we apply ourselves. But that wisdom is tied to penultimate reasoning. Ultimately, it's our culture that is broken, but it's a sacred brokenness! Until we see that, we may not be able to help ourselves. When we *do* see it, we are in a position to be touched by the pathos of it all. Nothing is dull anymore; absolutely nothing is two-dimensional.

In the *Chunupa* (Sacred Pipe) ceremony, the two pieces of pipe are joined together in a sacred manner. When not being used ceremonially, the stem and the bowl are kept apart in a sacred bundle along with other ritual objects used in the ceremony. (*Chunupa* is a merging of *cha* meaning "*a wood*" and *nunpa* meaning "*two*".) (15) Maybe this is what our "brokenness" looks like to Spirit—like those two pieces of the sacred pipe that belong together. (By the same token, that which a divided mind might perceive as irreparably shattered, to a healed mind might present as simply disconnected.)

The Australian Aborigines—the exclusive, continuous human inhabitants of the Australian continent for all but the last few centuries of the past 50,000 years—have survived more than one ice age.[3] And yet, on Tasmania—where all the evidence indicates that they got started—it appears that they wore little or no clothing and did not build fires! "The attitude of the Tasmanian Aborigines toward cold reflected either a conscious discipline or innate adaptation" (16). Is this because, instead of investing all of their energy in surviving, they had learned how to become one with their environment? In *The Quest: One Man's Search for Peace, Insight, and Healing in an Endangered World*, Tom Brown Jr. relates how he and his friend Rick, at a young age, were taught how to stay comfortably submerged in a frozen lake by raising their body temperatures through "spiritual fusion." By means of supreme concentration, they were able to overcome the "demon of distraction" and achieve "absolute oneness with all things" (17). There was no longer any inside and outside to the self, no duality, and therefore no cold versus hot.

As a writer, forever experimenting with the advantages of the subjective versus objective perspective, I am moved to ask my tribe (by which I mean writers and poets here): *As we delve deeper and deeper into our work, into this mind, are we not bound to put down our pens, if only as a symbolic gesture and long enough to question what impulse or directive is at the root of this thing we do?* Isn't language itself (referring now to non-indigenous language) the offspring of duality, being itself a dismemberment of Levy Bruhl's *participation mystique* or mystical participation in a pre-dualistic state of mind or one-mindedness? In our dominant Western mythology, initially, the *word* (logos), was synonymous with the act of creation or creation itself, or, according to the Gospel of John, the

---

[3] Research, from the Max Planck Institute for Evolutionary Anthropology, Leipzig, Germany, reveals, in the words of Professor Stoneking, "from looking at a large number of genetic markers from all across the genome that there was contact between India and Australia somewhere around 4,000 to 5,000 years ago." This discovery does not negate the Aboriginal's aboriginality. But it explains how, apparently, it was during this period that the dingo was introduced to the Australian continent.

divine incarnate (as Jesus). But such an identification of logos (Logos) with the spirit of creation glorified the power of the mind over all, and mind never knows when to stop. As soon as you start making language you start being a creator; you begin staking out territories of mind. But before pressing forward with "How?" "Why?" "Where?" "When?" "What?" you establish duality because to ask anything *of*, or to ask *for* or *about* anything, there must be a conscious subject outside of mind, a some-<u>one</u> who is curious or lonely or just wants to make something out of the power of thought.

How Native Americans kept/keep clear of falling into duality is tricky—hence the red path. Being outside of duality does *not* exclude being conscious of polar differences nor does it mean that there is no falling into extremes, it means honoring the opposites and the necessity of sometimes choosing sides while taking care to avoid becoming possessed, or warped into thinking that other choices carry any less validity in the eyes of Spirit. Being on the red path is not about merging with the instincts or becoming one with nature, it is about seeing oneself as a functioning part of nature in Wallace Black Elk's sense (if I understand him correctly) of sharing the same roots as the rock and the fire and the four-leggeds etc. It is about letting nature be the teacher, and applying those teachings to living in balance with, instead of exploiting, nature which would be tantamount to turning on one's teacher. As I say, avoiding the pitfalls of duality is a tricky business. Even a people who have been spared the inheritance of a dualistic strategy for living need help. They need trickster, *Iktomi* (spider), coyote, raven, they need *Heyoka*, thunder clowns, to personify the relativity of good and evil, and the ambiguity of what is considered normal or healthy or sane. They need *Tunkashila* and they need spirits, ancestral guidance and wise elders who know the medicines and the medicine stories to keep them humble and confident. The shaman is the role model for the versatility of human nature. In shamanic practice, gender isn't static but feminine and masculine identities relax to become modes of power or vehicles of healing serving the priorities of the shamanic work as they arise.

We Wasichu are clever, but we tend to think our clever way is the only way. Our cleverness has run away with us. That is one way to interpret our downfall. *Iktomi* was always ready to make fools of humankind. I think anyone who becomes involved with shamanism eventually learns that Spirit has an incredible sense of humor.

When Wallace Black Elk was institutionalized by his own Christian relatives and locked up in a padded cell, a spirit came and opened the door. But unlike the Chief in Ken Kesey's *One Flew Over the Cuckoo's Nest*, he doesn't leave the grounds of the hospital. There is no point. He isn't trying to escape the Wasichu. They would only come after him. So the spirit stays with him in his padded cell while the Wasichu are figuring out how he managed to unlock the cell and walk out. Here is a perfect example of a peaceful, harmless, effective application of power. He just stays put and lets them arrive at their own conclusion: that they have no power over him. He isn't playing Monopoly, he's playing a different game by different rules with a full deck!

So they test him just like in the fairy tales. If he fails to demonstrate his power for the king, then he's crazy; they'll indoctrinate him or medicate him. In other words, he'll be back in their game. This being our times, the "king" is four Wasichus: an archbishop, a doctor, a scientist, and a representative of the legislature. All of them add up to the king.

The king is treated to a *Chunupa* ceremony. Says Wallace Black Elk:

> So we began. We turned off the lights and started playing the noise-maker, the drum—Chununpa honoring song, four winds, calling song, medicine song. Then—boom—a bolt of lightning and that spirit came in. . . . When he landed you could see this man in the dark. Next the buffalo came in. . . . So he went over to that Christian guy and started poking him with his horns. (18)

*Right now the phone rings:*

*"This is an important announcement from the health enrollment center."*

*The fourfold king is getting nervous out there. It wants me/us to be happy playing by its rules. It doesn't want us smiling about archbishops being nudged by spirit buffalos. It would have us enroll for health benefits at the enrollment center, not go to the Yuwipi or sweat lodge to ask Spirit for health benefits.*

At the beginning of this chapter, Snyder describes following a dirt road between rice fields, within hearing distance of the freeway, when suddenly, "from nowhere", a flock of geese appears "wobbling and sideslipping down". Many of us Wasichu, if we think about it, have experienced something similar. We leave the highway for a secondary road and then an even smaller way, perhaps without knowing why, and something beautiful or exciting, or miraculous happens; we are in the right spot at just the right moment.

Let us reflect on those two kinds of roads that we all know so well. Both kinds are numinous as they carry the feeling tone of our journey. When the journey inspires us and fills us with a sense of adventure, the black road is our friend and ally; it might even incorporate qualities of the red road. When the journey is obligatory or impersonal, the road reflects that ethos with signs warning us not to stop, to wear seatbelts, telling us how fast to go, how far to the next exit. This is the road of the patriarchy, and the road of the four-fold king.

The freeway is not free, it is a costly, troubled way, and no matter how far we detour, spirit will keep reminding us that leaving it for long is not a realistic option. Talk about parallel worlds! We tear along our interstates at eighty miles an hour while red-tailed hawk majestically perches next to our accelerating race against time, scanning the shoulder of the highway for mice or rabbits, secure in its wisdom that we pose no danger, that is, except perhaps in our troubled dreams.

# 9

## Crossing as Writer

*I am crossing*
*Crossing this dangerous road*
*With mouse, deer and snake . . .*

I would like now to address how the archetype of crossing comes up for me as a writer and a poet.

A haiku is potentially a *super metaphor*. It is able to condense huge amounts of information, but it (at least, a master haiku) also facilitates a crossing. Just like a full-blown ritual, it triggers a quantum leap across the ?-threshold that Chopra discusses in *Quantum Healing*. The reader is given what he/she needs to make the leap. When you encounter a super metaphor in a poem, it reboots your imagination, tricking the brain into taking a leap of faith from what it already knows to what the soul knows. This benefits the brain in the same way that advanced yoga benefits the body.

*When I firewalked, the hardest part for me was articulating my intention and finding words to describe the part of me I was willing to consign to the flames. My rationale for excusing myself from this exercise was that it was almost too obvious: The way I was feeling, there was very little reason not to cross; there was little I wasn't willing to consign to the flames. But the truth was that I really didn't know exactly why I was crossing.*

*Maybe an animal doesn't either. Maybe the map that it goes by predates the road!*

It's hard to get down to the nectar of intention. And yet I have learned how important it is to say why I am doing something, or what I need for life, or what I need to return to life. Such declarations force us to focus all our attention on what needs to be transformed.

Tim Flynn (shamanic practitioner, teacher/blogger) discusses the nature of dismemberment in this day and age, and how it can take years to fall apart, "reflecting many different rounds of dismemberment and rememberment" (1). I believe he has hit on a basic truth about our current situation. But I am convinced we haven't much time left; hence, the numinosity of the archetypal crossing. There is an ecstatic element to it. Once we have crossed, we will know more about why we needed to.

Many of us are learning to evolve the capacity to sense energy, respond to energy, and metabolize energy. As we warm up to this new way of engaging with life and the world, we naturally turn to ritual as a means of expediting the process of stepping into what we know to be real. There is no thinking in ritual. In performing ritual, we are *living* metaphor. That may be where we are heading, as writers, as we press ahead in writing *whatever* we write and writing about whatever inspires us about this work. Isn't writing itself a powerful ritual that moves us ever closer to praxis?

Writers have their routines: time of day, special pen, special desk, special paper. With time, the routine deepens, maybe even slowing down our brain waves as happens in meditation and shamanic journeying and sleep. When we are able to achieve the state of mind that is conducive to writing, when we attain the groove, we quickly learn what works and we refine it.

*Let's see . . . how did I do that? Is this going to be easier next time?*

Cowan has compared the process of writing with hunting and gathering. In the initial stages, "I usually have lots of pieces of ideas and concepts and stories and images that somehow feel they go together but I'm not sure how." He is looking for the pieces while the phrases and images are autonomously sorting themselves by nature and kind. "I find myself trying to tame them as I put them into some kind of pattern that makes sense . . . like taming deer." As the process continues, the gathering and sorting might take on more of the nature of a hunting situation. In the end, the act of writing captures all of the satisfaction and ecstasy of the full-blown hunt, in which the writer is involved in a mystical exchange that incorporates the elements of gentle coercion and "bringing in the kill," but also of being "conquered" by something "into bringing it into existence" (2).

In the opening sequence of the film *The Last of the Mohicans*, Daniel Day-Lewis is stalking a buck with such mastery that he is not only following but also herding it to a spot below a ledge, from which he leaps to dispatch the magnificent animal with his knife. The action is shot in such a way that it is obvious that we are witnessing the playing out of a sacred agreement between the hunter (who is temporarily, ecstatically, more than a man) and the buck (who is more than simply his outmaneuvered quarry, but is complicit in its own ritual death).

I do prefer picturing myself as hunter rather than wordsmith. Way before a poem takes shape, I am aware of a charged atmosphere around an idea, a metaphor or phrase, and it is this charge—the equivalent of a fresh scent surrounding an animal's tracks—that announces the proximity of the object of the chase, the poem-to-be. This is the ecstatic phase of writing for me, and this is when I am most like the hunter: stalking, hyperaware of every trace of the pre-existent poem's corporality. I have to keep my focus on the big poem and not settle for a rabbit or grouse. But the big poem requires that I take risks: the risk of following the animal deep into its habitat, the risk of tracking an entity that is smarter and stronger than me. The ecstatic part, I believe, betrays the big poem's desire to be written, but not just by anyone.

It's a mystical seduction. It's a case of the writer tracking a lion and then coming upon his own tracks *and* the lion's. He/she has had to become more than himself to write the poem or he has *become* the poem that he is stalking. Merging is the key here; the poet is tracking himself. This is a fair description of my writing process.

Writing an ecstatic poem involves a sometimes circuitous circling back, and when the poem is finished, I am able to see how it is made out of me plus the fabulous entity I was stalking. The poem seduced me into thinking I could write it while neatly eluding me until I actually *could* write it. But to get to the point of being able to write it, I had to undergo a dismemberment and a *rememberment*. There is the crossing.

I found these words (in an email) by Ackor both courageous and perplexing: "I'd like to be a hunter, chosen by the hunted, or a hollow bone for gods and spirits. But most of the time I'm just an addled, ego-driven lunatic, chip-chip-chipping away until I've either shaped an idea or mangled it beyond recognition. My poetry is all about me or the great beautiful, bloody world as I experience it. (3)"

*After carrying around Rumi/Bark's, The Essential Rumi and The Soul of Rumi, and (as far as poetry goes) reading Rumi pretty much exclusively for about two years, my own poetry underwent a sea change. It was definitely a different kind of poetry, for me; sometimes I was mimicking Rumi, but gradually I was able to peel myself away from him and try my own kind of ecstatic verse. Something shifted.*

You know how a boy's voice starts cracking and going falsetto without warning as his vocal cords drop to a lower vibration? It was like that. I was aware that I was changing again, and it was affecting everything about me: my way of thinking and my way of feeling about people, community, nature, and the world. When Rumi writes, he merges with his subject. His personality shape-shifts into his words. He writes as a lover—a lover to another lover, a lover of life, a lover of suffering, a lover of wine, a lover of the market place, a lover of the divine. Whatever he is writing about, he is wide open.

Alfred J. Ziegler (author, Jungian analyst) writes about a different kind of seeing for a different kind of human being: seeing in terms of relationship, *cognito vespertina*, the vision of twilight (4). And for the writer who sees this way, language reveals its gnostic propensity. It becomes "the most suitable medium for the process of 'dissolving the over-materialistic' evaluations of the real.'"; Ziegler ascribes to it a *hybrid nature*. "On the one hand, language has roots in the unequivocalness and factuality of physical reality and, on the other, it possesses a sublime quality. . . . It is therefore mediatrix and magic wand par excellence". Ziegler continues: "It is as if nature (the physical universe) created a tool in language for preventing her own aggregate condition from becoming too pronounced" (5), allowing us to shape-shift out of the "stubborn restrictions" of what he means by "nature" (material nature)—out of the realm of our first birth.

In the realm of our first birth, we are never 100% sure of why we are doing anything; we are slaves to routine, and we are usually racing time. But this is sacred work: refining, sublimating, purifying, condensing, heating up, turning up the flame, moving closer, standing back. As writers, surely we have as much of a hand in our rebirthing as nature, because we are *dying to be reborn.*

If we stay in the birth canal or the womb, we're not fully alive. We might think we're doing important things, but we're in the dark. In other words, if we're not preparing for, or assisting in, our own delivery, then we are, in John (Fire) Lame Deer's words, *stumbling along.*

Andrew Harvey explains there are three possible impending fates for humankind: cataclysmic disaster, cosmic intervention, or painful birth. I think writers are intimately familiar with all three, sometimes in a single day!

It is when our writing routine becomes ritual—or when we realize that routine *is* ritual, or even that the act of writing itself is ritual—that we shape-shift out of our own stubborn restrictions. Everything that Ziegler says about language—for example, its hybrid nature—is true of the writer. The writer is potentially both alchemist and opus.

Every time we face a blank page, are we not in the birth canal? But Harvey says we have to be conscious during the whole birth process, with our eyes wide open, our minds taking everything in, because we aren't babies. We aren't starting fresh. Again, he is talking about the human being, but he might as well be talking about the evolution of writers. There is no such thing as "fresh" for a writer who is caught up in his art, because language itself is the distillation of experience; words are *used.* All by themselves, they already know a lot about life and what makes us tick. Many of our words are formed from nouns that are like cans that have been kicked down the street for centuries!

In the realm of our first birth, maybe we can fool ourselves into thinking that we are the first to say something, but language knows better. It reflects innocence, but it glows and burns with experience.

In the realm of our second birth, because we aren't starting fresh, we *see* with the vision of twilight as opposed to the vision of dawn. (Twilight, every twilight, offers a threshold over which we might cross into a *two-light world,* where the solar light of day fuses with and gradually yields to the lunar light of dreams, opening to the possibility of transcendent vision [6].) With twilight vision, we "see" (or realize) that we have seen before. We might even be treated to little epiphanies of re-cognition.

In the realm of our first birth, we don't ask any more questions than we absolutely need to because we don't want to know too much. *I don't get paid to worry. Don't rock the boat.*

> Only human beings have come to a point where they no longer know why they exist. They don't use their brains and they have forgotten the secret knowledge of their bodies, their senses or their dreams. They don't use the knowledge the spirit has put into every one of them; they are not even aware of this, and so they stumble along blindly on the road to nowhere—a paved highway which they themselves bulldoze and make smooth so that they can get faster to the big empty hole which they'll find at the end, waiting to swallow them up. It's a quick comfortable superhighway, but I know where it leads to. I've seen it. I've been there in my vision and it makes me shudder to think about it. (7)

As writers, we may escape this fate that Lame Deer so graphically describes. Second birth, no matter how it is managed, is a birth from semiconsciousness into full consciousness.

We're going to come out, and we're going to remember, again and again.

# 10

## Earth Will Show Us

When Tom Brown Jr. was only 12, his Apache mentor, Grandfather, brought him to the site of a long-abandoned homestead in the middle of the Pine Barrens, where he gently uncovered a vine-obscured grave into which was carved the words "12 years old." This was Grandfather's way of preparing Tom for a lesson that would change his life. That night, they made their camp on a nearby hill, and Grandfather recounted his visions of the four prophesies or warnings of the probable future of the earth. These disturbing visions came to him in the 1920s when he was in his early forties. He had just finished a vision quest and was resting at the mouth of the Eternal Cave when the first of the four visions was delivered by a warrior spirit. This same spirit manifested the second and third prophetic visions, a child spirit the last.

The first two prophesies revealed times of epic famine and plague and "holes in the sky" that bled like great wounds. In the third great vision, Grandfather beheld a red sky, succeeded by bleeding stars. The fourth warning depicted the end of humankind. The only survivors were those who had fled to the wilds and never turned back. Grandfather explained that the first two prophesies were not inevitable, but once the first two came to pass the third and fourth would follow within eleven or twelve years. He also said that, like a flock of geese flying in formation, the human race *can* alter its course. "One person, one idea, one thought can turn the flock of society from the destructive path of modern times" (1). How can this happen? Because the bird is in the flock but the whole flock *moves within* each bird.

> Grandfather spoke again, saying, "Trying to live a spiritual life in modern society is the most difficult path one can walk. It is a path of pain, of isolation, and of shaken faith, but that is the only way that our Vision can become reality. Thus the true Quest in life is to live the philosophy of the Earth within the confines of man. Our numbers are scattered; few speak our language or understand the things that we live. Thus we walk

this path alone, for each Vision, each Quest, is unique unto the individual. But we must walk within society or our Vision dies, for a man not living his Vision is living death" (2).

Grandfather is saying that people with vision, or those who are trying to walk their vision, though they are isolated are not as isolated as they often feel; he is challenging Tom Jr. and all people of vision to find their flock. But what if it is too late? What if we are in the times depicted in the last two prophecies? Isn't he saying two things?

*It is too late.*

*It is never too late.*

What if the Earth has a doppelganger, a soulful twin, out there somewhere in the universe, the cosmic analogue of the first shaman twin who could fly? In the case of planetary twins, let's just imagine that because these twin planets, in a sense, share the same soul essence, if one is destroyed, the survivor will be able to carry on for its twin who perished. If this were the case, I, for one, would rest a little easier—as I watch rain forests go up in smoke, our native land poisoned by hydro-fracking and our mountains fall prey to mountaintop removal at the hands of voracious coal-mining operations—just knowing that somewhere someone knows how to take care of a planet.

As soon as James Cameron was finished with *Titanic* (1997), the biggest box office hit in the history of cinema, he started working on *Avatar* (2009), which can still claim that distinction. These are grand-scale (Western) fairy tales for our times; they seem to satisfy our desire for a tale well spun that bypasses our cleverness for a while. In a cushy seat in the public/private cavern of the theater, we can allow ourselves to be pulled into a giant screen that dreams for us in three dimensions.

*Titanic* is the story of a young Irishman who wins passage on the *Titanic* in a game of poker. During the fateful crossing, he falls in love with a beautiful heiress whose impending marriage to an amoral tycoon will put her in possession of a priceless blue diamond. Her Irish lover goes down with the ship, but not before she pledges to him that she will live and marry and have babies. Her fiancé, the tycoon, looks for her but fails to recognize her among the survivors on the deck of the *Carpathia*. His only motivation to find her is to recover the blue diamond, which we see her (as an old woman) toss into the ocean in the very beginning of the movie. In the end, coming full circle, we realize that she never needed the diamond to secure her happiness. She fulfilled her promise to her Irishman; she lived a full life. Throwing the blue diamond into the sea at the end of her life was an ancient gesture of personal power and reciprocity, proving that she had figured out a way to live her truth without prostituting her heart. Meanwhile, *Titanic,* the flagship of the bankrupt industrial age, lies rusting in two pieces at the bottom of the North Atlantic.

*Avatar* fast-forwards to our future of a dying Earth. *Titanic* is now a mile-long military starship heading for an Eden-like planet. The blue diamond has morphed into a priceless element that is only found on Pandora, a lush watery world where nature and all its life-forms coexist in exquisite balance—much as we imagine Earth must have managed until something went haywire in the human psyche.

What Cameron is doing here is changing the story by giving us another chance in the parallel techno-universe of our Wasichu-style dream factory. The industrialists have shed their suits and bow ties to reveal their true cold-blooded nature. They aren't even *trying* to save, much less heal, Earth. They aren't much better than flies that lay their eggs on a host, where they hatch as maggots en masse and proceed to mine the host body for sustenance. They are still after one thing and one thing only: power.

Our hero, Jake, a paraplegic marine, has been summoned from Earth to fill in for his recently deceased identical twin brother who, when he died, was in the final phase of a cloning of his avatar, a transgenetic version of himself as a Na'vi, the indigenous humanoid race that inhabits Pandora. What makes Jake's avatar uniquely different from the avatar his twin brother would have created is that our damaged hero is right brained and highly intuitive; he is able to communicate with the ancestral soul of Pandora. Eventually, he chooses to fully inhabit his avatar, letting his old human self go. We might say that Jake is the human analogue of a crippled Earth being given a second chance.

Working this into our doppelganger theme, what we have here is a doppelganger triad: The Na'vi avatar combines genetic traits of both Jake and his identical twin, so this avatar is really the doppleganger for both brothers. It turns out that Jake, carrying the knowledge of what his race (his breed of human) is capable of, lacks only the indigenous/initiated wisdom of the Na'vi to fully embody the kind of leadership that can defeat the humans and send them back to their dying planet. At the end of the film, the whole screen is taken up by a close-up of the closed eyes of Jake's avatar. The real climax and finale occurs when Jake awakens to his new life on Pandora; his eyes open wide and alert to everything new: a new world with all new possibilities.

I like to think that Joseph Campbell would have been as excited about *Avatar* as he was about *Star Wars*, recognizing in Jake his "hero of a thousand faces" and a worthy hero for our times. A wounded warrior, Jake is also a suitable doppelganger for today's often well-meaning but, sadly, misguided soldier. Once initiated for his new life on Pandora, Jake, whose human soul has flowed into his Na'vi soul, has become someone who knows us, his human part, inside out, but who has chosen to live indigenously and soulfully in service of the tree of life.

It is no surprise that Cameron received much of his inspiration for *Avatar* from his dreams. In other words, the luminous forest and floating mountains of Pandora are not light years away—they are inside us. I say *us*, as it is clear from the overwhelmingly positive international response to *Avatar* that Pandora and the Na'vi, though fictional, are far more real than fact. And I think most of us can agree that the world we have created is dangling somewhere in the middle, between Pandora and that future Earth that is dying. If we want to be part of Earth's renewal, to be present when Earth re-members its dreaming, it's just possible that each of us, evolving at our own pace, must do the same. We must re-member ourselves, we must re-member each other and we must re-member ourselves in relationship to Gaia.

When a great ship travels over the ocean, it leaves a trail of oil and turbulence behind it. Similarly, a jet might etch its passing across the dome of the sky. We move around a lot on the face of the planet. We cross for trade, sheer entertainment, or business and sometimes for exposure to other cultures and environments. Are we connecting anything? Are we even aware of what is beneath us or around us when we cross back and forth? Are we aware that the earth is more than just a collection of places to visit or avoid?

The Internet is filling in the spaces that we summarily cross to reach our destinations. In a sense, it collapses the space between people and influences human interactions in real time and space in significant ways. Biz Stone, co-founder of Twitter, compares Twitter's contribution to human communications to the spontaneous choreography of a flock of birds on the wing who synchronize their flight in a collective pattern that poet Richard Wilbur described (in his poem "An Event") as a "drunken fingerprint". Stone imagines the "tweets" between users as allowing them to move in unison in virtual *and* physical space just like Wilbur's unified flock of birds. (3)

The Internet is not very warm or cuddly, and it doesn't help us check off all those ways to build community that I have taped to my refrigerator: "Leave your house, know your neighbors, greet people, look up when you're walking, sit on your stoop, plant flowers, use your local library, play together, buy from local merchants, share what you have, help a lost dog, take a child to the park." Maybe that work will have to come later. Building real robust, sustainable communities and the governing institutions to match may be for the next generation to achieve or the one after that. Our main job seems to be to build world community, sustain many long-distance conversations, refine protocols for networking, organize international movements, support worthy causes, collapse space, bask in the ecstasy of commonality, and prove to each other that post-1984, - 2000, -2012, there may be a future worth looking forward to—that is, if we attend to the healing of the extended family, the tribe, and the family of humanity. The Internet seems to be helping us do that. We have all seen again and again, how after a large scale catastrophe, communities pull together to assist the stricken and even those who have lost everything rally to assist their neighbors. Perhaps the twentieth century, with its Hiroshima and Nagasaki, Chernobyl, the two world wars, the Holocaust, the Korean War, Vietnam and the first diagnoses and spread of AIDS was our catastrophe out of the ruins of which we will discover our common humanity. Victor Turner (anthropologist) introduced the concept of *communitas* to account for a kind of social bonding that (in Robert Moore's words) "happens. . .not always under someone's leadership. . . but through the cracks in social structure and experience. . .that focuses on the equality of people"(4), the same universal equality that Lincoln evoked in his Gettysburg Address. With the Internet there is the possibility of experiencing *communitas*. (Paul Hawken, in *Blessed Unrest: How the Largest Movement in the World Came into Being and Why No One Saw It Coming* [2007], identifies a worldwide movement of progressive nonprofit groups and organizations [numbering in the millions] spontaneously constellating around environmental and social justice issues—and that was well over half a decade ago.)

When I take up dream work with people I find that, most of the time, the initial dreams are about soul retrieval—finding, recovering something that was lost—or soul renewal or cleansing, releasing something to liberate the soul (an object or a relationship). As soon as that work begins, people are able to expand, both inwardly and outwardly. There is a deep-seated, almost magnetic pull to do this work to clear the way for our full engagement with life. Now, with the ubiquitous Internet in our lives, we find we have access to a unique realm that seems to span the middle world's dreaming, a great web that is many things to many people, but clearly it has become a medium for soul retrieval on an unimaginable scale. There is a childlike quality to all of this sharing. Everyone wants a piece of the world's attention. People want to try things, show off a little, get to know each other a little, put something out there: a song, a dance, a piece of writing, a picture, a quirky talent, an intentionally unflattering photo, an artistic self-portrait. There is contagious movement, and the more sharing that happens, the more the excitement; the more excitement, the more sharing, and the soul of humanity begins to stir. (Now that, thanks to whistle-blower Edward Snowden, it is common knowledge that the National Security Agency [NSA] has redefined the concept of sharing to mean *whether you want to or not*, we must not let that deter us, but rather be encouraged to share all the more, without fear. The battle to exercise and defend our right to freely express ourselves is going to have to be fought against any number of hydra-like anti-democratic agencies/entities who will seek to control access to the Internet to serve their own secret agendas. [*A free and unpoliced Internet has the potential to humanize the kind of thinking that sees people in terms of demographics.*])

Returning to our discussion, as my son, Evan, reminds me, though, "Maybe (the Internet) does contribute to soul retrieval in very small ways, but it is spread across the world, and when it achieves something, it is rarely an epiphany. Sometimes it is, and sometimes it promotes revolution, or a movement in culture. But it's often something that someone will just scan over. It's like the Internet spreads things so thin because it is everywhere, all the time, and not potent and focused in one location." His point is well taken. I picture the Internet as the surface of the still, unplumbed sea of humanity. The sharing that happens might amount to nothing more than a slight perturbation in the surface tension of this sea, which may or may not affect or change anything dramatically, but perhaps it is because the Internet is spread so thin that it has the potential of touching everyone. (Subverting this potential is the Internet's almost uncanny, but calculated, ability to surround us with mirrors like a self-correcting feedback loop. Whatever we do or wherever we go on the Internet is observed, processed, packaged, and reflected back to us as something coming from the outside, creating the illusion that the Internet sees and understands us, when in fact it is enclosing us in a digital house of mirrors.)

Shamanic work is nonreflective and nonpsychological; it is about multidimensional connection. People who are new to shamanic journeying almost invariably ask if they are *just imagining* everything. The answer is yes and no. We may use our imaginations to get started, but as the work deepens, there is a point where our personal imagination can relax and recedes, allowing the archetypal imagination or the world's dreaming to take over. Eliade is very emphatic on this point. He could just as well have used the present tense when he wrote: "Shamans did not create the cosmology . . . of their tribe; they only interiorized it, 'experienced' it, and used it as the itinerary for their ecstatic journeys" (5). The experienced shaman locates him-/herself at the world's navel and journeys into Earth's dreaming without necessarily going anywhere. If we are open and ready, Earth will show us what She needs from us in a journey or perhaps in a dream.

A dream:

*I am looking outside, out the window (modest house, wooden, one story). I see a large hawk swoop down and pick up a snake in its talons. The snake struggles, but the hawk manages to fly off. Then I see the hawk return with the snake. The snake is much larger now and wriggling. The hawk knows it and has to drop it. The snake goes off in the direction of a swampy woods along the river (a park of sorts). Plenty of low brush, vines, and leaves. I keep looking, and now the snake is enormous, like an anaconda. I marvel at how this enormous snake has been able to coexist with people—even children—playing and camping in the woods, because obviously it could have easily caught and devoured people. I am discussing this with someone.*

A friend, Maryann Shadem (who has studied with Peruvian shamans), writes: "What comes to mind is the interplay of heaven and earth. I think of the spiritual work of this time as bringing heaven and earth into unity. You also bring together elements of North and South America, the hawk and the anaconda. In the Peruvian tradition, the condor (like the hawk and eagle) and the snake are *ways of seeing,* ways of knowing, *kinds of vision:* the bird, having the wide celestial view, and the snake, knowing the ways of the earth, embodiment, using the senses with knowledge and discernment. (6)"

The anaconda could well be *Yakumama*, the "immense mythical anaconda, considered the ancestor or 'mother' of the river-forest and all its creatures and possessed of the power to heal and impart healing powers" (7). (*Yacu* = water.)

It would seem that snake's journey into the upper world has awoken it to its dreaming, almost as if that fortuitous invitation to higher vision stirred snake's memory of its mythic ancestry. It saw something that pumped it up. As Shadem points out, in this dream "the nature of the snake is changed. (8)" The hawk and the snake have worked out some kind of truce, the hawk helping the snake to shed its negative or shadow aspect to reclaim its rightful protomythic domain.

The medicine stone I found that reproduces the medicine of the dragon/hawk feather addresses the west–east axis, just as the hawk/anaconda dream addresses the north–south axis and the up–down, earth–sky axis.

What is my role in this confluence of alignments, except as witness, visioner, observer? Shadem raises the same question with, I believe, a healthy anticipation that an answer is forthcoming:

*What may be carried? What may be held? What may be delivered?* And, *how do we know? How do we bring the elements together in understanding?* (9)

*In the big picture, in life, I have taken a few steps back from praxis because I feel alone.* But in the dream about the hawk and snake, I'm not alone. The dream ends with, "I am discussing this with someone." There are different kinds of feeling alone: alone in spirit, alone in time, alone in knowledge.

Holger Kalweit sheds light on how shamanic journeying for ancient knowledge cannot be divorced from shifting backward in time. "The journey to an alternative domain of consciousness . . . is . . . closely connected with a time journey undertaken by . . . cognition . . . into the historic past, that is to say, with a true return to the *illud tempus*[4] and to ancient knowledge" (10).

It is important to see that there are two levels to this dream: The dreamer in the house, witnessing, is one level, and what is going on outside is unfolding on an archetypal, one might say mythic, level.

I believe that the window is what makes this vision possible. My "modest" dream house seems to have but one window, but surely it is no ordinary window that allows me to observe such a mythic event. I am reminded of the marvelous house that Ganieda (Gwynedd), Merlin's sister, built for him when he refused to live in the castle—a magical house of many windows, and, depending on which legend one endorses, Myrddin Wyllt (Merlin) is still there, perhaps even watching us right now outside of time and space. It is so fitting that the house of perhaps the greatest of all druids (shape-shifter, magician, visionary, world-class soul) should offer myriad perspectives, perspectives on all times and places.

---

[4] illud tempus = time out of time, now and forever. Mircea Eliade used this phrase to refer to the dawn of time, primordial time, and dreamtime.

In this dream, the *snake* is the shaman, but my witnessing the shaman-snake's journey to the sky realm facilitates my own, albeit vicarious, return to *illud tempus and to ancient knowledge*.

It would seem that being alone in ancient knowledge is akin to being alone in time, and being alone in time is equivalent to being alone in spirit. But the dream does not leave me alone. Witnessing is not enough; I must share what I have witnessed with another soul who is standing near me in the house. At the same time, I am being reassured that the snake is no threat to those (picnickers) who are oblivious to its existence. To repeat, as I watch it move toward the woods, "I marvel at how this enormous snake has been able to coexist with people . . ." Marvel after marvel. But the most amazing teaching of this dream only sank in when it dawned on me that there is a subtle warp in the snake's relationship to time: Now that the snake re-members its mythic ancestry, it is as if it had never forgotten! It has found itself in time. It's almost as if the dream is saying that its smallness was just an illusion and that its journey to the sky was a vision that *I* needed to witness before I could *see* that *Yakumama* has always been here, in our own backyard!

As Shadem implies with her leading questions, this dream is an invitation to the dreamer to remember his own mythic ancestry, thereby enlarging his own perspective, and then to move to praxis.

Sometimes, if we're willing to embrace everything, including ourselves, we don't need to go anywhere. We just look outside the window in our dreams (or in real life), and everything is right there. Or we look inside: Again, everything is there, or whatever is there is everything. Surely that is how it is for the child, but it's also true for the re-membered adult.

Knowledge finds us because the earth wants us to know something. We're in the right place, or we're just ripe to receive. The right "place" in a dream might be an attitude that allows us to be open to what we are meant to "see" that will *return us to ancient knowledge*—but not just for ourselves.

As far as self and the big picture goes, ethnobotanist Kat Harrison has this to say: "Indigenous cultures use these (plant allies) to go beyond a daily perception, to step back and ask, *What is my work here? How am I doing with my relationships, my community and the larger world?*" (my italics) She admonishes, "We (Westerners) have to take it very, very seriously. It can't just be about personal growth. We too must look at the bigger picture . . . take on the charge of what we are going to contribute" (11). Originally the word *charge* referred to a *load*, or, in the case of the verb, *to load*. (12) So we see that Harrison and Shadem are saying the same thing. (Shadem: *What may be carried? What may be held? What may be delivered?*) Once we take in the bigger picture, whether we totally comprehend it or not, we are stepping beyond our daily perception and it does feel like a charge or a burden until we figure out a way to "take it on".

As quoted above, Tom Brown Jr.'s mentor, Grandfather, puts it this way: "We must walk within society or our Vision dies, for a man not living his Vision is living death." Many of us, if we are being honest with ourselves, might identify with that man who is not living his visions. And this helps explain why *Avatar*'s Jake must travel light-years, all the way to Pandora, just to come home to what Martín Prechtel refers to as our *Indigenous Soul*, which is not *just* human, but *more* than human. (13) When Jake wakes up, we wake up, at least ephemerally, to our own Na'vi souls. The ones who have caused all the trouble and don't know how to live in balance are sent back to their dying Earth. This is the reverse of what has been happening on our watch, during which plundering of resources and extinctions continue unabated—but don't we yearn to change the order of things, to banish that part of ourselves that can't live in harmony with the luminous forest?

# 11

## Our Great Mother Grows Impatient

> A few thoughts about the birthing. I wonder if
> some of us have been born salmon, that is, we
> look human but we are really salmon, our souls
> are salmons. The positive side of this is that we
> are still in the pool of wisdom, and live our lives
> in it, since all the waters of the world are related.
> . . . Maybe we salmonfolk are never totally born
> into the hard world of the earth, stone, logs,
> concrete, but are always swimming in a pool of
> knowledge that others don't share, and which
> we have such a hard time putting into language.
> —Tom Cowan (1)

Even the problem with language not being able to communicate real experience might be solved if we could just accept our lives as salmonfolk! Michael Dames observes that "In many Indo-European languages, the final part of several words meaning 'tongue' also serve as terms for 'fish.' This fish-tongue amalgam can be assigned to a very early date, with 'tongue' being derived from *fish*" (2) (my italics).

> We came up through the orchard . . .
> Passing between
> Old hollow trees,
> Wide as barrels
> Still holding golden green
> Apples to the sun.
> We were pleasantly
> Surprised
> By how warm it was too.
> It was an unseasonable warmth,
> Lush, generous,
> Hugging us to our surroundings,
> Sustaining us

Like two fish in a pond
Where one fish
Might comment to the other fish
About how warm the water is
And the other fish might concur
Or just smile . . .
But in any case,
They swim on, side by side,
Coming up through the orchard
Talking words.

— From author's poem, "Coming Up through
the Orchard"

Cowan says, "Perhaps if we live our lives in the water of the womb still in the great mother, we can see into the souls of things." (3)

The problem is that we live in a world in which our interior reality and exterior reality are hopelessly contaminated by each other. The middle world might be thought of as a womb of our own making, where there is no real inside or outside.

Ackor astutely sums up our predicament this way:

As individuals, most of us traverse at least two worlds. Obviously, for those engaged in shamanism, worlds can be myriad. The two primary worlds are OR (ordinary reality) and IR (interior reality), which I think of as being defined (as) the intersection of mind and soul, or the true self. For most of us, OR is the dominant world. I believe that as OR becomes more terrifying and complex to negotiate, it can impinge upon other worlds, especially IR—with cascading consequences. When the foundation of our OR lives becomes unstable, the angst and lack of control that we experience begins to make OR and IR seem like one and the same. (4)

*Escaping this confusion of realities is the shaman's destiny.*

Holger Kalweit goes into the training that shamanic initiates (of the Colombia *Siona-Tukano*) must undergo to prepare for the "proper learning of higher things" (under the tutelage of Ayahuasca). This phase can last two months.

> During this period (the novice) passes through various psychic phases, the first of which is merely marked by a sort of intoxication. Soon, however, the fear of death sets in, marking the beginning of the actual trial. Those who give up at that point will gain nothing, but whoever learns to overcome or face his fear will encounter the Jaguar Mother, who sheds tears at the fate of the initiate, because he feels that he is going to die. But this is only a further test of the initiate's steadfastness. When, at last, the novice begins to suckle at the breast of the Jaguar mother he reverts, as it were, to a state of infancy. . . . The return to childish innocence, purity, and an unscarred mind, is the most common prerequisite for further progress. (5)

Something in this description is missing. Kalweit doesn't make this clear, but the death that the initiate fears is in fact his birth.

When ordinary reality and interior reality get mixed up, there is disorientation, the *intoxication* phase. The womb of the middle world becomes intolerable; we can't go on living there anymore. But if we don't start down the birth canal, things can get much worse. And things *have* gotten much worse because we've been setting up shop in the womb for a very long time, making up all kinds of rules, adamantly denying that there is anything outside of our womb universe.

Often it seems like everything is testing us, and life is nothing but a series of trials, but that is the Mother just trying to get us out of her belly, and if we fight too long, we will lose. One way or another we have to come out. Some people respond to the Great Mother's contractions as a sign that the world is coming to an end, and they give up because they don't know what else to do. They start acting crazy in the worst way, falling apart, going numb, preparing to die. As Kalweit says, "those who give up at that point will gain nothing."

Because we Wasichu are all in this together, experiencing one phase or another of what we may not even have recognized as a birth or initiation, our whole culture is a buzz of bafflement and heartrending stories as well as epiphanies, depending on what phase is being experienced.

*On each of two mushroom journeys (two years apart), I was poignantly aware of being stuck at the threshold of my mortality. I had a terrible time extricating myself from the fear of approaching death. In the second journey, which took place in a ravine in the Green Mountains of Vermont, I had to retreat from the more secluded hollows of the gorge as I perceived the whole grotto to be waking up! Every stone and ledge was stirring and on the verge of enlarging, and I was afraid of being literally swallowed up like Dante into an epic journey from which, I probably rightly judged, my sanity would have been barred. I was sitting contemplatively by the stream when, right before my eyes, an embedded river stone came to life. Just to make sure that its metamorphosis wasn't "just" a vision, I reached over and laid my hand softly on its "skin," and it let me do this.*

*Just when I thought I had unplugged the journey by retreating with my precious mortality intact, just when being alone had become the warp and woof of my reality and I thought that I had closed the door, one single rock revealed its dreaming to me. In light of what Kalweit says, that nothing happens for the initiate until the fear of death is confronted or passed through, this, more than anything that has happened to me in my life, felt like a miracle. Even though I judged myself a failure, the mushroom didn't let me down.*

*But here's the thing: In many ways, yes, in very many ways in my 60 years, I have unplugged the journey just when things were stirring and waking up and enlarging, because I was afraid . . . afraid of not being able to find my way back to things familiar.*

*And every time this happens (unless there is a miracle) there is another bolt on the door.*

When we are trying to pass through our fear of death or crossing, whatever we glimpse of the other side is colored by this mortal fear. The point is, we can't do this alone. Something is pushing from behind, but how do we know that something will receive us on the other side? In Tarrant's *The Light Inside the Dark: Zen, Soul, and the Spiritual Life*, a Buddhist pilgrim naïvely asks the master: "I am pecking from inside, won't you peck from the outside?" (6) This question is somewhat irritating because it trivializes the role of the master, who might just be waiting for such wide-eyed earnestness to mature before offering any assistance. Suffice it to say that there are those who have made it through, and their eyes tell us that the new is familiar—even more familiar than the old familiar.

*I like to think that the little river stone that allowed me to touch its dreaming was the new familiar. It was, in effect, pecking from the outside.*

A dead or dying world is much easier to manipulate than a world that doesn't pander to our human expectations. In a dead or dying world, any movement or activity is accentuated, such as shopping, washing our clothes, or walking down the sidewalk with a friend. Regardless of the context, what we *do* becomes the whole proof that we aren't dead. But what if the world of so-called inanimate matter started to wake up? Wouldn't our habitual expressions of life begin to pale? Maybe this thought is a little intimidating. It even occurs to me that the real reason we keep animals locked up in zoos is because we are jealous of their zest for life; we want them to live like us.

I know I am not alone in worrying about the vital energy of Turtle Island waning—her energy, life force, or, more expressively, what the Australian Aboriginals call *guruwari*, a potency that the first ancestors injected into the land that infuses the soil and every living thing (7). But my dream of the hawk and the snake seems to be saying that nature is taking care of herself. Maybe it's not a question of either/or (of whether nature is managing to remain vital) but of *how much reality we are disposed to take in at any given time and place, and how much we are allowed to see into the inner workings of a beleaguered nature.* Right now my sense is that planetary energies are aligning: north–south, east–west, above–below.

*This is all very exciting, but I wonder about my role in this. I would like to be less passive without interfering.*

*I am becoming increasingly determined to wake up on both the shamanic level and the everyday level, to be in touch with the two worlds that I am most invested in.* Shamanically speaking, living in the middle world as if it is the *only* world is one way of guaranteeing the unsustainability of that world. It is accurate to compare a monopolistic middle world with a collective lucid dream in which the lucidity of the dreamers is all but unanimously lacking. Living shamanically in the middle world means living here lucidly, knowing there are coexistent worlds of equal or even greater significance that are readily accessible. I want to suggest that this is the great work of a lifetime precisely because so much of it is dead or dying.

We have all witnessed these dead zones, quasi-abandoned strip malls with vast parking areas, or what's left of once-thriving neighborhoods where the life energy has dried up, where people appear defeated and vacant and streets are a maze of permanent one-way detours with signs that read (to borrow from T. S. Eliot's "The Love Song of J. Alfred Prufrock") like a "tedious argument" (8). The same ennui or doldrums pervade certain forests where trees appear to be dormant or just biding their time, literally conserving energy. (One can only hope that the ancient giants of Sequoia National Park, the most polluted national park in the country, with an ozone level comparable to Los Angeles, will be able to make it through this time of trouble.)

Energetic partnership with the land is something our culture knows very little about. If the *guruwari* of a locale is strong, it can pass power or potency to people, and people, for their part, can enhance the life energy or *guruwari* of a place through timely ritual, but this symbiosis can reverse. If the energy of a place has been downgraded (or obliterated) by human projects or neglect—or, perchance, by a natural disaster—this can sap the energy of the people who inhabit that place, and they, in turn become sponges for the life energy of other locales. (The Sequoia National Park climate is hazardous to the health of the people who work or hike there; the ozone is depleting the life force of the place. It is conceivable that a visit there might actually trigger depression in an otherwise healthy person.)

Even people who tend to the land and enjoy a healthy relationship with a place cannot expect the reciprocating land to provide everything they need for life. In his discussion of the healing effect of song on both the human and natural environment, Peat, referring to Colin M. Turnbull's work, describes how certain African forest people (Turnbull calls them pygmies) thread through the forest, producing a kind of music that mimics the sounds of the animals because "it makes the forest happy" (9). The idea is that by serenading the forest, the forest will stay awake and will not forget them. Sad to say, our situation is such that our forests have mostly forgotten us. Few of us identify with a single locale anymore, and very few of us sing to our trees. Even if we want to sink roots, life pulls us in many directions. Our dreams are proof of this restlessness. The important thing is to recognize when the land is trying to tell us something and to pay attention.

What allows us to navigate the dead or energetically comatose regions is a shamanic attitude that never lets us forget that what we offer is essential even though what is unfolding is far beyond our comprehension. Cultivating that attitude is exhausting, but our sanity depends on it.

In the shamanic world, what happens in a dream like the hawk/snake dream is major. At the very least, it widens the scope of our vision.

*To think that I might not have jotted it down . . .*

When one is in a dream, it can be quite moving, but when one wakes up, it might not seem worth remembering. These two levels of functioning (the IR and OR) are hopelessly out of synch! What dreams have I dismissed because of this waking attitude? Often I wake from a dream and realize, dimly, that I was doing something totally outside of conscious comprehension. Clearly, I need to understand myself better! My conscious self doesn't seem to be able, or even want, to keep up; sometimes the shamanic part isn't even on its radar.

> Dreams float in deep green whirls under that fog . . .
> We bowed in a ritual I did not know I knew.
> — W. M. Ransom, "On the Morning of the
> Third Night above Nisqually"

*Yet, in the everyday world, my interests drift further from the mainstream; I am stumbling around somewhere in the middle. I don't want to be born. Perhaps I'm not miserable enough yet!* But the Great Mother is growing impatient. Cowan says:

> There was a time when hurricanes had no names. . . . There is a force or a source in the universe that cannot be named. . . . When we name it, it becomes the Mother of the Ten Thousand Things, the Mother of Everything Under Heaven, The Mother of All That Is. Some early Celtic people named this Life Force *Dana.* . . . Over time, she acquired other names: Brigid, Boanne, Shannon . . . and some terrible names . . . like Babh and the Morrigan. . . . And sometimes she is called simply the Cailleach, the Fierce Mother, the Dark Mother. (10)

Cowan quotes Mary Oliver's poem, "Shadows," in which she contrasts the "so-called senseless acts" of humanity, or the enemies of humanity, with the impersonal violence and cataclysms of nature (weather, the earth). Oliver concludes that "Whatever/power of the earth rampages, . . /whatever/the name of the catastrophe, it is never/the opposite of love." Muses Cowan, "And just possibly, when it comes to the Great Mothering spirit of the universe, there is no such thing as 'the opposite of love.'"

Our Fierce Mother is still our mother and, by some unfathomable logic, we know that whatever she delivers, we have it coming.

*I went to hear Andrew Harvey. Have you ever turned to look at the faces of the audience during a particularly moving scene at a movie? That's what Harvey's audience looked like, except there was a full range of emotions, the most prevalent being grief.*

When a mother is giving birth, her expression is contorted—during a difficult birth even more so. This is the face of the Mother that Harvey showed us. We will be born, but we will not be spared this truth—that as much as our Fierce Mother might make us suffer—with earthquakes, hurricanes, and tsunamis—we, by refusing to be born, by fighting her all the way, have made her suffer even more.

There are people in the world who are waging all-out war against nature—not just to subdue or control, but to destroy Mother Nature and anything that stands in the way. For example, there is the U.S. Department of Agriculture's, Bye Bye Black Bird program, which is responsible for poisoning birds as a service for farmers. In 2009, by their own posted count, using pesticides, they "euthanized" approximately four million brown-headed cowbirds, starlings, grackles and red-winged blackbirds, whose distinctive call from the edge of the marsh is a sure harbinger of spring. (11) Such a kill-off is far more disturbing than the die-offs that we are largely responsible for (but are not necessarily calculated or intentional) although the line between kill-offs and die-offs grows thinner by the day. The die-offs, such as what is happening with honeybees and Polar bears, a predictable consequence of destruction of habitat, are collateral damage in a war zone. In a war zone everything and everyone is vulnerable and is therefore on the endangered list. It doesn't matter whether you are living in a gated community or gathering pollen from a flower.

If one wanted to dream up a program for crippling the biosphere within a millisecond of geologic time, aside from actually blowing it up (which we may yet do), one might be hard pressed to fashion a more effective strategy than the one that is under way: namely, the flushing—Bill McKibben calls it "unburying" (12)—of all accessible coal and oil out of the earth and burning it, while clear-cutting and burning the rain forests of the southern hemisphere. Are people who promote and execute this environmentally disastrous agenda inherently amoral or evil? Or are they warped by some powerful Weltanschauung to behave in a way that defies reason, science, intuition, and common sense (but to them seems normal and reasonable)? Perhaps *warped* isn't the right word, because it implies mental illness; on second thought, maybe it is right! You can say that someone is addicted to oil, wealth, or power, but addiction or neurosis is treatable, and this problem goes much deeper. Weltanschauungs run deeper than mental illness which can be treated therapeutically. They are even supported by their own brand of psychology and religion, so the whole universe jumps in. When everyone is in the grip of the same madness, no one is mad. It is only when two Weltanschauungs are at odds in the same land that people begin to question their neighbor's sanity and right to exist.

The most violent wars are the wars fought between the adherents of conflicting Weltanschauungs. The Romans and the ancient Celts come to mind, as do the Aztecs and the Spanish, the Wasichu and the indigenous or First Nations people of Turtle Island, Imperialist Japan and the United States, and the North and South during the American

Civil War. But now we are living in a time when two people can look at an oil pipeline project or a power plant and see utterly different things because of the emotions that well up. Sadly, the day may soon come when those emotions will make or break governments, shatter social alliances, divide families, and foment civil wars.

*Let's clear the air. Gaia is alive.*

There are people who might glimpse that statement while skimming this book and put it down, never giving it a second chance. The Gaia "hypothesis" (that Earth is a complex self-regulating organism), as an hypothesis, is easy to dismiss or side-track as questionable science, but I'm not interested in the science here, I'm putting it out there as a raw, empirical, emotionally-charged fact—*Gaia is alive!* And it is essential that we realize that, because one measure of our health and sanity is how our lives reflect and channel this great life force that sustains us. In explaining his intention to live spartanly in the woods by Walden Pond for two years, Thoreau wrote: "I went to the woods because I wished to live deliberately, . . . I did not wish to live what was not life, living is so dear; . . . I wanted to live deep and suck out all the marrow of life" (13). The longest chapter in *Walden Pond,* the first, is titled "Economy," not *the* economy. I doubt that in his day there was such a thing. It had not yet reified into a global entity with its own agenda. In our day, the economy is like an old patriarchal god, or, more aptly, a Frankenstein on life support.

One reason that Thoreau took such great pains to flesh out what he meant by *economy* was that he was anxious—maybe even desperate—to challenge the new zeitgeist that was constellating around the time of his experiment: the zeitgeist of *the economy.* When Thoreau was writing *Walden Pond,* the United States was painfully converting to a new economic order characterized by a shift from farm to factory, artisan to industrial wage earner, and the family-run business to the conglomerate. To we who have served this golem (paying our taxes, fighting its wars, trying to keep our heads above water, not quite ready to jump ship or run for the hills, both tempting options), the health of the economy is an abstraction.

As long as we live in wooden houses, it is almost impossible not to distance ourselves from John Muir's sweeping condemnation, "Any fool can destroy trees" (14). Killing to maintain an unsustainable lifestyle is, to put it mildly, foolish! Killing for sustenance with reverence for the life that is taken is, in essence, a rechanneling of the life force. Very few people live this way, but there is a profound difference between my friend who reluctantly removed a tree that had established itself where he decided to build his house and a person who goes through life thinking that trees are just for shade or a resource or an asset or not.

Except ephemerally, say, at the climax of a crisis, like pigeons routed by a barn fire, we are completely swallowed by our subjectivity. The reality is that we don't care about *the* economy anymore. We care about being able to live our lives while providing for ourselves and our families, and we care about having a future—in other words, living *with* economy more like Thoreau was attempting to do in the middle of the nineteenth century. We just don't know how to get back to the humble cabin-by-the-pond-in-the-woods mentality or its contemporary equivalent.

*The* economy can function without a safe environment—that has been proven. Can people? Can what Thoreau meant by economy? We don't know the answer to that question yet. But what we really ought to be asking ourselves is this: Does *the* economy need people? Does it need consumers, or does it just need consumption?

Looked at from the historian's perch, economic forces are supremely impersonal and relentless. It (*the* economy) recedes into recession, it depresses, it lifts up and crests and crashes, it creates and destroys markets and currencies; it holds nations down, moves us this way and that. It pushes everything before it, everything that isn't deeply rooted or incredibly flexible. What drives this wave? The metaphor of the tsunami is apt, albeit the wreckage left in the wake of this destructive moving wall is only now becoming apparent.

*Is growth the new evil? What is evil?*

There is an archetypal *field* for evil, but in a world where the Weltanschauungs have hashed things out, when the dust clears, evil will fall away, like wooden masks. The word for *evil* in Hawaiian is *'ino,* meaning "harmful," in the sense of "too intense" (15), and that fits the behavior of those who are wreaking havoc with the environment (as well as those who took Hawaii from its Native people). They may not be evil in the Christian sense, but they are *'ino*—sowing chaos, out of control.

As Wasichus, much of our relationship to the soul of the land that we took from the Turtle Islanders has been way out of control. Intensity by itself is not the issue. It is when the intention at the heart of intensity is unbalanced that there is an issue; we wobble, we stagger, we spin out of control.

What if President Washington had been ruthlessly honest with the Indians?

*Here is how we feel about you, and here is what we are going to do with you: The land will run red with your blood. We will kill off your game, we will crush your spirit, and we will force you onto reservations. Any questions?*

In a dream:

*I am pacing around on my own (dream) property, talking to myself, and I realize I am being overheard by a friend, so I pretend that I am George Washington soliloquizing, practicing a speech that expresses the above sentiments. And the land is tinted red as if viewed through a red filter.*

Why do I pretend to be the Father of this country making a clean breast of his genocidal intentions when I suspected that my personal, depressive monologue was being overheard? It's as if this ruthless and restive shadow is my cover!

If I were to articulate my own Weltanschauung, I am quite sure that this Washington persona would represent its antithesis. This dream depicts a conflict as startling and shocking as the dream in which I try to pull the hawk into the car. In this dream, George Washington personifies, albeit almost surrealistically, the antithesis of the Red Man:

the archetypal Great White Father. He manifests out of nowhere, or out of the land; an archetype or a bad spirit, depending on one's viewpoint. Presumably because my own standpoint is depressed, this apparition steps right into the vacuum of the power gap and holds forth!

It is worth noting that about five months before the dream of George Washington, I had another dream about the founding father that was much more positive. In this dream, I am on a wooded hillside:

*I am agreeing to perform a ritual with streams running down from the top of the hill. Where the water surfaces farther down, I am working on a small span. The main stream represents a founding father, and each smaller stream is associated with a different boy. The ritual involves pouring some water into the stream while uttering some phrase about the patron or founding father. The water is brownish, not clear. When I'm done, a boy's mother, who has been waiting nearby on a path, asks me to do it again. I argue that it's not necessary, but she is firm and I relent. As the dream ends I wake with the impression that there is a spiral involved.*

This dream would seem to be about my serving the continuity or flow of the patriarchal stream, which issues harmlessly from the top of the hill. I am occupied lower down, where this main stream divides into individual *boy streams*, adding water to one of these boy streams while invoking the spirit of the founding father. The spiral alluded to at the end of this dream hints at the possibility of evolution and appears to be associated with my willingness to work with the mother, who, in addition to so much else, represents, in flesh and blood, the maternal aspect of the hill as source. She wants me to get it right, and I suspect that means that I need to do a better job invoking the ancestral spirit of the patriarch. Of more than passing interest is the possible relevance to the zodiacal Aquarian symbol of the water bearer who, as of the second half of the twentieth century (in the Western world) came to signify (echoing the words of the hit 1960s musical) *the dawning of the Age of Aquarius.* In this astrological reading of the dream ritual, the dreamer is fulfilling the archetypal role of the Aquarian man by attempting to wash out the impurities of the male-dominated past that has, in this instance, merged with the landscape but is muddying the fresh, new, forward-looking streams. Malidoma Patrice Somé reminds us that "ritual is a spirit-based activity performed by humans" (16). Nothing is achieved by simply going through the motions.

Marilou Awiakta, Cherokee/Appalachian storyteller and author, sheds light on this otherwise rather puzzling dream: "The Founding Fathers based much of the U.S. government on the Iroquois pattern (of governance) . . . (but they) left out a basic component the Iroquois always included—women" (17). This omission is perhaps not that shocking when one considers that patriarchy is all the Christian (Judeo-Christian) world has known going back "much farther than Abraham" (18).

Women of the Iroquois (Six Nations) Confederacy, for instance, wielded the authority to veto treaties or declarations of war. The members of the Grand Council of Sachems were selected by the clan mothers, and if any leader failed, by the judgment of the women of his tribe, to abide by the Great Law of Peace, the mother of his clan could demote him by knocking off his horns (removing his headgear), effectively returning him to private life.

Clearly, the founding fathers were only ready to incorporate those principles or tenets of this model of governance that mirrored their self-serving vision. They were unified in their desire to dissolve the monarchy but were adamant about preserving the patriarchy. Denying women any role in the framing of the new democracy and then barring them from contributing or participating in any meaningful way to the exercise of government was profoundly self-defeating; yet there was trouble in the land of the Wasichu that was even more ominous.

In Flynn's words:

> The presence of the sacred evaporated . . . as the power of women was diminished. The presence of the all-powerful father established itself as our own indigenous shamans were silenced. When a culture mutes the free expression of women and spiritual visionaries for centuries, it creates a void into which the most vibrant, spiritual activities must be banished. From a shamanic perspective, the void is real, and that which is cast

into the void does not disappear. It is alive and present within us the way an absentee parent haunts its children (19).

The George Washington dream raises a host of urgent questions, echoing and amplifying the questions with which we began: *Who am I? Why am I here? Where am I going? What am I doing?*

Yes, amplifying—asking the big questions: *Who are we? Why are we here? Where are we going? What are we doing?*

Are we not at the end of a great cycle? This would be the time to consult oracles.

*What is our Weltanschauung? What is the new spirit? And how do we deal with the old restive spirit? What is the new glue? What is the new role of the feminine?*

Many of us are plagued by an omnipresent quandary that transcends the personal—almost as if there are semiaudible whispered conversations being carried on within us, above us, and around us, causing us to question just about everything. The air is alive with signals and vibrations; how naïve it would be to assume that all of them are generated by our own business, or even human business, reducing them to mere projections of our dizzy brains. It's as if *we* are being discussed. Michael Conforti (Jungian analyst, author of *Field, Form, and Fate: Patterns in Mind, Nature, and Psyche*) calls the whisper of the ancestors, or the elders, a *sotto voce*. Whether we hear one whisper or many depends on the receiver, but gone are the days when hearing voices was a sign of madness. It could even be argued that those who hear only their own voice are potentially the craziest among us. "Perhaps," Conforti proposes, "we can find some modern amphitheater within which to amplify and listen to this message of underlying unity between individuals and between matter and psyche" (20). If we don't listen, choosing to ignore or silence or drown out the *sotto voce* with the chatter of mainstream culture, it/they (the ancestors) might resort to other ways of getting our attention.

There are plenty of examples in the literature of the reluctant future-shaman being picked up by the spirits and forced to undergo horrific trials geared to dismemberment and magical reconstitution because they know he won't take the initiative. The materialistic life is very lulling; our reluctance to change our ways is epic. Many of our receptors for spiritual information are switched off or blocked by excessive sugar, salt, TV, the whole over-the-top, self-perpetuating circus of pop-culture, compulsive sex, movies, meetings, street drugs, prescription drugs, music, Internet, coliseum-scale sports events, books, sightseeing (package tours), and propaganda coming in from myriad directions.

For an appreciation of how initiation works (or used to work) in a culture that is famously nonmaterialistic and initiation based, we can look to the Australian Aborigines. The Aborigines, until recently, seem to have had access to a fast track to shamanhood. In Aboriginal culture, the fine line between matter and energy, space and time, and spirits and nonspirits simply isn't there. Their middle world seems to rest as resiliently and delicately as a spider web upon an immense, genetically refined respect for the place they inhabit, which holds them and keeps them together like a vibrating gravity of ubiquitous connection.

Their dreamtime, an abstraction to us, is the essence and fruition of a 50,000-year-old, memory-steeped relationship with Earth! The word *aboriginal* is accurate and heuristic if we consider that the history of the Wasichu (and anyone, for example, of European descent) starts with our coming *to* a place. The suffix *ab-* means "of" or "from"; the Aborigines are *of* or *from* the beginning. They are the original inhabitants of the Australian continent. Robert Lawlor puts it this way: "The Australian Aboriginal culture is founded entirely on the remembrance of the origin of life" (21).

Dreamtime dissolves the line between yin and yang, releasing the dream power that dwells at the heart of every scintilla of creation. Compared with this kind of access, this living knowledge, this quality of reciprocity, nothing we know or have invented is worth a cent—not if we want to walk into the future, and not if it matters to us that our mother is about to abort us. We should be begging the Aborigines of Australia to teach us what they know. They are/were some of the most salmonlike people on Earth.

What if what we call reality, the middle world, is just an old-fashioned psychiatric hospital. All the psychotics and the depressives are medicated, but they are still miserable and ranting or dreaming about the end of the world. Who are the sickest? The ones who are staring out the window or having polite conversation or watching TV? Of course, the ones who are hardest to control are the ones who are about to walk.

There are spirits everywhere who want to help us. If we don't see them, it's because we are blind. Just as a blind person knows there are stars in the heavens and mountains and bats flitting around on a summer's night, just as we know there are creatures who shine like constellations in the deepest cellars of the sea, just so, there are spirits: ancestral spirits, spirits as old as time, mountain spirits, forest spirits, land spirits. The eyes and the ears to perceive these spirits do not just appear gratis any more than one would expect to see a bat in a hospital or a snake under the bed. Then again, it's not as if they aren't trying.

One of my favorite narratives of a full-fledged encounter with spirits is Joan Wilcox's unexpected seduction by faeries during her ten day ayahuasca retreat in the Amazon rainforest. She tells how (this was *after* a session with ayahuasca) she was in her tambo (an open shelter) when she found herself immersed in a "glowing darkness" that was "alive and vibrant. . .Then, from the darkly shimmering vegetation, fairies emerged. . .filling my inner and outer vision." She describes her situation as "being split between two dimensions" and this *split reality* "had a physicality to it unlike anything I had experienced under the influence of ayahuasca." (22) (I whole-heartedly invite the reader to delve into the whole story of her work with ayahuasca.)

*A while ago I was working as an aide and companion for a 30-year-old man with Down syndrome, a kind and gentle soul. One day he asked me if I would drive him to the next town over so he could visit with his uncle. When his directions led us to a secluded graveyard I wondered what he had in mind. We got out and he asked me politely if I would mind waiting. I watched him make his way to a grave and, for at least a half an hour, from my remove of about a hundred feet, I faintly overheard his conversation with this uncle and it was not at all one-sided. There were plenty of spaces in the "dialogue" during which, I presume, the uncle's spirit was responding and answering the many questions that my charge had for him. When he returned to the car I asked how his uncle was. He assured me that he was happy and we left.*

*Now I want to tell about the little bird who came to visit my father. He and I were sitting on his second-story deck, which my mother surrounded by chicken wire that extends high above the railing to contain the cat. We were sitting out there in this cage at a little table in the shade of an umbrella. He was reading to me from a Jungian monograph about synchronicity, when I became distracted by the activity of several varieties of birds in the foliage of the forest all along the edge of their narrow backyard. I interrupted him to bring this to his attention. "Dad," I said, "have you noticed the birds?" It was more than just their dipping in and out of the leafy branches, which they might do if they are gorging on something in the trees. Suffice it to say their energy was so pronounced as to be ecstatic. Just as he looked up or started to turn his head, a chickadee darted over, popped through the chicken wire, and hovered about two feet from his face for a few seconds—long enough for me to notice that a nuthatch had landed on the chicken wire and was trying to squeeze through. Then, as quickly as it appeared, the chickadee exited and vanished, along with the nuthatch. I had never seen anything like it.*

*Afterward, the party was over. Not a single bird was anywhere to be seen. Chickadee is Spirit's inconspicuous spy whose job is to keep its eye on us and report back. Its little black cap speaks to its medicine association with the head—not just the thinking process, but the higher mind (23). One can easily imagine that it excels at zeroing in on our innermost truths. I think that's exactly what it was doing. It was scanning my father, just like my white tiger. For what, I can only speculate. His readiness for crossing?*

*Another time, when I was visiting my parents, I was just letting myself in the front door, as was my habit, and there was my father, seated in the living room, peering at me with his mouth open in the shape of an O. The sound of the latch must have woken him from a deep nap, but it struck me that he looked exactly like an ancient carp haunting the depths of a fishing hole. He appeared ragged and spent and very, very wise. The solitary ancient carp is the proverbial fish of wisdom in the rich folklore of the Wasichu of Turtle Island. It has learned how to avoid the bait and the hook by staying put behind curtains of algae under ledge or log, revealing itself rarely. I think it is just as rare for a human being as for a fish to attain this right to be left alone by the middle world. Toward the end of his life, my father was like this—elusive and profoundly private, as if conserving his wisdom for some imminent otherworldly conversation.*

But let us return to Tom Cowan's identifying with salmon. We might say that salmon's wisdom is rooted in its instinctual unwavering connectedness to Self and to its kind, as well as to its life as a whole. We might say that it's rooted in its inborn sense of death and its knowledge of where it has to go to die and be reborn. But the most magical thing about salmon is that there is no contest between its inner and outer sense of reality: "At Connla, so at Ess Ruaid, the spots on the salmon's sides, its natural markings, were interpreted as the sign of supernatural origins, coming from within" (24).

# 12

---

## End to the Blind March

*In a dream I am hiking on a trail in a natural park. There are others ahead and behind, but I'm on my own. The path begins to ascend an exposed ledge with the hillside to the right and a drop-off to the left. The trail steepens to almost vertical. There are handholds to the left, closer to the edge where I can look over into the gorge, a hundred feet straight down. There is a young, excellent climber right above me who is waiting to see how I do. I am talking to him, or to the people directly below, to try to stay relaxed, but I'm stuck, afraid to chance it up or down, so I'm pinned on this protrusion of rock. I'm leaning toward descending when the whole piece I'm clinging to begins to move and falls. I go down with it a bit while the rest of the rocks tumble down. Thankfully, no one is hit, but right where this chunk of ledge was, there is a group of crystals. I begin to harvest them (without any ceremony). Apparently, I already have a smoky quartz crystal with me (one that I found before on the surface of the ground), but these newly exposed ones are of unusual beauty (in pristine condition). There is a clear quartz (scepter); an almost perfectly clear darker, shorter, and wider quartz; a yellow scepter crystal; and either a red or green scepter, both slightly shorter than the quartz. I am very excited and try to figure out a way to wrap them together. I hear them clinking together a little; this feels very real. (There is also a small fist-size cluster of clear and yellow crystals that falls, but it is the straight, taller ones that catch my eye, so I let them go.)*

Crystals express the potential for transmitting and/or receiving energy. The first radios (called crystal sets) used crystal receivers. They required no outside power source, but ran on the power received from (electromagnetic) radio waves. A fine copper wire, called a cat's whisker, was in contact with a crystal of a semiconducting mineral, forming a crude diode.

The properties of crystals have made them useful to industry and science as well as to the healing arts. According to Helen Dziemidko, "The simple, but exact, internal order of crystals seems to be important to healing function, making them a kind of natural hologram. They also contain energy in stable form. These crystal properties are used in technology, for example in clocks where exact time-keeping is the result of energy being released when the crystal is stressed" (1). (The so-called *piezoelectric effect* [the Greek *piezo* = push or press], discovered in 1880, accounts for how crystals, such as quartz, when compressed or subtly distorted, transduce mechanical energy into electromagnetic energy [2].)

As a newcomer to the wonders of crystals, I find it helpful to compare the relationship between crystal and crystal healer to those first radios, the healer's sensitivity being analogous to the cat's whisker. In general, though, to begin to understand the subtle or psychospiritual properties or potentials of crystals (and by amplification, for instance, the crystals in my dream), we must be open to the *intuitive science* of crystal-healing and not allow ourselves to get bogged down by confusing the natural sciences with the intuitive sciences, the latter being much older (culturally established), empirically based, and demonstrably effective.

For example, laser crystals are good at transmitting energy, but they can't store or retain energy. How a crystal functions is both specific and manifold. Some of the benefits depend on how you approach them or how you relate to them or how you are tuned to them—not just psychically, but electromagnetically and in ways that we Wasichu are just beginning to appreciate.

Dziemidko (MD, homeopath) explains:

> Healers believe that a crystal acts as a natural "tuning fork" to which the human energy field resonates. . . . The crystal helps restore harmony (to our energy bodies) by bringing them in line with the crystal's vibration. The clear focus of energy that crystals provide enhances our ability to work with subtle energies. They seem to have a particularly potent effect on the emotional body from which they can affect the etheric and physical body and release the mental body to align with the causal body. (3)

Robert Simmons, expert on the healing properties of stones, quotes biochemist, author and lecturer Mae-Wan Ho's description of the human body as essentially a liquid crystal, which Simmons defines for us as "a liquid whose component particles, atoms or molecules, tend to arrange themselves with a degree of order far exceeding that found in ordinary liquids and approaching that of solid crystals." Mae-Wan Ho says, "There is a dynamic, liquid crystalline continuum of connective tissues and extracellular matrix linking directly into the equally liquid crystalline cytoplasm in the interior of every cell" and this incredibly flexible responsiveness "enables the organism to function as a coherent, coordinated whole" (4). It is a shame that more of us don't experience ourselves as liquid crystals, but at least we can rest assured that certain gifted healers among us do.

In shamanic initiation, crystals might come up after dismemberment when the initiate is being re-membered or resurrected. His organs may be stuffed with crystals. "The Cobeno shaman introduces rock crystals into the novices head. . . . Elsewhere, the rock crystals symbolize the shaman's helping spirits" (5). In Aboriginal ritual, quartz crystals are associated with the Rainbow-Serpent and even have the same name (6). They may bestow the power to rise to the sky (7), said to be the place of their origin.

*Now it is imperative that I understand what they signify and how I might integrate or use them. It is all a fabulous resource for healing, which this dream would seem to be inviting me to access. There is an ecstatic element here, a chance to open to Zen Buddhism's beginner's mind. A musician friend once declared that if children were exposed to a room full of exotic instruments, including the standard Western band and orchestral instruments, and allowed to experiment to their heart's content, each child would naturally gravitate to the instrument that best expressed their unique personality. With the healing arts, let us open ourselves to the plethora of what is available in the field of alternative therapies, as clients or as potential practitioners.*

My frozen position in this progression of hikers, in front of the family and behind the single young man, dramatizes a classic dilemma for a man of my age (that is, well into the second half of life) trying to find his own way: To climb down would be equivalent to a regression, whereas to continue climbing up would be to rely on a younger man's assistance, thus denying myself an opportunity to individuate in accordance with the raw genius of the Self. My predicament is much like an old computer game my son used to play. When the player has progressed to a higher level of the game, options that worked before are eliminated by the program; each level has its own built-in objectives and restrictions.

This reminds me of a narrative, related by Kalweit, in which an Eskimo is off somewhere in the wilderness initiating. Things have been going pretty well for him except for one thing: He needs to find a seal-spirit. He knows this and is worried that he won't emerge successful from his initiation. After much anguishing and chanting and praying, a hole or cleft in a boulder transforms into the blowhole of a seal, and he becomes a powerful shaman (8). Was it always there, the seal in the rock? I might ask the same thing about my dream: Were these crystals always there waiting for the rock to take pity when I had suffered enough?

*At least for now, with the crystals safe in my dream pack or pocket, I'm not stuck. I'm my own person—with a lot to learn.*

Hypothetically, if this dream belonged to the young climber ahead of me, it would be carrying a completely different message. For him, the way forward is numinous; it is the way into life, into the future.

When one is young, the Self is within *and* without, but, above all, it is in what is coming. The whole process of individuation waits upon the individual's discovering that the path, if walked consciously, will not let one down. This is the walk or march in single file. Each person is aware of his/her fellows ahead and behind, traveling in the same direction, but autonomy provides what Jung might call the leitmotif (a recurrent guiding theme), and nobody knows where they are heading because there is no end in sight. Life is one riddle after another, underscoring the limitations of mortality. And if you would stray, there is Jung's admonition, which one might imagine him delivering tongue in cheek: "You always want to have at least one foot on paths not your own to avoid the great solitude. . . . As if you were not yourself! Who would accomplish your deeds?"(9) In the first half of life, we look for company, even though we (rightly) sense that solidarity is only an expedient solution. Soon one is back to the honest mirror.

In the dream of a man in his thirties or forties, it might be appropriate, from the point of view of individuation for the young expert climber (as positive shadow) to talk the dream-ego up or down, away from the edge, or back to a route that works for him. But at my age or, more to the point, at my stage of individuation, being stuck on the cliff assumes the form of crucifixion—a final exam. The ego has to surrender! The single-file march (or hike) to nowhere ends on the rock face. For it is only when I can't withstand the tension any longer and *I'm leaning toward descending* that something happens that changes everything. All of a sudden, the cliff face is unstable and begins to crumble, and from the crust emerges the crystals (green, red, yellow, and clear). Jung speaks of the "great way" in terms of a merging of the opposites: "In it the power of Below and the Power of Above unite. The nature of the way is magical, as are supplication and invocation; malediction and deed are magical if they occur on the great way" (10).

To put it another way: In the first half of life, when we are just heading out, the Self or the Tao, *the great way*, manifests through duality. When we are young, the opposites are sacred; when life boils down to either/or, it serves the autonomy of the ego. The hero archetype gets us into life by questing and sacrifice, but the ego can only persevere by making choices – choice after choice. The shadow crops up as both nemesis and sacred helper to both challenge and abet our progress.

In the second half of life, the Self shifts or shape-shifts into the archetypal field of the nonhuman or suprahuman. If duality illuminated the way into the game of life, this new dynamic is increasingly oriented around centering, soul-centering, merging, and repositioning oneself relative to the whole incomprehensible scheme of things, synchronizing with a shift from knowledge to wisdom as the new source for action or thought. And what is wisdom but a *knowing* that has passed the test of time? According to Jung, "To give birth to the ancient in a new time is creation. . . . It belongs to the essence of forward movement that what was returns" (11). Jung is talking about forward movement in terms of reclamation of something forgotten that is now the answer or the key that signals progress. (That "something" that was forgotten might be an archaic or "primitive" way to approach a relationship to something in nature, for example, with respect or awe or openness or humility, as *numinous* or *sacred* or even "teacher".)

Is healing with crystals old or new? The answer is, for *me* it is new, and for our culture it is relatively new, just as for the inventor of the crystal set, using crystals for receiving radio waves was new. It was the *essence of forward movement.*

Cynthia Bend reminds us that one of the responsibilities of the practicing shaman is to make sure that the medicine finds its way to where it is needed. For that to happen, we must not only know who our people are, but what makes them "tick" and what makes them sick. We must know them as well as we must know ourselves, inside out. *The oneness of our all sharing the same hoop, the same-sidedness is available to the modern shaman. The possibility of sowing the ample or wide furrow is within the shaman's grasp but only if the old (traditional) and new come together in the medicine.* Notes Bend: "Now (that) shamanism is experiencing a revival it is extremely important that the new shamans who are remembering and reviving the ancient skills be fully a part of today's society. A modern shaman is one who uses the ancient knowledge in the context of our present social and cultural environment" (12). It is for this reason that shamans (traditional healers and elders) from other regions, other countries, and other continents are publishing their wisdom or traveling the distance to teach. They are not trying to make converts to their way for selfish reasons. We are hearing from them because their knowledge is essential to the future.

I recently attended a workshop offered by Don Alverto Taxo, master shaman of the Atis people from the Cotopaxi region of Ecuador. We were seated in a circle in the backyard of a friend's house in rural Ashford, Connecticut, listening to this wise, gentle man. In front of him, arranged on the grass, were his medicine feathers and a half-dozen cell phones and various electronic devices. He had already explained several times that the time had come for the eagle to fly with the condor, and here was one way to show how that looked.

He, like Wallace Black Elk, has not discovered anything new. His genius is in his urging us to open our eyes to the potential of this technology that we mostly take for granted,—to fly with these devices, to use them as medicine, to get the word out instantaneously, to network with a new sense of vision and purpose.

Then it began to rain, and folks automatically reached for their phones as the circle broke up. Alverto just sat there smiling. Like Wallace Black Elk, he is part of the fire, part of the rock and the rain, and the rain was blessing our phones that were sharing ground with rattles and feathers in the land of the eagle.

Alverto is a great man, a great soul, but he will probably not be remembered for long in the land of the eagle because, again, he hasn't invented anything. The shaman is a timeless figure, not an historic figure. There are very few shamans associated with historic events, and only rarely are they credited with helping to usher in evolutionary shifts in consciousness such as the one we are witnessing—even though without great shamans, we would hardly know where to begin the rebuilding of old bridges and repairing old alignments. There are of course exceptions, but this work does not, as a rule, turn out great leaders and civic heroes. It is very personal and humbling work in that one is, in a sense, at the mercy of the elements but, at the same time, one senses that one is in good hands because one has, in Alverto's words, *befriended the elements.* But what if the elements overwhelm us and shatter our lives, like a hurricane? When we are dismembered (ritually or by life) we are only reliving what we have done to the Earth. When we re-member, we are working in tandem with the planet whose destiny is synonymous with our own. We're far from alone. Earth wants us to succeed as much as our ancestors do. The trouble is that we lack a *round vision* (13) because everything is coming together in a new way, a new Worldview, and nobody sees it yet. How we are going to succeed is just beginning to look like something. The alliance of smartphone and feather is an auspicious start.

Again, this dream marks the end of the blind march.

*The solution was neither to proceed, nor to retreat or regress, but to hold my precarious position until something shifted.*

*Now what?*

My son was raised on Jaime de Angulo's *Indian Tales*, which de Angulo wrote, toward the end of his life, with kids in mind. There is so much love in these tales, so much soul and family feeling and love for the Native peoples that anyone who picks it up is going to be pulled in.

De Angulo was a cattle rancher until 1919 when he met Alfred Kroeber and Paul Radin. He accepted an invitation to join Kroeber at Berkeley, where he taught Jungian psychology. According to Bob Callahan in his introduction to de Angulo's *Coyote Man & Old Doctor Loon*, "His presence alone, one suspects, would have been enough. His wonderful ear for language quickened the environment. In the company of those men he expanded his interests, seventeen new languages during the next fifteen years" (14). He left academic life in 1934. Stalked by a series of tragedies, he turned more and more to poetry and literature. But it wasn't until the late 1940s that he began to rework his early Northern California texts to the delight of his children; the project grew into *Indian Tales*.

Toward the end of his life, de Angulo became increasingly mysterious. "A tragic, dark figure, some would say . . . a north coast Poe. No, old friends replied, he was just wandering!" (15) De Angulo wrote:

> I want to speak now of a certain curious phenomenon found among the Pit River Indians. . . . They say of a certain man, "He has started to wander." It would seem that under certain conditions of mental stress an individual finds life in his accustomed surroundings impossible to bear. Such a man . . . will stop here and there at the camps of friends and relations, moving on . . . he will speak of what is on his mind to no one . . . he is not right. . . People will probably say of such a man: "He has lost his shadow." . . . The wanderer . . . remains in wild, lonely places. . . . Whenever anyone approaches, he runs away, throws sticks and rocks at his friends and relatives . . . (16)

But apparently, at some point, the true wanderer stops measuring his loneliness by what is missing and, with nothing to lose, begins to relate uninhibitedly to his surroundings. Then the spirits take notice.

> To (the Pit River Indian) the mysterious powers, the Tinihowis, are whimsical spirits living in the woods and . . . indifferent to the affairs of the Pit River Valley. . . . In order to gain their

friendship . . . it is necessary to become as wild as possible. Haunt lonely desolate places . . . yell and dance like a maniac . . . jump in the silent cold water . . . then perhaps some wild things will come to take a look at you. . . . When this happens the wandering is over, and the Indian becomes a shaman (17).

Callahan concludes his introduction with: "All white men are wanderers, the old people say; at the end de Angulo was trying to get home" (18).

When one wanders by choice or by fate, because one just can't take it anymore, one is essentially announcing that one is done with the middle world. But what then? Lacking map or guide, one enters the in-between realm where even the shadow has a hard time following, because the shadow will keep reminding one of the obligations of one's psychic journey (through the middle world) that will never let the soul be free. And when one wanders, one is, after all, siding with the soul, not the ego, so the shadow itself may wander. And yet, as long as we consent to remain earthbound and our wandering doesn't spirit us off with a one-way ticket to a land of dreams, we cannot permanently divorce our shadow. Even Peter Pan (leader of the Lost Boys in Neverland) has Wendy stitch his shadow back on because he needs that much grounding; it is his last vestige of humanness.

In Jungian terms, the personal shadow is, for the sake of this discussion, the distillation of one's personal unconscious. At the end of the day, when the sun is setting, our shadow grows longer and longer and less personal, eventually merging with the shadow of the pine and the ridge and then the night itself. Losing one's *personal shadow* is the prerequisite for any kind of merging with nature or being seen by the spirits.

Wandering and losing one's shadow are not the same thing. You might wander *because* you lost your shadow or you might wander because you *want* to lose your shadow. Or you might wander because your shadow is stalking you. But I think what de Angulo is writing about is *Wandering* writ large. It is, or can become, the ecstatic wandering of the Taoist sage, breaking from the linear progress of civilization and the single-file march—but it's not walking the red path, either. The red path wants our full attention and can be very demanding. There is nothing intentional in wandering. It is the soul's way of taking charge of the body for its own purposes. Maybe the spirits are noticing, maybe not, but when we're walking or driving straight forward, ever shortening the intervals between the dubious connections we call *life*, that's one-dimensional flatland behavior. Spirits are four-dimensional. I'll bet they can't even see us when we're in a line.

*Being shaken off the cliff is the Great Mother's invitation to wander!*

It is not unusual for the magic realm to open to a child, but rare is the adult who can follow a child's charmed lead. In Tom Cowan's *Fire In the Head*, he relates how W. B. Yeats was walking the beach with a little girl and they wound up standing before a "notable faery haunt . . . a shallow cave amidst black rocks, with its reflection under it." First the little girl and then Yeats "fell into a kind of trance," and he found himself chatting with the faery queen (19). Apparently the Sidhe *saw* him, because he was with the little girl and they thought he was OK; they *liked his looks.* When you are with children, unless you are trying to suppress their spontaneity, you are wandering, and you are in the magic realm. Wandering is a state of mind, as is letting oneself "go wild." I find it very interesting that the words *wand* and *wander* come from the same root word, the Old English *windan*—to wind, twist. So, to wander is to be open to the magical realm and to be free like the wind.

The spirits aren't trying to be mean by ignoring us. It's just that our straight, predictable, civilized ways make us transparent to them or dull or opaque. In any case, we are of no interest to them.

But wandering also connotes a lack of purpose. "All white men are wanderers, the old people say" (Callahan's words) must mean they regard us, Wasichu, as sleepwalkers, trying to shake off some great sorrow or grief or trauma. In spite of appearances, even *we* aren't very interested in what we are doing. Our hearts are heavy. We have a long way to go before our restlessness transforms into the ecstatic wandering of the Taoist sage; or of the east Indian *sannyasa*, marking the life stage of the renouncer of worldly existence, whereby a householder, at the threshold of the second half of life, dons a rob and goes begging; or of the prayerful walking from lodge to lodge that

Wallace Black Elk describes; or of the wildly random, crazy, dancing, boisterous exuberance that overtakes one who is about to be tapped by a spirit.

# 13

## Like Grass in a Burned-out Forest

The ancestral spirits, our ancestors, do (or would) keep tabs on us, but such gaps exist between people and their forebears nowadays! There is a real breakdown. The lines are down; the threads have snapped. In general, our kind, our civilization—call it what you will—is truly a civilization of drifters. We're spiritual orphans, but it's a one-way gap. We have divorced our ancestors. But there might be good reason for this. (There are times when I see my relationship with the United States as the dysfunctional relationship between a grown man and his abusive father, or his abused father's abused or abusive father. There are too many scars and bad memories, upsetting stories with unhappy endings. The aging son needs to focus on his own healing and leave the Great [estranged] Father to his fate to focus on his own legacy.)

To his great credit, Alberto Villoldo (Ph. D., founder of the Four Winds Society) models a novel approach to healing such a schism that yawned between him and his own father. Using his shamanic skills, Villoldo painstakingly taught his dying father how to journey to a gentle river, where the two of them spent their last days together in a shared consensual "reality of our dreamtime"(1), far removed from the world in which they could never find reconciliation. Following Villoldo's example, I can picture sitting by such a river with the spirit of my country personified. Such work offers the possibility of healing where little or no common ground exists in the middle world.

The human race has been passing through a protracted dark time for much longer than the living memory of our culture, which spans approximately 125–150 years or five generations. To illustrate how this five-generation-long memory works, when I was a child, there was still a handful of people around who remembered the Civil War. In the time of my father's youth, it would have been easy to sit down with a Civil War vet; that vet's grandfather might have fought in the Revolutionary War. Memory links to memory. Another example of this living memory is in the colorful language we inherit from our parents that they picked up from their parents that persists long after its currency. For example, I still use the phrase, "losing steam" to mean losing motivation or energy for a job or project. Because I embraced that phrase when my son was growing up, even if he doesn't use it and it falls out of usage with him, he knows exactly what it means and it links him to my mother's parents, four generations back. That phrase is his blood-link to the early twentieth century when steam power was the technology of the day. Family stories that tap that five-generational memory-well, although they are not the same as memory, serve to keep the collective memory of family, community, race and culture from atrophying. When stories are allowed to die, memories atrophy.

Many generations back have experienced upheaval after upheaval, and the memories never became stories. In other words, the memories were X-rated (for violent, traumatic content) and therefore never shared. For example, my father's father was a medic on the battlefield of World War I. He was undoubtedly a good and brave (posthumously decorated) but damaged man. My mother's father fought in the trenches and was exposed to mustard gas; he was never quite right. Few experiences alienate one's soul as effectively as war. (Still, every generation takes up the martial drumbeat.)

*On my last visit to my folks, I was going through stacks of piano music for my father when I came across a song that my grandmother (his mother) wrote. There was an old-fashioned copyright attached to it with an official red seal. The song was addressed to her "partner," who, in the song, had fallen in love with another. The backstory goes something like this: She was hoping the song would be a hit; it was her way of evening the score when her marriage was on the rocks.*

*My father's grandfather was a Norwegian orphan raised in a Danish orphanage run by the Danish Royal family. It is said that he came to this country with little else but a knife, fork, and spoon (bearing the royal Danish crest), which were pawned off during the Great Depression—not an atypical story, unfortunately. The trail goes cold a mere four generations back.*

*My great-grandmother on my mother's side (my maternal grandfather's mother), Lillie O'Brien, was Irish, from Tipperary. I confess, the first time my wife and I visited Ireland I did not know that I had Irish blood, but some of the Irish folk we met did! In 2005, the year I remarried and the year before we started losing my mother to Alzheimer's, I asked her to tell me about her ancestors. (For years she had been researching her family's genealogy.) She responded with two short e-mails, in which she wrote: "Although it has not been verified, it is believed that there is Indian blood in my mother's family."*

Thankfully, who we are at our core abides much deeper than personal and even familial memory. In my case, for example, I know in my heart that although my pacifism arose out of my conscientious response to growing up during the Cold War, coping with the social and racial upheaval of the sixties and, to some extent, compensating for my two grandfathers' traumatic journeys through the belly of World War I, my lifelong abhorrence for war is shallow compared with my love of life and nature, which carries the intrinsic watermark of essential self-recognition.

Shaman, master storyteller Martín Prechtel (whose workshops my wife and I have attended) tries to get people to contact their "first happy ancestor," describing this work as not just important, but indispensable for spiritual or soul growth.

*It was at a three-day workshop with Mehl-Madrona that I dreamed that I was back in the Middle Ages, walking up a street on a beautiful day, up this hill through a village, between my mother and father who were to my right and left. I was holding my father's hand. He was a stocky red-headed tradesman or artisan and a kind, warm-hearted, honest, well-liked member of the community. I dearly loved him. I was a child in this dream, but it was a lucid dream. I was aware that I was dreaming and was able to step out of the dream at will to express my uncontainable joy at finding myself reunited with this man. In the dream, my behavior was consistent with the circumstances, but when I pulled myself out, it was to jump up and down and shout ecstatically, "I love this man! I love this man!"*

*I am certain that this dream tapped the truth of what Prechtel and Mehl-Madrona have taken pains to empower us to do: to go back as far as we need to to repair that ancestral bond.*

The modern age has done enormous damage to the mycelia of tribe and clan. There is, for all intents and purposes, no *family of man*. We seem to have stepped beyond the pale of intrinsic recognition of consanguinity. (How many of us make the connection that the people we turn back from our borders are essentially members of our extended family?) So we have to head out like the youngest son in the fairy tale, the one who didn't inherit anything but a pair of walked-out shoes or an old swaybacked horse. We take what we have, and we don't quit until we figure out where the breakdown occurred, which is both endemic and pandemic. We ought to be doing this work en masse. If we were, it would probably result in a sort of collective stepping back from the precipice with a lot of crisscrossing of paths and intersecting. Eventually, the mycelia would return, and healings and benefits would multiply beyond our wildest dreams.

If cultures fall apart, what is left? What coheres that will keep the remnants of the family together as everyone drifts around without a compass?

Two stories on BBC News, from opposite sides of the planet, illustrate what is going on here. One story shows Chinese workers in hard hats with boxes of dynamite blasting a high Himalayan valley along the Kyirong River for a road that will connect Tibet and Nepal, and eventually Delhi (2). The Nepalese want this. For hundreds of years, they have been making this trek by foot along a narrow dangerous trail, using yaks and mules to carry their supplies. Soon, if the Chinese have their way (and they will, of course), there will be a direct road to India. The indigenous folk don't realize what this means for their culture, but if our experience serves as an example, they may soon be measuring their well being in terms of economic indicators.

The other story included a video of a crystal cave of giant selenite crystals, clear white and wide around as trees, some spanning floor to ceiling, glowing from within like giant fiber-optic columns. Some are leaning at gentle angles, allowing the reporter, speaking in hushed tones, to make his way through this subterranean temple of indescribable beauty on pure white crystal bridges. The Cave of the Crystals, connected to the Naica Mine in Mexico, was apparently discovered by coal miners by sheer accident.

No wonder the reporter (Professor Iain Stewart) is speaking in ecstatic whispers (3). Simmons describes selenite's metaphysical properties:

Selenite quickly opens and activates the third eye, crown chakra. . . . The intensity of energy delivered by selenite is greater than almost any other stone for the upper chakras. . . . It can clear congested energy or negativity from one's physical and etheric body. . . . When selenite . . . opens the inner eye the spiritual world enters (4).

He recommends lying down inside a grid of six or more wand crystals to "bring about experiences of spiritual ascension." (5) Just imagine what stepping into an entire cathedral of selenite could do for the aching soul of the Wasichu.

On one hand, the blasting wide of an ancient trade route in the Himalayas; and on the other, the discovery of a selenite *cathedral* in the womb of the earth. Research shows that such images and stories—the very ones that ignite the most powerful emotions of awe and despair— are being forwarded in all directions around the globe, around the clock, just short of the speed of light. There is no time for processing.

*What's going on? Whom should we listen to? What should we do? Is the sky falling or not?*

We are like chickens scratching for answers while the storm clouds gather overhead. It's not that we lack inspiration or information; on the contrary, we are stuffed with random bits of input. We can't take any more in.

How are we going to move from *Nature exists for our sake* to *Nature exists for her own sake* to *We don't know why Nature exists?* Perhaps if we figure out how to reverse the extinction sequence, we will begin to find out. John Muir's description of the passenger pigeon begs the question: *Is this the same bird that was hunted out of existence within a mere two or three generations?* "The breast of the male," he effuses, "is a fine rosy red, the lower part of the neck . . . changing from the red of the breast, to gold, emerald green and rich crimson" (6).

*Why, we might ask, would nature have bothered decorating a creature so magnificently if it was only meant to go down as another creature's meal?*

In his poem, "Enriching the Earth," Wendell Berry captures the ecstasy of mystic-ignorance: " . . . to serve the earth, not knowing what I serve, gives a wildness and a delight to the air. . ." (7).

Kalweit draws a distinction between the shaman's tribal-oriented relationship with nature spirits and with nature as matrix, and the modern biologist's empathetic, albeit science-based, involvement with the natural world:

> Tribal communities and peasant cultures . . . see the world not only as pervaded by life . . . but as something that is ruled by immaterial beings who, as it were, form the essence—the actual moving principle—of the various natural phenomena. The shaman . . . becomes the intermediary between nature and the tribal culture, between the living, the dead and the nonhuman spirit creatures. . . . A biologist may develop a deep understanding of loving empathy with profound admiration for the little miracles of the plant and animal kingdoms but the shaman goes beyond that; by extreme concentration he enters living nature so fully that he becomes able to see what lies behind its external forms. He beholds the matrix . . . or matrices of energy . . . the bioenergetic or the (Sheldrake) morphogenetic fields that form the framework of our visible world (8).

The *extreme concentration* that the shaman must master to enter *living nature* is akin to the concentration that we observe in the normal behavior of animals or even in the singular bearing of a plant or a stone. The difference is that the shaman must *learn* how to concentrate or distill him- or herself—in effect whittling down the ego-complex to become, in a very real sense, a condensed form of himself, at once less (less self-centered) and more (more nature- and spirit-centric). Not only must the shaman master this ability, but he must figure out a way to maintain this concentration, which usually means siding with nature and creating and fine-tuning a living space that nurtures shamanic work.

Shamans have one obvious advantage: They are so far off the grid that nobody pays too much attention to them, whether they are practicing alone or in public with other shamans. They can, for example, psychopomp for the souls in the rubble of Port-au-Prince, and nobody needs to know. That's how it should be. They can journey for a semi-somnolent client or for the planet in the privacy of their living room, and the benefits ripple out with nobody the wiser. They aren't asking for money or sucking up to the well-connected or campaigning for votes. They aren't selling anything. (Cowan belongs to a group that calls itself Shamanism Without Borders, whose mission is to heal places that have been compromised by the upheavals of the modern world, either by convening where the healing is needed or by journeying in synch from wherever they are to a specific location.)

Such first-line response from the shamanic community has to be extremely rewarding but equally stressful work. There are simply too few shamans to answer the call. In intact indigenous cultures, as in bygone Native cultures, the shaman, private or high profile, would be, in a very real sense, the keeper of the heart of the village, the one who taps the people's dreaming and knows when it is time to do the rituals.

Today's shamans, ideally, are not just mediators, multidimensional healers, and ritual masters. They—and, to a greater or lesser extent, all the other healers from various sympathetic modalities and alternative persuasions—are also purveyors of cultures that need to sprout up around them, of which they are the harbingers. These days, the new shamans are like maverick doctors who are called to practice medicine in a war zone, but it's a spiritual war zone. The new culture, which needs to sprout up to support these healers, is analogous to the new growth returning to a burned-out forest. In fact, we are depending on this new-growth culture to revitalize and repair the bio-spiritual-tribal-grid or net that used to hold the energy body of the planet together. The Wasichu, you and I, and maybe even the entire human race may never experience the ecstasy of immersion in unspoiled wilderness except vicariously in the accounts of eighteenth- and even nineteenth-century naturalists and explorers, those wide-eyed newcomers to Turtle Island (Lewis and Clark, Catlin, Muir, Thoreau). But before nature was "nature" and hence could be eulogized, it was a self-evident web of subtle and in-your-face values, uncanny relationships and ecstasy-provoking wonders.

One might have to travel to places as far afield as the Amazon basin to witness landscapes as enchanting as 29-year-old John Muir described in his journal during a marathon "walk" through the deep south in 1867: The forest wall above the Hiwassee River (on the Georgia–North Carolina line) was "vine-draped and flowering as Eden . . . overlaid and wrapt in the multitude of its everchanging notes of song" (9). I am struck by the similarity of Muir's journal entry and anthropologist Jeremy Narby's 2005 description of a clay "lick" or cliff deep in the tropical forest of the Peruvian Amazon, "epicenter of world biodiversity" (10). "The cliff had become a wall of spinning rainbow colors. . . . Magnificent colors and movements blended with dissonant sounds in a dazzling spectacle" (11).

Young Muir's Eden-like curtain of flower and song, that he rapturously described 150 years ago, reaches us from the extreme limit of living memory. What this means is, as we move even a little forward in time we cross a line of no return to that gift of enchantment that Muir felt so moved to share. Fortunately Narby's spinning rainbow wall of movement and sound, convinces me that Muir's rapture, although it may have receded beyond the powers of our collective memory to preserve, has not completely vanished from creation and that the earth can still produce Edens.

But there was a time, not so long ago (as the human soul marks time at least), when nature's magnificence and over-layering of color and song were not geographically remote nor was her wisdom lost on the human race. Rivers and mountains were sacred, snake was the possessor of mana and the master of rebirth and power objects had to be respected and when the souls of the dead hung around for a few days they just need a little help to pass on. You did ritual periodically to stay connected to the sun and moon and the seasons, people knew that a boy needed to pass through initiation to become a man, likewise man to metamorphose into husband, father, elder; woman, into wife, mother, crone. All of this used to be obvious, the *how* and the way collective wisdom was passed along or accessed, and not just wisdom, but very basic information that synchronized all of the elements of this multi-dimensional living wonder we call creation.

But it's not so obvious to the Wasichu because our great grandfathers didn't know any of this. It wasn't taught in the schools or anywhere. In fact, we were taught to believe the exact opposite—that everything in the material universe was as inanimate as a doorknob. Welcome to the land of the Wasichu. You might say that for the Wasichu, everything is externalized. We know how to put very complex things together—to materialize, structure, systematize, dissect, analyze, synthesize, digitalize, clone, reproduce, fuse, package and file—and we know how to blow everything up and how to clean up and rebuild after the explosions!

So, as shamans hone their skills, the world gives them more and more work to do. Strands of the web of life are snapping all the time. Just like in Dante's Hell, there are concentric rings of brokenness.

Up to a certain point, the earth, Gaia, is capable of healing herself. Bill McKibben, in *The End of Nature* (1989), sounds a saliently hopeful note that many of us who witnessed the 1986 meltdown at Chernobyl never thought we would hear: "Even the radiation from an event as nearly universal as the explosion at (Chernobyl) has begun to fade, and Scandinavians can once more eat their vegetables" (12). But there are limits to Gaia's recuperative powers.

In West Virginia, mountain-top removal is in full swing. After a couple of peaks have been decapitated and the valley between has been filled with the rubble from the massive excavation, the whole site is compacted and flattened. What's left is a true wasteland. They call it *reclamation*, but not even grass can grow there. Inside what remains of the mountains is a honeycomb of tunnels and shafts, artifacts of the old way of mining. Nothing can be safely built on these artificial plateaus because the new wasteland is hollow—a sacred threshold has been crossed. I think that this is obvious even to the ones who do this kind of work. The rationale for mountain removal, or more to the point, the mentality that rationalizes it, is beyond me, but my guess is that it's beyond most of us. It runs as deep as the Weltanschauung it serves; it is a complete vision with its own gods looking on. (Massey Energy, formerly the largest coal extractor in Appalachia, whose production obsessed mining operations yielded 40 million tons annually, made no bones of their ambitions, saying it all with their logo, a massive truncated 'M' with a flame shooting out of what's left of the "valley" between the leveled peaks of the letter.)

Sometimes it seems to me that there is a breathless, ecstatic element at work in the darkly mysterious ravishing—or, depending on who's reporting, gang-*rape*—of Earth. Here is yet another layer to consider as we peel back the skin of *why*.

The poet Federico Garcia Lorca wrote:

> On the withered, waveless solitude,
> the dented mask was dancing.
> Half of the world was sand,
> the other half mercury and dormant sunlight . . .
>
> But I'm sure there are no dancers
> among the dead.
> The dead are engrossed in devouring their own hands.
> It's the others who dance with the mask and its *vihuela*.
> Others, drunk on silver, cold men,
> who sleep where thighs and hard flames intersect. . .(13)

Marilou Awiakata (Eastern Band Cherokee author) recalls a film produced by Pueblo artists and scholars in which the people of *Selu*, the Corn-Mother, demonstrate that "Being peaceable does not preclude drawing the line on disrespect."

> The film opened with a view of a cornfield singing in the wind. A voice-over spoke about the significance of Our Mother Corn and other spiritual values. From there the story of Spanish oppression unfolded. The Pueblo people bore with it for many years—until they reached the limit of their endurance. On the land at a sufficient distance from the Pueblos, they drew a ceremonial line of cornmeal. The Spanish crossed it. And were defeated (14).

I suppose we might begin to forgive those "cold men" (the hydrofrackers, or the ones who are driven to remove mountains) once we comprehend that "the war against nature waged by the Industrial Growth Society arises from more ancient patterns" (15). But such rifts so plague the human race that any attempt to forgive one another is dwarfed by our measureless yearning to be forgiven for our own unwitting contribution to nature's undoing. Thirty years ago was the time for such soul-searching. At this juncture, we might be wise to cut our losses and concede that it is not up to us to heal the planet; even if it were possible, there isn't time, and the learning curve is too steep. It is more realistic to think in terms of protection and damage control. It *is* up to us to back off from making it impossible for Earth to begin healing herself. Let us hope that our civilization will not be known primarily for the scars we left behind.

Which side of the line are we on? Are we are on the same side as the ones who are removing mountain tops? Or are we on the side of the ones making the movies or writing the articles and the books, leading the workshops, or embracing so-called green technologies, trying to subsist off the grid? . . . In the sixties we held teach-ins to educate and focus our collective courage to stand our ground, but unlike the sixties, the choices that we face today transcend ideology. We are not innocents anymore.

As one grows more attuned to one's own energy body, it becomes easier to comprehend how Earth's energy body functions. We begin to re-vision ourselves in our Mother's image; then, as we learn to love our new selves, we realize that we are just like our Mother—that is, as we open to certain perceptions, or new, more subtle ways of experiencing ourselves, it begins to dawn on us that we are literally our Mother's children. As matter reanimates, and as we develop the senses to participate and rejoice in the return of spirit to matter, we naturally become more receptive to the vitality of the world around us and our imaginations expand to embrace what it really means to call the earth our Mother: Gaia.

As we step in to an energetic relationship with Gaia, we might find ourselves dispensing entirely with metaphorical thinking for long periods, the trend being to trust our senses more and, by degree, to credit them, as well as the accuracy of prescientific (or nonscientific) explanations, for what we are experiencing. Deepak Chopra is very clear on this point: "When Ayurveda says that the sun is our right eye and the moon our left eye, we mustn't sneer" at the primitive metaphor. "By bathing us in the moon, the sun, and the sea, Nature fashioned the bodies we inhabit" (16). And "There is good reason for all the ancient medicines to say that man is made of earth, air, fire, and water. . . . The human body does not look like the green meadow, but the fact remains that the breezes, water, sunlight and earth were merely transformed into us, not forgotten" (17).

Metaphorical thinking is a form of symbolic thinking. Symbolic thinking is self-explanatory because it is rooted in our collective psychic experience. It is the opposite of abstract thinking. When the mind thinks in symbols, it is presenting us with embodied equivalencies for realities that were not apparent before. But, absent its archetypal or cultural grounding, metaphorical thinking can easily function as our way of tricking ourselves into embracing the metaphysical without leaving the ring fort of rationality. When something is *as if*, we can grant it space to *be* without abandoning our standpoint of disbelief or skepticism. But it was Jung who said, "I don't have to believe . . . I know" (18). Knowing something deep down is powerful medicine because you don't have to build your argument or try to win people over to your side or provide proof in order to promote your own truth. You know what you know. In his foreword to *The I Ching*, Jung, then in his seventies and speaking from a position of unshakeable self-knowing, refused to cater to the inevitable skeptics; he simply asked the *I Ching* how it wanted to be introduced to the West, and the spirit of the *I Ching* sagely obliged, offering up a telling self-portrait.

*Belief* can be powerful. Believing has to do with allowing something to *be*—to be alive, to be what it is, to *be*, period. *Knowing* carries the sense of direct perception or direct cognition, closing the distance between the knowing subject (Jung, in the above example) and the object of his knowing (the *I Ching*) and opening to the possibility of personally experiencing something.

*Whatever we think a tree is, is not what a tree is. But somewhere deep inside, at the heart of our nature, we do know what a tree is. Yet the tragedy is that many of us will live and die thinking we know what a tree is! Drawing on Jung's example again, Jung did not think he knew what the I Ching was. He knew the I Ching.*

Probably the reason workshops are so popular is that people already *believe* and they just need a little push to step into their intuition and knowing. Jung was intuitive to the point of being swept away by what he "knew." He created *The Red Book* not as a calculated concession to his intuition but to open all the stops, to allow his intuition to take over and have its say. He became its servant. Intuition, if nurtured, quickly establishes its credibility. When it doesn't have to compete with the rational mind, we get the *news of the universe* (19). (Einstein saw knowledge and intuition as coequal opposites, but without intuition, knowledge lacked purpose, intuition being the conscience of intelligence.)

Later, Jung developed his theory of typology, by which he defined intuition as one of four primary functions of the personality (along with thinking, sensation, and feeling). But intuitive knowing is far more global: It ushers in a way of life, a viable way of being human. It is our way of communicating with all the intelligences that flourish outside of us, many of which are spirits.

# 14

## Believe It

Like the human body, Earth has its own chakras, which, as in the body, may be thought of as energy fields. To fully appreciate the soundness of this analogy, it might help to remember that the body of Earth came first, so it makes sense that the human body would copy Earth's body. We also have James Lovelock's geophysiology to warm us to the validity of the science of analogous (geo-human) creation (1).

Independent of the eastern (Tibetan and Hindu) chakra system, and half a world away, the Hopi elders of northern Arizona tell how the First People, their earliest ancestors, benefited from their own mystical system of vibratory centers located (like the chakras) along the vertebral column, the body's equivalent of Earth's axis. Corresponding almost exactly to the third through seventh chakras, these centers were / are attuned to the vibration of creation, the "living body of man and the living body of the earth (being) constructed in the same way" (2).

In Sanskrit, *chakra* means "wheel of light" (3). Why wheel? Because, in a healthy body, chakras are always moving; they are in fact, vortices of subtle energy turning in a clockwise direction that act as conductors to move energy through all the layers of the aura, focusing these energies toward specific regions of the physical body (4).

Because chakras are energetic and subtle, how they are perceived and experienced varies from culture to culture and individual to individual, and changes through time (from birth to death and, on the grand scale, with the passing of the millennia) because the human being, thankfully, is a work in progress. Associating colors with chakras is not new but the relatively recent attention paid to the healing properties of color has introduced a new dimension to accessing, stimulating and balancing chakras via color-visualization and exposure to colored light. Our cultural awakening to the therapeutic value of color is, simultaneously, an awakening to the reality of chakras, an exciting development in the history of Western consciousness. Rudolf

Steiner taught that contemporary people, with their overdeveloped brains, are in the process of evolving downward from the higher chakras to the lower—evolving, not devolving. That reasoning would help explain the growing (Western) interest in planet Earth versus space travel and eventual colonization of the solar system, ever since the Apollo program ended in 1972. Robert Johnson (Jungian analyst, author of *He, She, We*) identifies the motivation for the current *downward movement* as "nostalgia for the earthy" (5).

As quantum physicists have been telling us for a while now, what the universe reveals to us is as much a reflection of human consciousness as of what is there without us. (Even though fact is stranger than fiction, it is also a truism that, when it comes to unbridled exploration, our imaginations precede us in ways that we barely understand.) *I can't see chakras, but I am able to feel them. By simply suspending my finger over the opening of a chakra, my hand begins to rotate clockwise. If I resist this motion, it feels like I am trying to force the north poles of two magnets together. So, when it comes to chakras I am a blind man who must rely on his sense of touch to engage them physically, a strange irony for someone who does not see himself as a materialist. My being able to feel the circulation of my chakras (an ability that I discovered about 10 years ago), and knowing that not everybody can do this, has helped me appreciate how people might experience the chakras very differently, if not uniquely—or perhaps not at all.*

How, or whether, we experience subtle energy in ourselves or others rests on many factors. Certainly some people are gifted with extraordinary abilities, and many are born with aptitudes for developing extra senses and powers to heal. (Hinduism and Buddhism teach that the attainment of higher consciousness, with its attendant awakenings and special abilities, should follow a prescribed evolution that allows for moral enlightenment to parallel the spiritual, and this might take many lives or incarnations.) Special aptitudes aside, if we don't believe in the possibility of something, chances are we won't experience it. So, back to "belief": The dictionary defines belief as a "state or habit of mind in which trust or confidence is placed in some person or thing: faith" (6). And belief begets belief. Disbelief (or skepticism) is often based on lack of trust in or fear of what doesn't fit one's reality or Weltanschauung. Disbelief begets dogmatism and isolation. (I would like to suggest that it is what people *don't* believe that fosters fundamentalism: fundamentalist religion, fundamentalist secularism, and fundamentalist science.)

When a person's life is threatened by an illness, their fear of the illness or of death often overrides their disbelief in what is possible. For the sake of life, they dismantle a little of their Weltanschauung. Swayed by something they read or heard about, they might turn to unconventional therapies, even traveling great distances to exotic places, for a miraculous healing. There is nothing like the threat of death to dissolve paralytic disbelief.

This is where we are today as we begin to assume responsibility for the failing environment we live in. "Environment"—a word that has come to mean everything and nothing—has become a great mirror for our epic struggle to survive our contradictory nature. Most of us would agree that what we mean by environment is *that part of the world we are responsible for*, that part of the world that sustains us, and that part of the world that we are, nevertheless, destroying against the advice of our own science and conscience. Even as we try to make a difference, there is a sense afloat that it is too little too late, and this attitude is only the visible portion of a glacial inertia that affects every level of our global culture. Even though we might not show it, we are mortified by our own behavior. Even as we fear and disrespect ourselves, we continue to make choices that support our self-destructive and world-destructive addictions.

For some time now, everything we do has been colored by our attitude toward death, which for many amounts to a thinly veiled death wish or a surrendering to a downward spiraling outlook on life. What death happens to mean to each of us increasingly determines how we conduct ourselves. This widespread acceptance that the world as we know it is coming to an end—the Wasichu's version of the warrior's battle cry, "*It is a good day to die!*"—introduces a serendipitous softening of the structures of our disbelief, as well as a subtle but inevitable shift from a scientifically oriented political Weltanschauung to one that is spiritually–intuitively oriented. Against all odds, this has begun to change the way we experience that part of the world we affect: the environment!

As we face our own imminent demise and the demise of nature, we begin to realize that we aren't necessarily responsible for the environment, but only for ourselves. The whole notion of sending in the archeologists before the highway goes through is farcical and obsolete; so are all of those environmental impact studies paving the way for large ecologically risky projects. But, even though there is an obvious correlation between the sheer scale of our industrial presence and the magnitude of inevitable environmental disaster, what we're doing to the environment is not *the* problem; the problem is inside us. (We should have learned by now that we can't build a highway around the soul or cure our collective disillusionment with enthusiasms for the someday promises of greener technologies.) Even at this late hour, if we can remember how to be human, the rest will fall into place. The reason for this becomes clear if we can accept Mudrooroo's[5] definition of environment as "a community or family arranged in kinship patterns across her (Earth's) skin" (7).

Although the exact mapping of Earth chakras may be open to debate, the idea is very provocative: that different geographical regions of the earth correspond to different chakras. For example, in (CCH, RSHom [NA]) Ambika Wauters's *The Book of Chakras*, the root chakra is identified with "the sacred lands of all indigenous people, the sacral chakra, Brazil, solar plexus, the United States, heart chakra, Spain, throat chakra, Italy, Brow, Peru, Rocky Mountains, Crown, India" (8). (The best way to appreciate this spiritual science of geo-energetics is to experience it firsthand, which people are doing by the droves when they visit Machu Pichu or journey to Carnivale or Crater Lake in Oregon.)

To see the earth as a body, both in the physical and the energetic sense, is an evolution of our awareness of Earth as Mother. But I find it especially helpful and edifying that this author identifies the United States as home of the solar plexus chakra. The qualities and attributes of this chakra awaken us to the grounded vitality of the warrior archetype: selfhood, inner knowing, gut instincts, self-management,

---

[5] Mudrooroo, meaning *paperbark* to the Noongar, the aboriginal people from whom Mudrooroo claims descent, is the nom de plume of Colin Thomas Johnson, a novelist, playwright, essayist, poet, living in Nepal

self-worth, honoring ourselves through our interactions and negotiations with the world, personal power, mastery of duality by making wise choices, healthy connection with heart and ego maturity relative to Self, and our respective territory (9). The solar plexus also serves as a kind of womb for our grief or a safe harbor where our grief can weigh anchor while we try to carry on with our lives.

If Turtle Island is the terrestrial locus for the third chakra, then as reprehensible as our treatment of the Native Americans was and is, our methodical abuse of the land was—and still is—an epic crime in itself. This alone sealed our fate and guaranteed that nothing else will work for us.

Native Americans knew (still know) what it means to be a warrior in every way. The great spirit of this amazing land, the great solar plexus of the North American continent, taught them well what was expected of one who chooses to walk the red path. We systematically crushed that warrior heritage, that traditional Earth-human symbiosis, and we all but wiped out their access to that way.

> Some (Native American) men made a successful transition and found work as farmers or cowboys for the large ranches that moved into the vast prairies of former Indian country, while others literally joined the circus. . . . The army employed some as scouts . . . sent out from military posts to keep fellow Indians on the reservation (10).

*With that kind of karma in my blood, I can't expect the red path to want me. (My George Washington dream and pulling-the-hawk-into-the-car dream are simply calling me out to step into my karmic shoes.) If I am serious, if this is what I really want—to walk this strong path of balance—then I must, once again, faithfully revisit those questions that can, ultimately, be answered only by Spirit's spies:*

*"Who am I? Why am I here? Where am I going?" becomes, "Who is this? Why is he here? Where is he going?"*

*On my first vision quest, 17 years ago, I was violently woken in the middle of the night by the strident alarm of a great-horned owl. I had vowed to stay awake and had allowed my fire to go out! The next night, I was graphically warned by a vision that I would have surgery. One year later, I underwent four rapid-fire hernia-related surgeries all in 18 months, resulting in trauma to both the second and the third chakra. In retrospect, it is obvious that I was caught up in a biological, karmic, geo-energetic vortex and was in way over my head. I went up on the mountain to cry for a vision and was not disappointed. I received several. But there was no one in my life to help me interpret what had just happened—the ominous and the indelibly affirming!*

Given the world that my generation (we so-called baby-boomers) was born into (between the late 1940s to the early 1960s)—a brittle world on the verge of collapse or revolution, ripe for powerful archetypes to arise—I think it is likely that there are many shamanic late-bloomers out there who are destined to recover from their initiatory illnesses. We might even reasonably expect a late-blooming garden of shamanic types to appear over the next 10 years, precisely when they are most needed, followed by their progeny who, when pressed, will know better than they what to do. I am picturing desert turning into an exotic garden overnight! If this sounds like spontaneous remission on a collective scale, it is!

In my practice, I have been privy to clients' dreams of great power and medicine that seem to have been waiting in the wings for—how long? Who can say? Years or centuries? The shaman/shamanic practitioner is not as concerned as the psychiatrist about the capacity of the ego to withstand the strength of the medicine. In effect, shamanic techniques bypass the ego, fostering, to borrow Robert E. Ryan's phrase, "an inward relocation of the focal point of reality" (11).

More than twenty years ago, Michael Harner recognized the widespread interest in shamanism that he was witnessing as a return to "the original spiritual democracy of our ancestors in ancient tribal societies where almost everyone had some access to spiritual experience and direct revelation" (12). In fact, the *interest* Harner referred to in the late 1980s (thanks in large part to his teaching and example) has evolved into a vital movement fueled by excellent books covering a wide range of fields, journals, websites, online programs and courses, blogs, college-level courses, mentorships, workshops, pilgrimages, local gatherings, and drum circles. The firewall that organized religion and old-scientific anti-spiritual thinking erected between the individual and his or her soul and *direct revelation* has been thinning; at times it seems that it is only our individual psychologies that prevent us from taking our freedom. In fact, the growing importunity of the archetypes to manifest might call for a new kind of shaman, less a master *technician of ecstasy* (Eliade) than a spiritual midwife, assisting the birth of a new human being. (In Australian Aboriginal culture it is / was not unusual for a midwife to be a *putari* or shaman, the two callings being closely related.) (13)

Deepak Chopra sees a future blossoming of Ayurveda, combining knowledge of healing with compassion, which we might picture as a river of intelligence pushing back Maya, the illusion of boundaries (14). What we are witnessing now is a 1960ish experimental excitement associated with spiritual-psychic and shamanic questing, tempered by a twenty-first-century sense of coming of age. Halifax brilliantly sizes up our present situation thusly: "Many people today are interested in exploring Western Buddhism and neo-shamanism, in which elements from the older traditions relevant in today's world are combined—a kind of 'Bodhishamanism'" (15).

Here is Marilyn Zwaig Rossner's explanation of spontaneous remission: When a long-standing conflict in the soul-body is resolved, the physical body follows suit or conforms. "The soul-body is the mold around which the physical body is formed." It is the "three-dimensional blueprint (I would argue *four*) for the formation, dissolution and re-creation of the physical body." But the initiate has to be ready to emerge from the *initiatory illness*, and this, in a world still, albeit decreasingly, micromanaged by the allopathic (and techno-pharmacological) medical establishment, takes time. In addition, Rossner explains, "initiatory illnesses are not merely psychosomatic or psychologically caused; they are caused by the encounter of the same creative and destructive forces of the cosmos that have produced the material world—and our physical bodies—in their present mix: partly glorious and yet partly defective" (16).

# 15

---

## Going Deeper

What has been happening on the stage of the middle world has been building for a very long time; it is only now coming to a head. There is no more wiggle room. Although denial persists, something is shifting on a global scale. As the damage goes deeper, we are called to go deeper: into Earth's wound, through our own wounding.

It is the calling of the shaman to live beyond death. And it is the ethos, the unique character of a shaman's experience of death and resurrection that differentiates his/her power from a fellow shaman's. "He/she is able only to help with those elements whose source . . . has been given its proper share of shaman-flesh"(1).

The last DVD in the BBC series *Planet Earth* was a kind of eulogistic epilogue about the future of the planet, distinctly melancholic. The producers and the film crews had to carry on, knowing that many of the animals and life-forms they were documenting would never make it as a species. In the case of the Siberian leopard—the rarest cat in the world, according to their sources—only forty are left. These might as well be the earth's vital signs: one third of the planet's grasslands are gone (since we've been tracking these losses), one half of wetlands, one half of forests, one fourth of amphibians, and one fourth of mammals (2).

*I tried to watch one of the DVDs in this series, the one on caves, and the player refused to read the disc. I couldn't get past the menu, which was disintegrating into its digital substrate. But there was one image that kept patching in at odd intervals: the image of a man's body, spread-eagle, dropping into the immense maw of a vertical cavern. And just as the man was about to vanish into the abyss, this moth-eaten visual flickered off and returned to the menu.*

*That night I dreamed that I and another man, a friend, were being drawn into a vortex that was forming above the historic center of a stone village, back into another time. We were yelling this to someone as we disappeared into the whirlwind.*

Even though we are in the grip of a power with which we cannot communicate and over which we have no influence, there is never any sense of this being a random event such as finding oneself in the path of a twister might be considered random. But we are not shamans in this dream; a shaman might *invite* the whirlwind to take him somewhere. Halifax writes, "The center, axis mundi or nierika is the path or gateway to the realm of Death where the shaman confronts demonic forces that dismember. . . . This confrontation takes place in the cosmic womb of the Earth Mother, in the bowels of the underworld, in the primordial beginning before time" (3).

Why would the shaman risk losing everything, including his/her sanity, to undergo such a journey? Perhaps because he is not journeying for his own benefit, but for the whole community's well-being. (In Nicholas Black Elk's description of the *Inipi* or sweat lodge, the lodge leader calls out, "Behold me! . . . I am the people. . . . Help us" [4]). There is much more at stake than the shaman's personal health or even the health of the immediate community when one considers that the shaman's community is woven into the fabric of the nonhuman community and that illness, in the shamanic perspective, signifies that the immediate community has suffered some kind of unraveling or separation from the rest of the universe. Whatever needs healing becomes the pathway *to* healing. Although he or she might not characterize it as such, the shaman's work is a form of sacred activism aimed at reparation.

The propensity and know-how to journey shamanically lies in our own psychic depths but also in *protohistorical time*—that is, before our story was chronicled. "According to certain mythologies . . . the cosmos had total access to itself. There was one language for all creatures and elements, and humankind shared that language"(5). The innate power that comes with living and dying close to the source (a primordial birthright)—that was passed on through *seeing, experiencing,* and *knowing,* mastered through initiation and inherited via ritual and practice—was self-evident. In the course of millennia and countless generations, this ecstatic nexus, which amounted to a universal, all-encompassing protopsychic subjectivity, was compromised and abandoned, and the bonds of kinship were broken.

In a sense, our dreaming went underground to become the archetypal unconscious.

According to Halifax, "The shamanic world view still acknowledges this kinship among all aspects of nature; the primordial ancestors, Grandfather fire, Grandmother Growth, Our Mother the Sea, . . . Father Sun, Mother Earth . . . (are our) Nature-kin"(6).

*After my dream of the vortex, I decided to draw two cards from the Tantric Dakini Oracle. I asked the first card to show me where I am, what I am facing. The second card would speak to the larger picture, where I am heading.*

The first card was *Soma, 18*:

> . . . *signifying the entry of forces from the secret realms of the psyche and the assimilation of these forces for fulfillment. . . . The number of higher initiation . . . The image of the mushroom is depicted as a mirage or shadow, almost flickering across the side of a white glacier. . . . It is only in the interaction of the soma with the psyche, the inner water with the inner fire, that resolution of potencies can take place. Thus the mushroom is depicted as intangible . . . the glacier being (merely the visible tip) of the depths of the universal mind* (7).

According to *Webster's New Collegiate Dictionary*, soma = body (New Latin *somat-*, *soma*, from the Greek *somat-*, *soma* body) (8).

The second card was *Deep End, 51* (a mermaid is depicted as diving deep into bottomless water):

> . . . *path of the self as related to evolution of the psyche. The plunge of the seeker into the waters of the unconscious . . . the self is ready—adaptable (part fish) . . . prepared to make the plunge fearlessly* (9).

In the first card, soma, the body, is associated with the higher chakras. It is presented as somewhat holographic and a little unstable, like the menu of the *Planet Earth* DVD, which flickers miragelike to reveal the image of the diminutive spread-eagle body floating downward into the fathomless depths of the Earth Mother. Soma is the *body ecstatic*, the body holographic, the body through which we must eventually *see* or *pass* to go deeper. When we are ready, when life has tried us and tested us to the limits of what our conscious and physical standpoint can bear, and if we still identify with what remains of who we are after we have given our *share of flesh*, something in us releases, breaks, like a bag of water (we go back to the menu!). And, instead of flopping helplessly into some new reality that may or may not have us (to begin fresh), we discover that we are free and well adapted to make the plunge.

*In last night's dream, when I am passing into the vortex with my friend, there is no fear. I am simply calling out to someone outside the whirlwind to explain what is happening.*

I would like to suggest that the reason there is *no fear* is that the dream self is aware that its dream body can tolerate or survive this time journey through the vortex. This is not a lucid dream; the self has no control—or possibly even *desire* to control—what is happening in the dream, beyond its willingness to submit to the whirlwind. The dream self is, however, not alone and (it/I) am able to reassure an outside presence that what is happening is, in a sense, happening for a reason. Because the vortex is in an old stone village, this would seem to be a journey into the historic past, perhaps even into the troubled heart or soul of the village itself. So, even though much in this dream remains mysterious, a middle-world context is established; at least the starting place is made known; the village is the nierika.

In journeying into the vortex, this part of me is gone to consciousness, vanished like H. G. Wells's time traveler into that trackless other-dimension of time—except that my time-traveler self has no vehicle other than his faith in powers that operate outside his control.

The holographic mushroom (*Soma, 18*) represents this dream body with shape-shifting capacity. It can flicker in and out of its own way at will to navigate the universal mind or dive deep, plunge fearlessly (as half fish) into the *deepest depths*. This versatile dream-body self is still the self, but a self that has been refashioned by the forces of initiation into a body that is not confined to one reality or one dimension. And that body has work to do: "18 signifying the entry of forces from the secret realms of the psyche and the assimilation of these forces for fulfillment. . . . The number of higher initiation . . ."

*I would like to return to my childhood dream of standing on the beach and being told to bridge the ocean.*

According to Halifax's Eskimo shaman, "There is a power we call *Sila*, a great spirit supporting the world and the weather and all life on earth. . . . When all is well, *Sila* sends no message to mankind, but withdraws into his own nothingness. . . . So he remains as long as men do not abuse life but act with reverence toward their daily food" (10).

To this great Spirit who rarely speaks except when needed, children aren't *just* children as we tend to see them, with everything ahead of them and everything to learn. There is an aura about every child that is timeless, an air of wisdom that hovers around their brand-newness.

This intervention of a great vigilant spirit may be foreign to our rational conditioning, but it makes perfect sense to our dreaming self. According to Jung's empirical teaching, the psyche—upon which the nascent and individuating self floats, as upon a great ocean—contains not just the wisdom and shadows of one's culture, but the archetypal inheritance of the whole human race and, ultimately, world.

Jung was fond of personifying the collective unconscious metaphorically as a one-million-year-old man. But it was in his *Commentary* for *The Secret of the Golden Flower* (1928) that he began to refer to the archetype of wholeness as the Self, which is far more than a universal prototype for the self/ego. Transcending any attempt to categorize it, the Self *is* how it *manifests or transmutes,* alchemically, in nightly dreams or great religions. Sometimes it does personify, and when it does, we might call it God, Aion, Great Spirit, Atman. It is also the mandala, the sun, the 12-gated city, the source, the way, and the goal. Children, before they develop a sense of self, are tapped into the Self. That is normal, and indigenous people recognize this in them. (Robert Moss, author of *Active Dreaming: Journeying Beyond Self-Limitation to a Life of Wild Freedom*, points out that it is hardly unusual for children to dream the future; what *is* unusual is for the adults in their lives to recognize that children have this prophetic ability.)

Arnold Mindell observed how, in a Kenyan village he and his wife were visiting, the resident witch-doctor couple would give a penny to any child who came to their hut. Everyone in the village lived, by Western standards, in dire poverty, "but the spirit of the child was rich and central to the art" (11). This may sound like bribery but if we think about our own Halloween when children go around dressed as spirits and, as such, are treated, that is close to how the witch-doctors saw the village children except in the Kenyan village the children and their spirit are one.

When a baby is born to the Hopis, it is kept inside in the dark for the first 20 days of its life. During that time it has no name. Even though it is in this world, it is still under the protection of its spiritual parents, Mother Earth (Corn Mother) and Father Sun. It is only during his (the reference specifies male) initiation around the age of eight that he learns that while he is a member of an earthly family and clan, he is also "a citizen of the great universe to which he owe(s) a growing allegiance" (12).

*Sila* doesn't normally call on the Self to listen through the ears of a child because children should be allowed to play and grow up at their own pace. They should be allowed to hear the voice of *Sila* murmuring encouragement or warning through the myriad voices of nature or their parents. But sometimes, and only as a last resort, *Sila* has to call up the menu and jump ahead in the program, fast-forwarding past *innocence* or dispensing with the menu entirely, to communicate directly with the old soul or the Self that stands behind every new human being. When *Sila's* voice is heard by both the Self *and* the child, the child may be frightened, even traumatized, but that is a chance *Sila* is willing to take.

When *Sila* says, *Be a bridge across the ocean* to a 5- or 6-year-old, the child is frozen with fear because instinctively, intuitively, he/she knows that he can't run to his parents to ask what *Sila* is saying. (I didn't.) But the Self standing behind the child knows exactly what *Sila* means, and smiles. It knows that Spirit is talking to the man or woman that the child will become, the oak inside the acorn.

It used to be easier. There was a time when *Sila* was able to communicate through signs: by storm, snow, rain, wind, all the forces of nature; in the way animals behaved, in a bird's song; through dreams, visions, the moods of mountains; even in the way a cloud was shaped. All of these were the voice and poetry of *Sila*. There were elders and shamans who could routinely read these signs to make sure that *Sila* was being listened to.

When *Sila* asks something of a child in human language, that in itself is a sign that we need to listen because *Sila* doesn't like to turn a child old overnight, as it were.

In the dream of the vortex in the stone village, there are parallels to my early childhood dream of being called to bridge the ocean. In both dreams, there is no choice. Child and man are being pulled in or summoned by an irresistible power. The difference is that in the dream of the vortex, the dream self trusts that its dream body will not be annihilated and that it will return. In other words, unlike the six-year-old dreamer who identifies exclusively with the physical plane (his/her brand new home), my time-traveler dream self is closer to a living holograph (astral body), a step toward being able to shamanically travel wherever it is needed.

Perhaps we are all being asked in some way or other to suffer straight through our wounding, allowing it to become the vortex—our nierika, through which we journey fearlessly (through the very eye of our fear) to heal ourselves and our planet, our mother.

When one of the last survivors of the 2010 earthquake in Haiti, a young man, was pulled out of the rubble 12 days after the quake, he was interviewed by reporters, who were dying to know how he had managed to stay alive all that time. He said he had survived for his mother, so *she* would survive. If he had let himself die, he explained, she would have joined him shortly. His reasoning is numinous; it makes us feel proud to be human beings. His example goes a long way toward healing our despair.

We hear or read of people who have "died" to their bodies, who are sent back or given a choice to return to life to finish something. When they return, almost invariably, the way they live their lives reflects an attitude of choice—of having been given a second chance. The firewall that separates life and death has been removed. For them, as with the ancient Celts, the Otherworld is a hair's breadth, a heartbeat, a poem, a harp strum away. Stumbling along is no longer an option, and death is an ally, a manageable crossing.

The account of the young Haitian who survived the earthquake out of love for his mother reminds me of an infamous anecdote in the biography of Columcille, the founder and patron saint of Iona. The story goes that it was decided that a human sacrifice was in order to sanctify the foundation of a chapel that was resisting being built. Columcille asked for a volunteer, and a young monk, Oran, by some accounts a kinsman of Columcille, volunteered to be interred alive. In one version, after some time has elapsed, the saint, desiring to gaze once more on Oran's face, discovers that not only is Oran still alive, but he has plenty to say about how heaven and hell are not what we have made of them. Columcille's famous response is: *Earth, earth on Oran's eyes lest he further blab!*

This story is morbidly humorous, but there is a lot to it. Oran's journey in the underworld had apparently changed his Weltanschauung. He no longer saw the afterlife in terms of heaven or hell. Mother Earth had opened his eyes to a third possibility, to which Columcille was closed. Oran was the shaman, whereas Columcille personified the old Worldview.

When 200,000 people are buried by an earthquake and only a relative few survive, it helps to remember that matter is truly *mater* and that the earth is Gaia our Mother. As long as She is healthy, it is in our hardwiring to see how, although the grave on this side (the side of grief and loss) is heavy, from the other side, it is *gravid*, pregnant. The ground where a soul is buried is heavy with birth or rebirth.

*. . . as long as She is healthy.*

The way *Planet Earth* was filmed was new and completely captivating; I could not look away. The film crew used a camera with a powerful telephoto lens that allowed them to film animals from the air from a mile away. For example, they were able to follow a polar bear across its habitat without it sensing that it was being observed.

Watching animals with this eagle's eye worked a strange magic on my imagination. Whether it was a solitary baby elephant wandering in the wrong direction, searching for its mother that it would never find, or a herd of caribou surging across the tundra, there was no separation between life and life, life and world. The animals were just the moving part of a living body, the expression of an ecstatic holographic choreography. Holographic? Everywhere, on every continent, what we are being shown is the same spectacle, only from different angles, from the vantage point of different Earth chakras.

It was easy to imagine that when the grasslands, covering one third of the planet, were grazed by megaherds—Mongolian gazelle, caribou in the far north, bison on the Great Plains of North America, 50,000,000 strong—that Gaia was benefiting in ways that we may never appreciate.

When they sped up the film, these endless herds of caribou resembled a massive movement of solidified energy, an intelligent flood cascading over the land. It is thrilling to suggest that these megamigrations, representing major overland energy flows across the globe, were and may still be (albeit on a much diminished scale) performing some kind of deep massage or acupuncture for the energy body of the planet, stirring her vitality, keeping things circulating, charging things up. They are essentially in constant motion.

*And the ravenous flies are just Sila keeping them moving even faster.*

Wallace Black Elk humorously envisions the world as a giant carpenter's level with the migrating animals as the bubble that holds steady as the planet tilts (relative to the sun) (13). The sense of balance is built in. On a static, dead planet, the great ball would tip, and everything would stay right where it is, nailed or glued down, fenced in, built up, unresponsive.

# 16

## The Root Chakra

The root chakra, at the base of the spine, is the least subtle or most physical of all the chakras in our subtle or esoteric anatomy. The seventh, or crown chakra, at the top of the head is the most subtle or spiritually refined. Chakras, as already discussed, are energetic vortices that transmit, store, and assimilate earth energy (for example, magnetic energy) and cosmic energy (from above). We might also conceptualize them as a vertical garden of (seven) bio/spiritual, psychoenergetic *flowers*, each one unique. Like green plants (that use the energy of sunlight to convert carbon dioxide into food), chakras perform an equally "miraculous" process of synthesis and transmutation, converting universal energy into subtle energy for the maintenance and vital expressions of human functioning.

In her discussion of the root or base chakra, Wauters writes:

> Each time we define ourselves by the self-limiting ideas that dictate where we can and cannot go, whom we can or cannot participate with, and what we are allowed to do, we narrow our life choices. . . . Our root chakra, in order to be functional must be rid of narrow beliefs. . . . We heal the root chakra each time we affirm our right to the life we say we want (1).

Most of us are here to resolve something, and if we don't resolve it in this incarnation, we'll be back in some form or another to have another go at it. The root chakra keeps us from forgetting that we're here because creation wants us here and that first our business is to survive. To survive, we must make connections, or, more to the point, we must find "a steady and permanent connection with what is real and true" (2). First we have to find grounding and sustenance, and then we can begin to focus our energies on manifesting the *life we say we want*.

Back to the crystals dream:

*As I climb, the path grows steeper.*

Right away I think of the learning curve.

I climb as high as I can, and when I can't climb any higher and am *"leaning toward descending, the whole piece I'm clinging to falls."*

What is happening here is happening on the level of the root chakra.

Wauters says, "When we expand our consciousness to include the substratum upon which life is based, which is a spiritual consciousness, we can be unruffled by the changing tide of events that affect us" (3).

*"I go down with it a little, while the rest of the rocks tumble down—thankfully, no one is hit, but I see a group of crystals growing right where the rocks were."*

Wauters explains the difference between the ingrown, honor-bound clannishness and the harmonic unity that can result from a closed and open root chakra, respectively:

> When people live exclusively within the root chakra, they are overly attached to land, tradition, home, family, clan or tribal roots. . . . They do not . . . come to express their talents outside these perimeters. . . . We *open* the root (chakra) to be an anchor for our spirit and to manifest unity rather than separation (4).

If this cliff is the learning curve, then I have to learn that my way of manifesting unity and living the life I want is by breaking out of the linear progression that has been defining my relationship with the root chakra. The dream is showing me that I am ready for a dramatic shift in my life, from ground up, and this shift is fully supported by the root chakra. It might even be that this dream is confronting me with the fact that I am recovering from my *initiatory illness* and an unhealthy relationship with my tribe, the Wasichu.

According to Wauters, the core archetype of the root chakra is the Mother. She "feeds, nourishes and provides for our needs" (5). The crystals are a gift from the Mother.

*One of the hardest things about my life right now, as an aging son, is the knowledge that I am going to outlive my father. On the flip side, as a father, it has always been hard to imagine myself leaving my own son behind. It would seem that this is the time to reflect on these things: In light of these thoughts, the dream that I had the night before the crystal dream is self-explanatory:*

*I am at a house in the woods where I live. I am upstairs looking out over the drive and down at a large maple (growing between house and driveway), thinking I might clear out the weeds around its roots. Then I look out the windows in another direction, where there is a rise in the terrain close to the house that is overgrown by young trees and roots. I think of weeding or clearing around these roots as well. There is some scene with my father before this, which took place on the first floor.*

"Healing our roots is learning that we can do more than our parents did and be more than they were able to be," notes Wauters (6). I might add, as a father, that it also means understanding that our children will do and be more than we were able to do and be.

Continuing with this dream:

*I find myself looking at my reflection in a large mirror, "checking myself out." I have a longish-bearded face, but my eyes are sort of smiling or half closed or beguiling or sweet-looking; my face looks "hillbillyish." By this I mean foolish in an uneducated, unsophisticated way, a "little dreamy . . . a little like the fool on the hill."*

Even in the dream, I am wondering, on some level, *How can this be me?* One answer is, it doesn't have to be me. In dreams as well as in waking life, mirrors possess a shamanic function, to serve as "vessels for spirits and ancestral souls" (7). As I study this character, I am both puzzled and fascinated. Again, his beard is long and tapered, so this face combines the beard of a sage with the visage of a half-wit. The whole impression of the eyes and the beard together suggests that the one looking back at me is an idiot savant, Joan Halifax's wise fool who "emerges to dance the force of nature, to sing the songs of creatures, to dream the way to the future" (8).

The symbolism of the beard by itself connotes strength, virility, and old age (wisdom) or, in the instance of the V-shaped, downward-pointing beard, the grounding aspect of wisdom (9).

In Halifax's *Shaman: The Wounded Healer*, there is a detailed reproduction of the "Dancing Sorcerer" of the Magdalenian cave in Les Trois Frères (in central France), which Ryan discusses at length in his *Strong Eye of the Shaman* in terms of its theriomorphic (animal form) anatomy and what this signifies.

> We can now recognize how this uniting symbol in the cave recesses parallels Eliade's description of the cosmogonic function of the shaman as uniting the world creative polarities and in this way returning to the source of creation. (10)

In my dream, "my" reflection is not theriomorphic, but it does unite two polarities: the beard of the sage and eyes of the fool. The beard (in the reflection) is remarkably similar to the beard of the Dancing Sorcerer. Another bearded image comes to mind from Jung's *Red Book* (11). The ears in Jung's painting are identical to the ears of the Dancing Sorcerer. There are other parallels: Jung's image has nascent horns, and the hair on top bristles straight up, symbolizing rays of chthonic power. Both images are older than old, from that protohistoric time before time. The biggest difference between Jung's painting and the Dancing Sorcerer is that Jung's image is only a head embedded far down in Earth's matrix, held in the eternal embrace of fossilized bedrock. His eyes are shut against the passage of time, in deep-dreaming mode (reminiscent of the Celt's designation of the dismembered head as seat of the soul). The Dancing Sorcerer, as captured in these impressions of Ryan and Halifax, is whole, vital, and wide-eyed.

> He stands some fifteen feet above the level of the floor, ominously watching—a most numinous image, as if presiding over all . . . the God of the Cave, or the animal master . . . he seems to possess the antlers and ears of a stag, the rounded staring eyes of an owl or perhaps a lion (12).

> His ears are those of the wolf, and his face is bearded like a lion's. . . . The startling eyes seem to pierce through thousands of years (13).

> The dancing feet . . . are distinctly human, and as he rises to a semi erect position, his penetrating eyes look out from behind what appears to be a human beard (14).

The sorcerer's eyes are composed of concentric circles—mandalas, actually—indicating shamanic trance. One may also see them as twin nierikas, openings or portals into the mystery of Harner's *shamanic state of consciousness*; only in contrast to the spiral or one-directional vortex, his eyes might be thought of as two-way openings, for going and returning—for the initiate's two-way journey but also for the ancestor's journey out and his/her return to the dreamtime. Lynne Hume explains, "The generative power of the Ancestors comes from the center of the concentric circle. It is where the power resides" (15).

The discovery of the Dancing Sorcerer provides us with a portrait of what the Self looked like before it cut itself off (or was cut off) from the whole realm of nature. For Ryan, "the part-human, part-animal archetype is a 'uniting symbol,' bringing the human consciousness into fruitful contact with its deeper roots. The effect of the experience of such symbols, for the initiated is salvific . . . a tapping of the (primal) source of psychic power. . . . On the other hand, it points to the transpersonal world beyond our strictly individuated existence, a world characterized by universal or essential form" (16).

There were no mirrors then, but isn't it just possible that whoever painted the Dancing Sorcerer was painting his own transpersonal reflection—the reflection of some ur-alt ancestor, from the deep mirror of the cave ceiling, looking back at him?

My hillbilly-savant is the ancestor who represents my inherited relationship to my root chakra.

> On a physical level this chakra controls the adrenal cortex, which is the storehouse for inherited ancestral energy. The root chakra holds both our genetic inheritance for vitality as well as

our innate predisposition for disease. Within this domain are stored the qualities that helped our ancestors survive (17).

*All* of our chakras helped our ancestors survive, each holding its own formula or prescription for maintaining the vitality necessary for the "continuum of life" (18) based on countless centuries of ancestral experience. It makes sense that each might, in response to special circumstances (spiritual, emotional, psychic), reveal the primordial face or archetypal visage of the ancestor that best reflects or communicates the quality specific to that chakra that helped our most evolved predecessors survive (assuming that the least evolved of our ancestors would not have survived and would have left no lasting imprint).

*This linking of chakras to ancestors sheds light on the time I saw that ancient face looking back at me from the mirror: In 1973, I was facing a mirror, experimentally rotating my eyes rapidly in a clockwise direction, like two compasses, for the sheer entertainment of watching my eyes appear at regular intervals on the virtual circles that formed inches from my nose, which was centering the blurred field of my face. Thus preoccupied, I was totally unprepared for what happened next: I became gradually aware that somebody was watching me from where my own face should have been, in the mirror, watching me from a pair of almond eyes. Time seemed to stop as I found that I had become the focus of contemplation of a wise, compassionate being. The intensity of my curiosity was the perfect complement, or somehow the inverse equivalent, of a clarity and purity of focus the likes of which I had never before witnessed. I just stood there, basking in this intimate melding of attentions from both sides of the mirror, fearful of doing anything to break the spell.*

*I have always referred to this apparition as my "soul." Others with whom I have shared this story have offered that it might have been my higher Self. Here is a new theory: My random experiment with my eyes (rotating them rapidly clockwise) opened a kind of concentric portal or nierika by activating my sixth chakra, initiating a face-to-face encounter with the primordial ancestor who stands behind that chakra for me.*

*I'll never know who it was I saw, but the effect of his appearance was to take pressure off me for awhile by introducing a whole new perspective. It provided me with something worthy of a lifetime's pondering.*

Often spiritual people lack grounding, and spiritual disciplines become a way of escaping or padding reality while the woes of the middle world continue to monopolize our collective intelligence, consume Earth's resources and stress the land. This is understandable, but it's not helpful, nor is there any future in it! If spiritual people don't take on the responsibility of healing their tribe, the gap between realms will continue to widen. The worse things get, the more tempting it is to leave everything to the dogs. The image here is of the abandoned village, but someday soon, if we're not careful, we will be living in a world of abandoned cities or whole regions, as in the case of the meltdown of the (Soviet) Chernobyl nuclear plant in 1986. Chernobyl is still surrounded by a so-called Exclusion Zone extending 30 kilometers in all directions.

Fortunately, a growing number of us—equal numbers of men and women—have fallen deeply in love with the planet. Even Christians are waking up to the need to square the Trinity, to allow a little dirt in heaven, which has less to do with the formal recognition of the ascension to heaven of the Virgin Mary than the lowering of heaven so that it touches sacred earth. (Picture angels with dirt between their toes.)

One of my favorite lines in the Bible is "How beautiful are the feet of those who bring good news." (Isaiah, 40:9, NIV)

Now, the good news might be that the messengers are barefoot! Surely our barefoot ancestors are keeping an eye on us, but it seems as if we are waiting for a psychic earthquake. What's happening deep in the human psyche is building to become the psychic equivalent of the Big One. The fault lines between Weltanschauungs have been under intense stress for ages. Everyone senses that something has to give; we seem to be living in a time when disaster spells relief. Will any structure hold up? Certain questions are little more than the answer turned on its head. How about a different question:

*Does the answer have to be dreamed?*

If the problems are bigger than us, then the answer will have to come from outside or beyond us.

The ancestors are watching and waiting for us to realize how much more is at stake than the petty dreams of civilization; Earth's ability to dream is on the line. And many of us do realize; we *get it*. "As one shaman said (to Halifax): Many non-traditional people of the West seem not only to appreciate the 'road' of the shaman, but also appear to have an affinity for the 'Medicine Way.' The return to the middle world of today, then, involves a bridging of culture and time" (19)—a bridging, that is, to protohistoric time. Protohistory is antecedent history, the ground in which the great stories of cultures take root. More pointedly, it has no beginning and no end in the sense that it exists outside of time in the Dreaming. Protohistory contains the alpha and omega of all time-bound histories and tells the story that perseveres from age to age. Right now we are caught up in a culture of linear, chronological or (Eliade) *homogeneous* time, but the more we learn about shamanic healing and the medicine way, the less important that time-bound culture will be. We will dream a different dream.

By itself, the middle world is little more than the dressing of a void. It has impermanence written all over it, like a carnival that comes together overnight, and when it's over, it disappears just as quickly. For the sake of this discussion, there are two kinds of voids: the chaos that is breaking down into nothing (the dreamless void) and the nothing that is always on the verge of building into something unprecedented (the vacuum plenum). The middle world is a void trying to decide whether it wants to collapse in on itself or become *real and true*.

Sound far-fetched? Damien Broderick (internationally respected author, critic, and theorist) writes that some physicists find it useful to postulate the existence of a *probability field* to account for how *probability space* can "'bend' in the presence of some psi (paranormal) element of consciousness." He asks: "Can coupling between intention and matter or energy cause a warping of . . . the probability field?" (20) In the 1950s, when UFO sightings were a dime a dozen, some were so real they were pursued by Air Force jets. The government has never come clean about what they learned from all their classified midair encounters. But what was even more interesting to Jung (who coined the word *psychoid* to describe archetypal structures that straddle the psychic and material realms) was the relationship of ordinary people to the UFO phenomenon. Folks were so anxious to experience UFOs firsthand that some published sightings were nothing but homemade models of airships caught on film or a snapshot of a dish tossed over a suburban clothesline. Suffice it to say that the middle world is always in a state of flux. It is half-baked, floating on a vast relativity of values and dreams and barely functional systems, secretive bellicose governments, the ruins of ethnicities, great train wrecks of religions, the stirrings of new and renewed visions, and environmental breakdown. It is a soup of disparate energies: moral restlessness, continuous war, and cultural mayhem. Halifax notes: "As we have seen, shamans are trained in the art of equilibrium, in moving with poise and surety on the threshold of the opposites, in creating cosmos out of chaos. The middle world then, is still a dream that can be shaped by the dreamer" (21). But not just any dreamer: the Big Dreamer, the dream shaper, the Big Dream shaper.

# 17

## Now Our Story Is Beginning

In Black Elk's great vision, the fourth Grandfather, the Grandfather of the south, speaks, addressing Black Elk as "younger brother":

> With the power of the four quarters you shall walk, a relative. Behold, the living center of a nation I shall give you, and with it many you shall save. And I saw that he was holding in his hand a bright red stick that was alive, and as I looked it sprouted at the top and sent forth branches and on the branches many leaves came out and murmured and in the leaves the birds began to sing. And then for just a little while I thought I saw beneath it in the shade the circled villages of people and every living thing with roots or legs or wings, and all were happy. "It shall stand in the center of the nation's circle," said the Grandfather, "a cane to walk with and a people's heart and by your powers you shall make it blossom" (1).

While it is still in the hands of the south Grandfather, Black Elk is shown what is possible or what might be: This tree centers the hoop of all the nations, all the villages of the two-leggeds, and the nations of all living things. It supports the elderly, those who have walked the earth for four ascents (four generations), and it is, not metaphorically, but quite literally, a people's heart. First the Grandfather says, "With the powers of the four quarters you shall walk," and then he says, "By your powers you shall make it blossom." Ergo, his powers will come from his relationship with the four directions.

> Then when he had been still a little while to hear the birds sing, he spoke again: "Behold the earth!" So I looked down and saw it lying yonder like a hoop of peoples and in the center bloomed the holy stick that was a tree, and where it stood there crossed two roads, a red one and a black. From where the giant lives (the north) to where you always face (the south) the red road goes, the road of good . . . and on it shall your nation walk.

The black road goes from where the thunder beings live (the west) to where the sun continually shines (the east), a fearful road, a road of troubles and of war. On this also you shall walk, and from it you shall have the power to destroy a people's foes. In four ascents you shall walk the earth with power (2).

This fourth Grandfather isn't advising Black Elk to always face the south. In this vision, it is a given; south is the direction he is *always* facing. Even when he isn't physically facing south, he is still facing south on a deeper level. It is his destiny; it is who he is. Black Elk is only nine when all of this is unfolding. It is his destiny to grow. "In four ascents you shall walk the earth with power."

When Black Elk dictated this, via his son Ben's translation to Neihardt's niece, he was in the *third ascent,* or seeing the third generation. The middle world is fraught with danger. His nation will walk the good red road, but Black Elk is told that he will walk both the red road *and* the black road. The latter is "a fearful road," but it is also a road of power—a power *over,* one that can be used to destroy one's enemies. The tree of life rises right at the point where these two opposite roads cross.

As soon as the fourth Grandfather finished his speech, he "rose very tall and started running toward the south and was an elk" (3).

In these two brief passages, Black Elk is being handed a map of his destiny. The destiny of his nation is revealed, and he is told everything he needs to know to protect himself, everything he needs to know to grow and walk with power, and how to wield that power. What is so beautiful and, one might say, *elegant* about this teaching is that no words are wasted, and words are only the teacherly complement of what is shown.

What does it signify that the tree of life is rooted at the intersection of the red and black roads: the "good" medicine road and the road of troubles and war, the road of power for growth and wisdom and the road of power over/power of destruction? It seems that Black Elk's dilemma of having to walk both roads is our fate as well—the fate of those of us who have fallen deeply in love with the earth.

*I opened an e-mail this morning from Cindy Shogan, who represents the Alaska Wilderness League, an organization in the forefront of the effort to save the Tongass National Forest: "We all know that the forest's ecosystem is intricately balanced between salmon, bears, and old growth trees—but the network of human interest is just as complex. Conservationists, fishermen, Native groups, lumberjacks, and town governments—all depend on the forest's ecosystem for their livelihoods as well. . . . . A historic thing is happening in the Tongass right now as these groups put decades of conflict on hold to come to the table and try to fit all the pieces together, knowing that a sustainable vision of the forest awaits at the end."*

So here I am, picturing the "circled villages of people and every living thing" underneath the branches of the great tree.

She continues:

*"But the Sealaska corporation* (its very name reveals its ambitions), *having profited from years of intensive logging, doesn't like the way the picture is coming together."*

The puzzle-metaphor doesn't work for them, as it seems to work for the nations who are trying to learn to coexist beneath the tree.

*"Surprisingly, the U.S. Senate is moving forward on its proposal to dismiss the conservation piece of the Tongass puzzle and authorize more clear-cutting. The "Sealaska bill" will only perpetuate conflict in the Tongass, razing old-growth forests along the way."*

What can we expect from lawmakers whose whole world exists inside the beltway of the black road? Maybe they'll do the right thing, but for the right reasons?

As news, this story, in no time, will have run its course. Legislation will be passed, and the fate of the Tongass will be decided; everything is in flux. But regardless of how the Tongass fares, let this stand as a snapshot of what we face across the board. And let us not doubt that what is happening in and to the world is happening simultaneously in our souls. Sealaska by any other name is still Sealaska.

There are so many ways to take our power, to close the power gap, and to own our destiny. One way is to leave the familiar and start walking.

In 1971, John Francis (founder and director of Planetwalk) witnessed an oil spill in San Fransico Bay when two tankers collided under the Golden Gate Bridge. "It was nearly a year afterwards," he writes in *Planetwalker*, "that I gave up the use of motorized vehicles and started walking" (4). He walked for 22 years. In essence, he succeeded in reclaiming the planet by walking its skin, becoming a long-term pilgrim. In his introduction, he summarizes (Arnold van Gennep's) three distinct phases "through which every pilgrim must pass. The first is that of separation or detachment from the familiar; the second he referred to as (a) liminal . . . state during which the pilgrim is part of no fixed social structure and the third is the reaggregation, which occurs when the pilgrimage is completed and the pilgrim returns to society" (5). I love Francis's concept of environment. He says, at least for the pilgrim, that "environment is about how we treat each other when we meet each other" (6).

*Every time I visit my mother, we take rides down the old country roads around Storrs, Connecticut, enjoying the familiar landscapes. Some of those roads are almost animated the way they conform to the contour of the land, shadowed by old stonewalls, skirting swamps and ledge. Together, she and I avoid the liminal state of her Alzheimer's by searching out what little remains of the familiar. When she is gone I will most likely never drive these back roads again. She will soon be moving on and so must I, allowing my dreams to lead the way.*

In our dreams we are all eternal pilgrims:

*I dreamed that I was in a car with my son, and he was driving. At one point, as we were passing through a construction zone with heavy equipment to the right, he pulled the car over to stop, to let me drive. I could see right below my window that the edge of the road was exactly that—a clean edge that dropped off about five feet to where they were excavating. And where they had cut away from the roadbed, there was an almost surgically neat cross-section of the substratum of the highway. Even as I complained about my son's driving, our precarious proximity to the edge afforded me a glimpse of how the road was constructed of a thick layer of smooth, black oblong stones lying atop each other in a compact, overlapping fashion. Even in the dream, this struck me as an odd way to build a road.*

In this dream, I am curious as to why the road builders used smooth oblong stones for a roadbed instead of conventional compactable material, almost guaranteeing instability! But maybe that's the point: The black path is far from inert and fixed and devoid of life; it is a work in progress. It is black through and through, but the stones that hold it in place are egg shaped, underscoring that there is much more to this road than meets the eye. It might even have its own dreaming!

Anne Waldman (poet, performance artist, author) points out that in Navaho the word for *road* is "used as a verb". She explains: "Their whole relationship to *road* (my italics) has to do with how you travel it, who you are traveling with, what the environment might be, where you are headed, in what direction. . ." (7) This way of thinking returns us to Black Elk's description of *water* as a verb-noun, "*a living*", that is, a living mystery. What this dream is saying is, this road (in *this* dream) is also a living mystery in that it likes to change form and its medicine is life.

In my earlier dream, I was eating the asphalt; in this dream, I am learning something about the road's substructure or mantel. The black road, as archetypal symbol, is an unknown quantity; it is numinous. One might even say it is rapidly evolving to reflect our own metamorphoses.

Once, at night, my son and I were driving between meadows when I happened to catch sight of a group of deer ahead of us off to the right. I slowed down and came to a complete stop just in case more of the herd were trying to cross. Suddenly something crashed into my door with the impact of a quarterback. Dumbfounded, I peered out of the window to the left and there was this large deer standing back from the road, peering back at us. It hadn't seen our car! Why? Deer are used to seeing cars moving quickly past, toward, or away from them. A car stopped in the middle of the road did not compute. The black path is *darkly numinous*, a treacherous conundrum to both nature and to *man*, rife with contradictions.

We never know what unmarked trucks are carrying. (Perhaps they are transporting our dreams away!) We never know anything about the person we are passing or who is charging past us. Some of us are running away from something, some of us are seeking connection, some of us are running from ourselves, and some of us are just running, full speed, back and forth. The interstate highway system (originally referred to as the Dwight D. Eisenhower National System of Interstate and Defense Highways) was pushed through Congress by the Eisenhower administration in 1956 to facilitate the movements of military convoys. This is part of the history of the black path that intersects the red path at the tree of life.

To Maria Queta, Kofan healer, the road symbolizes the end of everything:

> When there wasn't a road . . . we just had good times, going hunting, fishing, just everything, we were so utterly content, and later the road came and with it colonization, and now we're nothing . . . the forest is lost, pure coca fields that the settlers plant, and we wind up with nothing, nothing (8).

When a Wasichu wants to walk the red path, he/she can do that. But we must also stay connected to the black path, because we don't know how to live without it. For our own survival, and for the survival of our descendants, we must understand this path inside and out, because it is also the path of the most powerful entities of our time, and they know nothing of the red path. For them, the tree of life is simply in the way. (In the land of the Wasichu, the [by volume] largest known tree in the world bears the name of William Tecumseh Sherman. Infamous for his scorched-earth marches through the deep south, he was considered by military historian Basil Liddell Hart to be "the first modern general" [9]. [Apparently there was a much larger sequoia but it was cut down in the 1940s.])

These two roads in Black Elk's vision form a cross. If they don't see each other, because the black road has most of the knowledge and all the power, it will triumph. The tree of life will be clear-cut, and all the puzzle pieces of the hoops of the various nations, *Mitakuye Oyasin*, who have been trying to coexist under the tree will scatter to the four winds. If the two roads clash and try to subdue each other, the tree will be crucified.

We who have fallen deeply and passionately in love with the planet, our Mother, must learn to dream the Big Dream, which is our mother's dream for us. We must commit ourselves to the red path while staying connected to the black path to defend our birthright of access to knowledge and power—power to subdue our foes.

We must always face south because, just like nine-year-old Black Elk, we have much growing to do. We must walk these two paths simultaneously and consciously, always keeping the full sun in front of us with wisdom and the ancestors watching our backs—always with the rising sun, the morning star, shining in our faces and with the thunder beings rumbling and shaking the heavens and drumming on the mountains behind us. This is our best way into the future because of the way we walked in the past.

*Have we abandoned the theme of crossing?*

Wallace Black Elk spoke of the red road as starting in the stone people's lodge, transecting the fire pit, and pointing straight out of the womb. This is one way of living a sacred life and one way of visualizing the red path. For a number of years, my wife and I have been meeting with a group of people every several months for sweat lodges; I can vouch for how walking from lodge to lodge is a way of rededicating oneself to the red path. But Nicholas Black Elk's vision is a high-up vision. From this height, the little stone people's lodges disappear into the landscape from which the great axis of the world tree looms upward, supported by a massive root system, spanning the three realms.

Black Elk's vision is truly a big vision. It is not literal; it is a mandala map, a shamanic map of how to live effectively and passionately as a two-legged in a world that has been steadily slipping away from us. Is this because we haven't been honest about the things we love and the things we fear? Shouldn't we be protecting what we love from the things we fear? Fear is not a bad thing, as long as our fear is well focused and not misdirected. As Barry Glassner (president of Lewis and Clark College) notes, "One of the paradoxes of a culture of fear is that serious problems remain largely ignored even though they give rise to precisely the dangers that the populous most abhors"(10).

*When we begin to deal with our root fear, then we are letting the universe know that we want to be initiated.*

As I contemplate this mandala map, this vision of a healthy middle world, I see it is a map for travelers and questers as well as for those who would stay put and live in peace with *all our relations*.

This crossing here is a crossing to a way of life that revisions our relationship to Earth and honors life. If we really are in love with Earth, our Mother, then we will defend her against her foes.

Pierre Teilhard de Chardin (philosopher, priest, paleontologist, geologist) said, "The day is not distant when humanity will realize that it is faced with a choice between suicide and adoration" (11). Teilhard de Chardin died in 1955. I think the day that he anticipated has dawned, in which case we are living on borrowed time. On certain days, it really feels like creation is just paying out the lifeline so that we might choose our next step consciously! Andrew Harvey would have us know that "Teilhard de Chardin . . . is referring to . . . the highest means of opening to the sacred truths of reality: that we must arm ourselves with love and clarity and protect our world" (12).

This is our story, and it is just beginning: the story of how the New Wasichu will behave when they grow up and take their power. They have seen what they have done through their own eyes and the eyes of their ancestors, and they have grieved for what has been lost that can never be replaced.

In his prophetic early-twentieth-century poem, "The Waste Land", T. S. Eliot wrote: "(Come into the shadow of this red rock) /. . .And I will show you fear in a handful of dust."(13) (Eliot's parentheses.) These are powerful words. When I first read that line many years ago, that handful of dust was all I could think of. I saw how much trouble that dust had caused, blowing into the eyes of warriors and politicians and lovers and explorers, poets, teachers, judges, and mothers and fathers. Holding it in the scoop of a hand is a powerful way of saying, *Let's start over.*

*Let us cross to a vision that puts us back in relationship with life and Earth and each other.*

On one level, the hourglass has run out of sand; no more time for discussion and analysis or experimentation. When a wisdom or a teaching is *shown,* as opposed to argued or explained, then we begin to use our middle eye; the pituitary gland begins to stir. "I will show you" is how the ancestors prefer to teach us after all.

> *Who hears may be incredulous*
> *Who witnesses, believes . . .*
> —Emily Dickinson (14)

So the Earth is red. Wallace Black Elk said, "Every living thing is red. My blood, my life is red. All the winged, four-legged, creeping-crawlers, mammals, fish-people, and two-legged, their blood is red" (15). The Tree of Life is red. So it doesn't matter where we walk on this planet, as long as we are walking as if each day is holy and all things are sacred. Then we are on the red path with the sun in our faces, and if we are walking in our power, then the morning star will always be rising in our souls!

# 18

## Nuts and Bolts and Three Fish

$B$ack in my father's time and his father's time and so on, the U.S. Patent Office was a busy place. People were inventing things left and right—all kinds of things. Invention was in the air. Technology and materials were still in the realm of hands-on. Mechanics, basic math, and electronics were understandable. If you could draw it, chances are someone could make it. When I was a little boy you could still say you wanted to be an inventor when you grew up; being an inventor was right up there with being a teacher or a lawyer or an engineer. My brother subscribed to *Popular Mechanics*, a magazine that told you how to build all sorts of contraptions and machines. And they actually worked!

Like most kids who grew up in the 1950s, I tried my hand at inventing. (My most successful invention was a wooden vending machine that my Irish setter used to dispense herself biscuits.) But it was my destiny to stick with language. I became a poet (among other things). I could almost hear, or at least sense, a faint humming inside language like a tuning fork. Poetry for me was full of wonder and utility. It was plugged in to a current.

I am presently the resident poet for an Internet journal: a blog. *Blog* is a contraction of *web log*. *Weblog* was coined by Jorn Barger in 1997, but *blog* was coined by Peter Merholz, who broke Barger's weblog into the phrase *we blog*. Then Evan Williams at Pyra Labs used *blog* as a noun and verb: *to blog* means to edit one's weblog or to post to one's weblog. (1)

A blog is an invention that "facilitated the posting by non-technical users," including poets. Until around 2009, blogs were the work of single individuals or small groups and were limited to a specific subject. Previously, a working knowledge of such technologies as HTML and FTP had been required to publish on the Web (2). Blogs are linked to other blogs, websites, and journals with rapid-fire sharing of posted material. (According to Wikipedia, in 2011 there were 156 million public blogs in existence. It wouldn't surprise me if that number has since doubled.) My poem might be read by tens of thousands of people within a week of my writing it. (One day alone, my work was read by more than 8,000 people.) Sometimes a poem (and the attached image) floats to the surface of this virtual sea months after its posting. The font has changed or the ending has been dropped, but I recognize it as my offering.

This is not to brag. In fact, blogging is not personally satisfying; it is not about recognition. This is an example of how the world has changed overnight. I don't know any of the people who read my poem, and I rarely hear from them. Feedback is not to be expected. The point is, when I post a poem, it instantaneously dissolves into a sea of blogging. (One time I heard from someone in Panama who knew somebody who knew somebody who was friends with someone who knew *of* me.)

When I wake up in the morning, often I have a hard time getting started. I don't want to do many of the things I have to do to maintain the order of my life, to sustain my reality. I would rather write or walk or work on certain projects. I'm sure that there are people, for example in business, who would rather farm for a living, disappear for a few weeks or at least daydream of rescuing themselves from their routines; and I know that there are farmers who would rather spend all day tinkering with machinery than milking the cows.

Life requires us to make choices in real time. The choices we make are not always ones that will guarantee us happiness in the long run. We are complex. That complexity is often masked by our willfulness and impulsiveness and the ongoing social experiment that has turned most of us into *consumers* and other monstrosities.

Who would deny that earning money is our main reason for getting up these days? And that earning money isn't really working?

We have reached a point in our evolution when we are all making important choices that will affect our future and *the* future. My gut tells me that the thousands of people who go to the sorts of blogs and websites that post the kinds of poetry I have been writing all know what I'm talking about even though I have no proof of that.

Meaning is elusive, but unless our lives are meaningful, we are going to care only enough to limp along but not enough to reinvent ourselves, which is what we are being challenged to do.

Poets are among those who can help people reinvent themselves.

You know the phrase "You can't get there from here"? Many of us who lived through the Cold War know that nothing that we did can account for how we made it to "here," wherever "here" is. (*Here*, it turns out, is a place in time, a place made of "now." In other words, *here* is *now*.) Nor was it anything our leaders did that got us through to here. We were quite literally facing the end of the world when something shifted and the old structures couldn't hold up any more. Such a shift has to do with how we use our minds and how we don't use our minds.

Logic works for logic. In other words, logic builds a world around itself where it sets the agenda. But out in nature or in the "real world"—or even in certain countries—logic doesn't get one very far.

People function differently. Going by Jung's typology, people can be *intuitive* types, *sensation* types, *feeling* or *thinking*, and they can be introverted or extraverted *intuitives, feelers,* etc. Each of these four functions can combine (unless they are polar opposites such as *feeling* and *thinking* or *intuition* and *sensation*), so there can be introverted *intuitive-thinkers* or extraverted *intuitive-feelers*, etc. Isn't it a wonder that we can agree on anything at all? In fact, it is the individuality of our functioning that accounts for the richness of human interactions.

In spite of this richness, it is also true that different periods in history have favored certain functions over others. One way to look at a collective shift in consciousness is to see it in terms of a rallying around a new standard for human functioning, for example, *feeling* or *intuition* or something in between.

With the dawning of the computer age, people who function by pure logic have been caricatured as Spocks: brilliant but shallow and, in certain contexts, bumbling or even stupid. Circumambulating an issue or arriving at a conclusion indirectly makes sense when the issue is blurry at the edges. When edges blur, logic fails.

What we are facing today is different than anything we faced during the Cold War. The reality of "now" is more complex than two nations facing off across the ocean. We are, in fact, losing control of a logic-based reality.

Rumi, incomparable mystic and the most-read poet in the world today, narrated (he never wrote down a poem himself) a poem that goes by the title "The Three Fish."

There are three fish in a lake. One is intelligent, one is half intelligent, and one is stupid.

Some men with nets show up, planning to catch the fish. The intelligent fish decides to leave immediately and make his way to the ocean. He decides not to consult the other two for fear that any discussion would weaken his resolve. He knows they will stay put and take their chances.

And he is right.

The half-intelligent fish's strategy is to pretend that he is dead. He flops out of the lake and lies still as a corpse. His ruse works; the fishermen ignore him and he is able to slip back into the water undetected.

The stupid fish panics and tries to escape the net by darting and thrashing about but he is caught and winds up in the frying pan, where he swears to himself, "If I get out of this . . . I'll make the infinite my home." That is his last thought.

Meanwhile, the intelligent fish manages to reach the sea by making his "whole length a moving footprint."

These three fish are aspects of ourselves: The stupid fish is the part of us that stays because he can't conceive of changing anything that he is doing. He simply hopes that he will be able to avoid the net of fate. The half-intelligent fish escapes, at least for the time being, by faking death, but without the intelligent fish to lead and inspire him, he remains where he has no future. His way of surviving is to become invisible and remain invisible.

The intelligent fish realizes that the lake was never his real home anyway. Even though his journey requires everything he has, he knows that "your real 'country' is where you are heading, not where you are" (3).

Right now, the intelligent third of the human race is on the move, flopping over land to the sea. But two thirds of us are like the other two fish, one of which will wind up in the frying pan and the other of which doesn't have it in him to leave his pseudo-home, where he will most likely eventually be caught or simply die pretending to be dead.

This is the time for us to reinvent ourselves, to shape-shift, like the fish who turned himself into a foot. None of us wants to wind up in the frying pan hoping for a miracle. The fact is that our real home is the infinite ocean, the shoreless sea, where there are no limits to our intelligence.

Most likely, I don't know you. But maybe you know someone who knows someone who knows someone who knows me. Regardless, I will tell you the same thing I would tell a dear friend. That is:

*If you haven't already, flop out of the pond and head for the sea!*

The boundless sea is the Tao, the Dreaming, the realm of the archetypes, Earth-centered consciousness, the new age, the place of two-light vision, the place of our second birth, where we know what we know and belief is a given, where we are in relationship with the elements and the directions and the ancestors and each other. It is where magic is possible and matter animates. It is the place where the red and the black road meet and continue on from the tree of life. It is the side of life. And it is an attitude that has less to do with philosophical positioning and spiritual questing than with intensity.

We, the New Wasichu, have to care enough to rescue ourselves from *not* caring. Once we care, we begin to move. And we find our coordinates. We fish-flop, and the earth moves under us. We are like the point on an Etch A Sketch sliding along the meridians. Our position changes, but the self remains in place at the intersection where the path of power and the path of balance come together. Instead of walking these paths separated by 90 degrees of divergence, we remain centered on the invisible crosshairs of perpetual convergence. We *become* our walk as we learn to let the two paths move through us. And we never forfeit the integrity of our hard-earned two-in-oneness, no matter where we go: in and out of time and dreams and never-ending realities, "still and still moving" (4) into ever greater intensity.

## Postscript

When I started writing this book, I suppose I knew that my father had less than a few years to live, and it concerned me deeply that he didn't seem ready to die.

He and I had enjoyed a rare closeness ever since we both began studying Jung back in the mid-1970s. I was at college when I became passionate about Jungian psychology and launched into dream analysis. At the same time, he was ripe for a complete change of direction, having just retired at age 55 from his 25-year career as professor of electrical engineering at the University of Connecticut. An MIT graduate, he was hardwired to adopt a rational, logical approach to the large questions about life and the meaning of his own life. The day in 1974 that I handed him Jung's autobiography, *Memories, Dreams, Reflections*, I was very excited. I knew that he would respect Jung's prodigious intellect and integrity as an empiricist, and I was right. That day was truly the first day of the rest of his life. Within three years, my father had graduated from the Zurich Jungian Institute as a certified analyst and had launched a new career that would span 30 years.

Ataxia gradually wore him down, but he continued to see clients right up to the last six months of his life. For his last two years he worked on a weekly basis with a remarkable woman, Jennifer (his yoga teacher), whom I credit with opening his heart and his higher chakras to the possibility of spiritual transformation. Still, it concerned me, even as his vitality ebbed, that he was being hounded by his rational mind. It was obvious that his heart was opening, but he was straddling worlds and could not seem to shake the habit or *program* of identifying with his head, or the thinking function. He was forever struggling to let go, the way Jung had so brilliantly modeled in *The Red Book*.

During his last week, he was transferred from rehab to hospital with pneumonia. In compliance with his living will, the family chose to bring him back to rehab. The day the hospice people showed up, Jennifer, who had just been working with him, advised us to be with him. In her words, he was "very clear" and she urged us to "take advantage" of this. Sure enough, when I saw his eyes, I was struck by their crystal clarity. He was gazing straight up at the ceiling, and his pupils were following the movement of something that I could neither see nor detect. Then he raised his hands (which, until then, had been lying at his sides) slowly upward with fingers spread in a classic ecstatic religious gesture. If someone had described this to me, I might have chalked it up to poetic license. After all, this was my father who, in spite of his Jungian background, was not given to believing in anything he couldn't see or sense. It was an uphill battle to convince him that human consciousness wasn't the ultimate source of "reality." And here I was, watching him having a religious experience! I have no doubt that he was *crossing alive*.

Those of us who saw him off were struck by the profound irony that, because of the eventual loss of control of his throat muscles, he, who, as I say, always wrestled with just letting things be or happen on their own terms without interpretation or explanation, couldn't articulate a single word of what he was experiencing. There is a lesson here: that we can't always have it both ways. But I saw him see what he saw. And what's more, I believe he would have wanted me to.

# Notes

## Foreword

1. Black Elk, Wallace and William S. Lyon. *Black Elk: The Sacred Ways of a Lakota*. New York: HarperSanFrancisco / HarperCollins Publishers, 1991, p. 23.
2. Ibid., p. 21.
3. LaDuke, Winona. *All Our Relations: Native Struggles for Land and Life*. Cambridge, MA: South End Press, 1999, p. 142.
4. Halifax, Joan. *Shaman: The Wounded Healer*. London: Thames and Hudson, 1982, p.25.
5. Tedlock, Barbara. *The Woman in the Shaman's Body*. New York: Bantum Books, 200, p.24.

## Chapter 1

1. Mehl-Madrona, Lewis. *Coyote Medicine*. New York, NY: Fireside Book, 1998, p. 28.
2. Jung, C. G. *Children's Dreams: Notes from the Seminar Given in 1936–1940*. Princeton and Oxford: Princeton University Press, 2008, p. 288.
3. Moore, Wes. *The Other Wes Moore: One Name, Two Fates*. New York: Spiegel and Grau, 2010, xxi, xxii.
4. Sheldrake, Rupert. *The Rebirth of Nature: The Greening of Science and God*. Rochester, VT: Inner Traditions, 1991, 109.
5. Ibid., p. 116.
6. NPR, Books segment. Fresh Air interview of V.S. Ramachandran: "V.S. Ramachandran's *Tales of the 'Tell-Tale Brain'*", (from WHYY), July 14, 2011.
7. Beston, Henry. *The Outermost House*. New York: Penguin Books, 1977, p.10.
8. Kalweit, Holger. *Shamans, Healers, and Medicine Men*. Boston: Shambhala, 2000, p. 10.
9. James P. Blair. *Yugoslavia, Six Republics in One.* National Geographic, Vol. 137, No. 5, May 1970.
10. Quoted in Bly, Robert. *News of the Universe: Poems of Twofold Consciousness*. San Francisco: Sierra Club Books, 1980, p. 39.

11. Lockhart, Maureen. *The Subtle Energy Body: The Complete Guide.* Rochester, VT: Inner Traditions, 2010, p. 52.

12. Barks, Coleman (transl.). *The Essential Rumi.* Edison, NJ: Castle Books, 1995, p. 2.

13. Kalweit, Holger. *Shamans, Healers and Medicine Men.* Boston, MA: Shambhala, 1992 , p. 12.

14. Lockhart, *The Subtle Energy Body*, p. 28.

15. Chopra, Deepak. *Quantum Healing: Exploring the Frontiers of Mind/Body Medicine.* New York: Bantam Books, 1989, p. 149.

## Chapter 2

1.  Dames, Michael. *Merlin and Wales: A Magician's Landscape.* London: Thames and Hudson Ltd, 2002, p. 18.

2.  http://lewisandclarkjournals.unl.edu, text of Nebraska edition, edited by Gary E. Moulton.

3.  Traxel, William. *Footprints of the Welsh Indians.* New York: Algora Publishing, 2004., p. 148.

4.  Ibid., p.149.

5.  Ibid., p.24.

6.  Fell, Barry. *America B.C.: Ancient Settlers in the New World.* Muskogee, OK: Artisan Publications, 2004, p. 134.

7.  MacEowen, Frank. *The Mist-Filled Path: Celtic Wisdom for Exiles, Wanderers, and Seekers.* Novato, CA: New World Library, 2002, p. 45.

8.  Ellis, Peter Berresford. *A Brief History of the Druids.* Philadelphia: Running Press, 2002, p. 39.

9.  Ibid., p. 43.

10. Cowan, Tom. *Fire in the Head: Shamanism and the Celtic Spirit.* HarperSanFrancisco, 1993, p. 111.

11. Ellis, p.40.

12. Matthews, Catlin and John. *Encyclopedia of Celtic Wisdom.* Shaftsbury, Dorset: Element, 1994, p. 188.

13. Ellis, p. 73.

14. Lady Gregory. *Gods and Fighting Men: The Story of the Tuatha Danaan and the Fianna of Ireland.* London: J. Murray, 1904., Part I, Book III.

15. Matthews, Caitlin and John. *The Encyclopedia of Celtic Wisdom.* Shaftesbury, Dorset: Element, 1994, p. 9.

16. Lady Gregory.

17. Kirkey, Jason. *The Salmon in the Spring: The Ecology of Celtic Spirituality.* San Franciso: Hiraeth Press, 2009, p.21.

18. *In Search of Ancient Ireland.* DVD, directed and produced by Leo Eaton (Café Productions, 2002).

19. Quoted in Hume, Lynne. *Ancestral Power: The Dreaming, Consciousness and Aboriginal Australians.* Melbourne, Australia: Melbourne University Press, 2002, p. 4.

20. Ibid. (Hume's words).

21. Dames, Michael. *Merlin and Wales: Magician's Landscape.* London: Thames and Hudson Ltd, 2002, p.8.

22. Neihardt, John. *Black Elk Speaks.* Albany, New York: State University of New York Press University of Nebraska Press, 2008, p.291.

## Chapter 3

1. Kalweit, Holger. *Shamans, Healers, and Medicine Men.* Boston: Shambhala, 2000, p. 163.

2. Ibid., p. 164.

3. Tedlock, Barbara. The Woman in the Shaman's Body. New York: Bantum Books, 2005, p.134.

4. Doore, Gary. *Shaman's Path: Personal Growth and Empowerment.* Boston: Shambhala, 1988, p. 94.

5. Chopra, Deepak. *Quantum Healing: Exploring the Frontiers of Mind/Body Medicine.* New York: Bantam Books, 1989, p. 267.

6. Tedlock, Barbara. The Woman in the Shaman's Body. New York: Bantum Books, 2005, p. 153.

7. Wilcox, Joan. *Ayahuasca: The Visionary & Healing Powers of the Vine of the Soul.* Rochester, VT: Park Street Press, 2003, p. 4.

8. *Webster's New Collegiate Dictionary.* Springfield, MA: G. & C. Merriam Co., 1976, p. 532.

9. Quoted in Ingerman, Sandra and Hank Wesselman. *Awakening to the Spirit World: The Shamanic Path of Direct Revelation.* Boulder, CO: Sounds True, 2010, p. 164.

10. Ibid., p. 165.

11. Harvey, Andrew. *The Hope: A Guide to Sacred Activism.* Carlsbad, CA: Hay House, Inc., 2009, xv.

## Chapter 4

1. Brown, Joseph Epes. *The Sacred Pipe: Black Elk's Account of the Seven Rights of the Oglala Sioux.* Norman, OK: University of Oklahoma Press, 1953, p. 59.
2. Kalweit, Holger. *Shamans, Healers, and Medicine Men.* Boston: Shambhala, 1992, p. 63.
3. Aniela Jaffe. *Children's Dreams: Notes from the Seminar Given in 1936–1940.* Princeton and Oxford: Princeton University Press, 2008, p. 289.
4. Cowan, Tom. *Fire in the Head: Shamanism and the Celtic Spirit.* San Francisco: HarperSanFrancisco, 1993, p. 64.
5. Ibid., p. 36.
6. Black Elk, Wallace and William S. Lyon. *Black Elk: The Sacred Ways of a Lakota.* San Francisco: HarperSanFrancisco, 1991, p. 11.
7. O'Donohue, John. *Anam Cara: A Book of Celtic Wisdom.* New York, NY: Cliff Street Books, 1997, p. 37.
8. Heat –Moon, William Least. *The Hidden Yosemite.* National Geographic, Vol. 207, #1., p.103.
9. Black Elk and Lyon, p. xix.
10. Ibid., p. 4.
11. Ibid., p. xix.
12. Ibid., p. xx.
13. Whitman, Walt. *Leaves of Grass.* United States: A.S. Barnes & Company, 1944, p. 165, 167, 168.
14. Mary Schmidt quoted in Nicholson, Shirley J. *Shamanism.* Wheaton, IL: The Theosophical Publishing House, 1987, p. 68.
15. St. Pierre, Mark. *Walking in the Sacred Manner: Healers, Dreamers, and Pipe Carriers—Medicine Women of the Plains.* New York: A Touchstone Book, 1995, p. 151.

## Chapter 5

1. Black Elk, Wallace & Lyon, William. *Black Elk: The Sacred Ways of a Lakota.* HarperSanFrancisco, 1991, p.24.
2. Kirkey, Jason. *The Salmon in the Spring.* San Francisco: Hiraeth Press, 2009., p.6.

3. Ibid., p. 146, quoting Snyder from: *The Gary Snyder Reader: Prose, Poetry, and Translations.* New York: Counterpoint, 2000, p. 332.

4. Ibid., p. 100.

5. Black Elk, Wallace and William S. Lyon. *Black Elk: The Sacred Ways of a Lakota.* San Francisco: HarperSanFrancisco, 1991, p. 48.

6. Chopra, Deepak. *Quantum Healing: Exploring the Frontiers of Mind/Body Medicine.* New York: Bantam Books, 1989, p. 2.

7. Ibid., p. 17.

8. Ibid., p. 6.

9. Carl Jung, quoted by Richard Noll in Nicholson, Shirley J. *Shamanism.* Wheaton, IL: The Theosophical Publishing House, 1987, p. 60.

10. Lachman, Gary. *Jung the Mystic: The Esoteric Dimensions of Carl Jung's Life and Teachings.* New York: Penguin, 2010, p. 132.

11. Ziegler, Alfred. *Archetypal Medicine.* Dallas, TX: Spring Publications, Inc., 1983, p. 4.

12. Jung, C. G. *Children's Dreams: Notes from the Seminar Given in 1936–1940.* Princeton and Oxford: Princeton University Press, 2008, p.283.

13. Johnson, Robert. *Balancing Heaven and Earth.* New York, NY: HarperCollins Publishers Inc., 1998, p.125.

14. Black Elk and Lyon, p. 61.

15. Peat, F. David. *Blackfoot Physics.* Boston: Weiser Books, 2002, p. 139.

16. Bruchac, Joseph. *The Native American Sweat Lodge: History and Legends.* Freedom, CA: The Crossing Press, 1993, 81.

17. Lawlor, Robert. *Voices of the First Day: Awakening in the Aboriginal Dream Time.* Rochester, VT: Inner Traditions, 1991, p. 270.

18. Ibid.

19. von Franz, Marie-Louise. *Psyche and Matter.* Boston: Shambala, 1992, p. 28.

20. Watts, Alan. *The Way of Zen.* New York: Pantheon Books Inc., (division of Random House Inc.), 1957, p.4.

21. Hume, Lynne. *Ancestral Power: The Dreaming, Consciousness and Aboriginal Australians.* Melbourne, Australia: Melbourne University Press, 2002, p. 1.

22. Peat, p. 311.

23. Black Elk and Lyon, p. 71.

24. Ibid., p. 70.

25. Ibid., p. 69.

26. Kalweit, Holger. *Dreamtime and Inner Space: The World of the Shaman.* Boston & London: Shambala, 1988, p. 66.

27. Ibid., p. 67.

28. Ibid., p. 62.

29. Hume, p. 94.

30. Brown, Joseph Epes. *The Sacred Pipe: Black Elk's Account of the Seven Rights of the Oglala Sioux.* Norman, OK: University of Oklahoma Press, 1953, p. 29.

31. Kalweit, p. 66.

32. Quoted in Faulkner, Raymond O. and James P. Allen. *Ancient Egyptian Book of the Dead.* New York: Barnes & Noble, 2005.

33. Kalweit, p. 65.

34. Ibid., p. 64.

35. Ibid., p. 62.

## Chapter 6

1. Kalweit, Holger. *Dreamtime and Inner Space: The World of the Shaman.* Boston & London: Shambhala, 1988, p. 213.

2. Peat, F. David. *Blackfoot Physics.* Boston: Weiser Books, 2002, p. 75.

3. Black Elk, Wallace and William S. Lyon. *Black Elk: The Sacred Ways of a Lakota.* San Francisco: HarperSanFrancisco, 1991, p. 119.

4. Chopra, Deepok. *Quantum Healing.* New York: Bantam Books, 1989, p. 127.

5. Hume, Lynne. *Ancestral Power: The Dreaming, Consciousness and Aboriginal Australians.* Melbourne, Australia: Melbourne University Press, 2002, p. 90.

6. Roberts, Jane. *Seth Speaks.* Pdf, esotericonline.net., p.29.

## Chapter 7

1. Jung, C. G. Foreword. In Richard Wilhelm and Cary F. Baynes. *The I Ching or Book of Changes.* Princeton, NJ: Princeton University Press 1950, p. xxiv.
2. Progoff, Ira. *Jung, Synchronicity, and Human Destiny: C. G. Jung's Theory of Meaningful Coincidence.* New York: Julian Press, 1973, p. 87.
3. Vitebsky, Piers. *The Reindeer People.* Boston: Houghton Mifflin Company, 2005., p.269.
4. Noble, Vicki. *Motherpiece: A Way to the Goddess Through Myth, Art and Tarot.* New York, NY: HarperSanFrancisco, Harper Collins Publishers, 1983, p.188.
5. Douglas, Nik and Penny Slinger. *The Tantric Dakini Oracle.* Rochester, VT: Destiny Books, 2003, p. 74.
6. von Franz, Marie-Louise. *Psyche and Matter.* Boston: Shambala, 1992.
7. Douglas, Nik. *The Tantric Dakini Oracle.* Rochester, Vermont: Destiny Books, 1979., p.75.
8. Black Elk, Wallace, and William S. Lyon. *Black Elk: The Sacred Ways of a Lakota.* San Francisco: HarperSanFrancisco, 1991, p. 92.
9. Lawlor, Robert. *Voices of the First Day: Awakening in the Aboriginal Dreamtime.* Rochester, VT: Inner Traditions, 1991, p. 88.
10. Black Elk and Lyon, p. 125.

## Chapter 8

1. Thomas, George, PhD, MD.
2. http://ghthomas.blogspot.com/2011/02/medical-research-errors-or-dont-believe.html.
3. Buhner, Stephen Harrod and Brooke Medicine Eagle. *Sacred Plant Medicine: The Wisdom in Native American Herbalism.* Coeur d`Alene, Idaho: Raven Press, 1996, p. 77.
4. Ibid., p. 69.
5. *Webster's Third New International Dictionary.* Springfield, MA: Merriam-Webster INC., 1986, p. 57.
6. Campos, Don José. *The Shaman & Ayahuasca: Journeys to Sacred Realms.* Studio City, CA: Divine Arts, 2011, p. 28.

7.  Black Elk, Wallace and William S. Lyon. *Black Elk: The Sacred Ways of a Lakota*. San Francisco: HarperSanFrancisco, 1991, p. xii.

8.  Mehl-Madrona, Lewis. *Coyote Medicine*. New York, NY: Fireside Book, 1998, p.122.

9.  Black Elk and Lyon, p. 4.

10. *Webster's Third New International Dictionary*, p.1436.

11. Black Elk and Lyon, p. xxi.

12. *Webster's Third New International Dictionary*, p. 2111.

13. Dylan, Bob. *Chronicles, Volume One*. London: Pocket Books, 2004, p. 196.

14. Black Elk and Lyon, p. 6.

15. Ibid., p. xix.

16. Ibid., p. 51.

17. Lawlor, Robert. *Voices of the First Day: Awakening in the Aboriginal Dreamtime*. Rochester, VT: Inner Traditions, 1991, p. 83.

18. Brown Jr., Tom. *The Quest: One Man's Search for Peace, Insight, and Healing in an Endangered World*. New York: Berkley Books, 1991, p. 61.

19. Black Elk and Lyon, p. 130.

## Chapter 9

1.  Tim Flynn. http://www.alchemistsjournal.com/2010/01/over-edge-writing-as-re.html.

2.  Cowan, Tom. Email, 10/2010.

3.  Achor, Jefferson. Email, 10 /2010.

4.  Ziegler, Alfred J. *Archetypal Medicine*. Dallas, TX: Spring Publications, Inc., 1983, p. 5.

5.  Ibid., p. 7.

6.  Halifax, Joan. *Shamanic Voices: A Survey of Visionary Narratives*. New York: Dutton Paperback, 1979, p. 16.

7.  Erdos, Richard and John (Fire) Lame Deer. *Lame Deer, Seeker of Visions*. New York, NY: Simon and Schuster, 1972, p. 157.

## Chapter 10

1. Brown Jr., Tom. *The Quest: One Man's Search for Peace, Insight, and Healing in an Endangered World.* New York: Berkley Books, 1991, p. 12.
2. Ibid, p. 13.
3. Jesse Finfrock. http://www.motherjones.com/media/2009/ /interview-biz-stone.
4. Moore, Robert. *The Archetype of Inititiation.* Xlibris Corporation, 2001, p.42.
5. Eliade, Mircea. *Shamanism: Archaic Techniques of Ecstasy.* London: Penguin/Arkana, 1964, p. 266.
6. Maryann Shadem. Email, 1/11/2010.
7. Williams, J. E. *The Andean Codex: Adventures and Initiations among the Peruvian Shamans.* Charlottesville, VA: Hampton Roads Publishing Company, Inc., 2005, p. 189.
8. Maryann Shadem. Email, 1/11/2010.
9. Ibid.
10. Kalweit, Holger. *Dreamtime and Inner Space: The World of the Shaman.* Boston & London: Shambhala, 1988, p. 130.
11. Kathleen Harrison, quoted in Harpignies, J. P., ed. *Visionary Plant Consciousness: The Shamanic Teachings of the Plant World.* Rochester, VT: Park Street Press, 2007, p. 123.
12. Merriam-Webster's Collegiate Dictionary (Tenth Edition): Springfield, MA: Merriam Webster, Inc, 2001, p.192.
13. Prechtel, Martin. *The Disobedience of the Daughter of the Sun.* Cambridge, MA: Yellow Moon Press, 2001, p. 113.

## Chapter 11

1. Cowan, Tom. Email conversation, 1/11/2010.
2. Dames, Michael. *Mythic Ireland.* London: Thames and Hudson, 1992, p. 191.
3. Cowan. Email, 1/11/2010.
4. Ackor, Jefferson. Email, 1/12/2010.
5. Kalweit, Holger. *Dreamtime and Inner Space: The World of the Shaman.* Boston & London: Shambhala, 1988, p. 161.

6.  Tarrant, John. *The Light Inside the Dark: Zen, Soul, and the Spiritual Life.* New York: HarperPerennial, 1998, p. 122.

7.  Hume, Lynne. *Ancestral Power: The Dreaming, Consciousness and Aboriginal Australians.* Melbourne, Australia: Melbourne University Press, 2002, p. 62.

8.  Eliot, T.S. *T.S.Eliot: The Complete Poems and Plays.* New York: Harcourt Brace & Company, 1980, p. 3.

9.  Peat, F. David. *Blackfoot Physics.* Boston, MA: Weiser Books, 2002, p. 143.

10. Cowan. Email, 11/2010.

11. Jonsson, Patrik. http://www.csmonitor.com/layout/set/r14//Society/2011/01 20/Bye-Bye-Blackbird-USDA-acknowledges-a-hand-in-one-mass-bird-death

12. McKibben, Bill. *The End of Nature.* New York: Random House, 1989, p. 11.

13. Bode, Carl, ed. *The Portable Thoreau.* New York, NY: Penguin Books, 1982, p. 343.

14. Quoted in Rowthorn, Anne. *The Wisdom of John Muir: 100+ Selections from the Letters, Journals, and Essays of the Great Naturalist.* Birmingham, AL: Wilderness Press, 2012, p. 147.

15. Nicholson, Shirley. *Shamanism.* Wheaton, IL: Quest Books, 1987, p. 196.

16. Somé, Malidoma Patrice. *Ritual: Power, Healing, and Community.* New York: Penguin, 1997, p. 53.

17. Awiakta, Marilou. *Selu: Seeking the Corn-Mother's Wisdom.* Golden, CO: Fulcrum Publishing, 1993, p. 121.

18. Snyder, Gary. *Danger on Peaks: Poems.* Washington, D.C.: Shoemaker Hoard, 2004, p. 107.

19. http://www.alchemistsjournal.com/2010/02/stepping-over-edge-dancing-with-dark.html.

20. Conforti, Michael. *Field, Form, and Fate: Patterns in Mind, Nature, and Psyche.* New Orleans: Spring Journal Books, 1999, p. 60.

21. Lawlor, Robert. *Voices of the First Day: Awakening in the Aboriginal Dreamtime.* Rochester, VT: Inner Traditions, 1991, p. 14.

22. Wilcox, Joan. *Ayahuasca: The Visionary and Healing Powers of the Vine of the Soul.* Rochester, VT: Park Street Press, 2003, p. 193.

23. Andrews, Ted. *Animal-Speak: The Spiritual & Magical Powers of Creatures Great & Small.* St. Paul, MN: Llewellyn Publications, 1996, p.125.
24. Dames, Michael. *Mythic Ireland.* London: Thames and Hudson, 1992, p. 174.

## Chapter 12

1. Dziemidko, Helen E., MD. *The Complete Book of Energy Medicines: Choosing Your Path to Health.* Rochester, VT: Healing Arts Press, 1999, p. 112.
2. Simmons, Robert. *The Book of Stones: Who They Are & What They Teach.* East Montpelier, VT: Heaven & Earth Publishing, 2005, p. xxi.
3. Dziemidko, p. 112.
4. Simmons, p. xxii.
5. Eliade, Mircea. *Shamanism: Archaic Techniques of Ecstasy.* London: Penguin/Arkana, 1964, p. 52.
6. Ibid.
7. Ibid., p. 138.
8. Kalweit,, Holger. *Dreamtime and Inner Space: The World of the Shaman.* Boston & London: Shambhala, 1988, p.119.
9. Jung, C. G. *The Red Book.* New York: W. W. Norton & Company, 2009, p. 308.
10. Ibid.
11. Ibid., p. 311.
12. Bend, Cynthia. *Birth of a Modern Shaman.* St. Paul, MN: Llewellyn Publications, 1989, p. xiv.
13. St. Pierre, Mark. *Walking in the Sacred Manner: Healers, Dreamers, and Pipe Carriers—Medicine Women of the Plains.* New York: A Touchstone Book, 1995, p. 89.
14. Callahan, Bob. Introduction. In: Jaime de Angulo. *Coyote Man & Old Doctor Loon.* San Francisco: Turtle Island Foundation, 1973, p. 13.
15. Ibid., p. 16.
16. Ibid.
17. Ibid., p. 18.
18. Ibid.

19. Cowan, Tom. *Fire in the Head: Shamanism and the Celtic Spirit.* San Francisco: HarperSanFrancisco, 1993, p. 50.

## Chapter 13

1. Villoldo, Alberto. *Island of the Sun: Mastering the Inca Medicine Wheel.* Rochester, VT: Destiny Books, 1992, p. 135.
2. Jolly, Joanna. BBC News. *Highway will bring Nepal and Tibet 'in from the cold'.* January 27, 2010.
3. BBC News. *Mexico's Cave of Crystals* from BBC series, How the Earth Made Us. January 18, 2010.
4. Simmons, Robert. *The Book of Stones.* East Montpelier, VT: Heaven & Earth Publishing, 2005, p. 338.
5. Ibid., p.339.
6. Quoted in Rowthorn, Anne. *The Wisdom of John Muir: 100+ Selections from the Letters, Journals, and Essays of the Great Naturalist.* Birmingham, AL: Wilderness Press, 2012, p. 71.
7. Berry, Wendell. *New Collected Poems.* Berkeley, CA: Counterpoint, 2012, p. 125.
8. Kalweit, Holger. *Dreamtime and Inner Space: The World of the Shaman.* Boston & London: Shambhala, 1988, p. 219.
9. Quoted in Hunt, James B. *Restless Fires: Young John Muir's Thousand-Mile Walk to the Gulf in 1867–68.* Macon, GA: Mercer University Press, 2012, p. 86.
10. Narby, Jeremy. *Intelligence in Nature.* New York: Penguin, 2005, p. 7.
11. Ibid., p. 13.
12. McKibben, Bill. *The End of Nature.* New York: Random House, 1989, p. 57.
13. Mauer, Christopher, Editor. *Federico Garcia Lorca: Selected Verse.* New York, NY: Farrar Straus Giroux, 1997, p. 211,213.
14. Awiakta, Marilou. *Selu: Seeking the Corn-Mother's Wisdom.* Golden, CO: Fulcrum Publishing, 1993, p. 236.
15. Macy, Joanna and Molly Young Brown. *Coming Back to Life.* Gabriola Island, BC, Canada: New Society Publishers, 1998, p. 48.
16. Chopra, Deepak. *Quantum Healing: Exploring the Frontiers of Mind/Body Medicine.* New York: Bantam Books, 1989, p. 112.
17. Ibid., p. 114.

18. Jung, Carl Gustav. 1959 BBC interview with John Freeman: BBC television series *Face to Face*, produced by Hugh Burnett.
19. Bly, Robert. *News of the Universe: Poems of Twofold Consciousness.* San Francisco: Sierra Club Books, 1980.

**Chapter 14**

1. Sheldrake, Rupert. *The Rebirth of Nature: The Greening of Science and God.* Rochester, VT: Inner Traditions, 1991, p. 155.
2. Waters, Frank. *Book of the Hopi.* New York: Ballantine Books, 1963, p. 11.
3. Wauters, Ambika. *The Book of Chakras: Discover the Hidden Forces within You.* London: Quarto Publishing, 2002, p. 14.
4. Ibid.
5. Johnson, Robert. *Balancing Heaven and Earth.* Harper San Francisco, 1998, p. 292.
6. *Webster's Third New International Dictionary* (unabridged). Springfield, Massachusetts, 1986, p. 200.
7. Mudrooroo quoted in Hume, Lynne. *Ancestral Power: The Dreaming, Consciousness and Aboriginal Australians.* Melbourne, Australia: Melbourne University Press, 2002, p. 175 (from his book, *Us Mob*).
8. Wauters, pp. 41, 51, 61, 71, 81, 91, 101.
9. Ibid., pp. 60–63.
10. St. Pierre, Mark. *Walking in the Sacred Manner: Healers, Dreamers, and Pipe Carriers—Medicine Women of the Plains.* New York: A Touchstone Book, 1995, p. 202.
11. Ryan, Robert E. *The Strong Eye of Shamanism: A Journey into the Caves of Consciousness.* Rochester, VT: Inner Traditions, 1999, p. 39.
12. Michael Harner, quoted from an interview with Gary Moore in Nicholson, Shirley J. *Shamanism.* Wheaton, IL: The Theosophical Publishing House, 1987, p. 15.
13. Tedlock, Barbara. *The Woman in the Shaman's Body.* New York: Bantum Books, 2005, p. 70.
14. Chopra, Deepak. *Quantum Healing: Exploring the Frontiers of Mind/Body Medicine.* New York: Bantam Books, 1989, p. 255.
15. Quoted in Nicholson, p. 218.

16. Quoted in Bend, Cynthia. *Birth of a Modern Shaman*. St. Paul, MN: Llewellyn Publications, 1989, p. xxi.

## Chapter 15

1. Halifax, Joan. *Shaman: The Wounded Healer*. London: Thames and Hudson, 1982, p. 20.
2. *Planet Earth*. DVD, produced by Alastair Fothergill (BBC Video, 2007).
3. Halifax, p. 7.
4. Brown, Joseph Epes. *The Sacred Pipe: Black Elk's Account of the Seven Rites of the Oglala Sioux*. Norman: University of Oklahoma Press, 1953, p. 38.
5. Halifax, p. 11.
6. Ibid.
7. Ibid.
8. Douglas, Nik and Penny Slinger. *The Tantric Dakini Oracle*. Rochester, VT: Destiny Books, 1979, p. 73.
9. *Webster's New Collegiate Dictionary*. Springfield, MA: G. & C. Merriam Co., 1976, p. 1107.
10. Douglas and Slinger, p. 139.
11. Halifax, p. 11.
12. Mindell, Arnold. *The Shaman's Body: A New Shamanism for Transforming Health, Relationships, and the Community*. San Francisco: HarperSanFrancisco, 1993, p. 189.
13. Waters, Frank. *Book of the Hopi*. New York: Ballantine Books, 1963, p. 11.
14. Black Elk, Wallace and William S. Lyon. *Black Elk: The Sacred Ways of a Lakota*. San Francisco: HarperSanFrancisco, 1991, p. 39.

## Chapter 16

1. Wauters, Ambika. *The Book of Chakras: Discover the Hidden Forces within You*. London: Quarto Publishing, 2002, p. 45.
2. Ibid., p. 42.
3. Ibid., p. 43.
4. Ibid.
5. Ibid.

6. Ibid.
7. Halifax, Joan. *Shaman: The Wounded Healer.* London: Thames and Hudson, 1982, p. 92.
8. Cooper, J. C. *An Illustrated Encyclopaedia of Traditional Symbols.* London: Thames and Hudson, 1978, p. 19.
9. Ryan, Robert E. *The Strong Eye of Shamanism: A Journey into the Caves of Consciousness.* Rochester, VT: Inner Traditions, 1999, p. 55.
10. Jung, C. G. *The Red Book.* New York: W. W. Norton & Company, 2009, p. 122.
11. Ryan, p. 52.
12. Halifax, p. 82.
13. Ryan, p. 53.
14. Hume, Lynne. *Ancestral Power: The Dreaming, Consciousness and Aboriginal Australians.* Melbourne, Australia: Melbourne University Press, 2002, p. 81.
15. Ryan, p. 55.
16. Wauters, p. 19.
17. Ibid., p. 15.
18. Halifax, p. 94.
19. Broderick, Damien. *Outside the Gates of Science: Why It's Time for the Paranormal to Come in from the Cold.* New York: Thunder's Mouth Press, 2007, p. 278.
20. Halifax, p. 94.

**Chapter 17**

1. Quoted in Neihardt, John G. *Black Elk Speaks: Being the Life Story of a Holy Man of the Oglala Sioux.* Lincoln: University of Nebraska Press, 1979, p. 28.
2. Ibid., p. 29.
3. Ibid.
4. Francis, John. *Planetwalker: 22 Years of Walking. 17 Years of Silence.* Washington, D.C.: National Geographic, 2005, p. 7.
5. Ibid, p. 9.
6. Ibid., p. 8.
7. Waldman, Anne. *On All Kinds of Roads,* interviewed by Kurt Jacobsen. Internet journal, Logos: a journal of modern society and culture, 2011. Logosjournal.com. (accessed 11/12/13).

8.  Quoted in Frisch, Cynthia. "Gathering the Shamans to Save the Land." *Sacred Fire* (Issue 12), p. 43.
9.  Hart, Basil. *Sherman: Soldier, Realist, American.* Boston: Dodd, Mead & Co., 1929, p. 430.
10. Glassner, Barry. *The Culture of Fear: Why Americans Are Afraid of the Wrong Things.* New York: Basic Books, 1999, p., xviii.
11. Teilhard de Chardin, Pierre. *The Divine Milieu.* New York & Evanston: Harper Torch Books, Harper & Row, 1960, p. 66.
12. Harvey, Andrew. *The Return of the Mother.* New York: Penguin Putnam Inc., 2001, p. 16.
13. Eliot, T. S. *The Complete Poems and Plays.* New York: Harcourt Brace & Company., 1952, p. 38.
14. Bly, Robert. *News of the Universe: Poems of Twofold Consciousness.* San Francisco: Sierra Club Books, 1980, p. 71.
15. Black Elk, Wallace and William S. Lyon. *Black Elk: The Sacred Ways of a Lakota.* San Francisco: HarperSanFrancisco, 1991, p. 116.

## Chapter 18

1.  Wikipedia.org. Blog, 11/27/2013.
2.  Ibid., Blog, History, 11/27/2013.
3.  Barks, Coleman (trans). *The Essential Rumi.* Edison, NJ: Castle Books, 1995, p. 195.
4.  Eliot, T. S. *The Complete Poems and Plays.* 1909 – 1950. New York: Harcourt Brace & Company, 1980, p. 129.

## Bibliography

Andrews, Ted. *Animal Speak: The Spiritual & Magical Powers of Creatures Great & Small.* St. Paul, MN: Llewellyn Publications, 1996.

Awiakta, Marilou. *Selu: Seeking the Corn-Mother's Wisdom.* Golden, CO: Fulcrum Publishing, 1993.

Barks, Coleman (translator). *The Essential Rumi.* New Jersey: Castle Books, 1995.

Bend, Cynthia. *Birth of a Modern Shaman.* St. Paul, Minnesota: Llewellyn Publications, 1989.

Berry, Wendell. *New Collected Poems.* Berkeley, CA: Counterpoint, 2012.

Beston, Henry. *The Outermost House.* New York, NY: Penguin Books, 1977.

Black Elk, Wallace and William S. Lyon. *Black Elk: The Sacred Ways of a Lakota.* New York, NY: HarperSanFrancisco / HarperCollins Publishers, 1991.

Bly, Robert. *Lorca and Jimenez: Selected Poems.* Boston: Beacon Press, 1973.

Bly, Robert. *News of the Universe: Poems of Twofold Consciousness.* San Francisco: Sierra Club Books, 1980.

Bode, Carl, ed. *The Portable Thoreau.* New York, NY: Penguin Books, 1982.

Broderick, Damien. *Outside the Gates of Science.* New York: Thunder's Mouth Press, 2007.

Brown, Joseph Epes. *The Sacred Pipe.* USA: University of Oklahoma Press, 1953.

Brown, Jr., Tom. *The Quest.* New York: Berkley Books, 1991.

Bruchac, Joseph. *The Native American Sweat Lodge*. California: The Crossing Press,1993.

Buhner, Stephen. *Sacred Plant Medicine*. Idaho: Raven Press. 1996.

Cahill, Thomas. *How the Irish Saved Civilization*. New York: Random House, 1995.

Campos, Don Jose'. *The Shaman & Ayahuasca*. California: Divine Arts, 2011.

Chopra, Deepak. *Quantum Healing*. New York: Bantam Books, 1989.

Conforti, Michael. *Field, Form, and Fate*. Louisiana: Spring Journal Books, 1999.

Cooper, J. *An Illustrated Encyclopaedia of Traditional Symbols*. London: Thames and Hudson, 1978.

Cowan, Tom. *Fire in the Head: Shamanism and the Celtic Spirit*. HarperSanFrancisco, 1993.

Dames, Michael. *Mythic Ireland*. London: Thames and Hudson, 1992.

Dames, Michael. *Merlin and Wales:A Magician's Landscape*. London: Thames and Hudson Ltd, 2002.

De Angulo, Jaime. *Coyote Man & Old Doctor Loon*. California: Turtle Island Foundation, 1973.

Doore, Gary. *Shaman's Path*. Boston, Massachusetts: Shambhala, 1988.

Douglas, Nik. *The Tantric Dakini Oracle*. Rochester, Vermont: Destiny Books, 1979.

Dylan, Bob. *Chronicles, Volume One*. London: Pocket Books, 2004.

Dziemidko, Helen. *The Complete Book of Energy Medicines*. Rochester, VT: Healing Arts Press, 1999.

Eliade, Mircea. *Shamanism: Archaic Techniques of Ecstasy.* London: Penguin / Arkana, 1964.

Eliot, T.S. *T.S.Eliot: The Complete Poems and Plays.* New York: Harcourt Brace & Company, 1980.

Ellis, Peter Berresford. *A Brief History of the Druids.* Philadelphia: Running Press, 2002.

Faulkner, Raymond. *Ancient Egyptian Book of the Dead.* New York: Barnes & Noble, 2005.

Fell, Barry. *America B.C.* Muskogee, OK: Artisan Publications, 2004.

Ford, Patrick. *The Mobinogi and Other Medieval Welsh Tales.* Berkely: University of California Press, 1977.

Francis, John. *Planet Walker.* Washington, D.C.: National Geographic, 2005.

Glassner, Barry. *The Culture of Fear: Why Americans Are Afraid of the Wrong Things.* New York: Basic Books, 1999.

Green, Miranda. *Dictionary of Celtic Myth and Legend.* London: Thames and Hudson, 1992.

Halifax, Joan. *Shaman: The Wounded Healer.* London: Thames and Hudson, 1982.

Halifax, Joan. *Shamanic Voices.* New York: Dutton Paperback, 1979.

Harner, Michael. *The Way of the Shaman.* HarperSanFranciso, 1990.

Harpignies, J. *Visionary plant consciousness.* Rochester, VT:Park Street Press, 2007.

Harvey, Andrew. *The Hope.* California. Hay House, Inc.,2009.

Harvey, Andrew. *The Return of the Mother*. New York: Penguin Putnam Inc.,2001.

Heat –Moon, William Least. *The Hidden Yosemite*. National Geographic, Vol. 207, #1, 1/2005, p.103.

Hume, Lynne. *Ancestral Power*. Australia: Melbourne University Press, 2002.

Hunt, James. *Restless Fires*. Georgia: Mercer University Press, 2012.

Ingerman, Sandra. *Awakening to the Spirit World*. Boulder, Colorado: Sounds True, 2010.

Johnson, Robert. *Balancing Heaven and Earth*. HarperSanFrancisco, 1998.

Jung, Carl. *The Red Book: Liber Novus*. New York: W.W. Norton & Company, 2009.

Jung, Carl. *Children's Dreams*. Princeton and Oxford: Princeton University Press, 2008.

Kalweit, Holger. *Dreamtime and Inner Space: The World of the Shaman*. Boston & London: Shambhala, 1988.

Kalweit, Holger. *Shamans, Healers and Medicine Men*. Boston: Shambhala, 1992.

Kirkey, Jason, *The Salmon In the Spring. San Franciso:* Hiraeth Press, 2009.

Kondratiev, Alexei. *Celtic Rituals: An authentic guide to ancient Celtic Spirituality*. Scotland: New Celtic Publishing, 1999.

Lachman, Gary. *Jung the Mystic*. New York: Penguin, 2010.

Laduke, Winonoa. *All Our Relations*. Cambridge MA: South End Press, 1999.

Lame Deer / Erdos, Richard. *Gift of Power.* Santa Fe, NM: Bear & Company, Inc., 1992.

Lawlor, Robert. *Voices of the First Day.* Rochester, Vermont: Inner Traditions, 1991.

Leadbeater, C.W. *The Chakras.* Wheaton, Illinois: Quest Books, 1927.

Lockhart, Maureen, *The Subtle Energy Body.* Rochester Vermont: Inner Traditions, 2010.

MacEowen, Frank. *Spiral of Memory and Belonging.* California: New World Library, 2004.

MacEowen, Frank. *The Mist-Filled Path.* California: New World Library, 2002.

Macy, Joanna. *Coming Back to Life.* BC, Canada: New Society Publishers, 1998.

Malidoma Patrice Somé. *Ritual: Power, Healing, and Community.* Arkana, Penguin, 1997.

Matthews, Caitlin and John. *Encyclopedia of Celtic Wisdom.* Shaftesbury, Dorset: Element, 1994.

Mauer, Christopher, Editor. *Federico Garcia Lorca: Selected Verse.* New York, NY: Farrar Straus Giroux, 1997.

McKibben, Bill. *The End of Nature.* New York: Random House, 1989.

Mehl-Madrona, Lewis. *Coyote Medicine.* New York, NY: Fireside Book, 1998.

Mindell, Arnold. *The Shaman's Body.* San Franciso: HarperSanFrancisco, 1993.

Moore, Wes. *The Other Wes Moore: One Name, Two Fates.* New York: Spiegel and Grau, 2010.

Moss, Robert. *Active Dreaming*. Novato, California: New World Library, 2011.

Narby, Jeremy. *Intelligence in Nature*. New York: Penguin, 2005.

Neihardt, John. *Black Elk Speaks*. University of Nebraska Press, 1979.

Nicholson, Shirley. *Shamanism*. Illinois, USA: The Theosophical Publishing House, 1987.

O'Donohue, John. *Anam Cara*. United States: Cliff Street Books, 1997.

Peat, David. *Blackfoot Physics*. Boston, MA: Weiser Books, 2002.

Planet Earth, BBC Video. Series producer: Alastair Fothergill, 2007.

Prechtel, Martín. *The Disobedience of the Daughter of the Sun*. Cambridge, MA: Yellow Moon Press, 2002.

Progoff, Ira. *Jung, Synchronicity and Human Destiny*. New York: Julian Press, 1973.

Rees, Alan and Brinley. *Celtic Heritage*. London: Thames and Hudson, 1961.

Rowthorn, Anne. *The Wisdom of John Muir*. Birmingham, AL, 2012.

Ryan, Robert. *The Strong Eye of Shamanism*. Rochester, VT: Inner Traditions, 1999.

Sheldrake, Rupert. *The Rebirth of Nature*. Rochester, Vermont: Inner Traditions, 1991.

Simmons, Robert. *The Book of Stones*. East Montpelier, VT: Heaven & Earth Publishing, 2005.

Snyder, Gary. *Danger on Peaks*. Washington D.C., Shoemaker Hoard, 2004.

St. Pierre, Mark. *Walking in the Sacred Manner.* New York: A Touchstone Book, 1995.

Sullivan, Robert. *The Thoreau You Don't Know.* New York, NY: Harper Collins, 2009.

Tarrant, John. *The Light Inside the Dark.* New York: HarperPerennial, 1998.

Teilhard de Chardin, Pierre. *The Phenomenon of Man.* New York: Harper & Brothers Publishers, 1959.

Teilhard de Chardin, Pierre. *The Divine Milieu.* New York & Evanston: Harper Torch Books, Harper & Row, 1960.

Ueda, Makoto. *The Master Haiku Poet: Matsuo Basho.* Tokyo: Kodansha International, 1982

Villoldo, Alberto. *Island of the Sun.* Rochester, Vermont: Destiny Books, 1992.

Vitebsky, Piers. *The Reindeer People.* Boston: Houghton Mifflin Company, 2005.

Von Franz, Marie Louise. *Psyche and Matter.* Boston: Shambala, 1992.

Waters, Frank. *The Book of Hopi.* New York: Ballantine Books, 1963.

Watts, Alan. *The Way of Zen.* New York: Pantheon Books Inc., (division of Random House Inc.), 1957.

Wauters, Ambika. *The Book of Chakras.* London: Quarto Publishing, 2002.

*Webster's New Collegiate Dictionary.* United States: G. & C. Merriam Co, 1976.

*Webster's Third New International Dictionary* (unabridged). Springfield, Massachusetts, 1986.

Whitman, Walt. *Leaves of Grass*. United States: Random House, 1944.

Wilcox, Joan. *Ayahuasca: The Visionary & Healing Powers of the Vine of the Soul*. Rochester, VT: Park Street Press, 2003.

Wilhelm / Baynes. *The I Ching or Book of Changes*. Princeton University Press, 1950.

Williams, J.E. *The Andean Codex*. Charlottesville, PA: Hampton Roads Publishing Company, Inc., 2005.

Ziegler, Alfred. *Archetypal Medicine*. Dallas, TX: Spring Publications, Inc., 1983.

## Index

CPSIA information can be obtained at www.ICGtesting.com
Printed in the USA
BVOW01s1110050514

352229BV00001B/27/P

# REAL OR FAKE

# REAL *OR* FAKE

## Studies in Authentication

*Joe Nickell*

THE UNIVERSITY PRESS OF KENTUCKY

Scholarly publisher for the Commonwealth,
serving Bellarmine University, Berea College, Centre
College of Kentucky, Eastern Kentucky University,
The Filson Historical Society, Georgetown College,
Kentucky Historical Society, Kentucky State University,
Morehead State University, Murray State University,
Northern Kentucky University, Transylvania University,
University of Kentucky, University of Louisville,
and Western Kentucky University.

*Editorial and Sales Offices:* The University Press of Kentucky
663 South Limestone Street, Lexington, Kentucky 40508-4008
www.kentuckypress.com

09  10  11  12  13      5  4  3  2  1

Library of Congress Cataloging-in-Publication Data

Nickell, Joe.
Real or fake : studies in authentication / Joe Nickell.
p. cm.
Includes bibliographical references and index.
ISBN 978-0-8131-2534-3 (hardcover : alk. paper)
1. Forgery. 2. Fraud. I. Title.
HV6675.N53 2009
364.16'68—dc22          2008051816

This book is printed on acid-free recycled paper meeting
the requirements of the American National Standard
for Permanence in Paper for Printed Library Materials.

Manufactured in the United States of America.

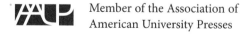

Member of the Association of
American University Presses

# CONTENTS

# CONTENTS

# ILLUSTRATIONS

# ACKNOWLEDGMENTS

THE WORK FEATURED in this book spans decades, and I must acknowledge the efforts of many people. In addition to those mentioned in the text, I am especially grateful to some who have passed away: autograph expert Charles Hamilton, who tutored me in the fine art of forgery and its detection; photographer Robert H. van Outer, whose expertise was always at my service; and microanalyst Walter C. McCrone, who provided inspiration with his sophisticated analyses and his motto, "Think Small."

I am also indebted to many experts for both their professional assistance and their friendship. Among them are librarian Timothy Binga (Center for Inquiry), forensic anthropologist Emily Craig, forensic analyst John F. Fischer, identification expert Alfred V. Iannarelli, ink chemist Antonio Cantu (U.S. Secret Service, retired), forensic document examiner Gideon Epstein (U.S. Bureau of Immigration and Naturalization, retired), and historical manuscripts authority Kenneth W. Rendell. Gerald Richards (formerly a forensic document examiner for the FBI) was kind enough to read the manuscript and make many helpful suggestions, as was Antonio Cantu. Any errors or deficiencies are, of course, my own responsibility.

I am further indebted to the editors and publishers of several of my earlier works from which portions of this treatise were abridged or adapted (listed in the references under my name).

I am grateful to Paul E. Loynes for his expert manuscript preparation. I also wish to thank the entire crew at the University Press of Kentucky for their continued encouragement, professional assistance, and friendship. They are a pleasure to work with.

ACKNOWLEDGMENTS

For their patience and support, as always, I thank my colleagues at the Center for Inquiry—notably, chairman Paul Kurtz, CEO Ronald Lindsay, and CSI executive director Barry Karr—and my family, including my wife, Diana Harris; my daughter, Cherie Roycroft; and my grandchildren, Chase, Tyner, and Alexis.

# INTRODUCTION

THE DISTANT PAST presents us with countless mysteries that challenge our collective intellect and imagination. Time typically obscures the contexts, erases the links, and removes the ancillary evidence that would allow us to fully comprehend ancient events. Yet the past can also yield fragments—even whole treasures—that serve as clues, pieces of the puzzles that engage us.

## The Recovered Past

For years, I have kept a file labeled "The Recovered Past." Here are some examples of the clippings it contains.

"Found: A Legendary City that History Forgot" (1995) reports on a remarkable discovery by a team of archaeologists led by UCLA's Giorgio Buccellati. After eight years of excavation, they located Urkesh, the fabled capital of the Hurrians, beneath a modern town in Syria. Many historians had doubted the existence of either the people or the city, due to a paucity of evidence: only brief mention in the Old Testament and other ancient literature and a pair of bronze lions inscribed *Urkesh*. The archaeologists discovered clay figures and pottery, metal tools, and the signature seals of the ancient city's king and queen dating from some 4,300 years ago. Buccellati observed that the discovery would give the neglected Hurrians and their rich city their deserved place in history. "The footnote will become a chapter."

"Unknown Goya Canvas Discovered" (1996) relates how a previously unrecorded painting by Spanish master Francisco de Goya (1746–1828) was found by workers renovating a government building in Madrid. The eight- by six-foot canvas, discovered in an attic storeroom, depicts redeemed souls being swept from purgatory up into heaven. It was tentatively dated to the early 1780s, when Goya painted mostly religious themes. A Prado museum curator who helped authenticate the painting enthused, "From the moment we saw it, it was marvelous."

"Smithsonian Acquires Long-Lost Photo of Noted Abolitionist" (Ruane 1996) details how a missing portrait of radical abolitionist John Brown resurfaced after being presumed lost for most of the twentieth century. A pair of collectors spotted the daguerreotype—the original of an image thought to exist only in copies—at an auction house in Pittsburgh. It had been mistaken for the image of obscure nineteenth-century novelist George Lippard. The collectors purchased it for $12,000 and then sold it to the Smithsonian for $129,000. Curator of photographs Mary Panzer, noting that Brown's image had been recorded by black daguerreotypist Augustus Washington at a time when both men were attempting to rid America of slavery, stated: "You don't come across something this powerful very often. I feel very fortunate. I don't think there will be anything more important that I will ever buy for any museum anywhere."

"Mary Shelley's Lost Children's Story Found in Italian Palazzo" (1998) presents the discovery of a thirty-four-page manuscript by the famed author of *Frankenstein* and wife of poet Percy Bysshe Shelley. The story, known to have existed from a mention in Mary Shelley's journal and in a letter written by her father, was assumed to be irretrievably lost. However, it was found by Andres and Cristina Dazzi in a wooden chest in a neglected room of the family mansion in the Tuscany hills. Andres was descended from Lady Mountcashell, a member of the Shelleys' circle when they sojourned in Italy. The story, titled *Maurice, or the Fisher's Cot,* had been written for Lady Mountcashell's eleven-year-old daughter. It is a morality tale about a boy who runs away from a cruel stepfather and is adopted by a grandfatherly fisherman. Two experts authenticated the manuscript. Claire Tomalin, author of *Shelley and His World,* described the story as "a very exciting find," and Catherine Payling, curator of the Keats-Shelley Memorial House in Rome, stated,

"The discovery adds greatly to our understanding of Mary Shelley's mind and imagination."

The file goes on and on: "Dead Sea Scroll Gives Up Its Secret" (Schmemann 1997), "4,500-Year-Old Family Tomb of Governor Found in Egypt" (1998), "Ancient Texts Shine New Light on Taoism: Find Is Likened to Dead Sea Scrolls" (Ribadeneira 1998), "*Titanic*'s Locater Finds Two Sunken Phoenician Vessels" (Kilian 1999), "Draft of Eichmann Memoir Discovered" (Geitner 1999), "Ancient Works of Archimedes to Be Restored and Studied" (Webber 1999), "Russia to Display What It Says Is a Fragment of Hitler's Skull" (2000), "Expert Says 'Lost' Score Is Mozart's" (Leeman 2001). Historical treasures continue to appear—from an archaeological dig, a neglected attic, or some other cache—as if from forgotten time capsules.

Treasures can turn up in the most unlikely places. For instance, a 1,200-year-old Psalter was unearthed by a construction worker in an Irish bog. Officials from Ireland's National Museum in Dublin said they were impressed that the Book of Psalms had survived for such a length of time in boggy terrain and that the worker had been able to halt his mechanical digger fast enough to keep the Psalter from being destroyed. A museum news release called the discovery "the greatest find ever from a European bog" (Cowell 2006).

Like most authentication specialists, I have helped bring some lost treasures to light. For example, while in graduate school, I took a course in colonial American literature, taught by noted scholar John Shawcross, and became intrigued by one of the most perplexing literary mysteries of that era: the missing edition of Ebenezer Cooke's Hudibrastic satire *The Sot-weed Factor*. Cooke published the first edition in 1708 and the third in 1731, but not a single copy of the second edition could be found—until I discovered it had been on the shelf in plain view all along! It happens that in 1730 Cooke had published a sequel, *Sotweed Redivivus* (which could be translated "Sotweed reissued"), and that his handwritten notes "design'd for a preface" to "this Second edition" of *The Sot-weed Factor* were similar in many words and phrases to those in the preface of *Sotweed Redivivus*. I recognized that the latter was, indeed, the "missing" edition. The discovery, published as part of my doctoral dissertation, subsequently appeared in one of my books (Nickell 2005, 110–22) and in a critical journal (Nickell 2006a).

While doing research for another book (Nickell 1990), I became fascinated by the history of the first paper mill in the early American West, founded by Craig, Parkers and Company in 1793. Its exact location—somewhere on Royal Spring Branch in Georgetown, Kentucky—had been lost, and I set out to find it, alternating between searches of land records and visits to the creek (on one of these visits, I fell into a hole on the bank, emerging unhurt but covered with burrs). Eventually, local resident David Stuart and I discovered that what had appeared to be a rock outcropping was actually a stone foundation. Kentucky archaeologist Nancy O'Malley subsequently visited the spot with us, along with a local historian and a photographer. She showed us the outline on the ground where the old mill pond had been and made other important observations. She then prepared a survey form to document the features as a Kentucky archaeological site (Nickell 1994c, 22).

In another case, I was able to supply the who, what, where, when, and why of a homely little notebook that had turned up in my home county of Morgan in eastern Kentucky. It had been found behind an office cabinet when the historic courthouse was being renovated. I studied it for some time, observing that—because it contained jotted notes on collecting taxes, impaneling jurors, and making arrests—it must have been a sheriff's book. It bore scattered dates in the early 1850s, at which time William Mynhier (later an officer in the Confederacy) was sheriff. I was able to compare the notations with recorded specimens of his handwriting and establish that it had indeed been his personal pocket notebook. Its discovery in the office of the circuit court clerk was explained by Mynhier's having been elected to that post after serving as sheriff. One interesting feature of the notebook was a list of jurors' names for the county's only hanging—carried out by Sheriff Mynhier in late 1853.

Apart from my own uncovering of treasures, I have often helped others by authenticating—or not—their documents, photographs, and other artifacts. I have been consulted on some very famous and controversial cases. And in some of them—the Shroud of Turin, for example (Nickell 1998)—I have weighed in with my own opinions, sometimes with the encouragement of interested outsiders.

My entry into the world of authentication began early and progressed slowly. As a child, I merged some of my collections—stamps, fossils, heirlooms—and an occasional borrowed item, thus establishing a museum in my upstairs playroom at about the age of nine. Even then, I was aware that occasional items, such as a tiny pre-Columbian Inca figure a friend of my mother's had brought me from Peru, were probably not authentic. I also knew, of course, that my Declaration of Independence was reproduced on "parchment" paper and "antiqued" to look old.

Through high school and college, I ran a profitable summertime sign-painting business that developed my hands-on skills in pen calligraphy and brush lettering (using dozens of historical and modern styles), the mixing of paints and varnishes, gilding, silk-screening, copying trademarks and pictures, altering and repairing commercial artworks, and other crafts that would prove useful to an authenticator. In high school I was president of the Chemistry Club, and in college I learned other analytical skills, such as how to use a light microscope (in microbiology and botany labs). I majored first in art, learning the history and techniques of painting, sculpture, printmaking, and so forth, and worked as an art gallery assistant. Then I majored in English, which helped prepare me (much later) for advanced studies in linguistics, literary investigation, and folklore.

My checkered career—modeled somewhat on the lives of participatory journalist George Plimpton and the "Great Impostor" Ferdinand Waldo Demara—included stints as a carnival pitchman, stage magician and mentalist, private investigator and undercover operative, and assorted other personas, including paranormal investigator (see www .joenickell.com). All these were useful in the process of sorting the real from the illusory. I also worked in a couple of museums, completing a course in museology from the Canadian Museums Association, and today I am curator of a virtual museum (www.skeptiseum.org).

Meanwhile, while doing graduate work and teaching at the University of Kentucky, I began an extensive collection that culminated—ten years later—in the publication of my profusely illustrated book *Pen, Ink, & Evidence: A Study of Writing and Writing Materials for the Penman, Collector and Document Detective* (1990). To produce that book, I studied and imitated old writings, and I learned to cut quill pens, concoct ink from oak galls, make paper, and apply sealing wax—among many other useful crafts. I practiced how to decipher antiquated scribbles, use ultraviolet light to read faded texts, and scan documents with a stereomicroscope to reveal hidden clues. I researched watermarks, studied how erasures and corrections were made, and endeavored to identify the various types of pens from the strokes they produced. I sought the raison d'être of writing sand, collected ink recipes, and cataloged stationers' embossments. My friend, the late Robert H. van Outer, made hundreds of professional photographs for the book, illustrating everything from advertising blotters to Zaner-method copybooks—all items contained in my collection now at the University of Kentucky.

During the course of my research, I would occasionally be asked—by a dealer or a collector or someone acquainted with an archivist or some other person who knew me—to take a look at some questioned object, typically a document, and determine whether it was genuine, a forgery, or a reproduction. As I realized that my increasingly specialized knowledge could be useful in solving document cases, I also began to take up the art of forgery, tutored in part by one of my mentors, manuscript expert Charles Hamilton. I promised him that if he helped me learn to produce forgeries as a means of learning how to better detect them, I would never turn to a life of crime.

Eventually, I also began to study old photographs, a pursuit that led to more cases and culminated in my *Camera Clues: A Handbook for Photographic Investigation* (1994a). Another book, focusing on historical enigmas—*Unsolved History: Investigating Mysteries of the Past* (Nickell

2005)—included questioned artifacts other than documents and photos, such as a "Daniel Boone" rifle and the Shroud of Turin.

Some of my early cases were quite simple. For example, even from across the counter of a bookshop, it was possible to identify as fake a document signed "Daniel Boone" that the bookseller had hoped to authenticate. A closer inspection revealed that it was merely a photocopy, "antiqued" by what appeared to be tea stains. But even at a distance, one could see that the ink was positively black—unlike the rusty brown color of the oxidized iron-gall ink of genuine Boone writings.

More challenging was a *carte de visite* photograph of a famous Confederate commander signed in ink "RE Lee/Genl." A collector had purchased it at a price that was disarmingly—and thus suspiciously—low. Although the photo was authentic for the period, magnification revealed tremors in the pen strokes, indicative of a slowly drawn forgery. They were not attributable to the shakiness that can result from age. And notably, genuine Lee signatures from the last year of his life had been smoothly penned. That fact, coupled with tests showing the ink was inconsistent with inks of the period, revealed the autograph to be a forgery (Nickell 1990, 188–89).

Much more challenging were some of my later cases—not because they were fundamentally more difficult to assess, but because their high-profile, controversial nature meant that I had to counter perverse arguments made on their behalf. Examples are presented in some of the chapters that follow.

I am often asked whether I am disappointed to discover that some sensational item is inauthentic. The answer is no; I am always pleased when I can make a confident determination one way or another. It is wonderful to be able to verify the genuineness of a treasure, and it is also cause to celebrate when one can purge a bogus item from the historical canon.

## Principles of Authentication

Determining authenticity is easier said than done, and there is no one simple procedure that works for every case. With organic materials (those from plants or animals), radiocarbon dating may be effective, but a small amount of the material must be sacrificed, and the accuracy is only within about 150 years. Thus, carbon dating would be useless for determining whether a 1795 U.S. coin were an authentic gold half eagle, an adulterated counterfeit, or a brass reproduction (as discussed in chapter 16); however, measuring the coin's specific gravity could prove decisive.

Neither carbon dating nor specific gravity would be useful in determining the genuineness of a sensational diary that surfaced in 1990 that supposedly verified the crash-landing of a flying saucer near Roswell, New Mexico, on July 8, 1947. The penned text related how members of a family had come upon a crashed alien craft containing injured extraterrestrials while rock hunting in the desert. In this case, however, analytical tests performed by a forensic chemist proved that the diary's ink had not been manufactured until 1974, disproving its authenticity (Nickell 2001, 120).

As these diverse cases demonstrate, a single discerned fact may be decisive in establishing that something is a fake. One must consider not only what is right about an artifact but also, and more importantly, what is wrong. For instance, radiocarbon dating of the controversial Vinland map, purportedly drawn by a fifteenth-century monk, showed that its parchment was genuinely old. Unfortunately, that was not sufficient to authenticate the map because forgers often use genuine old materials on which to produce their fakery. Indeed, radiocarbon dating of a coating on the parchment—possibly used by the forger to resurface it—yielded a modern date (Donahue, Olin, and Harbottle 2002). Moreover, the map's ink was found to contain traces of anatase, a titanium pigment that was not synthesized until the twentieth century (McCrone 1974).

Ideally, one should carefully consider as many of an artifact's attributes as possible, because a single finding that appears conclusive may be in error or may be challenged. With the Vinland map, for example, microanalyst Walter McCrone's finding of anatase was subsequently challenged by scientists from another laboratory using a different analytical technique (particle-induced X-ray emission, or PIXE); they concluded that the finding of trace amounts of titanium was not proof of anatase pigment and was, in fact, consistent with authenticity (Cahill et al. 1987). Later analysis by yet another lab, using a technique called Raman microprobe spectroscopy, confirmed McCrone's original findings (Brown and Clark 2002). This was supported by carbon dating of the parchment coating and by other additional evidence (Nickell 1996a, 189–91). Whenever possible—and especially in controversial cases—the use of such corroborative evidence is highly recommended.

Therefore, it is wise to take a multifaceted approach to questioned artifacts. If there is some reason to suspect an object, every aspect of it should be thoroughly examined. In a sensational artifact, the various factors to be considered include provenance, content, material composition, and the results of scientific analyses. Let us look briefly at each of these.

*Provenance* refers to the origin or derivation of an artifact. When employed by experts in the fields of rare manuscripts and valuable objets d'art, it refers to a work's being traceable to some particular source or quarter. The provenance of a valuable piece helps establish its historical origin and, potentially, its authenticity. Naturally, provenance has more significance in the case of a sensational item, and a missing provenance is unfortunate but not necessarily insurmountable. Of course, provenances themselves can be forged in much the same manner as the works they are supposed to authenticate. Dealer markings, penciled notations, and the like are sometimes falsely added to a work to indicate previous ownership. Fake repairs and other restorative efforts may be added to create the impression that the work is of sufficient age to require such measures. Evidence of prior framing or mounting may be faked to suggest that an earlier owner considered a work authentic. Moreover, bills of sale, dealers' certificates of authenticity, and other papers, including written statements allegedly from prior owners, can all be fabricated by a determined forger. Thus, although provenance is important, it is not unimpeachable and carries less weight than an examination of the work itself. Nevertheless, contradictory stories with regard to provenance or evidence that provenance may have been faked is a serious warning sign and should prompt a very careful investigation.

*Content*—or the "internal evidence" of a document, photograph, or artwork—may provide crucial evidence. Many a document forger has been tripped up by inattention to such details as format, grammar and spelling, and various historical elements, such as using words and phrases that are inappropriate to the period in question. Similarly, in the case of old photographs, clues may be found in the scene depicted. For instance, a daguerreotype portrait of poet Emily Dickinson's mother, Emily Norcross Dickinson, was authenticated on the basis of several internal clues: a brooch she was wearing, which was found in the poet's possession at her death, and studio props—such as a distinctive table-cloth—that also appeared in the daughter's daguerreotype (De Santis 1993; Longsworth 1990, 40–41, 129). Regarding artworks and other artifacts, even the style of an object may be telling. Although more subjective than other evidence, matters of style can be critical when they are assessed by knowledgeable experts. For instance, an old rifle purporting to have belonged to frontiersman Daniel Boone and carved with the words "BOoNs bESt FREN" was pronounced by experts to date from after Boone's death, based on the style of the stock and other features. Moreover, the stock's fifteen cut notches—supposedly for the number of Indians shot, according to the rifle's seller—was a practice dating from the much later Wild West era (discussed more fully in chapter 14).

*Material composition*—or what artifacts are made of—can have significant evidential value. As an amusing example, consider the forger who rendered a "Byron" manuscript on paper bearing a watermark reading "1834"—ten years after the celebrated poet's death. Likewise, some forgeries of Benjamin Franklin lacked the characteristics produced by the common quill pen of his time; instead, they had an ink trail indicative of the later steel nib (Nickell 1996a, 110, 117). Similarly, a triptych painted and gilded in fifteenth-century Sienese style was exposed as a fake when X-rays revealed it had modern hinges and machine-made nails (Nickell 2005, 77). Although not all cases of material inaccuracies are so conclusive or so dramatically and clearly revealed, with careful study, the artifact detective can spot the clues to a forgery, or perhaps simply discover that a piece, though genuine, is not of the period alleged.

*Scientific analyses*—properly conducted and correctly assessed—can be conclusive in many cases of questioned artifacts. However, carelessness, bias, faulty methodology, and other factors may intrude. And sometimes, a clever forger may have used means to subvert scientific testing. For instance, notorious art forger Han van Meegeren produced paintings in the style of Dutch master Jan Vermeer (1632–1675). To circumvent the experts, van Meegeren used genuinely old canvas and stretcher bars, hand-ground colors, paintbrushes made of badger hair, and so on, artificially "aging" his fake Vermeers and even adding clever touches of "restoration." Van Meegeren fooled even art experts by giving them what he knew they would look for. Later, however, in a wonderful example of scientific one-upmanship, experts reexamined the paintings using more sophisticated techniques: additional microscopic and microchemical tests, as well as radiographic, spectroscopic, and other analyses. These revealed telltale traces of formaldehyde, used by van Meegeren to speed up the drying of his paints, and the presence of cobalt blue, a pigment not used before 1802 (Waldon 1983, 50–69; Mills 1973, 76–77). (See chapter 12 for a fuller telling of the van Meegeren story.) In addition to uncovering the true nature of the materials used in a work, scientific analyses can lead to other crucial discoveries. For instance, thermoluminescence is important in dating pottery, and X-rays can reveal that underneath an alleged "El Greco" is a painting from a later time, uncovering a modern forgery (Mills 1973, 42, 85).

Over the years, I have learned that, with regard to authentication, people often allow bias to creep in. There is a tendency to start with the desired answer and work backward through the evidence, picking and choosing the "facts" that support their convictions. Investigation must be predicated on a rational, scientific approach, keeping emotionalism in check and focusing only on learning the truth. A few practical principles apply. One is that extraordinary claims require extraordinary proof—meaning that the evidence must be commensurate with the extent of a claim. Another is the principle of Occam's razor, which holds that the simplest tenable explanation—the one requiring the fewest assumptions—is most likely correct. Yet another important maxim is that the burden of proof is on the advocate of the idea—meaning that the person who asserts that an artifact is genuine or fake has the responsibility to prove that assertion. Following these principles should help inquirers avoid a rush to judgment and keep focused on the evidence.

Each of the three parts of this book—on documents, photographs, and other artifacts—begins with an introductory chapter on authentication, followed by chapters presenting illustrative cases I have investigated. The cited cases and illustrated methodologies do not cover all contingencies, but they characterize the field of authentication, provide some essential criteria for consideration, and suggest some specific approaches, possibly even inspiring the creation of new ones. The category of artifacts is especially varied, consisting of almost anything made by human hands: books, glassware, furniture, jewelry, objets d'art, toys, paper ephemera, tools, quilts, firearms, vintage clothing, clocks—the list is practically endless. Not even an experienced antiques dealer—who is, of necessity, a generalist—is capable of authenticating everything. That is what experts are for. Yet an intelligent layperson can acquire the means—the tools, knowledge, and experience—to uncover many types of fakes. With this book as a beginning, you can start to develop a discerning eye and an analytical mind—essential qualities of an authentication detective. Another essential quality is good judgment—one that may be lacking in otherwise brilliant people.

We must realize that, like everyone else, we are fallible. As I told *Autograph Collector* magazine (Grossberg 2007), "The person who thinks he can't be fooled has just fooled himself." To avoid being deceived, we must look at questioned artifacts from different points of view and not jump to conclusions. We must begin with the evidence, assess it carefully, and let it lead us to the truth. In short, instead of being zealots for a position pro or con, we must be investigators seeking an honest answer to the question: Is a purported historical treasure real or fake?

# PART I

## DOCUMENTS

## Chapter 1

# INVESTIGATING DOCUMENTS

JUST AS A talented impersonator can mimic a person's voice or manner-isms, a skillful forger can convincingly simulate someone else's hand-writing. To uncover such fakery, ancient or modern, the document sleuth must grasp all aspects of writing, including its evolution (see figure 1.1). The following discussion is not meant to replace more detailed treatises such as Albert S. Osborn's *Questioned Documents* (1978) or my own *Pen, Ink, & Evidence* (1990) and *Detecting Forgery* (1996a). This introduction to writing materials, handwriting identification, warning signs of forgery, and the detection of nonforgery fakes is intended to acquaint the student with some of the basics.

## Writing Materials

The materials used to produce a document—writing implements, ink, paper, and other materials—have evolved over time and thus have significant evidential value. They can often be decisive in exposing a forgery.

### *Writing Implements*

From the ancients' stylus, brush, and reed pen, writing implements have steadily evolved, especially during the past two centuries (see figure 1.2). The quill pen, the mainstay of penmanship through the medieval period, underwent a transformation. Its old broad-pen form, which was cut with a chisel edge, gave way to the pointed nib during the Renaissance, mak-ing possible the tapered shadings and hairline flourishes of round-hand script (see figure 1.1).

Apart from isolated references to metal pens over the centuries,

Figure 1.1. The evolution of handwriting, from Roman square capitals through medieval Gothic to modern systems, is an important aspect of historical document study.

steel pens were not significantly employed until after they were manufactured in Birmingham, England, beginning in 1780. Even then, they were not produced on a large scale until 1824 and were not fully accepted until about 1845. By the end of the American Civil War, they had largely

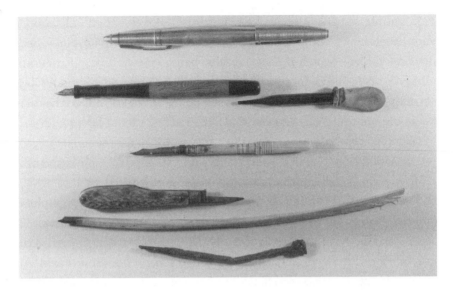

Figure 1.2. Writing implements have also evolved over time. Shown here (bottom to top) are a Roman stylus, a Renaissance-type quill pen with a late-eighteenth-century penknife, an early steel pen on a bone penholder with a cap, a nineteenth-century fountain pen with its dropper filler, and America's first ballpoint pen, made by Reynolds and dated 1945.

supplanted quill pens. Other durable pens included gold nibs (which, by 1810, were being tipped with rhodium or other hard substances to reduce wearing) and glass pens. The latter were known for their smooth writing from as early as 1850, but their fragility made them impractical.

Fountain pens were known only in experimental form during the seventeenth and eighteenth centuries but were patented in England in 1809. By the 1870s, metal nibs had completely supplanted quills, and there was a proliferation of reservoir pens. The first truly successful fountain pen with an effective "feed" (or flow mechanism) was marketed by Lewis E. Waterman in 1884. Thereafter, fountain pens were sold in great quantities.

Fountain pens were displaced by the ballpoint, first produced in its modern form in Prague in 1935 and marketed in New York in 1945 by Milton Reynolds (see figure 1.2). Later developments included the liquid lead pencil (a ballpoint with erasable graphite ink), introduced in

1955 but phased out in the early 1960s; the "roller ball" pen (a ballpoint with free-flowing ink like that of a fountain pen), in the late 1960s; and the Eraser Mate (which had an erasable ballpoint-type ink), introduced in April 1979. Porous-tipped pens were first manufactured as refillable "brush pens" in the 1940s, and the wick-like "markers" introduced in 1951 led to the fiber-tip pen, marketed in Japan and the United States in 1964.

Pencils have never been used to prepare legal documents, owing to the erasability issue, but they have been employed for much legitimate writing. The pencil's forerunner was the silver (or lead or lead alloy) stylus used by Renaissance artists. In 1564 the discovery of a vast graphite deposit in England led to the use of wooden pencils. By 1662 cut-graphite sticks began to be replaced by sticks molded from a mixture of powdered graphite and adhesives. Later, clay was added and the sticks were fired in a kiln, a process that permitted the hardness of the "lead" to be regulated. In 1822 mechanical pencils were introduced, and in 1866 indelible "ink pencils" were developed; the latter contained dyes that could be converted to an ink-like form by wetting.

The ability to identify each type of pen by the way it writes (see figure 1.3) enables a document examiner to determine whether the instrument used was appropriate for the apparent period and alleged authorship. (This is not always easy, however, even for an experienced expert. Ideally, identification of the writing implement should be correlated with the type of ink used.) For example, the quill pen produces hairline upstrokes and heavy, shaded downstrokes. So do metal pens, but they leave definite scratches—called nib tracks—that retain additional ink and become clearer after the ink fades with time. The "stub" pen, a metal pen with its tip clipped off, yields a distinctive ribbon-like line. Fountain pens produce a continuous ink flow, whereas "dip" pens leave a line varying from dark to light then dark again as the pen is refilled. Stylographic fountain pens (not extensively used) produce a fine line of near uniform width on both upstrokes and downstrokes. So does the ballpoint, which is readily identifiable by the distinctive line produced by the viscous ink and rotating ball application (Nickell 1996a, 146–48).

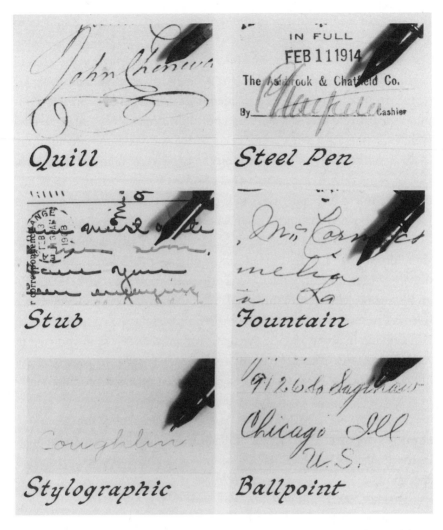

Figure 1.3. From the ancient quill to the modern ballpoint, pens leave evidence of their form in the lines they produce. (Photograph by Robert H. van Outer)

## Inks

The ancient Egyptians and Chinese used a simple carbon ink made by mixing soot with gum or glue. Since carbon is a stable element, such inks do not fade; nor can they be bleached by chemicals, although—because they remain on the surface of the writing material—they are subject to abrasion and easy erasure.

A later ink—possibly in use on Greek parchments by the second century—eliminated this problem. Known as iron-gallotannate (or simply iron-gall) ink, it was an aqueous decoction of an iron salt (copperas, or hydrated ferrous sulfate) and tannin (usually gallotannic acid from oak nutgalls), with some gum added for viscosity and binding. With age, iron-gall ink blackened on the page from its initial dark gray; then it eventually oxidized to a rusty brown. It was corrosive and "bit" into parchment or paper, making it less subject to abrasion, although it frequently burned through a page where the ink was heavily applied.

To render iron-gall ink fully black at initial use, carbon ink was sometimes mixed with it (especially during the Middle Ages), and during the eighteenth and nineteenth centuries, dyes such as indigo and logwood were commonly used. An indigo and iron-gall blue-black ink was produced in 1834, followed by a potassium chromate type of logwood ink in about 1848. A synthetic indigo variety was introduced in 1861, and certain other colored inks were made possible by the discovery of aniline dyes in 1856. Nigrosine ink was first produced commercially in 1867.

Fountain pens had various specially formulated inks, notably Sheaffer's popular Skrip of 1922 and a blue "washable" variety developed in the 1930s. As noted earlier, ballpoints and porous-tip pens also had special inks.

Various other mineral, animal, and plant materials were commonly used in inks from the Middle Ages to the nineteenth century. For example, pokeberry ink was reportedly used on the American frontier.

Forgers have attempted, with varying degrees of success, to obtain—or simulate—suitable inks, but the chemistry is not always right. For example, the ink used by Thomas McNamara in his forgeries of William Carlos Williams was not manufactured until a year after the poet's death. Even Mark Hofmann—who followed old recipes to produce iron-gall ink—was uncovered due to evidence of his artificial aging techniques (such as heating with a hand iron or applying certain chemicals).

As these cases illustrate, knowledge of inks and their history can be of inestimable value.

## Paper

The ancients made a rather heavy, brittle writing material from criss-crossed strips of pith sliced from the papyrus plant. The resulting sheets were then glued end to end to form a scroll, an early form of the book. By Hellenistic times, a more flexible material—parchment, made primarily from sheepskin—had been developed. (A particularly fine type, made from the skin of young animals—mostly calves, but also kids and lambs—was called vellum.) Since parchment could be creased without breaking, it gave rise to the modern type of bound book, called a codex. Codices had displaced scrolls by the fourth century A.D.

Eventually, paper displaced parchment. It was apparently first made in China during the Han dynasty (206 B.C.–A.D. 221), then spread to Arabic regions in the eighth century, and thence to Europe (largely via Constantinople) in the early twelfth century. The earliest known European paper document was a deed made by King Roger of Sicily in 1102. Paper mills were subsequently established in various European countries. Paper was first used in England in 1309, and a paper mill was built there in 1495. England and Holland supplied paper to the American colonies. The first American paper mill was built in 1690 by William Rittenhouse near Germantown, Pennsylvania.

Early paper was handmade, with the pulp being dipped by a framed wire mold in the "laid" pattern. (The brass screen was composed of heavy, widely spaced "chain" wires and finer, more closely spaced "laid" wires crossing the chain wires at right angles; see figure 1.4.) About 1755, a second mold pattern, called the "wove" pattern, was introduced but was not widely used in America before 1800. As its name implies, it was formed of wire mesh woven on a loom, similar to today's window screening, which left only a barely perceptible pattern in the paper (Nickell 1996a, 113–15).

Emblematic devices bent from wire and sewn to the mold's laid or wove screen produced designs called watermarks (see figure 1.4). These

Figure 1.4. Backlighting reveals characteristic lines in paper with a laid pattern and an identifying watermark. (Photograph by Robert H. van Outer)

have significance in terms of dating, and there are guidebooks for the identification of watermarks (Briquet 1907; Churchill 1935; Gravell and Miller 1979, 1983). A simple light box, such as photographers use to look at transparencies, facilitates the examination of watermarks, as well as the identification of the type of paper and the detection of erasures and other markings.

Machine papermaking was patented in France in 1798 and was instituted in England by 1809 and America by 1817. Early machine-made paper was necessarily of the wove pattern and lacked a watermark (the paper being formed on a belt of wire mesh). However, in 1825 a patented roller—a "dandy roll"—was used to impress a watermark-type imprint or a pseudo-laid pattern into the tender, newly formed wove paper (Nickell 1996a, 115–16). Thus, the mere presence of a laid pattern or watermark is no longer proof that the sheet was handmade, although handmade paper can be distinguished from the machine-made variety by use of a microscope. This allows the examiner to see that the lines made by the machine's dandy roll—the pseudo-laid pattern or watermark

—are pressed into the upper side of the paper, while the wove wire marks of the continuous wire belt are visible on the underside (Nickell 1996a, 151).

Linen and cotton rags were initially used to make paper pulp, and other materials were added later. Ground wood pulp was first produced commercially in Saxony in 1847; commercial production in the United States commenced in 1867, when wood-pulp paper was manufactured at Curtisville, Massachusetts. Chemical processes used to eliminate lignin and other extraneous materials destructive to the cellulose in paper were first employed in 1851 in England. Thus, microscopic and chemical tests may demonstrate that the paper used for a document is correct or incorrect for the period in which it was allegedly produced (Nickell 1996a, 178–79).

Forgers sometimes make blatant errors in their choice of paper, as in the previously mentioned case of an alleged "Byron" manuscript on paper with a watermark reading "1834"—ten years after the poet's death. A more modern example is the presence of optical brighteners in the "Hitler diaries," which emitted a strong white fluorescence under ultraviolet light. This was an early indicator that the diaries were fake, since such whitening agents were not used in paper prior to the 1950s. Even if a forger uses a credible sheet of paper, he or she may use it improperly. For example, the notorious "white salamander letter" (one of several Mormon-related papers forged by Mark Hofmann) was folded and sealed incorrectly for a letter dated 1830—before envelopes were common (Nickell 1996a, 117–18, 186).

Apart from forgeries, laypersons are often fooled by printed facsimiles of documents that an expert may be able to spot at a distance because of the imitation antique "parchment" paper on which they are frequently printed (discussed later in this chapter).

### Other Materials

In addition to pen, ink, and paper, a variety of other materials can provide clues to the validity of documents. These include paper fasteners.

The old ribbon-and-wax method appeared by the thirteenth century, an extension of the use of sealing wax, which has an even longer history. Wafers (thin disks of flour, gum, and coloring matter) were used instead of wax to close letters or fasten sheets of paper together from as early as 1635. Staplers were introduced in about 1875, but practical, lever-action models (which did not require whacking with a mallet) appeared early in the next century, replacing the use of straight pins. Paper clips were a British invention of about 1900, and cellophane tape an American one of 1930.

Envelopes, not common until the 1840s, invited a variety of methods of closing them, including mucilage and printed stickers called "motto seals." The adhesive or "self-sealing" envelope of the late 1840s eventually prevailed, but the clasp envelope, patented in 1879, also continued in use.

Other implements that leave their marks on paper include the paper knife, probably as old as paper itself and used to slit a folded sheet. About the middle of the nineteenth century, with the advent of the envelope, the rounded paper knife evolved into a companion implement that was more slender and tapered to a point—the letter opener.

Another desk knife, the ink-eraser knife, was used to scrape off mistakes—first on medieval parchment, then on paper throughout the dip-pen era. Often the roughened area that resulted would be polished by rubbing with a burnisher of some sort to minimize the spread of ink during rewriting. Other ink erasers were the gray "sand rubber" type, sold as early as 1867 and still in use, although they now receive competition from electrically powered rubber or vinyl erasers. Chemical "ink erasers" or "ink eradicators" were usually chlorine bleaching solutions (with a second solution, typically limewater, used to neutralize the first). This process was common from the latter nineteenth century but was rendered obsolete by the ballpoint pen's oily ink, which repelled the eradicator liquid. Subsequently, white correction fluid was marketed to paint over penned or typed text.

In addition to erasures, blotting of ink left identifiable traces on old documents. While medieval scribes typically let their ink air-dry, from the sixteenth century, sand was frequently dusted on wet writings to dry them (by coagulating the ink, increasing its surface area, and exposing it to the air). Traces of writing sand—or a speckled appearance where it once was—can occasionally be seen in old writings. By the mid-nineteenth century, however, blotting paper (known from 1465 but seldom used until about 1800) had effectively supplanted sand. It too eventually became obsolete with the advent of ballpoints (Nickell 1990, 59–67; 1996a, 118–22).

Still other implements and materials—bill spindles, various embossing devices (such as notary seals and check writers), rubber stamps, scissors, hole punches, and so forth—may have left their marks on a document. All such traces should be carefully examined to reveal potential anomalies or anachronisms.

## Handwriting Identification

The individuality of handwriting has been recognized since antiquity. It is the basis for both the pseudoscience of graphology (which supposedly divines personality from handwriting) and the forensic science of handwriting comparison. (For a discussion, see Nickell 1992a; 1996a, 17–24.)

It is crucial for the investigator to understand that many similarities may exist between two or more handwriting samples simply because their authors learned penmanship from the same writing system or even the same copybooks. Those writing features common to a group sharing the same general penmanship style are called "class characteristics." In contrast are "individual characteristics," or variations that evolve in mature handwriting. These individual peculiarities—in combination—will not be exactly duplicated in another's handwriting (see figure 1.5).

Failure to distinguish between class and individual characteristics is the mark of the layperson or rank amateur. Document examiner Ordway Hilton (1982, 160) noted, "The most common error of the unqualified examiner is to describe an unusual characteristic as being individual when in fact it merely belongs to a writing system outside the sphere of his experience." Such errors have actually resulted in persons being wrongly convicted of forgery and other crimes. To avoid such serious

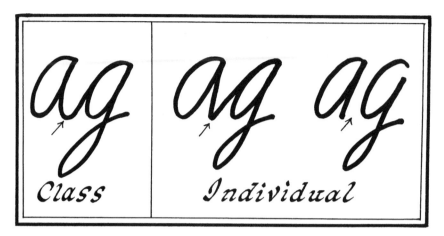

Figure 1.5. Class characteristics are those common to a copybook system or a group norm, whereas individual characteristics differ in specific ways (for example, instead of rounded connecting strokes, there may be angular or even missing connectors).

problems, the examiner must become familiar with all the basic styles of penmanship (see figure 1.1), including, if he or she is working with historical documents, antiquated handwriting systems. As a rule, the less familiar one is with a handwriting system, and the more ornate such a system of penmanship is, the more likely one is to mistake class characteristics for individual ones.

According to Charles E. O'Hara in *Fundamentals of Criminal Investigation*, "The majority of questioned document cases are concerned with proving authorship" (1973, 785). The manuscript detective may seek to determine, for example, whether an unsigned document was written by a particular individual (an anonymous letter by a suspect, for instance) or whether a letter or other document was actually written by the individual whose signature is affixed to it. In such cases, the correct procedure involves obtaining known *standards* (authentic specimens of a subject's handwriting), which are then compared with the questioned writing. As O'Hara explains (1973, 785–86):

The principles underlying the comparison of handwriting are similar to those on which the science of fingerprint identifications is based. No two products of man or nature are identical, and differences are perceptible if a sufficiently close study is made. Through years of practice each individual acquires permanent habits of handwriting. The group of characteristics which form his script constitutes an identifiable picture. In comparing two specimens of handwriting the expert searches for characteristics which are common to both the questioned and standard writing. If the characteristics are sufficient in kind and number and there are no significant unexplainable differences, he may conclude that the writings were made by the same person.

However, before such a comparison is made, the examiner must carefully examine the questioned writing. Gideon Epstein (1987), a noted document expert, stated: "In the comparison and identification of handwriting, the first thing that must be done is that the disputed writing or the disputed signatures . . . must be examined to determine that the signatures are naturally executed, freely executed, executed with what we consider careless abandon or unconscious effort, and that the habits that are there are in fact unconscious, habitual movements. . . . And that they were not drawn or traced or in some manner forged." Next, according to Epstein, the expert examines the known standard writings to determine the genuine handwriting habits of the individual. And finally, the examiner compares the disputed writing with the standards.

Characteristics that form a basis for comparison include *quality of line* (affected by pen position, pressure, rhythm, speed, tremor, skill, and other factors), *form* (including proportion, slant, beginning and ending strokes, and flourishes), and *arrangement* (spacing between letters, words, and lines; their alignment; width and evenness of margins; positioning of the signature relative to text). (For a discussion, see Nickell 1996a, 35–42.) It should be noted that modern forensic document analysis (in contrast to the practice of some graphologists) eschews the use of exact measurements of height, spacing, and the like (instead, ratios are considered) because of the normal variations that occur (Nickell 1990, 192).

To compare a questioned signature or other writing with known specimens, the document sleuth must carefully collect several of the latter. These should be as similar as possible to the questioned writing. Therefore, one should compare a questioned signature with other signatures, a scrawled or a carefully written specimen with similarly written standards, and a ballpoint writing with other ballpoint writings. In obtaining standards, it is desirable to seek those with words and letter combinations similar to those of the questioned writing. And since handwriting can change over time, standards should be chosen that are relatively contemporaneous with the questioned writing.

Of course, obtaining standards for historical document cases can be challenging. Several sources are available, however, although they provide printed copies for standards rather than the much more desirable originals. For the autographs of famous personages, a number of books contain facsimiles, notably Charles Hamilton's *The Book of Autographs* (1978), *The Signature of America* (1979), and the two-volume *American Autographs* (1983). Other valuable sourcebooks include Ray Rawlins's *Four Hundred Years of British Autographs* (1970) and *The Guinness Book of World Autographs* (1977); Herbert Cahoon, Thomas V. Lange, and Charles Ryskamp's *American Literary Autographs from Washington Irving to Henry James* (1977); and John M. Taylor's *From the White House Inkwell: American Presidential Autographs* (1968). In the case of signed art prints and signatures on paintings, one can consult such reference works as Radway Jackson's *The Visual Index of Artists' Signatures and Monograms* (1991).

Most large university and public libraries have at least some of these sourcebooks, possibly in their special collections departments. One may also find original letters and other papers written by famous historical figures. (At the University of Kentucky, for example, I was able to use several Charles Dickens letters, a survey document by Daniel Boone, and a long letter by Mary Todd Lincoln for authentication purposes.) To find which libraries, historical societies, and other archival sources have the papers of the person of interest, consult the *National Union Catalog of Manuscript Collections*. Then, to obtain the library's address, consult the current edition of the two-volume *American Library Directory*. The *Directory of Archives and Manuscript Repositories in the United States* is another guide to locating sources of archival materials. Where the targeted figure is more obscure, the *Biography and Genealogy Master Index* may lead to clues about the person's will and other handwriting sources.

It goes without saying that the standards must be of unquestionable authenticity in order to have evidentiary value. Consider the case of the notorious "Hitler diaries," which consisted of several volumes of fake writing by the forger Konrad Kujau. In 1983 three examiners declared the diaries genuine. Unfortunately, they had allowed their client, *Stern* magazine, to supply the alleged standards, and it turned out that some of those were also Kujau forgeries (Rendell 1994, 113–15).

A word should be said about typewriting. Since the first commercial model was introduced in 1873, typewriters began to replace handwriting, first in the field of business, then in other areas. In 1883 Mark Twain became the first author to submit a typewritten manuscript, *Life on the Mississippi*, to a publisher (*Story of the Typewriter* 1923, 72–74). Like handwriting, typewriting has both class characteristics (those of a particular make and model of machine, identifiable from the typeface) and individual characteristics (those that develop through use and abuse, such as wear and faulty alignment). Also like handwriting, comparisons of typewriting must begin with the acquisition of suitable standards. The importance of typewriter comparison was demonstrated in the Alger Hiss espionage case. Expert examination proved that copies of classified government papers had been typed on Hiss's personal Woodstock typewriter. Numerous distinctive points of similarity were found, including damage to the lower serif of the *d* and consistently heavier printing on the right side of the *O* (Hilton 1982, 232).

## Warning Signs of Forgery

It is probable that documents have been altered to change their meaning or value since writing began. In earlier centuries, widespread illiteracy meant that forgery was largely confined to the upper classes and often entailed the imitation of a seal rather than a signature. Forgeries flourished in European churches in the fifteenth century: "Clerics comprised the majority of those who could read and write, and a number of them forged and sold papal bulls and dispensations for high prices. On occasion they also supplied themselves with documents that could improve their own power or position; university professors not infrequently engaged in the same practice" (Thornton and Rhodes 1986, 7).

With the advance of literacy, forgery grew increasingly common and became a statutory offense in England in 1562. Eventually, daring forgers began to achieve a measure of notoriety, ranging from George Psalmanazar (ca. 1679–1763), who posed as a Japanese and fooled scholars with fictitious writings on Formosa (*Encyclopaedia Britannica* 1960, s.v. "forgery," "Psalmanazar, George"), to Mark Hofmann, who in the 1980s forged Mormon and other papers, then turned to bombing and murder in an attempt to prevent exposure (Naifeh and Smith 1988).

Detecting forgeries can be a challenging endeavor. Among the factors to be weighed are provenance (discussed in the introduction) and writing materials (examined earlier in this chapter). Other signs that can point to forgery are discussed in the following paragraphs. Although this section does not constitute a complete treatise on the subject, it should prove helpful for autograph collectors, archivists, and others with an interest in manuscript material. Of course, some indicators are just that—they do not in themselves prove inauthenticity but require additional evidence—whereas others (such as a watermark originating after the date penned on the document) immediately betray a forgery.

*Incorrect writing characteristics.* The style and form of a writing should be consistent with its supposed time and place of production. For instance, I once dismissed a Daniel Boone letter as a fake because it was penned not in Boone's English round hand, but in Palmer-method script. The same rule applies to individual handwriting features, since handwriting and signatures evolve over time. For example, in his old age, Benjamin Franklin's writing became more tremulous and he had some difficulty forming his capital *F* and properly rounding his *n*, yet forger Joseph Cosey's elderly "Franklin" was as elegant as his youthful one (Hamilton 1980, 93, 99).

*Uncommon forms.* Beware of any form of writing—particularly a signature—that differs from a writer's usual one. For example, in a letter supposedly written by Charles Dickens, a forger "neglected to note Dickens' normal complimentary close" (Rendell 1978, 75). As another example, amateur forgers have frequently used the wrong form of signature for Abraham Lincoln. The sixteenth president customarily used "Abraham Lincoln" for official papers but rarely for letters, which he signed simply "A. Lincoln" (or, in letters to intimates, "Lincoln" or merely his initials, "A. L."). He never used "Abe" (Hamilton 1980, 264).

*Off-scale writing.* Quite often a forger unconsciously shrinks the writing of his or her subject. For instance, Robert Spring's "George Washington" was typically one-half to two-thirds the size of the first president's own signature (Hamilton 1980, 48, 264–65). Conversely, a forger may inadvertently enlarge a diminutive handwriting by copying it from a published facsimile that is not to scale. However, particular situations (such as a small signature box on a printed form) might change the size of a genuine writing.

*Blunt beginnings and endings.* Forgers who are slowly copying or tracing a signature or other writing tend to produce blunt starts and stops. These are in contrast to the tapered strokes that result from speedy writing, in which the pen is in motion before it touches the paper and continues moving as it is lifted from the paper (Osborn 1978, 109, 283).

*Evenness of pen pressure.* Another characteristic of writing that is copied or traced is an unnatural evenness in pen pressure, manifested by uniformly heavy strokes. In contrast, normal handwriting that is freely and rapidly executed is typified by light upstrokes and heavier downstrokes—even in writing with ballpoint and felt-tip pens, which tend to minimize this contrast between strokes.

*Uncertainty of movement.* The forger's lack of certainty in terms of the direction a stroke should take may result in an abrupt shift in the movement of the line. This can give the line a kinked appearance rather than a smoothly curved one (Hilton 1982, 185).

*Unnatural hesitations.* In genuine writing, there are certain places where the pen naturally hesitates or stops, whereas in a forgery—which is usually produced in the manner of a drawing—there may be hesitations anywhere. To study these and other handwriting features, the authentication specialist employs the stereomicroscope, which uses relatively low magnification (20 to 30 power is especially useful for document work) in direct light. The binocular eyepiece provides a high-resolution, three-dimensional image, enabling the examiner to accurately view subtle and even depth-related features such as nib tracks or pen furrows.

*Unnatural pen lifts.* Beyond hesitations, there may be evidence that the forger paused frequently to check his or her progress and actually lifted the pen in the process. This is especially true of an unskilled forger—a drawer or tracer. Conversely, some writers have the distinctive habit of lifting the pen before or after making certain letters, which may go unnoticed by the imitator (Osborn 1978, 114–15). These elements are clearly revealed by use of the stereomicroscope.

*Forger's tremor.* Another trait that indicates slow drawing rather than natural writing is called forger's tremor (Nickell 1996a, 68–69). However, this must be distinguished from the tremulous writing caused by age, illness, or "illiterate writing" (Osborn 1978, 110–15).

*Evidence of tracing.* Traced signatures may be so amateurish as to retain evidence of their method of production, such as carbon or graphite traces, the erasure of such traces, or out-of-line indentations (Hilton 1982, 187–89; Nickell 1996a, 67–68, 70). Indentations are best seen by oblique light examination (light striking the document's surface from one side at a low angle) in conjunction with varying degrees of magnification.

*Patching.* Although a writer may occasionally touch up a faulty stroke or writing feature (in fact, the habitual retouching of certain letters can represent a point of identification), such repair is typically done in a bold, even slapdash manner. In contrast is the surreptitiously careful "patching" of forged writing. Again, such minute features are revealed by use of the stereomicroscope.

*Context of signature.* Sometimes a forger adds the signature of a famous person as a witness or cosigner to a genuine but relatively worthless old document. For example, one forger added the exceedingly rare signature of Button Gwinnett (signer of the Declaration of Independence from Georgia) to a leaf from a 1760 edition of the Book of Common Prayer. Anything that suggests a signature's addition—such as a crowded appearance or its presence on a document there was no need for the celebrity to sign—should serve as a warning (Hamilton 1980, 69, 210–11, 213; Rendell 1994, 16).

*"Feathering" of ink.* Since paper often loses its sizing with age, new writing added by a forger can leave a suspicious, fuzzy appearance. If the old paper had been folded before the writing was added, the ink may have spread along the fold, since folding can render the paper more porous (Rendell 1978, 79, 80; Hamilton 1980, 100, 266–67).

*Other factors.* A careful study of a disputed document might reveal factual errors, an incorrect format, or many other anomalies that signal forgery, including lines of handwriting that tend to undulate or excessive attention to detail (forged writing is often more legible than the targeted writing) (Nickell 1990, 190; 1996a, 72–77).

It must be kept in mind that many of the indicators of forgery—tremulous writing, pen lifts, and patching—may be found in genuine writing. It is the particular way the feature appears, or the combination of features, that may point to forgery.

## Detecting Nonforgery Fakes

Some writings are neither genuine nor forgeries. I have dubbed them "genuine fakes" (Nickell 1990, 192). They are frequently encountered and are the bane of autograph collectors. They fall into several categories.

Some represent cases of mistaken identity, in which lesser-known people of the same name are confused for a celebrity. For example, Thomas Lynch Jr. (1749–1779), signer of the Declaration of Independence, obviously had a father of that name, and there was also a merchant from New York City with the same appellation. Matters are made more confusing by the fact that the merchant's handwriting shares some similarities (class characteristics) with the signer's. In an article titled "Confused Identities," Joseph E. Fields (1984) lists several such notables who share their names with others, as does Mary Benjamin in *Autographs* (1986).

A second category of genuine fake signatures can be divided into several subtypes. In a *clerk's copy*, the entire document, including the writers' signatures, is in the handwriting of the clerk who made it, possibly as a file copy. Similarly, a specially *prepared copy*—by a clerk or a notary—is in another's hand, but that fact is usually noted on the reverse side. Then there is the *proxy signature*, in which someone else (such as a secretary) legally signs for the named person. This is the case with many presidential signatures, such as those on old land grants. However, the secretary's name is usually indicated below, immediately following the word "by." Distinguished from the proxy signature, which is usually identified as such, is the related *secretarial signature*, whereby an autograph is essentially forged deliberately by someone hired to do so. Many presidents employed secretaries (John F. Kennedy had more than a dozen) to sign their names for them (see figure 1.6). Most of these secretaries learned to imitate their employers' signatures so well and penned them with such speed and confidence that they lack the obvious signs of forgery and are often deceptively similar to the autographs they simulate. Many movie stars also employ secretaries and others to sign autographs for them. Detecting such signatures begins by being forewarned, followed by research and careful study of known standards of both genuine and secretarial signatures from compendiums such as Vrzalik and Minor's *From the President's Pen* (1991).

There are several types of reproduction signatures. Among them is the *rubber-stamped signature* that dates at least to Edwin M. Stanton (1814–1869), Lincoln's secretary of war. Document expert Ordway Hilton (1982, 74) observed that stamp impressions have uneven line edges, faulty line thickness, and "difficulties exhibited in the tapering of ending and beginning strokes." Also, stamp-pad ink differs in appearance from writing inks under magnification, which also reveals a lack of identifiable pen strokes. Stray ink marks from dirt on the stamp or areas around the signature may also be encountered.

*Autopen signatures* represent another type of reproduction. Produced by robotic devices with brand names such as Autopen and Signa-Signer, they are now referred to by autograph dealers and collectors generically

Figure 1.6. John F. Kennedy frequently employed secretaries to sign autographs for him, as in this example from the author's case files.

as "autopen" signatures. President Kennedy began using the autopen in the White House in 1960, and he has been followed in that regard by his successors. Kenneth Rendell (1994, 105) observed, "It should always be assumed that any letter, signed photograph, or other piece not of a truly personal or important business nature could have been signed by a machine if it is from a well-known person who receives many routine letters requiring an answer." Although a person's penned signature differs slightly with each writing, autopen signatures match exactly—or nearly so, given the use of different pens and the way they are attached to the device. Nevertheless, by superimposing a questioned specimen over a known autopen one (using a window or light box to provide illumination), many autopen signatures have been detected. Other identifiable characteristics of autopen writing include machine-produced waverings, a staccato dot-dot-dot quality to the line (especially near the beginning and end of the signature), uniformity of stroke thickness, and blunt rather than tapered stroke endings (Nickell 1996a, 84–87).

Among the most numerous types of reproductions are *facsimiles*—exact printed copies—of historical documents. They may appear on paper of varying degrees of resemblance to the original and may be printed by any of several methods, including lithography and halftone process, as well as photocopying. Commonly encountered facsimiles include those of the Declaration of Independence and the U.S. Constitution; Lincoln's Gettysburg Address; General Order No. 9, relating to the surrender of the Confederacy and signed by General Robert E. Lee; various historical letters by Thomas Jefferson, Benjamin Franklin, John Brown, Lord Byron, and Abraham Lincoln (especially his consolation letter "To Mrs. [Lydia] Bixby, Boston, Mass," dated November 21, 1864); and other documents, including colonial American and Confederate currency (see figure 1.7). Detecting facsimiles is not difficult. The following procedures should be helpful.

First, learn to recognize parchment paper. Imitation parchment was invented in about 1857 and first manufactured in the United States in 1885. It is heavy, crinkly, and usually of the "antiqued" or browned variety. It is quite distinctive, and facsimiles printed on it are sold at most historic sites' gift shops. Although it is supposed to provide an authentically old look to documents, never was currency or Jesse James wanted posters or any other authentic document printed on anything resembling it. Neither Jefferson nor Lincoln (or anyone else) had stationery like it, and it bears scant resemblance to genuine parchment (on which the Declaration and Constitution were originally written). In brief, genuine documents were written on parchment or paper, not on imitation parchment paper.

Use a magnifier to look for a dot-screen pattern indicative of halftone printing (like that of newspaper photos) or the telltale appearance of color photocopies or other evidence of mechanical reproduction. (I carry a 10× Bausch and Lomb illuminated Coddington-type magnifier, essentially a penlight-loupe combination, for this purpose.) Studying old prints in this way helps one become familiar with printing processes.

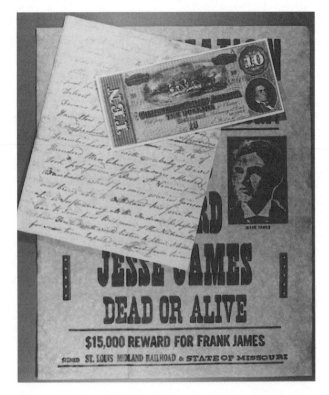

Figure 1.7. Facsimiles, such as those shown here of Confederate currency, a handwritten document, and a wanted poster, are the bane of amateur collectors.

(An excellent treatise is Bamber Gascoigne's *How to Identify Prints* [1988]).

Employ the stereomicroscope to look for characteristics of genuine handwritten documents, such as nib tracks, indentation from pen pressure, and the irregular deposit of ink. Facsimiles lack these features. If printed in black ink, a facsimile's text will be uniformly black from beginning to end, without shadings of gray. Keep in mind that most old, once-black writing ink was iron based and will have turned a rusty brown with age, unlike printer's ink, which is carbon based and remains black forever.

Be alert to anomalies, such as paper of the wrong size or apparent watermarks that are not translucent when the paper is held up to the light. I helped debunk an old document that, at first glance, appeared to be a genuine clerical copy of General Order No. 9, relating to the surrender of the Confederacy and bearing General Lee's signature. It had been discovered folded in an antique book purchased at an estate sale. But when it was held to the light, its large watermark was nowhere to be seen. A loupe revealed that the document was a halftone reproduction. In the case of another facsimile, an 1803 letter from Thomas Jefferson to Craven Peyton was accompanied by an envelope; however, envelopes were not used in the United States until 1832 or later and were not common until the 1840s (Nickell 1996a, 78–84).

The foregoing is only an introduction. The serious student should study the sources referenced and obtain and learn to use the basic equipment, such as a loupe (or, for the very serious student, a stereomicroscope), ultraviolet light, light box, and other aids.

We turn now to several case studies that demonstrate how one authenticates—or exposes—sensational and controversial documents.

# Chapter 2

# DIARY OF JACK THE RIPPER

SOMETIME IN 1991, the purported diary of one of the world's maniacal serial killers surfaced. If genuine, the volume solved the century-old mystery of London's Whitechapel murders, proving that the fiend known as "Jack the Ripper" had been a fifty-year-old cotton merchant from Liverpool, James Maybrick. But was it real or fake? (See figure 2.1.)

A series of grisly murders took place in London's East End in 1888. Although it is inaccurate, as sometimes reported, that they "all occurred in the 'Whitechapel area'" (Wilson 1989, 35), the first three slayings did take place in that district, inspiring the label the "Whitechapel Murders." Subsequent victims were discovered in the adjacent district of Spitalfields. In all, five prostitutes were brutally slain.

The first murder occurred early on August 31, when Mary Ann "Polly" Nichols had her throat cut and her abdomen ripped open, leaving her intestines protruding. A week and a day later, Annie Chapman died in a similar manner, nearly decapitated and disemboweled. On September 30, two more prostitutes fell victim: Elizabeth Stride, whose throat was cut but whose body was spared further mutilation when the killer was interrupted, and Catherine Eddowes, who experienced the frustrated killer's full fury. The latter suffered a slashed throat, which resulted in her death by "haemorrhage from the left common carotid artery," as the coroner wrote in his postmortem notes; she was also disemboweled, with her kidney and uterus removed. Finally, Marie Jeannette "Mary Jane" Kelly was murdered during the morning of November 9; her grossly mutilated body, with its heart missing, was the only one found indoors. The gruesome serial murders went unsolved (Fido 1993, 3–100).

Figure 2.1. Robert Smith, British publisher of a book on the alleged Jack the Ripper diary, examines remnants of pages that were excised from the volume—one of many suspicious elements.

According to an 1894 memorandum by M. L. Macnaghten, chief constable of Scotland Yard's Criminal Investigation Department, there had been at least three prominent Ripper suspects: M. J. Druitt, who was "sexually insane" and committed suicide (by drowning) after the Ripper murders; "Kosminski" (apparently Aaron Kosminski), a Polish Jew who resided in Whitechapel, had a hatred of prostitutes, and was subsequently imprisoned in an asylum for the insane; and Michael Ostrog, allegedly a Russian doctor who was a "homicidal maniac" and whose "whereabouts at the time of the murders could never be ascertained" (Begg, Fido, and Skinner 1994, 116–21, 241–45, 279–90, 340–44).

After the death of Annie Chapman, letters began to be received by the Central News Agency and the Metropolitan Police signed "Jack the Ripper" (Evans and Skinner 2001). The earliest one (recently discovered) was received on September 17 (Cornwell 2002, 211). Most "Ripperologists" today accept the mounting evidence that these letters were the work of one or more journalists (Begg et al. 1994, 209–11). Nevertheless, the sobriquet "Jack the Ripper" stuck.

As the horrible crimes remained unsolved, popular writers began to propose suspects. Over the years, something of a Ripper industry has grown up, with authors proposing first one candidate and then another. For instance, mystery writer Patricia Cornwell (2002) has spent a fortune in a failed attempt to prove that artist Walter Sickert was the culprit (Nickell 2003b). Ripperologist Martin Fido (2001) took the words out of my mouth when he said of some of these books, "The common reader like myself found each identification quite convincing as he read it, and kept changing his mind about which was the Ripper."

More than a century after the slayings, in 1991, a Liverpool scrap-metal dealer named Mike Barrett allegedly came into possession of a remarkable diary that, if genuine, solved the gruesome mystery. The diary's author was a fifty-year-old cotton merchant from Liverpool named James Maybrick (who died of poison in 1889). Entries in the diary explained how Maybrick, seeking revenge on his unfaithful wife, committed the murders in drug-induced frenzies. Here is a sample entry (Harrison 1993, 275):

I have taken a small room in Middlesex Street, that in itself is a joke. I have paid well and I believe no questions will be asked. It is indeed an ideal location. I have walked the streets and have become more familiar with them. I said Whitechapel it will be and Whitechapel it shall. The bitch and her whoring master will rue the day I first saw them together. I said I am clever, very clever. Whitechapel Liverpool, Whitechapel London, *ha ha*. No one could possibly place it together. And indeed for there is no reason for anyone to do so.

The next time I travel to London I shall begin. I have no doubts, my confidence is most high. I am thrilled writing this, life is sweet, and my disappointment has vanished. Next time for sure. I have no doubts, not any longer, no doubts. No one will ever suspect. Tomorrow I will purchase the finest knife money can buy, nothing shall be too good for my whores, I will treat them to the finest, the very finest, they deserve that at least from I.

Not surprisingly, Barrett sought to capitalize on his find. Robert Smith of Smith Gryphon Publishers announced a forthcoming book presenting the diary along with a narrative by Shirley Harrison. It was to be copublished in the United States by Warner Books and titled *The Diary of Jack the Ripper: The Discovery, the Investigation, and the Authentication.* Almost immediately, however, skeptics questioned the reported "authentication," and at the eleventh hour, with the text already set in type, the publisher sought an expert opinion.

## The Investigation

Warner executives naturally turned to Kenneth Rendell, the manuscript authority who had investigated the notorious "Hitler diaries" for *Newsweek* magazine. Rendell in turn contacted me. While arrangements were made for the diary to be insured for $1 million and brought to the United States, I proceeded to secure a forensic laboratory and assemble a team of ink chemists and other experts (Nickell 1997).

Meanwhile, a number of the diary's features—provenance, internal evidence, and writing materials—were concerning, and as a historical investigator, I addressed them. The first issue was the diary's complete lack of provenance (or historical record). Although remarkable items occasionally surface that are lacking in provenance, suspicious circumstances attending such a discovery should immediately place the investigator on alert. This was the case with the questioned diary. According to owner Mike Barrett, it had been a gift from a barroom acquaintance—one who consistently refused to explain his possession of such an apparently valuable item. The suspicious circumstances were magnified by the fact that the benefactor had conveniently died before the diary was made public, and his family was utterly unaware of his reputed ownership of it (Harrison 1993, 7; Smith 1993a). Although

Barrett claimed that he had bought numerous Jack the Ripper books in an attempt to research and verify the diary's story; unfortunately, he kept the purported discovery a secret during that time. Therefore, there was no incontrovertible proof that the diary preceded the research, and not the other way around.

The diary's text also cast doubt on its genuineness. Its author seemed to go out of his way to include Ripper trivia, insignificant material intended solely to make the diary appear genuine. For example, the police list of the possessions of Ripper victims Catherine Eddowes (finally published in 1987) mentioned "1 Tin Match box, empty." The diarist indicated that he had wanted a match to provide light for his grisly work, but "damn it, the tin box was empty" (Harrison 1993, 78–79, 281). As another example, a witness had seen the last victim, Mary Kelly, go off with a man who gave her his red handkerchief when she mentioned she had lost hers. One of the many versified entries in the diary read: "a handkerchief red, led to the bed" (Harrison 1993, 98–99, 285). There were many similar heavy-handed examples inserted throughout the diary (Nickell 1993a).

However, the diarist did not always get his facts straight. For instance, in relating the death of Mary Kelly, he wrote that he had "left [the breasts] on the table." But Martin Fido (n.d., 14) responded: "*Wrong.* This was reported, and the only published photograph has long shown a flattened piece of flesh that could be a breast. In fact the breasts were left on the bed." Fido observed that the diarist's account of the Kelly murder "reads like a description by someone who had read many of the books/press reports of the subject *before* the recovery and release of [police surgeon] Dr. [Thomas] Bond's [1888] report in 1988 told us what was really found in the room."

Moreover, the diary was definitely—though suspiciously—tied to a letter allegedly written by the serial killer. Dated September 25, 1888, it was addressed "Dear Boss" and signed, like the diary, "Jack the Ripper" (see figure 2.2). Also, as diary promoter Shirley Harrison (1993, 88) acknowledged, "the use of language in the letter repeatedly echoes

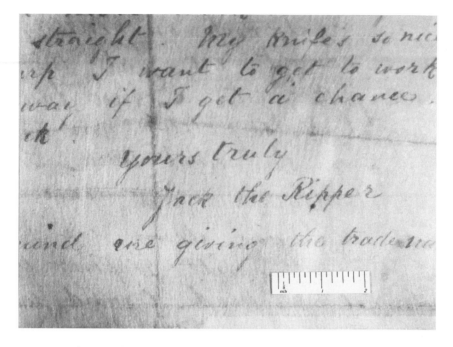

Figure 2.2. Photographic exemplar of handwriting from the 1888 "Dear Boss . . . Jack the Ripper" letter fails to match the penmanship in the reputed Ripper diary.

that of the diary." Both, for example, contained the phrases "down on whores" and "funny little games," both referred to the "red stuff," and both repeated the underlined interjection "*ha ha.*"

Whether the letter was genuine or not—and a journalist eventually confessed that he had produced it and other "Jack" writings "to keep the business alive" (Harrison 1993, 87)—the diary accepted it as such. Therefore, the characteristics of the two writings should have matched. Yet, immediately apparent was the fundamental difference between the antiquated round-hand script of the "Dear Boss" letter and the relatively modern appearance of the diary's handwritings. There were also profound differences in punctuation between the two writings, as previously noted by handwriting expert Sue Iremonger of East Sussex (Harrison 1993, 179). (Particular features of the handwriting were addressed by Maureen Casey Owens and are discussed later.)

Additional evidence involved the nature of the diary itself. It had actually been manufactured as a scrapbook, based on the presence of spacers between the leaves to allow photographs, postcards, and the like to be inserted without stressing the binding. Indeed, it had previously been used as an album, as demonstrated by the characteristic rectangular areas of yellowing (cellulose degradation) remaining on the flyleaf. However, the pages containing the items that left their imprint—some four dozen leaves—had been removed with a knife. Since the diary began in midsentence, the implication was that someone had removed the pages (and with them a portion of the text) after the entries had been written. But why would someone mutilate an item so boldly identified as the diary of Jack the Ripper? Actually, all the evidence (including traces of peeled-off material at two places inside the front cover—consistent with a stationer's sticker and an identifying bookplate) suggests a different scenario: that a forger purchased the album from an antique shop as a means of obtaining credibly old paper and then, possibly with an old pen and bottle of ink from the same store, used it for his purpose.

All these elements—the suspicious circumstances surrounding the diary's alleged discovery, the internal evidence suggestive of the text's derivation from books and other publications, and the implausible nature of the scrapbook-turned-diary with its cut-out pages—are symptomatic of an amateurish forgery (Nickell 1993a).

### Forensic Analysis

On August 21, 1993, our team of experts met at the Chicago laboratory of noted handwriting analyst Maureen Casey Owens. The assembled experts took turns examining the volume and its handwriting under the stereomicroscope. We observed Owens as she conducted infrared and ultraviolet light examinations on the diary, as well as an examination for indented handwritten impressions using an electrostatic detection apparatus (see figure 2.3). Each step in the examination of the diary was photographed, including Owens's photographing of the pages of the diary and ink chemist Robert Kuranz's taking of tiny core samples of ink and paper for his own and Roderick McNeil's ink tests. (Subsequently, Kuranz [1986] performed a thin-layer chromatographic analysis, and

Figure 2.3. The author assists noted forensic document examiner Maureen Casey Owens in applying electronic static detection analysis (which can identify even very slight impressions on paper) to the alleged Ripper diary.

McNeil [1994] used a new, controversial ion-migration test in an attempt to determine how long the ink had been on the paper.)

I had emphasized the need for the ultraviolet examination because old ink—especially old iron-gall ink—frequently leaves a faint image of itself on a page it is in contact with for a long period. Sometimes this is not apparent to the unaided eye but may be revealed—often dramatically—by ultraviolet illumination (or by argon laser light). Since such offsetting is rather unpredictable, its absence means little, but its presence could be a sign of apparent age in a document (Nickell 1990, 193–94).

However, the various instrumental tests showed little of consequence, and Kuranz's techniques (which basically replicated those previously conducted by Dr. Nicholas Estaugh in England) revealed nothing that was inconsistent with the purported date of the diary. McNeil's analysis, which used a scanning Auger microscope to measure the migration of ions from the ink into the paper, yielded a median date of 1921, plus or minus twelve years (McNeil 1994). Although this indicated that the diary was a forgery, it gave an implausible date for its creation (based on the evidence cited earlier). A potential explanation for the error was the diary's paper having been unsized and therefore being extra absorbent (Rendell 1993).

## The Handwriting

The most significant evidence was provided by the handwriting. Owens, who had sixteen years' experience as a forensic document examiner for the Chicago Police Department before turning to private practice, compared the questioned writing of the diary (see figure 2.4) with two groups of known standards: a photograph of the "Dear Boss" letter (see figure 2.2) and the accompanying envelope, and copies of authentic writings of James Maybrick—his signature on his marriage certificate and his holographic two-page will (see figure 2.5).

Owens (1993) reported: "The characteristics of the Dear Boss letter follow closely upon the Round Hand writing style of the time and exhibit a good writing skill. The Will shows a fine hand and exhibits significant shading in the writing. Both of these items contain a writing skill superior to that of the Diary." She went on to observe: "The diary contains many varieties in letter forms. Some letter forms are significantly different in design and movement. Shading seems to be incidental to the writing as opposed to by design and lacks uniformity." Owens concluded that neither of the writers of the standards had written the diary. In other words, the handwriting failed twice. The diary had

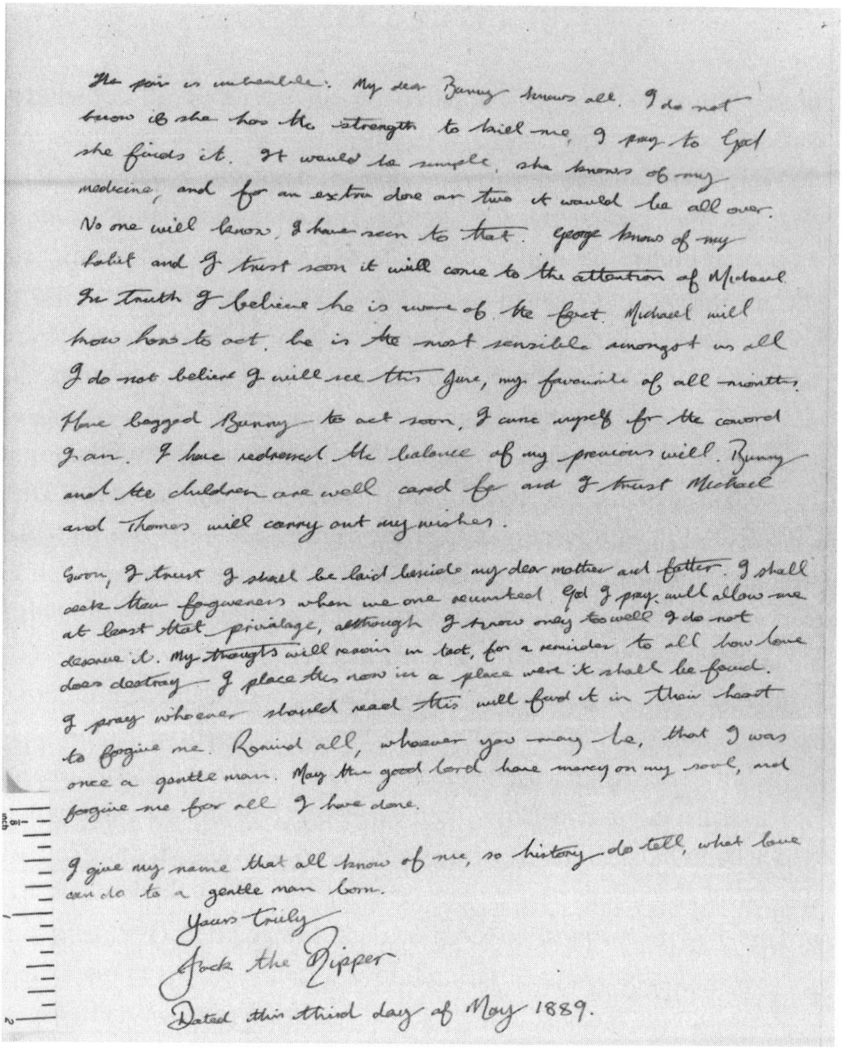

The pain is unbearable. My dear Bunny knows all. I do not know if she has the strength to kill me. I pray to God she finds it. It would be simple, she knows of my medicine, and for an extra dose or two it would be all over. No one will know, I have seen to that. George knows of my habit and I trust soon it will come to the attention of Michael. In truth I believe he is aware of the fact. Michael will know how to act, he is the most sensible amongst us all. I do not believe I will see this June, my favourite of all months. Have begged Bunny to act soon, I curse myself for the coward I am. I have redeemed the balance of my precious will. Bunny and the children are well cared for and I trust Michael and Thomas will carry out my wishes.

Soon, I trust I shall be laid beside my dear mother and father. I shall seek their forgiveness when we are reunited. God I pray will allow me at least that privialge, although I know only too well I do not deserve it. My thoughts will remain in tact, for a reminder to all how love does destroy. I place this now in a place were it shall be found. I pray whoever should read this will find it in their heart to forgive me. Remind all, whoever you may be, that I was once a gentle man. May the good lord have mercy on my soul, and forgive me for all I have done.

I give my name that all know of me, so history do tell, what love can do to a gentle man born.

Yours truly

Jack the Ripper

Dated this third day of May 1889.

Figure 2.4. Last page of the Ripper diary, supposedly written by James Maybrick, fails to match known standards of Maybrick's script, including that from his holographic will.

not been written by the author of the "Dear Boss" letter; nor had it been authored by James Maybrick. This evidence alone was fatal to the diary's authenticity.

Both Rendell and I had independently studied the handwriting and concurred with Owens's opinion. In his report to Warner Books, Rendell (1993) stated:

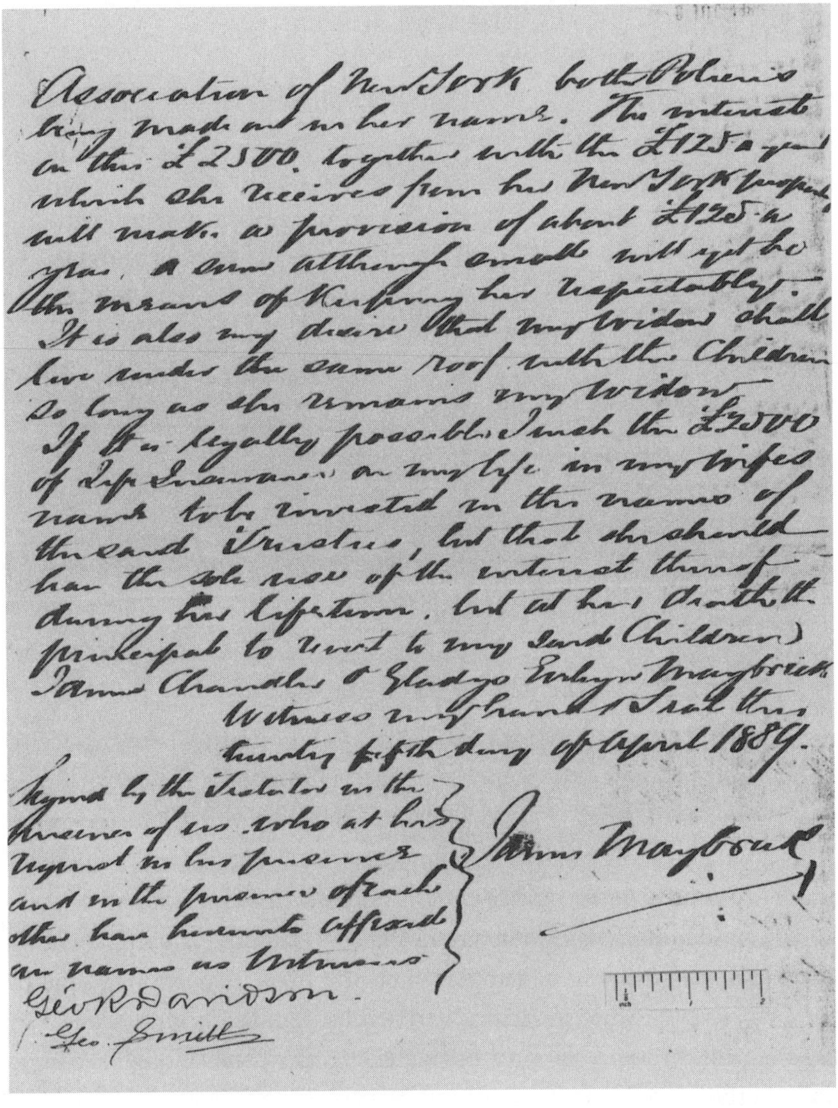

Association of New York both Policies
being made out in her name. The interest
on this £2500. together with the £125 a year
which she receives from her New York property
will make a provision of about £125 a
year, a sum although small will yet be
the means of keeping her respectably.
It is also my desire that my widow shall
live under the same roof with the Children
so long as she remains my widow.
If it is legally possible I wish the £2500
of Life Insurance on my life in my wifes
name to be invested in the names of
the said Trustees, but that she should
have the sole use of the interest thereof
during her lifetime, but at her death the
principal to revert to my said Children
James Chandler & Gladys Evelyn Maybrick.
Witness my hand & Seal this
twenty fifth day of April 1889.
Signed by the Testator in the
presence of us who at his
request in his presence
and in the presence of each
other have hereunto affixed
our names as Witnesses
Geo R Davidson.
Geo. Smith
James Maybrick

Figure 2.5. The handwriting in James Maybrick's will is completely unlike that found in the notorious diary supposedly penned by Jack the Ripper.

The question concerning the "Dear Boss" letter was whether it was possible for the diary's author to have disguised his or her own writing by adopting a different style. Mrs. Owens has two and a half decades of experience in detecting situations where a person is attempting to write in a manner to cover up his own handwriting. She is definitive in her opinion that this is not the case with the "Dear Boss" letter. . . .

Our further examination of the writing in the diary confirmed what Dr. Nickell, Mrs. Owens, and myself suspected the first time we saw the diary: the writing is not consistent with letter formations of the late 1880s; there is a uniformity of ink and slant of writing in going from one entry to the next (supposedly written at different times) that is unnatural and very indicative of a forger writing multiple entries at one time. A lack of variation in layout also leads to the same conclusion.

Rendell's report (1993) concluded: "there is no credible evidence whatsoever that this diary is genuine. Every area of analysis proves or indicates the Jack the Ripper diary is a hoax."

## The Debate

As a result of our team's work, Warner Books immediately canceled publication of *The Diary of Jack the Ripper*, "exactly one month," noted the *Washington Post*, "before 200,000 copies of the Victorian serial killer's purported ramblings were to go on sale." The *Post* added, "What was once touted by the publisher as the historical find of the century has collapsed into a hoax" (Streitfeld 1993). Noting that a prepublication ad in Warner's catalog had represented the book (based on claims by the English publisher) as being "verified by experts" and "reviewed by premier authorities," the *Post* concluded wryly: "Not enough of them, apparently."

Hyperion seemed to lack Warner's concerns and published the book with an altered subtitle: *The Discovery, the Investigation, the Debate*. The "debate" consisted of Rendell's report followed by a "Rebuttal" from Robert Smith (1993b) of Smith Gryphon Publishers. In the latter, Smith continued to demonstrate a naiveté about forgeries and hoaxes—or a stubbornness to admit his error. However, as Rendell told the *Washington Post*: "If I wrote my own book about this episode, a chapter would be called 'yes but.' Everything I say, Robert says, 'yes, but.' . . . The English attitude has been, 'Prove it's a fake.' Well, I have. But that's the wrong approach. They should be proving it's real" (Streitfeld 1993).

I subsequently debated the author of the book's narrative, Shirley Harrison, on the Washington, D.C., Mutual Radio program *The Jim Bohannon Show* (October 20, 1993). When Harrison boasted that we debunkers were only helping the book become a best seller, I replied that she and the publisher might well be laughing all the way to the bank, but before they counted their take, they should reflect on the ethics of the matter. I was referring to facts that had come to light in England. As it happened, prior to our examination, the *Sunday Times* of London had assembled its own panel of experts who had likewise determined that the diary was a fake. Smith Gryphon attempted to hold the newspaper to a confidentiality agreement (signed in connection with an option on serial rights), but the newspaper issued a writ in the High Court, citing misrepresentation and fraud, and prevailed (Chittenden and Lloyd 1993). On September 19, 1993, the *Sunday Times* published a two-page exposé, headlined "Fake!" One bombshell was that Smith had withheld an early report prepared by an experienced forensic document expert, David Baxendale, who had determined that the diary was a modern fake. Among other analyses, Baxendale had done a simple ink-solubility test that indicated—much more accurately, in my opinion, than the doubtful test conducted by McNeil for our team—that the writing had probably been done within the past three years (Chittenden and Lloyd 1993).

The controversy did not end there. In late June 1994 Mike Barrett finally confessed that he had forged the Ripper diary. His methodology had been just as I had deduced. First, he spent ten days composing the text on a word processor. Then he obtained an old photograph album from which he removed the used pages and purchased a traditional ink from an art store. Next, he transcribed the fake text into the "diary" and made up a story about receiving it from an elderly friend on his deathbed. Perhaps not surprisingly, according to the *Sunday Times* (Chittenden 1994), "Barrett's agent and publishers were still maintaining the diary was a true document." In fact, although Barrett had first confessed to Shirley Harrison and then had given a signed admission to reporter Harold Brough of the *Liverpool Post,* he soon retracted his confession (Lay 1994). This came just as I was writing a short chapter on the diary for a British book on Jack the Ripper (Wolff 1995).

However, British investigative author and Ripperologist Melvin Harris decided to pursue the clue in Barrett's confession that he had used a reproduction Victorian ink. Harris soon learned that the ink contained a modern preservative. He arranged to have tests done but got no cooperation from the British publisher with regard to obtaining new samples. So Harris turned to our team. At my request, Kuranz gave him half our remaining samples, and subsequent analysis confirmed the presence of a modern preservative; however, tests at another laboratory were negative, reporting only a trace that was "put down to contamination" (Linder, Morris, and Skinner 2003, 158–59).

Although it is apparent that no amount of evidence will convince those with a vested interest in the diary's authenticity, the proof of its spuriousness is overwhelming.

# Chapter 3

# NOVEL BY AN
# AMERICAN SLAVE

A FASCINATING LITERARY mystery surfaced in 2001 when the distinguished scholar Henry Louis Gates Jr.—chair of the Department of Afro-American Studies at Harvard University—purchased at auction a 300-page holographic manuscript (one written in the author's own handwriting; see figure 3.1). Its title page read, "The Bondwoman's Narrative / By Hannah Crafts / A Fugitive Slave / Recently Escaped from North Carolina." Gates (2002a, xii) immediately recognized that "if the author was black, then this 'fictionalized slave narrative'—an autobiographical novel apparently based upon a female fugitive slave's life in bondage in North Carolina and her escape to freedom in the North—would be a major discovery, possibly the first novel written by a black woman and definitely the first written by a woman who had been a slave."* Beyond the excitement, of course, was the question: was *The Bondwoman's Narrative* authentic?

To address that crucial question, I was commissioned to examine the manuscript by Laurence J. Kirshbaum, chairman of Time Warner Trade Publishing, which was planning to publish the novel. I had been recommended by document expert Kenneth Rendell (see chapter 2). In a letter dated April 24, 2001, Kirshbaum referred to Professor Gates's finding that the manuscript appeared to date from around 1855. "We need your investigative expertise to authenticate this date," wrote Kirshbaum. I had subsequent discussions with him, Gates, and Rendell, who had taken a preliminary look at the manuscript. We agreed that I would make a detailed examination of the manuscript's physical makeup as well as any internal evidence relating to its date and authorship. Meanwhile, Gates

---

*The first novel published by a black woman was *Our Nig* (1859), written by Harriet E. Wilson, who had been born free in the northern United States.

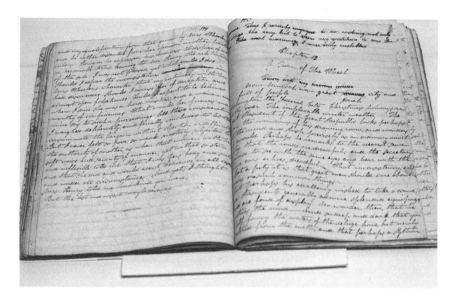

Figure 3.1. Titled *The Bondwoman's Narrative,* a 300-page manuscript could be the earliest novel written by a black woman.

and other researchers were attempting to verify the historical existence of a Hannah Crafts.

Subsequently hand-carried to my lab by courier, the manuscript began to give up its secrets and slowly yield clues about its mystery author. For six weeks I subjected the ink, paper, and other traces to a battery of tests—stereomicroscopic (see figure 3.2), chemical, and spectral (ultraviolet). At night, I read a typescript of the novel, looking for clues in the text.

Of my subsequent findings, Gates (2002a, xxx) wrote, "Nothing in my experience as a graduate student of English literature or a professor of literature for the past twenty-five years had prepared me for the depth of detail of the results of Nickell's examination, nor for the sheer beauty of the rigors of his procedures and the subtleties of his conclusions."

## Results of the Examination

Gates published my report as an appendix to *The Bondwoman's Narrative* (Nickell 2002). It treats the following aspects: provenance,

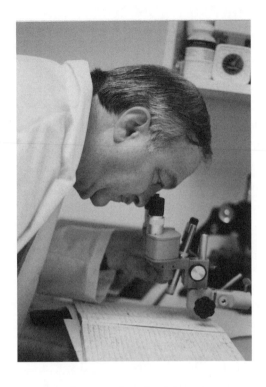

Figure 3.2. The author examines the alleged slave-written narrative using a stereomicroscope. (Photograph by Thomas Flynn, Center for Inquiry)

paper, ink, pen, handwriting, erasures and corrections, binding, and textual matters. My findings are summarized here.

Professor Gates provided some letters regarding the known provenance of the manuscript. It could be reliably traced back to a 1948 catalog from Emily Driscoll, who operated an autograph and book business on Fifth Avenue in New York City. Driscoll subsequently sold the Hannah Crafts narrative for $85 to Dorothy Porter of Howard University. Driscoll told Porter she had "bought it from a scout in the trade" and that all she knew of its prior history "was that he came upon it in Jersey!" (Driscoll 1951). This information showed that the manuscript's provenance was incomplete but not suspicious, being traceable back half a century, to a time when it was not so valued and therefore not such a target for forgery.

Mrs. Porter's typed record described the work as a "Manuscript Novel" and a "fictionalized personal narrative" that had been "written in a worn copy book" (Nickell 1993c). Actually, it was penned on stationery (subsequently bound) that consisted of folio sheets (sheets of paper folded in half and thus having two leaves and four pages). The manuscript consisted of four different types of stationery sheets, two of which bore embossed stationers' crests (designs impressed in the upper-left corner of letter folios beginning in the late 1830s). These crests were from the Southworth paper manufacturing company, one of which appeared in examples from 1856 and 1860 (as shown in a catalog I compiled of more than 200 such marks [Nickell 1993c]).

As part of my detailed examination, I studied the paper's rag content (Nickell 2002, 291):

> Stereomicroscopic examination of the surface of the various pages reveals the presence of bits of thread, occasionally still colored red, blue, etc., indicating the paper pulp was not bleached but was made largely of white cloth. I obtained some small slivers of paper from frayed outer edges (slivers that were about to become dislodged in any case), moistened a sliver with distilled water and teased it apart on a microscope slide, stained it with Herzberg stain [see Nickell 1996a, 178–79], and observed the fibers microscopically. I identified rag—linen and cotton—fibers (the latter with their characteristic twist) but found no evidence of ground wood pulp (first successfully commercially produced in North America in 1867).

Among other analyses, I employed transmitted light (backlighting), which showed that the wove paper lacked a watermark. However, I was excited to discover a type of "accidental" watermark consisting of translucent stitch-type markings running across some leaves; I recognized them as having been produced by the seam of the wire belt of an early paper machine.

The ink proved to be ordinary iron-gall ink. To learn this, I used a nondestructive procedure I had developed with forensic analyst John F. Fischer. Whereas some document examiners either make tests on the document itself or remove samples of ink by scraping with a scalpel or punching out tiny disks of inked paper, we devised a technique that is much less destructive. As I reported (Nickell 2002, 294):

> In this procedure, a small piece of chromatography paper is moistened with distilled water, placed over a heavy ink stroke, and rubbed with a blunt instrument using moderate pressure, by which means a small trace of ink is lifted onto the paper. Such samples were taken randomly from several locations throughout the manuscript. The chemical tests were then conducted on the chromatography paper.
>
> Two reagents were used. First, hydrochloric acid was applied, which produced a light yellow color typical of an iron-gall ink that lacks a provisional colorant. (A blue reaction would have indicated a colorant such as indigo; red would have indicated logwood.) This was followed by potassium ferrocyanide which yielded a Prussian-blue color, thus proving the presence of iron and indicating an iron-gallotannate ink. This type of ink was the most common in use during the middle of the nineteenth century.

Rarely in the manuscript, the ink was blotted with the application of sand, but never with blotting paper.

Significantly, examination with ultraviolet light revealed that there were numerous instances of "ghost writing"—mirror-image, fluorescing traces of writing caused by ink corrosion from the facing page. Its presence here was in marked contrast to its absence in the fake Jack the Ripper diary (discussed in the previous chapter), and this was one of several signs of age in the manuscript.

That *The Bondwoman's Narrative* was written with a dip pen was evidenced by sequences of writing that became progressively lighter and then abruptly dark again, as the writer recharged the pen. Also, sometimes the pen strokes became finer, indicating a shift from a blunt to a sharp nib—a characteristic of the quill pen. Stereomicroscopic inspection showed the absence of nib tracks and other features that

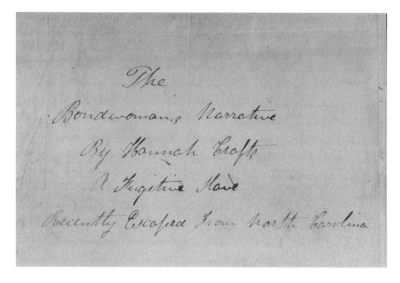

Figure 3.3. *The Bondwoman's Narrative,* purportedly by one "Hannah Crafts,"
is in a modified round-hand style of script, consistent with its purported
1850s authorship.

confirmed the use of quills (which were largely abandoned by the end
of the Civil War). I determined that standard goose quills had been
used, rather than the crow quills employed to produce the tiny script
sometimes affected by Victorian ladies as an expression of femininity
(see Nickell 1990, 3–4).

The handwriting throughout the narrative was of a class succeeding American round hand (circa 1700–1840), called modified round
hand (see figure 3.3). It dominated from about 1840 to 1865 (before
being supplanted by the Spencerian system of 1865–1890). Of course,
a handwriting cannot be precisely dated by style, since people tend
to continue their manner of writing into old age. Because the writing
materials of the manuscript indicated it had been written in the 1850s,
the absence of archaic forms (such as the long *s*) suggested to me that the
writer was relatively young. The penmanship was of a quality I described
as "serviceable" (neither elegant nor untutored), and though it was a
natural, genuine handwriting, it had been penned relatively slowly, as

if to render it legible. The punctuation was eccentric (lacking periods, having apostrophes and quotation marks on the baseline like commas).

The author used a wide variety of correction and revision techniques, ranging from making strike-outs with the pen and providing careted insertions (using an inverted *v* to indicate placement) to scraping with an ink-eraser knife. Sometimes, while wet, the ink had been wiped off with the little finger (the direction indicating the right hand; see figure 3.4), a common practice of the quill pen era. (The later steel pen dug into the paper too much and eliminated the practice [Nickell 1991].) More extensive revisions had been made by covering the old text with slips of paper bearing the new text; these were affixed with halves of moistened vermilion-colored paste wafers (see figure 3.5). To make a better bond, the pasted areas were impressed not with the usual seal-like device bearing a waffle iron–like pattern but apparently with a thimble—one of several indicators that the author was probably a woman.

Since the manuscript was composed not in a blank book but on sheets of stationery, it needed to be bound. Evidence of pinholes (see figure 3.6) indicated that it had originally and amateurishly been sewn with needle and thread, apparently by the author (just as Emily Dickinson did with her poems [Shurr 1983]); the author then numbered the pages. Much later (as indicated by soiling and abrading of the manuscript's original first and last pages), the manuscript was professionally bound with a black cloth-covered pasteboard binding (Nickell 2002). This appeared to date from sometime after 1880 (Rendell 2001).

In short, the author's writing accoutrements included quill pens, a penknife, a container of iron-gall ink, folded stationery sheets (including those produced by the Southworth paper company), an ink-eraser knife, a sander (filled with common sand for blotting ink), a box of vermilion paste wafers, a pair of small scissors, and possibly a paper knife (to slit an occasional folded sheet into two leaves). These items could have been kept in a combination writing and sewing box that included a thimble (used to press down the wafers to make a better bond) and needle and thread (to sew the pages into a book). All these materials were consistent with the 1850s.

Figure 3.4. Evidence that ink was wiped off by the little finger before drying—a common practice for making corrections in the quill pen era—is consistent with the period in question (and indicative of a right-handed author).

Figure 3.5. To correct the manuscript, its author used vermilion paste wafers to attach slips of paper over the replaced text.

Figure 3.6. Evidence of pinholes reveals that the manuscript had been bound in an amateurish manner using needle and thread.

The text of *The Bondwoman's Narrative* offered further information about the author and the date of composition. The narrative was not that of an unread person, despite many misspellings: *meloncholy* for *melancholy* (59), *benumed* for *benumbed* (285), and *your* for *you're* (109). Polysyllabic words such as *magnanimity* (94), *demoniacal* (127), and *ascertained* (230) flowed from the author's pen. The admixture of good vocabulary skills and poor spelling suggested that the writer had struggled to learn to write. The readability level of the novel—determined by applying a common formula (Bovée and Thill 1989)—was high. The following passage, describing the protagonist's visit to a gallery of ancestral portraits in the stately mansion Lindendale (18), was assessed at the eleventh-grade level:

Though filled with superstitious awe I was in no haste to leave the room; for there surrounded by mysteryous associations I seemed suddenly to have grown old, to have entered a new world of thoughts, and feelings and sentiments I was not a slave with these pictured memorials of the past They could not enforce drudgery, or condemn me on account of my color to a life of servitude As their companion I could think and speculate In their presence my mind seemed to run riotous and exult in its freedom as a rattional being, and one destined for something higher and better than this world can afford.

The author's erudition was even more impressive, referring to "the laws of the Medes and Persians" (23), suggesting appearances that "were enough to have provoked a smile on the lips of Heraclitus" (173), and speaking of "the meaning of nature's various hieroglyphical symbols" (252).

I found many indications that the work was a novel, despite the author's protestations in the preface that "being the truth it makes no pretensions to romance." There were, for instance, Gothic elements, including the shadowy gloom of Lindendale, a curse-containing "legend of the Linden," and suggestions of various supernatural elements. The novel's lengthy exchanges of dialogue, as well as elaborate scene-setting descriptions and other conventions, stood in contrast to the true slave narrative of Frederick Douglass (1845).

Yet there were indications that the novel may have been based on certain actual experiences. For example, one clue in the manuscript led to a North Carolina slaveholding politician. I noticed that the name "Wheeler" in the novel had often been underlined, and when I inspected closer using the stereomicroscope, I discovered that the word had originally been written as if to conceal the identity—for instance, "Mr. Wh____r" and "Mrs. Wh____r"—and later filled in with the missing letters to complete the name. I related this to Professor Gates, who learned that the reference was to an actual North Carolina slave owner, John Hill Wheeler (Gates 2002b, 331–36).

There were many literary influences in *The Bondwoman's Narrative*. As discovered by astute Princeton graduate student Hollis Robbins (who went on to become director of the Black Periodic Literature Project at the W. E. B. DuBois Institute at Harvard), there were many outright borrowings from Charles Dickens, in particular from *Bleak House,* which was published in the United States in 1853, following serialization in 1852 and 1853. The following two examples show nearly verbatim borrowing (Gates 2002b):

| *Bondswoman's Narrative* | *Bleak House* |
| --- | --- |
| Gloom everywhere. Gloom up the Potomac; where it rolls among meadows no longer green, and by splendid country seats. Gloom down the Potomac where it washes the sides of huge warships. Gloom on the marshes, the fields and heights. Gloom settling steadily down over the sumptuous habitations of the rich, and creeping through the cellars of the poor. Gloom arresting the steps of grave and reverend Senators; for with fog, and drizzle, and sleety driving mist the night has come at least two hours before its time. . . . | Fog everywhere. Fog up the river, where it flows among green aits and meadows; fog down the river, where it rolls defiled among the tiers of shipping, and the waterside pollutions of a great (and dirty) city. Fog on the Essex marshes, fog on the Kentish heights. Fog creeping into the cabooses of brigs; fog lying out on the yards, and hovering in the rigging of great ships; fog drooping on the gunwales of barges and small boats. Fog in the eyes and throats of ancient Greenwich pensioners. . . . Most of the shops lighted two hours before their time. . . . (chapter 1) |
| It is a stretch of imagination to say that by night they contained a swarm of misery, that crowds of foul existence crawled in out of gaps in walls and boards, or coiled themselves to sleep on nauseous heaps of straw fetid with human perspiration and where the rain drips in, and the damp airs of midnight fatch and carry malignant fevers . . . | Now, these tumbling tenements contain, by night, a swarm of misery. As on the ruined human wretch, vermin parasites appear, so, these ruined shelters have bred a crowd of foul existence that crawls in and out of gaps in walls and boards; coils itself to sleep, in maggot numbers, where the rain drips in; and comes and goes, fetching and carrying fever. . . . (chapter 16) |

Throughout *The Bondwoman's Narrative,* numerous distinctive words and phrases had date significance. I found that selected words from the text were correct for the mid-nineteenth century. In addition, historical references rang true, as in the mention of "vagabond

Irishmen" (248), which may have been prompted by the increase in immigration resulting from the great Irish famine of 1846–1847. One very specific indicator was mention of "the equestrian statue of Jackson" in Washington (246); that sculpture was completed in 1853, thus providing a date before which the manuscript could not have been written. As to the latest date the novel might have been written, I reasoned as follows (Nickell 2002, 307–8):

> Throughout the narrative, references to slavery are in the present tense (as in the Preface's mention of "that institution whose curse rests" over the nation). This would make no sense if written after the war. Neither would the author's claim to being "A Fugitive Slave" who had "Recently Escaped from North Carolina." Mentions of "a deed of manumission" (p. 53), "a slave state" (p. 104), and "an Abolitionist" (p. 202) are all correct for the pre–Civil War period. To have omitted any mention of secession or the outbreak of war itself would have been counterproductive if written after 1861. Following the war, the story would have seemed passé, perhaps thus helping to explain why it went unpublished.

I concluded that, considering all the evidence, a date of 1853–1861 was indicated, supported by consistent evidence from the writing materials.

## Search for an Author

The link between the narrative and John Hill Wheeler meant that either Hannah Crafts had been an escaped slave of Wheeler's or she had created a persona as such. Gates (2002a) demonstrated that the novel's mention of the Wheelers' runaway slave "Jane" was surely based on the real-life escape of Wheeler's slave Jane Johnson. She and her two young sons had traveled with Wheeler to Philadelphia, where they were assisted in their escape by black Underground Railroad activist William Still and white abolitionist Passmore Williamson. Jane subsequently faded into obscurity (Gates 2002a, xlvi–lvi; Flynn 2004, 372–73).

In 2004 Gates and Robbins published *In Search of Hannah Crafts,* their edited collection of critical essays on the narrative. Some of those fascinating essays proposed "suspects" in the quest for the identity of the author. I was asked to contribute a chapter assessing each possible candidate in light of my original findings and, conversely, to reconsider my profile of the author in light of the new evidence (Nickell 2004).

Gates himself conducted an extensive search for Hannah Crafts. He found a black Hannah Kraft in Maryland, but she was too young and happened to be illiterate. He also found a Maria H. Crafts in New Orleans, but her signature did not match the "Hannah Crafts" on the title page. Expert genealogical sleuth Katherine E. Flynn (2004) uncovered two more possibilities—a white Boston teacher and her mother—but their handwriting also failed to match.

Two other candidates for authorship mentioned by Gates were revisited by Flynn and distinguished English professor Nina Baym. Flynn (2004) reopened the case on Jane Johnson, whose candidacy Gates (2002c) had rejected because she had apparently been illiterate, having signed court documents relating to her escape not with her signature but with her "mark." I cannot do justice here to Flynn's excellent and important research, but she found several obstacles to Jane's being Hannah. For instance, according to Jane's co-rescuer, William Still, "she has never been allowed to read" (quoted in Gates 2002a, xlix), which contradicted the *Narrative* author's claim that she had been taught reading and writing as a child by an elderly white couple. Moreover, although Jane Johnson commendably became literate five years after her escape, it seems unlikely that she could have progressed from total illiteracy to writing a novel of the *Narrative*'s quality in so short a time. Thus, there are many reasons to doubt that Johnson was Hannah (Nickell 2004, 411–12).

Baym (2004) also returned to a candidate rejected by Gates: a free black woman from New Jersey named Hannah Vincent. However, Vincent remains only a possible author until stronger evidence—such as handwriting—confirms or disproves her authorship.

We must remember that the burden of proof is on the proponent;

it is not up to others to disprove a claim. We must also guard against wishful thinking, being careful to follow the evidence and not get ahead of it.

Here is my updated profile of Hannah Crafts: She was a talented female writer who had read much imaginative literature and probably produced other literary works, such as poems or short prose pieces, both before and after *The Bondwoman's Narrative*. She was relatively young when she composed the novel, which was written between 1855 (when Wheeler's slave Jane Johnson escaped) and 1861 (the advent of secession and the Civil War). Her identity as an African American slave rings true, but as Baym (2004, 316) observed, that might be because "the account rings *imaginatively* true" (emphasis added). Whatever her race, it appears that she struggled to become educated. That, along with some indications of frugality (she recycled paper for correction slips and used quill pens rather than the more expensive steel variety), suggests that she was not a middle-class Victorian lady. She was surely a Christian and likely a Methodist, just as Hannah was portrayed in the novel. We have a copious quantity of her handwriting and may someday discover her true identity.

# Chapter 4

# LINCOLN'S LOST GETTYSBURG ADDRESS

SIX SCORE AND seven years after Lincoln's famed address at Gettysburg, a copy of it surfaced. Had the Holy Grail of American manuscripts been discovered at last, or was the document too good to be true?

As an essential historical document relating to American freedom, as well as an admired example of profound oratory, the address given by President Lincoln when he dedicated the national cemetery at Gettysburg on November 19, 1863, would be priceless. If the final draft, or reading copy, were discovered, it would be, stated David Warren (1990–1991), "a national treasure."

Artist and renowned Lincoln collector Lloyd Ostendorf believed he had found just such a document—page two of the very copy that Lincoln had taken from his breast coat pocket to read at Gettysburg. It surfaced in mid-1990 when an acquaintance asked Ostendorf to appraise it, claiming it had been discovered at a northern Ohio antique fair, lodged between the pages of *The Lincoln Memorial*—a book about the sixteenth president's life and funeral published in 1865.

The first page was missing, but the second one contained the last eleven lines of the famous text and was autographed on the verso, "For Hon Judge David Wills from A. Lincoln Nov 19, 1863." Lincoln had stayed at Wills's home at Gettysburg, and in a later letter, Wills had asked Lincoln for the "original manuscript" to be placed at Gettysburg "with the correspondence and other papers connected with the project" of creating the national cemetery (Wills 1863).

The page looked credible to Ostendorf, but many of his fellow collectors and Lincoln scholars were skeptical. Where was the first page? Its absence made the document appear more like a single-page forgery than a treasure, half of which someone had carelessly lost. As Warren (1990–1991, 17) observed, "Connoisseurs look at three aspects before investing in a single-page historical document: provenance, provenance, provenance." How was one to account for what Warren called "that incredible time gap, 1863 to 1990?" Yet Ostendorf rationalized, "We collectors all know that fine Lincoln items continue to turn up at this late date, some with and some without any provenance" (quoted in Warren 1990–1991, 10).

If authentic, Ostendorf's copy would take its chronological place as the reading copy of the address, following two drafts (working copies) and preceding three fair copies (neatly penned after the final corrections had been made). Neither of the drafts contained the words "under God," but all the fair copies did. What about the reading copy? At Gettysburg, an Associated Press reporter had borrowed the president's original to correct his own transcription for publication, proving that Lincoln had actually said "under God." Here is a summary of the different copies (see Mearns and Dunlap 1963):

*1. First draft.* Known as the Nicolay copy (after Lincoln's secretary John Nicolay, whose heirs gave it to the Library of Congress), it is the first known draft. It consists of two pages, the second in pencil, and it was never folded.

*2. Second draft.* Called the Hay copy (after Lincoln's other secretary John Hay, whose children donated it to the Library of Congress), it is similar to the first and also lacks folds (see figure 4.1).

*3. Reading copy.* This is the final draft that Lincoln took from his pocket and read at Gettysburg. It was lost, but its second page was supposedly discovered by Ostendorf. It has folds and a signed inscription to David Wills.

*4. First fair copy.* This copy was requested by Edward Everett (who also spoke at the Gettysburg dedication) for a book he was writing on the event. He was informed that Lincoln's reading copy was no longer available; to produce the copy, the president referred to the newspaper report.

*5. Second fair copy.* Penned at the request of educator George

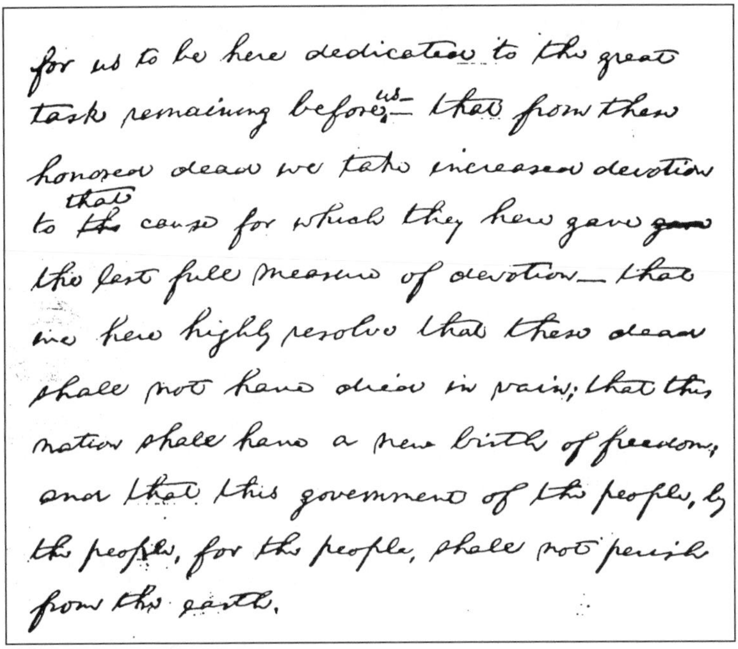
for us to be here dedicated to the great
task remaining before us— that from these
honored dead we take increased devotion
to that cause for which they here gave gave
the last full measure of devotion— that
we here highly resolve that these dead
shall not have died in vain; that this
nation shall have a new birth of freedom,
and that this government of the people, by
the people, for the people, shall not perish
from the earth.

Figure 4.1. Lincoln's Gettysburg Address (page 2 of the Hay copy, the president's second draft) in his rugged handwriting.

Bancroft to benefit the Baltimore Sanitary Fair (a Red Cross–like organization), it was written in late February 1864 and mailed the same day as the Everett copy.

6. *Third fair copy.* Colonel Alexander Bliss asked for a copy to be used for printing. Lincoln wrote it on lined paper provided by Bliss for that purpose. Lincoln signed it, as requested, making it the standard version.

Ostendorf studied the purported reading copy (see figure 4.2) in light of the drafts and fair copies, and he decided to purchase it. He traded thousands of dollars in cash together with several items from his collection, including a rare 1865 tintype of Lincoln with his son Tad. The seller insisted that his name not be revealed, giving the document not only a "dead-end provenance" (Warren 1990–1991, 9) but also a suspicious one.

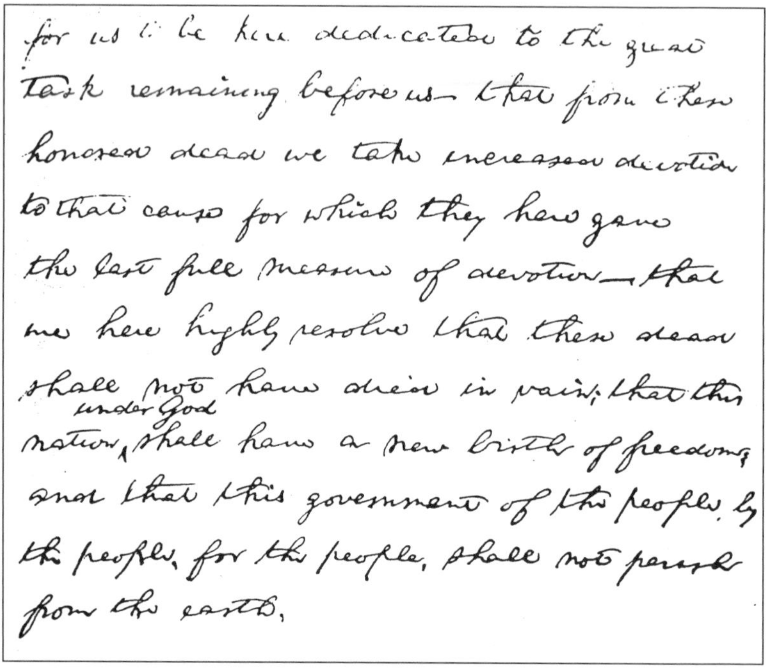
for us to be here dedicated to the great
task remaining before us— that from these
honored dead we take increased devotion
to that cause for which they here gave
the last full measure of devotion— that
we here highly resolve that these dead
shall not have died in vain; that this
nation, under God, shall have a new birth of freedom,
and that this government of the people, by
the people, for the people, shall not perish
from the earth.

Figure 4.2. Ostendorf copy of the Gettysburg Address may simply be a tracing of the Hay copy. (Courtesy of Lloyd Ostendorf)

## Document Examination

Following a Sunday telephone call to me about his find, Lloyd Ostendorf and his son came to the University of Kentucky, where I was teaching, on September 25, 1991. I set up my stereomicroscope and other equipment in a room I had booked for the purpose, and for the next three and a half hours I examined Ostendorf's treasure, which at first look, certainly appeared genuine.

It consisted of a single, approximately legal-size sheet of machine-made paper, dandy-roll imprinted with a pseudo-laid pattern and a "Britannia" watermark. The paper was a light blue color—known to manuscript experts, ironically, as "Lincoln blue," due to the large number of legal pleadings Lincoln wrote on such paper (Nickell 2003a, 88)—and the previously folded sheet appeared to be consistent with paper from the period in question. However, under ultraviolet light, the paper brightly fluoresced, unlike numerous old documents from my reference collection, including several sheets of Lincoln blue. Moreover, the fluorescence was spotty, giving the document the appearance of having been swabbed, possibly indicating that it had been resized (a step used by forgers to prevent "feathering" of new ink on old paper) or that a chemical had been applied to "age" the ink.

I tested the ink by viewing it with ultraviolet and infrared illumination. Under both, its appearance was consistent with an iron-gallotannate variety, but it seemed somewhat dimmer under the infrared light than expected. The fluorescence shown by the ultraviolet light may have masked any contact traces of writing often found in old folded documents due to offsetting, caused by the corrosiveness of the iron-gall ink.

Also suspicious was the presence of anomalous folds in addition to the main ones: the sheet had been folded in half and then in half again, with the folds running across its width. The two extra folds ran the length of the sheet (one near each edge). Here and there, on each side of the document, some of the ink had spread into a fold, indicating that the paper had been folded before being written on. This suggested that an old sheet had been recycled for this use, as did the fact that neither long edge of the paper was original.

Under stereomicroscopic examination, the handwriting, done with a steel pen, exhibited considerable tremor that I associated with "forger's tremor," caused by being slowly drawn rather than swiftly penned. It was evident, for example, in the *D* of "David Wills." However, Chris Coover of Christie's auction house told Ostendorf (quoted in Warren 1990–1991, 12): "Shakiness in handwriting often is evidence of forgery. But in this case, if the tremor appears in other authentic Lincoln letters and documents of the period, it might in fact, serve to confirm authenticity of your find. A 24 November 1863 letter from Lincoln to Seward was sold recently at Christie's. It showed the same shaky qualities because Lincoln had a mild case of smallpox at that period." The handwriting certainly resembled Lincoln's, but the inscription (on an outside panel of the folded sheet; see figure 4.3) exhibited a number of specific flaws. Among these were uneven slant, occasional faulty pen pressure, and a

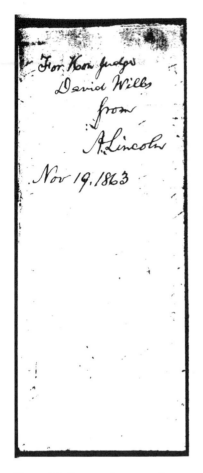

Figure 4.3. Purported autograph of Lincoln in an inscription to Judge David Wills has telltale signs of forgery. (Courtesy of Lloyd Ostendorf)

signature with glitches (including an uncharacteristically rounded second hump on the final *n*).

Taken together, all these factors pointed to forgery. The ink was subsequently tested by Roderick J. McNeil, whose scanning Auger microscopy technique for dating ink proved faulty in the case of the Jack the Ripper diary (see chapter 2). He reported to Ostendorf (quoted in Warren 1990–1991, 14–15) that "the body of the document showed a median age of 1869, plus or minus 10 years, based on seven samples measured in triplicate," making it consistent with authenticity. However, he found that the inscription had a later median age, 1875 plus or minus fifteen years, which he attributed to sampling problems. It appears to me, however, that McNeil's technique—whatever its accuracy with genuine historical documents—cannot be trusted in cases that might involve forgery. According to James Gilreath of the Library of Congress (who phoned me to discuss the Ostendorf document after he learned I had actually examined it), "Who can doubt that an enterprising and knowledgeable (or even lucky) forger might beat the McNeil test at some time in the future?" As Gilreath told Ostendorf, "McNeil's test, like every other analysis, must be used in conjunction with the full range of information about the document, and considered with a clear and open understanding of the manuscript's provenance" (quoted in Warren 1990–1991, 14).

## A Comparison of Copies

Ostendorf had brought a transparency of the questioned draft, which we superimposed over the Hay copy (version number 2, described earlier). Although it did not fit precisely, it showed a remarkable coincidence of word configurations—even with regard to the anomalous elements (e.g., an unusually heavy stroke on the second *p* of the first "people" in the next-to-last line). The effect was as if someone had copied the text.

Famed microanalyst Walter C. McCrone, of the McCrone Research Institute in Chicago, noted that the Hay and "Wills" (Ostendorf) versions of the second page "bear much more than a superficial relationship." He added, "I was surprised to see that the match was as good as it is. I can see why Nickell and others think that this must be a tracing." He was not convinced, however, noting "a fluidity and continuity" that he thought would be difficult to duplicate by tracing (McCrone 1992). Nevertheless, he recommended consultation with a handwriting expert who had experience with tracings and copies: Maureen Casey Owens (familiar to readers from chapter 2).

Owens weighed in on the issue, stating (as quoted in Warren 1990–1991, 16): "The uncanny similarity in handwriting characteristics is evident not only in form and proportions but also particularly significant in writing movements, beginnings, endings, and pen emphasis throughout the writings. Even margins and line spacings are close." She concluded, "These similarities are too striking to be coincidence and are highly suggestive of simulation." In her opinion, the writing quality and details were too good for a tracing, and she thought it more likely to be "the well practiced simulation of a skilled penman." In contrast, I continue to believe that it was traced by just such a skilled penman who used more freehand smoothness than usual with a slow, careful tracing.

Owens noted another significant observation: elements of the questioned draft that were not part of the Hay copy (the careted insertion of "under God" and the signed inscription on the reverse) were wrong. As she observed, the uppercase *G* of "God" was inconsistent with other forms of that letter in the Everett, Bancroft, and Bliss copies, as well as in other Lincoln writings available for comparison. She noted similar inconsistencies in other uppercase letters—*H, N,* and *W*—in the inscription. This evidence is suggestive, since a forger would have had to look elsewhere (other than the Hay copy) to find samples of those elements and apparently did not give them the proper attention.

## Other Historical Factors

Examination of the paper and handwriting had betrayed the forger's work, but there was even more evidence from the historical record. For example, Wills family historian Michael McKee—a great-great-grandson of David Wills—observed that Wills had not been appointed a judge—as he is referred to in the inscription of the Ostendorf copy—until 1871. In 1863 he was only a justice of the peace, although a justice might have been called "judge" in practice (Warren 1990–1991, 11).

In addition, if Lincoln had indeed autographed the document on the day of the address, as it indicates, why would Wills have written later, on November 23, to request it? It might be argued that Lincoln had backdated the inscription, but if so, then Wills ought to have mentioned that he had it when, in about 1889, he signed a statement for Charles McCurdy (quoted in full in Warren 1990–1991, 10):

> I was President of the Soldiers' National Cemetery Association at Gettysburg, having organized the Association in July, 1863, shortly after the Battle.
>
> I had charge of all the arrangements for the dedication of the Cemetery, and it was on my official invitation that President Lincoln came to Gettysburg on that occasion. Edward Everett, who had been selected to deliver the oration, preceded the President several days, and was my guest. I also invited the President to my house and he arrived there on the evening of the 18th of November, 1863. After spending part of the evening in the parlors he retired to his room. Between nine and ten o'clock the President sent his servant to request me to come to his room. I went and found him with paper prepared to write,

and he said that he had just seated himself to put upon paper a few thoughts for the to-morrow's exercises, and had sent for me to ascertain what part he was to take in them, and what was expected of him.

Wills continued:

> About eleven o'clock he sent for me again, and when I went to his room he had the same paper in his hand, and asked me if he could see Mr. Seward. I told him Mr. Seward was staying with my neighbor, next door, and I would go and bring him over. He said "No, I'll go and see him." He went and I went with him, and Mr. Lincoln carried the paper on which he had written his speech with him, and we found Mr. Seward, and I left the President with him. In less than half an hour Mr. Lincoln returned with the same paper in his hand. The next day I sat by him on the platform when he delivered his address, which has become immortal, and he read it from the same paper on which I had seen him writing it the night before. He afterwards made a copy of it, of which I have a fac simile and have had a photograph of it taken. There are but two or three changes in this copy from that as taken by the stenographers on the day it was read from the platform.

The facsimile Wills referred to was a photo of the Bliss copy (Warren 1990–1991, 10).

Moreover, if the book in which the "Wills" (Ostendorf) copy of the address had been found—the 1865 volume *The Lincoln Memorial*—had belonged to Wills, it uncharacteristically lacked the inscription of his name found in most of his books. This was pointed out by McKee, who also noted that Wills was not known to file documents in books and in fact scrupulously maintained proper files of his considerable correspondence.

## The Forger

As the evidence demonstrates, a forger seized on the fact that the reading copy of Lincoln's Gettysburg Address was missing and decided to bring it to light as a forgery. Lacking two sheets of appropriate paper, he made a single one do, probably obtaining it from the blank second half of a two-page folio. He resized the paper and smoothly traced the necessary last lines from the Hay copy, careting in "under God" as a clever touch. He penned an inscription on the back to "Judge" Wills, then chemically treated the sheet to artificially age the iron-based ink. Lacking any provenance for the creation, he reverted to the trick of placing it in a book where it was to be presumed to have reposed for 127 years.

Who was the forger? Warren (1990–1991, 7) noted, "It's unlike any known Lincoln forgery." Regarding a rather obvious suspect, "the notorious, talented forger, and convicted murderer, Mark Hoffman [*sic*]," Warren insisted that "Hoffman was incarcerated in 1987, too long ago to have done this piece; forgers do want to cash in on their work promptly." Therefore, Hofmann "was discounted quickly" as a suspect.

But wait: If we can believe that an authentic Lincoln document supposedly remained hidden for 127 years, why is it so difficult to imagine that a Hofmann "Lincoln" failed to surface for a mere three or four years? In fact, a Hofmann "Emily Dickinson" poem did not appear until much later (Worrall 2002, 4, 23).

Could Hofmann have forged the Ostendorf copy of the Gettysburg Address? The forger's modus operandi in that case was exactly the same as that of Mark Hofmann. And Hofmann's output was enormous, eventually involving works purportedly by such historical characters as Betsy Ross, Daniel Boone, Abraham Lincoln, Billy the Kid, and 125 others. He penned hitherto unknown letters, placed posthumous autographs in old books, and even created early printed documents. According to one writer, "A favorite strategy was to forge a document that was known to have existed but had disappeared" (Worrall 2002, 151)—the very scenario behind Ostendorf's Gettysburg Address.

To deal with the troubling issue of provenance, Hofmann used a variety of techniques. One of these was the so-called dead-man provenance—that is, to claim that a document had come from a dealer or some other person who had since died (as Mike Barrett did with the Jack the Ripper diary). Another dodge was the one Hofmann used for a forged Mormon document called the Anthon transcript: he simply claimed that the man he had purchased it from did not wish his identity to be revealed (a fairly common practice in the antiques and collectibles trade, usually for tax purposes or because of publicity or security concerns). Still another ploy (also used for the Anthon transcript) was to "discover" the item in an old book (a Bible, in that instance) (Worrall 2002, 43, 101, 102). After Hofmann became notorious, dealers tended to omit his name from the provenance, no doubt rationalizing that because Hofmann often sold genuine documents, it was unfair for one to be branded spurious just because it had passed through Hofmann's hands.

That Mark Hofmann had the skills necessary to forge the Ostendorf Gettysburg Address is certain. Consider, for example, his "Oath of a Free Man," known to historians as the first example of printing in America, although no actual specimen of the printed text had ever come to light. Then, in the mid-1980s, when the young Hofmann's talent for discovering long-lost treasures was at its zenith, first one and then another copy surfaced. Despite the suspicions naturally raised by this equivalent of lightning striking twice, and despite other warning signs, including a lack of provenance and anomalies in the typography, one scientist concluded that the ink's bonding to the paper was consistent with an age of some 300 years—supposedly proof that the document was authentic.

As it happened, however, Hofmann had used some pioneering techniques to produce amazingly authentic-looking fake historical documents. To create the "Oath," he researched early-seventeenth-century printing; obtained a blank sheet of seventeenth-century laid paper from a book; made ink from carbon (using burned paper of the correct date in case a carbon 14 test was done), boiled linseed oil, tannic acid, and beeswax; had a printing plate made from a pasteup of the text, using cutout letters from the contemporary Bay Psalm Book; "aged" the metal letters by grinding and rubbing to simulate wear on the type; and inked and pressed the plate. He created a false provenance by forging a bookstore receipt, then convinced a clerk that she remembered the item. As Hofmann told investigators, "By the time I forged the 'Oath,' I considered myself a pretty good forger. I thought I had a pretty good knowledge of different techniques that would be used in analyzing it" (quoted in Naifeh and Smith 1988, 437, 546–47).

Similarly, in creating the Anthon transcript, Hofmann obtained the right paper by excising an end sheet from an 1830s biblical history text. He then dipped the sheet into a hot gelatin solution to resize the paper so the fresh ink would not "feather." He made iron-gall ink according to a recipe in a German book he had stolen from the Utah State Library, and with it he carefully drew the hieroglyphics supposedly revealed on gold plates to Mormon prophet Joseph Smith. Then he washed off the gelatin and applied hydrogen peroxide to turn the ink brown. He added other touches, creating "foxing" (rustlike patches on old paper) by spraying the manuscript with milk and gelatin, followed by heating with an iron. He even used the iron to cause acid in the transcript's paper to bleed into the pages of the Bible in which it was allegedly found, thus creating browning like that which would occur over time (Worrall 2002, 100–101).

Despite such attention to detail, however, Hofmann's work was imperfect. With the "Oath of a Free Man," typographical anomalies would prove fatal, enabling scholars to demonstrate the document's spuriousness despite scientific pronouncements to the contrary. For example, printing experts observed that there was an overlapping of descenders (the tails of letters such as *j*) with ascenders (letters such as *b* and *d*) in the following line. Such overlapping would not happen with authentic hand-set type, wherein each line is self-contained (Sillitoe and Roberts 1988, 299–318, 546; "Scandal in America" 1988). In the case of the Anthon transcript, the brown staining on the document "had ridges consistent with scorching done by a hand iron," among other problems (Throckmorton 1988, 531).

Just such a mixture of cleverness and error characterizes the work of the best forgers, Hofmann being no exception. Everything about Ostendorf's Gettysburg Address—the "discovery" of a lost sensational document, the found-in-a-book-by-someone-who-wishes-to-remain-anonymous provenance, the skilled penmanship, the "aged" writing materials—points to Mark Hofmann. If it is not his work, then it is that of his equally evil twin.

# Chapter 5

# AN OUTLAW'S SCRIBBLINGS

A JAIL NOTEBOOK containing the purported writings of legendary outlaw Billy the Kid and his nemesis Pat Garrett surfaced more than a century after Billy's death. It was certainly a sensational item, and I was commissioned to determine whether it was real or fake.

## Historical Background

Billy the Kid was a common outlaw—a rustler, horse thief, and gunfighter—with an engaging personality. His brief and tragic life (1859–1881) made him the stuff of legend. Born in New York City as Henry McCarty, he moved west with his family as a teenager. He later took the name of his stepfather, becoming Henry Antrim, before adopting the alias William H. Bonney and gaining infamy as Billy the Kid.

He was drawn into New Mexico's bloody Lincoln County war. Eventually indicted for murder, he reneged on his bargain with Governor Lew Wallace to testify against others in return for a pardon. He later fled custody and was captured by Sheriff Pat Garrett and lodged in the "squalid" jail at Mesilla. Tried in "a rundown adobe building" and sentenced to hang, he was afterward confined in a room in the new Lincoln Courthouse (a former store), from which he escaped, killing his two guards in the process. Garrett eventually tracked Billy to a ranch, where he was shot and killed under circumstances that are still disputed (Utley 1989).

Another controversy involved an album containing alleged writing by Billy, Garrett, and others, as well as a framed page with a letter signed "WH Bonney." (Another page—bearing another "Bonney" letter—had reportedly been removed from the album.) The owner of these items,

80

George E. "Polka" Scott, stated that he had obtained the album from Tom Dooley, "a world-renowned western artist" and "a western antique dealer/collector." Dooley reportedly obtained it from a "buddy" known as "Woody," who was "purportedly a heavy gambler." Woody allegedly discovered it in the drawer of a dresser belonging to his late mother-in-law. Scott paid for the "notebook" (as it was called) "in trade for a Sioux Ghost Dance shirt and cowboy chaps from London that had been part of the Buffalo Bill Wild West Show in the early 1900s" (Scott 2004a).

Pasted on the inside front cover of the album was a three-by-five-inch ruled index card bearing an unsigned, hand-printed text headed "Family History of Mesilla Sheriff's Book owned by Eusavio Gonzalez" (see figure 5.1). It states: "Eusavio Gonzalez was born in Las Vegas, N. Mex. in 1859. He knew 'Billy the Kid' as they were the same age. Gonzalez worked doing errands for Mesilla Sheriff's Office. When his daughter Mary Gonzalez Martin, passed away in Mar. 2000, this book was found in her effects." Note that the passive-voice construction "was found" avoids stating who discovered the book. Presumably, this person was "Woody," but even so, that is only an alleged provenance. In fact, Scott (2004a) reported a contrary claim as to the provenance of the album, citing the efforts of appraiser and collector Stephen Elliott of Tombstone, Arizona:

> Elliott through his contacts discovered that the old Mesilla courthouse buildings were renovated and cleaned out of historical documents about ten to twelve years before the jail notebook was traded to me. Among the historical items was a cabinet of old documents that were to be taken to the State Archives by police officers. But allegedly some of the personnel doing the moving kept some of the documents, the jail notebook being one of these. A friend of Elliott's knows the man who took the Mesilla Jail Notebook and they often discussed it. Therefore, this would dispute Woody's claim of [it] belonging to his mother-in-law. Woody does have trading partners in New Mexico.

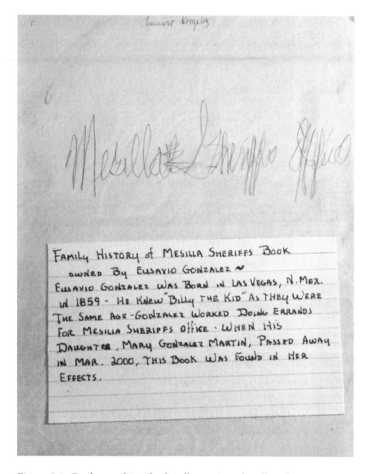

Figure 5.1. Card pasted inside the album gives the alleged provenance of the Mesilla sheriff's book.

Hypothetically, Woody may have gotten the jail notebook in a trade and realized it had been pilfered—waiting years till the statute of limitations expired and used [his] mother-in-law as an excuse.

Conflicting stories as to provenance represent grounds for suspicion, but they do not by themselves constitute proof of theft or forgery. Scott (2004b) later wrote to say that Elliott had contacted a man—unnamed—who had allegedly seen a book of that description "twelve years past." This is hearsay at best and does not authenticate the book. The man might have seen a "Mesilla" autograph book or one converted into a forged "jail notebook."

## The Album

The album measures approximately 18 by 21.5 cm overall (about 7 by 8⅜ inches). It has padded covers of red velvet, and the gilt-edged leaves are hand-numbered in ink. Pages 7, 10, and 11 bear handwritten entries, and page 25 features a cartoon of a prisoner behind bars at "Hotel Mesilla" (see figure 5.2). Written in pencil on the inside front cover are the words "Mesilla Sheriffs Office."

In basic form, the book is an autograph or a sentiment album—not a photograph album, postcard album, ledger, blank book, or notebook. Stylistically, it seems to match such albums from the late nineteenth or early twentieth century. It might be consistent with the purported 1881 date, except that on the cover is the faint word "MESILLA," with traces of "gold" still on the lettering (as shown by stereomicroscopic examination). The form of the letters indicates that the album was commercially imprinted with the word (as opposed to "MESILLA" having been hand-printed by its purchaser). Thus, we have a commercial autograph album that was apparently sold as a souvenir of Mesilla, New Mexico. However, during the period in question, Mesilla was a frontier "Hispanic village" (Utley 1989, 5), not a tourist destination, dating the album from a later period.

An indication that the Mesilla book was originally used for its intended purpose—as an autograph or a sentiment album—is found on the back of page 16 and the front of page 17. Those pages contain some brown stains that resemble Rorschach ink-blot designs and are surely the imprints of pressed flowers, which were in the album for a long time. The presence of these floral imprints, along with the fact of removed pages, suggests that this sentiment album was converted into

Figure 5.2. Cartoon in the purported jail notebook or sheriff's book.

a pseudo–jail book. Also suspicious is the fact that the front flyleaf (of heavy embossed paper) was removed—possibly because it contained a statement of ownership or some other unwanted trace.

The hand-numbering of the pages seems unusual for an autograph album. If the intent was to convert it to a record book of some kind, then why was it used so cavalierly to dispense paper for notes or letters? It might be suggested that pages were removed because paper was scarce on the frontier, but it seems to me that plush-velvet autograph albums sold as souvenirs of Mesilla would be even more scarce. I have never seen a sheriff's office book improvised from an autograph album or a sheriff's book used in this way. Certainly, there have been instances of genuine old books being used for forgery, notably the blank notebooks used to produce the "Hitler diaries" and a scrapbook transformed into a "Jack the Ripper diary" (Nickell 1996a, 34–35, 45–48).

The paper of the album showed nothing definitive as to authenticity. It was a machine-made, wove variety without a watermark. I obtained a small sample (from the remaining stub of a removed leaf) and examined it with the use of Herzberg's stain and a microscope. I identified the presence of wood pulp—specifically, I discovered tracheids (cells) of angiosperms. Ground wood pulp used for paper was first produced commercially in the United States in 1867 (Nickell 2003a, 201). Ultraviolet examination showed the absence of optical brighteners; their presence would have indicated manufacture after 1950 (Nickell 1996a, 156).

## The Ink

The ink of the album and that of the framed letter from Bonney to Wallace had been tested by a professional ink chemist before my investigation. Scott had offered the items for sale through John Gangel's Little John's Auction, and appraiser Warren Anderson had raised some suspicions. As a result, Gangel had submitted the items to Federal Forensic Associates Inc., where chemist Albert H. Lyter III used a variety of analytical techniques, including thin-layer chromatography (this necessitated punching pinhead-size holes out of the paper, which I discovered during my own examination).

Among the forensic findings was that four different inks had been used in the writings, none of which contained iron, "a common component in inks of this time period." The writing of the framed Bonney letter and that on page 10 of the album were from an ink formulation with "characteristics similar to dye based fountain pen ink, which were routinely commercially available in the 1920's." Writings on pages 7, 11, and 25 "also contained characteristics of dye based fountain pen ink. It is likely that these writings were not prepared in 1881 as suggested" (Lyter 2003).

Lyter (2003) noted: "The ink on page 7 . . . was blue in color and consistent with standard formulations manufactured by Papermate and Parker with commercial availability dates from the 1960's and 1970's." The blue ink on page 7 was not from the extant writings on that page but was found in traces of writing that had been scraped off with a sharp blade. It was a very bright blue and may have been removed because, applied on the page, it did not look like an old ink. Oblique lighting showed the indented traces of this writing. Remnants of this blue ink were also found in the inside front cover, above the penciled "Mesilla Sheriffs Office." However, what appeared to have been an *M*—as if to write "Mesilla," possibly in the same hand as the penciled works—had been partially erased. Lyter (2003) added that the ink of the page number on page 25, "and most likely on the other page numbers, was brown in color and consistent with standard ink formulations having commercial availability dates in the 1950's."

Lyter's report has been criticized by album defender Stephen K. Elliott (2003). Elliott faulted Lyter for being only "an expert on inks of the 20th Century—not the 19th Century." Actually, Lyter was involved in the Hofmann case and helped conduct numerous experiments with iron-gall ink (Throckmorton 1988, 532). Besides, the inks in the questioned album were found to be from the twentieth century, so Lyter's expertise applied. Lyter was also correct about the prevalence of iron-based inks during the period in question. Elliott cited Kenneth Rendell's *Forging History* (1994, 27) regarding aniline inks being invented in 1856; however, Elliott (2003) concluded that "no iron based inks would have been used after the 1860's," which is absurd, since dye inks did not *replace* iron inks but only joined them (see Nickell 2003a, 35–39; Osborn 1978, 450). Rendell never said otherwise. Are we to imagine that there was a genius ink chemist on the frontier who invented certain formulations decades ahead of their known manufacture?

I reviewed Lyter's report, which Scott also questioned. I decided to test the brown ink of the "Bonney" writing on page 10 of the album, lifting a sample onto chromatography paper dampened with distilled water. It transferred surprisingly easily (and thus suspiciously) and tested negative for iron (using hydrochloric acid digestion followed by potassium ferrocyanide reagent). The ink thus had the characteristics of a brown-colored ink and not a black iron-based ink that had turned brown with age through oxidation.

The availability of a brown-colored ink in 1881—especially on the western frontier—seems very unlikely. It could well be that the forger used brown ink to avoid the difficulty of having to artificially age an iron ink and thus transform it from black to brown. This is such a common forger's technique that expert Charles Hamilton (1996, 129) referred to brown ink (specifically Waterman's brand) as "the forger's friend."

A significant aspect of the ink in the Mesilla jail book is what is known as "feathering," the spreading of ink into the fibers of the paper. It is especially noticeable in the first line of the framed letter. According to Mary A. Benjamin (1986, 151–52):

> When paper, acting in a manner somewhat similar to that of a blotter, unduly absorbs ink, there is cause for suspicion. A good grade of freshly manufactured paper, of any period, is rarely soggy. Ink used on it leaves a fine, clean impression. This same paper in aging, however, and especially if subjected to dampness and mildew, becomes readily absorbent. Ink of a later date, when applied to it, tends to spread in being absorbed, but it will for this very reason not run. The effect differs widely in appearance from the clearly defined pen stroke made by the original signer at a time contemporary with the publication of the printed material or not too long thereafter. Forgeries may often be spotted because the fraudulent overlook these facts.

Rendell (1994, 28) observed that feathering could occur in a genuine writing "in unusual circumstances"—which I considered and eliminated—but "it is generally an immediate indication of forgery." In my opinion, it is an indication of forgery in the case of the "Bonney" writings.

## The Handwriting

Writings attributed to William H. Bonney include an 1878 bill of sale for a "sorrel hosse" (horse), owned by the Panhandle-Plains Historical Museum in Canyon, Texas (Utley 1989, illus. 19), and an 1881 letter to Governor Lew Wallace requesting a meeting, owned by the Indiana Historical Society (reproduced in Hamilton 1979, 89). Pat Garrett observed of Billy that he "wrote a fair letter" (Hamilton 1979, 88), and even in facsimile, these specimens showed a serviceable handwriting of the period. They had the qualities associated with natural writing, including "flying" starts and endings (tapered strokes resulting from the pen being in motion before it touches the paper) and hairline upstrokes and shaded downstrokes (the latter caused by the points of the pen separating with pressure to produce accented lines), among other characteristics (see Nickell 1996a, 38). In contrast, the questioned Bonney writings were unnatural and exhibited signs of "forger's tremor"—a result of the slowly produced nature of the script. In brief, they had been *drawn* rather than freely written (see figures 5.3 and 5.4). (For a discussion of forger's tremor, see Osborn 1978, 110–12.) Other evidence of slow drawing includes an uneven base line, with an upward tendency of many words (discussed in Osborn 1978, 103), which was evident in the framed "Bonney" letter I examined (bearing a date of March 14, 1881).

It has been suggested that the handwriting quality was diminished by Bonney's having been in handcuffs or, alternatively, that he could not have written at all because of being fettered (Scott 2002). Neither view is correct, in my opinion. I experimented with writing in handcuffs and found that one can certainly do so. Although there is some effect on the writing, it by no means necessitates the result seen in the "Bonney" writing. Indeed, while many things can cause "bad handwriting," that particular effect is, in my opinion, due to forgery; coupled with the "feathering" of the ink, described earlier, forgery is clearly demonstrated.

Presumably, Sheriff Garrett was not wearing handcuffs when *he* wrote, yet when his purported note and signature are compared with known exemplars (Hamilton 1979, 89; see figure 5.5), it is clear that

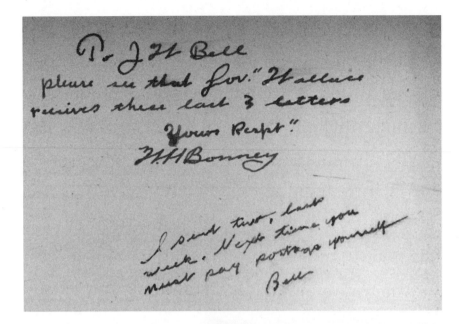

(Above) Figure 5.3. Writing (at top) is purportedly by "W. H. Bonney"—Billy the Kid—but has the signs of an inept forgery.

(Right) Figure 5.4. Blunt endings, "forger's tremor," and ink feathering are among the signs of an amateurish forgery.

they were slowly drawn, resulting in blunt endings and forger's tremor. This "Garrett" writing is clearly unnatural, a poor-quality forgery that provides evidence of its own spuriousness (see figure 5.6).

In addition, the pencil writing on the album's inside front cover, "Mesilla Sheriffs Office," looks like nothing so much as *disguised* writing. With such features as a peculiar *S* (resembling a *G*), mismatched lowercase *s*'s, adventitious strokes on the *ff* combinations, and elongated, crowded letters, the script is unconvincing as a natural handwriting of the period in question.

Territory of New Mexico }
County of Lincoln } SS.
I hereby certify that on the
16th Day of September A.D.
1881. At Tularosa in the
County of Don Ana. I
executed the within writ
by arresting the body of
the within named Jose
Zamora who afterwards
Gave bonds in the sum of
$500.00
Pat F. Garrett
Sheriff

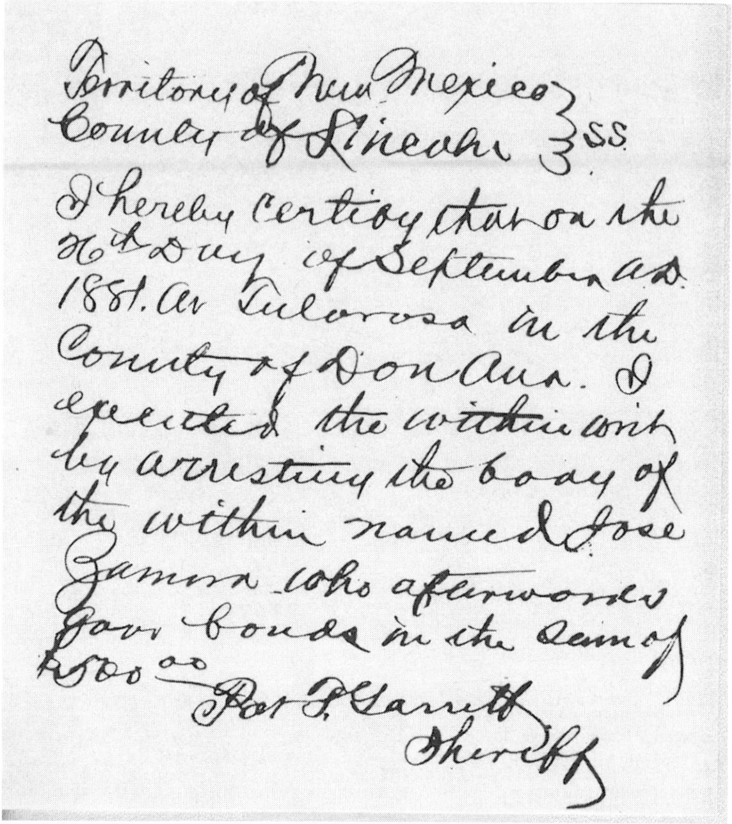

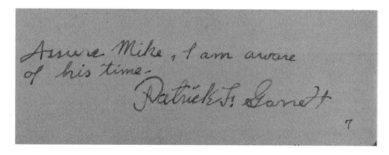

Figure 5.5. Authentic writing of Pat Garrett is far superior to the slowly drawn imitation shown in figure 5.6.

Assure Mike, I am aware
of his time.
Patrick F. Garrett
7

Figure 5.6. Alleged Garrett writing was obviously not penned by the famous sheriff.

## Suspicions Confirmed

Before I examined the album, several other people had already raised doubts about it. A historian at a commercial museum stated, "One of the enigmas is that all of the entries appear to have been made in Santa Fe while the cover clearly has the word 'Mesilla' on it." An East Coast dealer was suspicious because, he said, "In my 25 years of dealing with historical documents I have never seen a 'Billy the Kid' signature or document" (Scott 2002). Appraiser Warren Anderson (2001) proclaimed the items "phony as a three dollar bill," even though he never examined the originals. The National Civil War Museum's curatorial staff examined the album, "notably the signature purported to be that of William Bonney," but their results were "inconclusive" (Reed 2001).

Following my examination, I concluded that, taken together, the various findings with regard to provenance, ink, and handwriting point unmistakably to a forgery—and a rather unskillful forgery at that.

*Chapter 6*

# OUT OF THE ARCHIVES

NOT ALL CASES of questioned historical writings are as sensational as the ones examined thus far, but even lesser documents and manuscripts can have great significance to the collector, archivist, and historian. They can present puzzles as profound as any and deserve their "day in court." Here is a selection of such cases from my files.

## More Hofmanns

As indicated in the previous chapter, anything sold by the notorious forger Mark Hofmann carries the taint of suspicion—one that many have ignored at their peril. For example, just two weeks after Hofmann was arrested for murders he had committed in an attempt to cover up his crimes, Sotheby's auction house sold a rare Daniel Boone letter for $31,900. It was accompanied by an inspiring tale of Boone's frontier heroism, but there was more to the letter than met the eye. As it happened, it had been consigned by Salt Lake City businessman Kenneth Woolley, who turned out to be Hofmann's cousin. Not only was the letter a forgery, but according to Simon Worrall (2002, 56–57), "If anyone had looked closely they might also have noticed that the letter was dated April 1."

My involvement with Mark Hofmann began with his prosecution by the Salt Lake City district attorney's office. Eminent manuscript dealer Charles Hamilton, one of my mentors, was acting as a consultant to the prosecutors. Hamilton had written the foreword to my *Pen, Ink, & Evidence* (Nickell 1990, vii), in which he stated, "had I owned this volume sixty years ago, it would have enormously eased my entry into the manuscript world and spared me countless hours of trial and error in deciphering old scripts and identifying forgeries, as well as adding a more polished background to my court testimony as an expert in forensic documents."

In preparing to bring Hofmann to trial, and at the personal recommendation of Hamilton, prosecutor Gerry D'Elia telephoned me at the University of Kentucky about the suspected forgeries that were central to the case. D'Elia was interested in what I could tell him about iron-gallotannate ink—specifically, how it could be made and aged artificially. I went over the natural ingredients and the traditional procedure— soaking crushed oak galls in rainwater to extract tannic and gallic acids, straining the resulting decoction, mixing it with copperas (hydrated ferrous sulfate) to cause a chemical reaction that yields a black color, and adding gum arabic (acacia gum) to increase viscosity and act as a binder (see Nickell 1990, 37, for a photo essay on this procedure). I also told D'Elia how one could make a similar ink using an ordinary chemistry set or even improvise an iron-gall ink from household items, such as using instant tea for the tannic acid.

Then our discussion turned to "old" iron-gall ink as it typically appears on historical documents. How, D'Elia inquired, would one artificially age the ink I had just described to simulate such rust-colored writing? I explained that there are basically two methods. One involves heating (slowly baking the document), which might give the paper itself a browned and suspicious appearance. The other uses chemicals. He indicated that Hofmann had apparently used the latter because, under ultraviolet light, the document looked as if it had been dipped in some solution and then hung up to dry. I told D'Elia that two chemicals would "age" the ink suitably: hydrogen peroxide and ammonium hydroxide. A forensic report on the Hofmann documents, which were compared with some 6,000 historical documents used as standards, stated (Throckmorton 1988, 533):

Entire Hofmann documents were found to exhibit a certain discoloration under ultra-violet light. Our questions thus became: Why had these documents been chemically treated and with

93

what chemical(s)? Many possible answers were considered. In the end it was determined that hydrogen peroxide and ammonium hydroxide could cause the characteristics exhibited by these Hofmann documents. These two chemicals cause rapid oxidation of the iron in iron-gall ink and also cause a slight blue-hazing effect on the paper itself. There is no reason why genuine nineteenth-century documents would legitimately be treated with these chemicals. However, such chemicals artificially age the appearance of iron-gall ink. Only those documents which coming [sic] from Hofmann among the over 6,000 documents examined exhibited this blue-hazing effect.

A book on Hofmann's crimes pointed out that a certain manuscript expert, one of many who had been deceived by the forger, "was not a trained forensic document examiner" (Sillitoe and Roberts 1988, 109). However, even the FBI laboratory had been unable to uncover evidence that one of Hofmann's sensational Mormon documents—the so-called white salamander letter—was a forgery. I later spotted it as a fake from a photograph—it had been folded incorrectly for a pre-envelope cover. I reported this to D'Elia in a letter of March 28, 1986, while Hamilton and forensic examiners were preparing their case against Hofmann (Nickell 1990, 188).

As indicated in chapter 4, I now believe that the Ostendorf Gettysburg Address was probably a Hofmann production. And in 1993, I came in contact with other works by the prolific forger. During the annual meeting of the Manuscript Society in Albuquerque, I headed a symposium on forgery that included Walter McCrone and an expert from the U.S. Secret Service. I was approached by a man who had known Hofmann and had purchased several documents from him. He asked for my help in sorting out the real from the fake, and I agreed to the task.

Among the half dozen documents, I immediately spotted a Hofmann forgery. It was a promissory note dated October 5, 1852, and signed by famed mountain man James Bridger with his "mark" and by Louis Vasquez, with William H. Hooper as witness. I focused on the Hooper

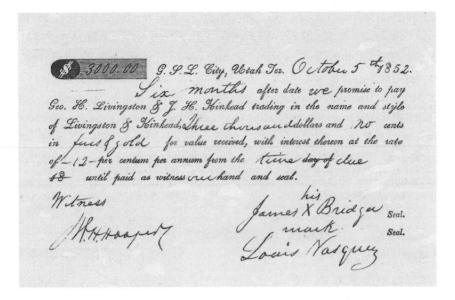

Figure 6.1. Forger Mark Hofmann created all types of fake American documents, including this bogus promissory note "signed" by famed mountain man Jim Bridger. (Courtesy of Steven Barnett)

signature, comparing it with known Hooper standards as well as with Hofmann forgeries of the same, and determined that it was the latter. Hofmann had failed to capture the quality of line (especially the distinct contrast between hairlines and shaded strokes) evident in the genuine signatures (see figure 6.1).

Most of the other documents were of modest value, including a J. R. R. Tolkien letter that I authenticated on the basis of the freely penned writing in Tolkien's distinctive calligraphic hand and by the use of correctly watermarked and printed Tolkien stationery. For the latter, I consulted an archivist at a college repository of Tolkien papers.

One document came in for special scrutiny: a small list of marriages recorded and signed by Cotton Mather in 1715. The paper was watermarked and consistent with a known example from 1704. The ink, confirmed as iron-gall by microchemical tests, appeared to show signs of genuine age, such as ink corrosion resulting in cracks of light showing through the paper in two heavily inked areas. A particle embedded in the ink was examined using polarized light microscopy at the University of Kentucky geological laboratory by Warren Anderson. He confirmed my identification of mica, which I interpreted as evidence of writing sand (used to dry ink before the mid-nineteenth century). Stereomicroscopic inspection revealed a jotted-down appearance of quickly written script produced by a quill pen. There were no signs of forgery, and—significantly—the provenance could be traced prior to Hofmann. Two distinguished experts, familiar with Hofmann's forgeries, thought it was genuine, as did I. Hofmann was good, but not that good (Nickell 1994b).

## Charles Dickens's Notes

Did famed English author Charles Dickens record the title of a major novel, along with the name of one of its characters, four years before he actually composed the story? In a semblance of Dickens's distinctive script, both "Great Expectations" and "Magwitch" (the surname of Pip's benefactor in the tale) appear in blue ink on the flyleaf of an old dictionary, along with the date—1856 (see figure 6.2). Because of the implications to literary criticism, noted Dickens scholar Jerome Meckier (one of my former professors) asked me to help settle this interesting controversy.

The issue arose in 1986 when Dick Hoefnagel labeled the flyleaf notations "An Early Hint of *Great Expectations*." This was significant because it meant that the story and title had not first occurred to Dickens in September–October 1860, as he himself had claimed. Hoefnagel believed that the dictionary—a copy of Samuel Johnson's *Dictionary of the English Language* (in the Special Collections of the Dartmouth College Library)—had been Dickens's own. Conversely, Kathleen Tillotson (1987) accepted the notations as authentic but rejected Dickens's monogram "C. D.," the address "Tavistock House / London W. C.," and the year "1856"—which she insisted had been added by "an imitator." In her opinion, the notes were not evidence of an "early dating of the author's plans for his 1860 novel."

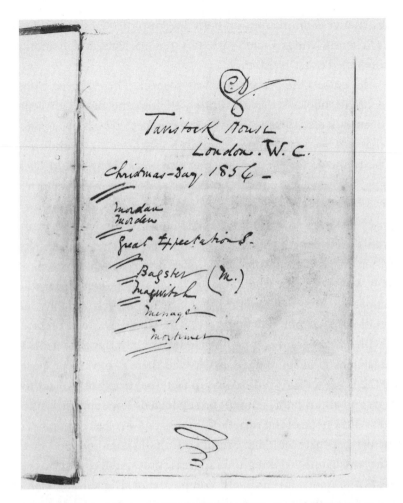

Figure 6.2. Flyleaf of a copy of Samuel Johnson's *Dictionary* of 1825, bearing alleged notes by Charles Dickens. (Photograph by University of Kentucky Photographic Services)

My examination of the dictionary was facilitated by Stanley Brown, Dartmouth's curator of rare books, who graciously entrusted the volume to the University of Kentucky's special collections library so that I could examine it there. I was able to study the notations and compare them with several authentic writings by Dickens in Kentucky's own collection, and I performed stereomicroscopic, infrared, ultraviolet, and other nondestructive examinations on both. I also studied facsimiles of many other Dickens writings, including letters, manuscripts, and memoranda, and conducted other research.

At the outset, the provenance was suspect. There proved to be no record of the book's existence until well into the twentieth century. Significantly, it also lacked either Dickens's expected bookplate or a sales label that had been placed in each of his books after his death in 1870.

The rationale for the writing was also weak. Why would Dickens not once but repeatedly make notes—as suggested by the alternation of two different blue inks—when he had a memorandum book for that purpose? The lines "Bagster (M.)" and "Magwitch" are written in an ink that vanishes when viewed under infrared light, whereas the remainder is written in an ink that darkens under infrared light (Nickell 1989, 163–64). Moreover, why would one of Dickens's notations ("Magwitch") also appear in the memorandum book, while others (notably, "Great Expectations") do not? Furthermore, why would Dickens preface his *notes* with a monogram and mailing address? Or, if those elements were added later, as Tillotson suggested, why was there a convenient space left above the notes for those additions? In fact, the theory of two authors—Dickens and an imitator—cannot be supported. The supposed different portions show none of the variations in ink, pen strokes, or handwriting characteristics that would have resulted from dual authorship.

The amalgam of monogram, address, notes, and gratuitous spiral dingbat represents an unlikely composite of Dickensian elements compiled from disparate sources and times. For example, the "Tavistock House" does not match the particular configuration of those words found in authentic Dickens letters of the same period. As to the appearance of these elements on the flyleaf of a book, forgers have commonly used that strategy.

Although written with a quill in two different blue inks and in a writing imitative of Dickens's, the work actually exhibits unmistakable signs of forgery (see figure 6.3). The script has been drawn rather than written, and "forger's tremor" is evident throughout. Although, compared with the steel pen, the quill is more forgiving of retouchings,

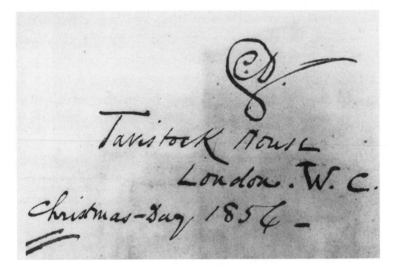

Figure 6.3. Detail of figure 6.2 showing that the script, particularly the
"C. D." monogram, is drawn rather than written.

various pen lifts, retracings, and patchings can be seen. These are most
obvious in the "C. D." monogram, leading a previous seller to conclude
that it "and probably other words are evidently in a hand other than
Dickens'" (quoted in Tillotson 1987, 17–18); they can also be detected in
the final *e* of "Message" and the *M* of "Mortimer."

For a second opinion on the handwriting, I submitted photographic
enlargements of some of the details to Hamilton. He concurred with my
opinion, stating, "You are right on target with the Dickens forgery. On
a scale of one to ten I'd rate this forgery about five. Not lower, because
the forger has caught pretty well the movement and vitality of Dickens's
script. Not higher because there are many obvious flaws in the forgery."
Among these flaws, he noted that "the 'forger's tremor' is obvious in
almost every letter," that "the letters are in many cases spliced," and
that "every stroke has a labored character to it"—unlike Dickens's own,
which "rolls across the page like wheat in the wind" (Hamilton 1989).

Following my report to him (Nickell 1989), Professor Meckier
(1992) published his definitive treatise on the pseudo-Dickens notations.
After a litany of telltale signs of spuriousness—lack of provenance,

doubtful context, questionable formatting, and a too-clever date, along with the forged handwriting—he concluded that the notes were the work of a single imitator. His identity is unknown, but Meckier (1992, 128–29) convincingly demonstrated that the evidence points to "a New York–based forger operating after 1902 (when the prices of Dickens material began to skyrocket) but before 1928 (after which the notes' existence is established)."

To the credit of Dartmouth, curator Brown (1992) wrote to Meckier, "Your arguments are most persuasive toward the conclusion that the purported Dickensian notes in our copy of Johnson's dictionary are a forgery." He added that the library would "adjust the cataloging" to so indicate and also separately catalog Meckier's article, "linking it to the dictionary, so the whole matter will be clear to any newcomer on the scene." This admirable scholarly response is a model, both ethical and procedural, for others to follow in similar circumstances. Brown also raised an interesting point:

> Our forger may not have been a particularly good one, but he certainly went to some pains to doctor this book, and succeeded well enough to fool quite a few people. With that in mind it seems unlikely that he didn't do likewise to other items to enhance their value. I have no notion of how many hundreds or perhaps thousands of flyleaves there are out there with inscriptions attributed to Dickens, but it seems highly probable that at least some of them are the work of our forger. Should the alarm be raised?

## Boones—Real or Otherwise

Daniel Boone is at once a justifiable quarry for collectors and an understandable one for forgers, who frequently set their sights on the famed frontiersman but often end up wide of the mark. "Boone's autographs," wrote Charles Hamilton (1996, 213) "are rare and valuable and frequently tempt forgers." He noted, "a common practice of forgers [is] to add a rare signature to an authentic old paper," such as having Boone "sign" an inexpensive document dated 1799. As shown in Hamilton's *Great Forgers and Famous Fakes* (1980, 213), it compares poorly with the real McCoy—or the real Boone, in this case.

Many Daniel Boone rarities are holographic survey documents (he was a surveyor in Kentucky for a time) or letters, mostly about land or financial transactions. One interesting but absolutely authentic letter of 1782 was not in his handwriting but had been dictated by Boone (a practice the reluctant writer took advantage of on occasion); it concerned "the intended Expedition against the Shawnese" (reproduced in Hamilton 1979, 5).

Top American document dealer Joseph Rubinfine, sought my expertise regarding Boone's handwriting in another letter he was examining. Its provenance was good, Rubinfine (1993) wrote, having been "in a Virginia collection formed in the nineteenth century—predating autograph dealers!" I went over a photocopy of the letter, which concerned a list of land parcels:

Enter 2000 akers on goos Crick about 25 milds from the mouth beginning a half mild below a high yellow Bank an old Indin Camp and 2 or 3 well painted trees. Runing up said Crick for quantity on booth sides there may be more than that quantity the botam is a half mild wid and 4 or 5 in Lenth and very good

I recognized Boone's quill-penned, round-hand script and, of course, his creative spelling. This was generally consistent and represented a phonetic version of his southern Appalachian speech. Hoaxers have often tried to mimic Boone's spelling on various artifacts—"BOoNs bESt FREN" on a rifle stock, for instance (see chapter 14)—but their carelessly conceived caricatures are typically pathetic.

As I subsequently told Rubinfine, "with the caveat that one cannot authenticate a document from a photocopy (although one may well be able to disauthenticate one), the handwriting looks good to me, as does the phonetic spelling." I also commented that the show-through on the reverse seemed consistent with the corrosiveness of ink over time and thus indicative of genuine age in such a document. Rubinfine (1993) responded, "Through your assistance I can now say that I wish everything was as easy as the Boone Letter!" I concurred.

I have already mentioned some of the forged Boone documents I have encountered: an "antiqued" photocopy (see the introduction), a letter amateurishly written in the wrong style of penmanship (see chapter 1), and the Hofmann forgery that brought $31,900 (later refunded) at Sotheby's (see earlier in this chapter). According to Worrall (2002, 199), Hofmann had once "been able to ward off his creditors by dashing off a forged inscription in a book, or faking a Daniel Boone autograph, then selling it for a few thousand dollars." Hofmann "was a poet and a magician; a conjurer of ink and paper; a ventriloquist and shape-shifter. He was Joseph Smith and Walt Whitman; Abraham Lincoln and Daniel Boone" (Worrall 2002, 162).

Boone remains a forger's target. I was once asked by a distinguished jurist to help him decide whether to purchase a Daniel Boone letter he had on approval. I met him in the law library of his office suite, and as I began to unpack my stereomicroscope and other paraphernalia, he took the document out of a briefcase and laid it on the other end of the long table (see figure 6.4).

At that point, I felt a bit like my mentor, Charles Hamilton, because as soon as the judge laid out his would-be treasure, I knew instantly it was spurious. Hamilton's obituary in the *New York Times* (Thomas 1996) spoke of his flamboyance, occasional snap judgments, and hyperbole, summing up: "If he was exaggerating a bit when he claimed he could spot a forgery from across the room, by the time he branded the so-called Hitler diaries 'patent and obvious forgeries,' in 1983, Mr. Hamilton had been proved right so many times—that even Hugh Trevor-Roper, the British historian who had authenticated them, would have to accede to his opinion." My reaction to the two Boone fakes previously mentioned had been just as instant and just as negative—one due to its ink, the other to the penmanship. This time, there were several factors that my brain analyzed in a flash. Slowed down, the thought process

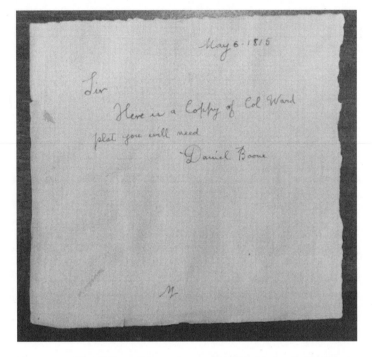

Figure 6.4. Alleged Daniel Boone letter of 1816 is on genuine old paper.

went something like this: probably genuine paper, ink of the right color, but too much wasted space around the text (I have never seen the frugal Boone use such a full sheet for such a brief text), and the handwriting is a very poor imitation.

Closer inspection did not improve the document's credibility. Although it was on a genuine sheet of handmade, watermarked laid paper of Boone's time, it lacked folds and had a surprisingly clean appearance. Its torn edges appeared to be recent, consistent with having been removed from a book. Ultraviolet light revealed a rectangular area at the top, consistent with a slip of paper having been used as a bookmark.

The writing (see figure 6.5) could not have been worse. It exhibited blunt endings and a uniformity of pressure (lack of contrasting hairline upstrokes and shaded downstrokes), giving it a slowly drawn appear-

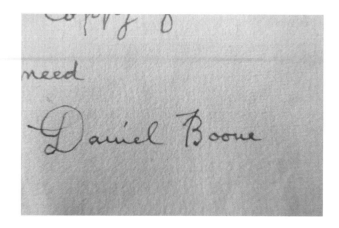

Figure 6.5. The signature exhibits blunt endings and other clear signs of forgery.

ance, complete with a lack of proper slant. The letter forms were widely off the mark. For example, the capital *C* was totally unlike Boone's, which invariably extended below the line and was separate from the rest of the word. The lowercase *d* of "need" and "Ward" lacked the final flourish typical of Boone's writing.

I learned that the document had been featured in a manuscript auction catalog. The entry stated (Cowan 1995, 13): "This note undobtedly [*sic*] relates to the financial problems Boone was experiencing in the spring of 1815 when he was forced to liquidate much of his Missouri property." It was estimated that the piece would bring $1,000 to $3,000. I was told by the judge that it had been offered to him with a word of caution: It had been questioned by a prospective bidder, leading to an inquiry, and an archivist had offered the opinion that it was not a genuine Boone writing. It had consequently been withdrawn from the auction.

Quite intrigued, the jurist looked over my shoulder as I examined the paper and its text. He studied each feature as I pointed it out and clearly understood every implication. As I compared the handwriting with facsimiles of Boone's that I had brought with me, he nodded in recognition that the questioned script was a poor simulation of Boone's. "Once you know what to look for," he said, "it becomes obvious."

A more difficult case came my way in 1984 when an antiques dealer in Georgetown, Kentucky, asked my opinion regarding a cache of thirteen Daniel Boone survey documents from the 1787 period. A hush-hush status on the provenance, together with the sheer quantity, made me suspect a forgery factory.

These were not spot-them-across-the-room fakes, however. First, the paper was absolutely genuine, handmade paper in the antique laid pattern, exhibiting a darkening along the chain lines caused by the chain wires being sewn to the mold's ribs; as a result, as the sheet is formed, the paper pulp lies more heavily along them (see Nickell 1990, 81, for a photograph). Of course, a clever forger could have obtained sheets of old paper, so this in itself could not authenticate the documents.

The texts were also completely correct, line for line, as to content and orthography (spelling). For example, one "Survaid for James Dickey" had a boundary that ran to "a hickory and Rad oke." Such spellings as "Rad" for *red* are best appreciated when read aloud, whereupon one can almost hear the frontiersman pronouncing them in his eastern mountain accent. However, a determined forger could study genuine Boone surveys, as I have done, and copy his vocabulary and spelling.

Then there was the handwriting, penned with a quill in a perfect flowing rendition of Boone's own hand, with none of the symptoms of forged writing. This was a skillful, practiced forger indeed—if the documents were actually forgeries and not the genuine rarities they appeared to be!

In time, I gave up my suspicions and recognized that these documents appeared astonishingly real because they *were*. One detail is worth noting. In each document's plat sketch—a small scale drawing of the property surveyed—was a detail that few people knew about: the presence of a pinprick at each corner of the boundary. Their purpose was simple: they facilitated making copies of the drawings. Although the text had to be written out by hand for each copy (one to the property owner, one for the surveyor's office, and so forth), the plat drawing was carefully plotted only once (using a protractor and scale). Then the pinpricks were used to transfer the corners of the boundary onto a stack of sheets placed beneath, and, in connect-the-dots fashion, the boundary lines were inked using a straightedge.

I would eventually publish this discovery (Nickell 1990, 166), but at the time, I did not expect a Boone forger to be aware of this old process. Indeed, on the questioned surveys, the pinpricks were not apparent, the paper fibers having somewhat refilled the holes over time. That detail, along with many others—the fact that everything rang true—convinced me of the authenticity of the documents. The questioned provenance was not fatal, and it was later explained. It turned out that the elderly owner's family had been secretly selling his collection to pay for his care. They had sold the documents one at a time so as not to flood the market and lower the price at auction houses.

I think Daniel Boone would have been pleased to see his authentic writings separated from the spurious ones, like wheat from chaff. Honest and fair dealing in his relationships, he would have wanted anything connected to him after his death to reflect, as he said, "a man of my pri[n]sepel" (quoted in Lofaro 1978, 129).

# PART II

## PHOTOGRAPHS

## Chapter 7

# PHOTO SLEUTHING

THE FIRST SUCCESSFUL photographs were taken in 1839, and by the mid-nineteenth century, photography had become commonplace. Following the introduction of the Brownie camera in 1900, anyone could take a snapshot. As photos proliferated, so did the questions they eventually posed: Who were the individuals in those antique family photos? Where and when were they made?

Photographs may raise many questions for the historical detective, but in terms of authentication, there are primarily two issues: (1) Is a given photograph authentic (that is, is it a genuine original, a copy, or a deliberate fake)? (2) Is the person in the photograph the actual person it is believed to be? The following discussion—adapted from my book *Camera Clues: A Handbook for Photographic Investigation* (Nickell 1994a)—covers how to identify and date old photos, identify people in photos, and distinguish originals from copies and fakes.

## Identifying and Dating Old Photos

Photographs exist in a variety of forms, posing a challenge to genealogists and historians who may need to date them for research purposes. The following brief guide may make the task less bewildering for the nonexpert.

For practical purposes, old photographs can be divided into three broad classes: photos on metal, glass-plate images, and paper prints. The earliest photographs were on polished silver-coated copper plates and are called *daguerreotypes*. They are easily recognized by their mirror-like surfaces and images that shift from positive to negative when tilted in the light (see figure 7.1). They date from 1839 to about 1860. Another

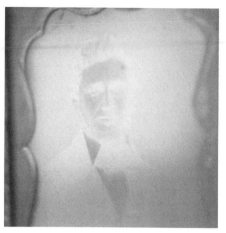

Figure 7.1. Identifying daguerreotypes is easy: their mirror-like images shift from positive (left) to negative (right) when tilted.

kind of metal-plate photo is the *tintype* (actually on a varnished iron plate, attractable by a magnet). The tintype was patented in 1856 and was used until after World War II (see figure 7.2). Both daguerreotypes and tintypes are "direct-positive" images—that is, left and right are reversed as in a mirror (unless the reversal was corrected by use of a special device, such as a prism or mirror, in front of the lens).

Glass-plate images (except for old lantern slides) are called *ambrotypes*. They are negative images but appear positive when backed with black varnish or paper. Though direct-positive images, because they were usually on clear glass, they could be reversed to correct the backward images. Ambrotypes date from about 1855 to 1865.

Instead of being backed to create an ambrotype, a glass-plate image could be used to make photographic prints on paper—as many as desired. After the picture was developed on the glass, that negative image was projected with light onto specially treated paper and chemically developed to make a positive print. Such pictures were typically mounted on card stock. Those on cards measuring about 2¼ by 4 inches were known as *cartes de visite* (from the French for "visiting cards") and were used from 1854 until about 1925 (though rare after 1905).

Larger paper-print photos, mounted on cards measuring about 4½

Figure 7.2. Like daguerreotypes and ambrotypes, tintypes are "direct-positive" images—reversed, as in a mirror. Therefore, women's and men's garments (which are buttoned oppositely) appear to be fastened backward, and wedding rings appear on the wrong hand, as in this portrait.

by 6½ inches, were called *cabinet photographs*. This practice began in 1862 but was not common until approximately 1873 and lasted until the 1930s. Card-mounted photos of other sizes were not as popular as the *cartes de visite* and cabinet pictures but existed from about 1872 until the present. Unmounted paper prints were uncommon until the late nineteenth century but proliferated after 1900.

A special type of paper photograph that is common in family collections is the very large portrait known as a *crayon enlargement*. Resembling a cross between a photo and a charcoal or pastel drawing, such pictures were produced by an enlargement process that usually required enhancement (resulting in obvious crayon strokes in hair and beard areas, outlining of the irises of the eyes, and so forth). They date from the late nineteenth and early twentieth centuries.

Dating old photographs is complicated by the fact that pictures made by one process were often copied many years later by other photo processes. For example, a paper photo of my great-great-great-grandfather, the Reverend Joseph Nickell (1792–1874), was unlikely to have been made when he was a young man, as he appears in the portrait. A washed-out appearance at the bottom probably resulted from glare on the mirror-like surface of a daguerreotype original. Likewise, a crayon enlargement of a young man in a Civil War uniform would indicate a copy. If the buttons and insignia are reversed (as in a mirror), the original photograph was likely a direct-positive picture, such as a tintype.

Dating also has a bearing on authentication. For instance, a tintype portrait depicted a young man identified as Edmund Wells (1777–1846), the founder of Morgan County, Kentucky (and my ancestor). But since Wells died before tintypes were invented, the picture was at best a copy of an earlier one. However, even the earliest daguerreotype of Wells could not have shown him as a young man, and the photo is now thought to be that of Wells's grandson of the same name.

Properly investigated, authenticated, and dated, old photographs can be treasures to those attempting to reconstruct and preserve the historical record. After the first step of identifying the photographic process that produced it, there are other useful clues to dating photos. One is the photographer's name and address, which sometimes appears inside the case holding a daguerreotype or may be printed on the front or back of a card-mounted photo. These can be researched (see Nickell 1994a, 38–40; Palmquist 1991), perhaps with the assistance of the photo archivist in the department of special collections of the nearest university library.

Another clue may be found in the style of the case or card mount, in the printing style of the *carte de visite* or other card, or in the portrait style. Some tintypes and *cartes de visite* have a revenue stamp on the back (having been among the articles taxed to raise funds during the Civil War; see figure 7.3). These were supposed to be dated as well as canceled, but the mere presence of the stamp is helpful because it dates the photo to within a twenty-three-month period from September 1, 1864, to August 1, 1866. Later photos offer other stylistic clues (see Nickell 1994a, 30–44; Darrah 1981). The serious collector or photo analyst can easily assemble a useful reference collection, as I have done, purchasing old photos that have printed or written dates and keeping

Figure 7.3. Revenue stamps were affixed to the backs of old photographs—tintypes and *cartes de visite*—from September 1, 1864, to August 1, 1866.

them chronologically in an album suitable for archival photos. These known standards can serve as comparisons for dating photographs on stylistic grounds.

Another means of dating a photograph of any type is a consideration of the "internal evidence," such as the style of dress (bustles, men's collars, and hats all having dating significance) or, if an external shot, the style of a motorcar, street sign, or other feature. In one of my local history cases, a photo surfaced of the interior of a historic bank building that had burned on November 9, 1931. Careful examination of the photo with a loupe revealed a calendar on the wall. It was partially obscured, but I could decipher "RUARY" and the final digit of the year, a "1." It was also possible to see that the first Monday fell on the second of the month. With this information, I consulted a perpetual calendar and learned that Monday was the second day of February in 1891, 1931, and

1981. Since the bank had not opened until 1905, the picture had been snapped sometime in February 1931, a few months prior to the bank's demise (Nickell 1994a, 57).

Another example of dating by internal evidence involved a view of my hometown, West Liberty, Kentucky, on a real-photograph postcard (not the printed-on-a-press variety, but a genuine photo developed onto a piece of card stock printed with a postcard back). The picture's time frame could be closely approximated to the year 1915, by the presence or absence of buildings of known date; to the fall season, because of leafless trees, fodder shocks, and other clues; and to the time of day—8:23 in the morning—as shown by the clock on the distant courthouse's cupola (Nickell 1994a, 55–57).

## Identifying Individuals

Questions of identity are among those most frequently posed by old photos. Fortunately, the photo detective has a number of techniques at his or her disposal that may prove illuminating or even decisive. These can be divided into historical investigation and facial-feature analysis.

### Historical Investigation

Such elements as handwritten annotations, stylistic clues, internal evidence, provenance, and the like can help substantiate—or discredit—the identification of someone in an old photograph. Consider, for instance, a photograph purportedly of Edgar Allan Poe (1809–1849). It was a *carte de visite*, an albumen print made from a glass negative. That process was not invented until 1851—two years after Poe's death. The identity could also be dismissed on stylistic grounds, since "the small bow tie, Prussian shirt collar, and swallow-tailed coat were accouterments not introduced until the 1850s" (Deas 1989, 132).

Another spurious Poe was an oval photograph that supposedly depicted him as a child. Discovered in Virginia in 1940, it was accompanied by an attached inscription: "Edgar / on his fifth birthday / Born on the 19th day of January 1809" (Poe's birth date). Several persons testified as to its authenticity, but all that is needed to expose the hoax is to consider that in 1814 (1809 + 5), photography had not yet been invented. Apart from purely experimental images, photography was not available until 1839, at which time Poe was thirty years old (Deas 1989, 137).

Frequently, false attributions of identity are written on photographs, especially those alleged to depict persons of notoriety. For example, an old ambrotype I examined at the Woodford County, Kentucky, historical society supposedly depicted a sister of Frank and Jesse James, the American outlaws. They were born in 1843 and 1847, respectively, and their siblings included a brother Robert (who was born in 1844 but died a few days later) and a sister Susan Lavinia (born in 1849). Another sister, reputedly born in 1848 and named Mary, has occasionally been attributed to the family, and the ambrotype in question was inscribed "(Prudy) / Mary Eliz James" (Nickell 1994a, 78). The inscription, however, was in a modern hand, and the name "M. E. [COBURN?]" had been partially erased. Given the girl's apparent age of about seventeen and the reputed birth of Mary James in 1848, the picture would be a rather late example of an ambrotype. In any event, James family researchers relegate her to the realm of myth by noting strong negative evidence: the absence of her name both in Missouri census records and in the James family Bible (Beamis and Pullen n.d., 19; Triplett 1882, 65).

In a lengthy discussion in *Camera Clues* (Nickell 1994a, 76–84), I demonstrate how various types of historical evidence—provenance, handwriting, dress styles, jewelry, photographers' props, and many other factors, including genetic traits and occupational clues—can help establish or discredit an identification. The tools for attempting to solve such questions are a magnifying glass (see figure 7.4) and a sharp eye to look through it, along with a creative imagination, a capacity for critical thinking, and a willingness to persevere.

### Facial Features

The methodology applied in many sensational cases consists of comparing facial features in the questioned image with features in a known portrait. One approach utilizes the measurement of facial "landmarks"—individual features on the human face that can be easily identi-

Figure 7.4. A stand magnifier is among the useful tools for studying old photographs. (Photograph by Robert H. van Outer)

fied and charted for comparison. Another technique is to superimpose one image over the other, looking for similarities and differences.

An attempt to objectify this process led to a computerized analytical technique that received national attention when it was used to compare a photo of one Ollie L. "Brushy Bill" Roberts with a tintype of Henry McCarty, also known as William "Billy the Kid" Bonney. Roberts, who died in 1950, was among several people who had claimed to be Billy the Kid, having escaped death and living out his life in the Southwest. On other occasions, Roberts had claimed to be Frank James.

Oklahoma forensic anthropologist Clyde Snow led an identification team commissioned by historians from New Mexico's Lincoln County Heritage Trust. They supplied authenticated photos of both men that were then copied and fed into a scanner linked to a VAX mainframe computer. It reduced the images into pixels and enhanced portions of them where necessary. To determine identity, the technique used a "similarity index," mathematically derived from twenty-five facial landmarks. The computer also matched the photographs to a database consisting of 150 people of both sexes and of various facial types. This would show how many persons in the sample, if any, were more similar in appearance to William Bonney than Roberts was. If Roberts were actually Billy the Kid, his picture should have ranked second, after Bonney's own picture, which was ranked first for the analysis. Instead, however, he came in a distant forty-second. "That means," explained Heritage Trust director Robert L. Hart, "there were 40 individuals [in the database] who look more like Billy the Kid than Brushy does." He added, "Brushy doesn't look very much like Billy the Kid at all" ("Computer" 1990).

One aspect of facial identification has proved decisive in many important cases—the ear. Jacques Penry (1971, 82, 84), developer of the PHOTO-FIT method of producing composite pictures of suspects, has discussed this at length:

> Although as unique to every face as a fingerprint is unique to each person, the ears have been almost entirely ignored as a means of identification. . . .
>
> . . . The ears of mankind in their infinite permutations and combinations of angle, thickness of rim, length, width, position of head, size and shape of lobe, if any, and many other smaller pattern factors are such that *no two people* are likely to have ears which tally exactly in their detail any more than they are likely to have exactly matching fingerprints. . . .
>
> . . . Since the ear-pattern is unique to every person, its importance in facial identification from photographs cannot be too greatly stressed, especially in cases where a missing person with a doubtful fingerprint record (or none at all) has deliberately tried to alter his facial appearance.
>
> A selection of photographs may well reveal clear views of the ear which, when examined and compared, may decide whether any photographs of faces A, B, C, and D, et cetera—taken at various stages from infancy—are pictures positively of the same person. Such a decision could be conclusive even when time, hardship, illness or artifice have made changes in the face. . . . It may be hoped that at some time not far hence, methods of unravel-

ing problems of identity—both of malefactors and innocent people—will take far more into account the enormous assistance the conclusive ear evidence can provide. The ironic situation at present, as it has been for centuries, is that the ear-shape, the only feature which can (apart from fingerprints) provide fundamental proof, remains virtually ignored while every other scrap of photographic evidence is microscopically scanned and debated. It is as if a small number of witnesses were most methodically and intensely cross-examined for the evidence they could offer regarding some ambiguous situation, while the star witness holding the key to the matter stood by, mute and ignored.

One who has made a career of attempting to rectify that neglect is Alfred V. Iannarelli, a distinguished identification expert with decades of experience in law enforcement. He is the author of the comprehensive textbook *Ear Identification* (1989) and, over the years, has been involved in many important cases of identification, including some in which he generously assisted me (see chapters 9 and 10).

Whether the quest is to identify unattributed or questioned photos of one's ancestors or resolve a sensational international controversy, challenging questions of identity continue to be raised. As the foregoing discussion indicates, there are techniques—and experts who know how to use them—that can be brought to bear on these authentication issues.

## Original or Not?

Properly dating a photograph depends, of course, on its being an original and not a copy—especially not a multiple-generation copy or possibly even a cleverly faked one. Therefore, similar to the procedure with a questioned document, whenever a photo comes under scrutiny, all possibilities should be carefully considered. Let us look at which factors suggest authenticity, indicate copying, or reveal outright forgery.

Authentic old photos have an intrinsic value that is lacking in copies and prints. A photograph is considered an *original* if it is the very daguerreotype, ambrotype, or tintype that was made at the subject's sitting, or—in the case of prints from negatives—a print made from the original negative. It is considered a *vintage* print if it was made within about a year of the negative. However, in the case of a photographic art print made in a second edition or any print made after considerable time has elapsed—such as a modern print made from an antique glass negative—then the terms *reprint* and *modern reprint* apply, respectively (Blodgett 1979, 16, 18, 238). Although it is not always possible to determine whether a photo is original, it may be accepted as genuine to the degree that there is evidence in its favor and the absence of evidence to the contrary. Therefore, it is essential to be able to recognize signs of copy prints and modern fakes.

Copies of earlier photographs have been made since the beginning of photography. One encounters not only tintype copies of daguerreotypes but also daguerreotype copies of earlier oil paintings. One indicator that a picture is in fact a copy is the obvious presence of the original within the margins of the copy—in one case, secured to a board by pushpins visible at the top and bottom.

Another potential indicator comes from elements in a picture that may be anachronistic. For instance, a cabinet photograph (circa 1880s) depicted a woman from the daguerreotype era, as indicated by her dress and hairstyle, which were inappropriate for the 1880s but consistent with about 1850. Corroborative evidence came from a washed-out appearance near the picture's extremities, a result of glare from the mirror-like surface of the daguerreotype (see figure 7.5).

Still another indicator comes from the direct-positive nature of daguerreotypes, ambrotypes, and tintypes. This results in the image being reversed, as in a mirror (unless an optical device—a prism or a mirror—was used to correct this defect). In one old tintype, for example, the reputed subject seemed younger than she should have been after 1856, the year tintypes were invented. Was it really her picture, as oral tradition maintained? As it happened, a photo archivist called attention to the way her dress was buttoned. (Traditionally, men buttoned left over right, women right over left.) The fact that the woman's dress was but-

Figure 7.5. This cabinet photograph is actually a copy of an earlier daguerreotype portrait, indicated by both the woman's dress and the washed-out appearance near the extremities, resulting from glare on the daguerreotype's mirror surface. (Original photograph courtesy of Mr. and Mrs. Oscar Dillon)

toned *correctly*—not *reversed*—indicated that the image was a copy (that is, the mirror imaging of the tintype had reversed a prior mirror-image picture), supporting the conclusion that the original was an earlier daguerreotype (Nickell 1994a, 47–48).

Many copy prints may not be easily identified as such, but copying often results in a diminishing of quality—a loss of fine detail and an unnatural contrast buildup with the loss of intermediate gray tones—that may be apparent to an experienced eye. If a known original is available, direct comparison with the questioned print should settle the matter.

Modern, fake tintypes are now showing up at antique shops and shows with increasing frequency. These include forged Civil War tintypes. Fortunately, many can be spotted with the aid of a magnifying loupe; this reveals a mechanical pattern of halftone dots, betraying the fact that the photo was copied from a printed book or magazine. Since halftone illustrations did not appear until about the mid-1880s, their presence in an ostensibly old tintype (probably somewhat fuzzy from being copied) is a fatal anachronism.

An article in *Antique Week* reported other signs of fakery evident in a photo sold at an antique mall (MacLean 1992, 29):

> Remember that a tintype, like an ambrotype, is a negative image viewed against a black background. Close examination of this image suggested that it wasn't a negative image at all, but was a positive image against an off-white background. A little poking and probing and, lo and behold, the top emulsion can be peeled back and underneath isn't the black of a tintype base but a creamy off-white surface. So not only is the image faked, it isn't even a tintype. It is an entirely different process deliberately made to appear as if it were a tintype. Because there would be little financial incentive to have faked a Civil War tintype before they became highly collectible, this imitation is probably of very recent vintage.

A chemical test (Nickell 1994a, 51) can differentiate between the collodion emulsion that was used on all early tintypes (from their invention in 1856) and gelatin emulsions, which began to be marketed in the mid-1870s and were used in producing later tintypes.

Even very early process prints are apparently easy to counterfeit, as shown by a 1974 exhibition at London's National Portrait Gallery. It featured a hitherto unknown photographer's remarkable series depicting street urchins and child prostitutes of Victorian London. All was well until a visitor recognized one of the urchins as a professional child model. She and others had been dressed in period garb and hired to pose for some novel pictures for the portfolio of an advertising photographer. That photographer gave a set of prints to a painter and collector of Victorian photos named Ovenden. He transformed seven of the prints into "original" Victorian photographs by obtaining old paper—in one instance, watermarked 1835—and impregnating it with the appropriate chemicals for producing a calotype print (also known as a "salt print," because common salt is used in the developing). Scientific tests on the prints were reportedly inconclusive (Nickell 1994a, 53). However, one expert noted, "Part of the photograph's impact derives from the appearance of the little girl's flinging her hands up as if to protect herself, but to get this effect in an 1840s or '50s calotype the pose would have to be held for at least two or three minutes, quite an improbable feat for a young street urchin." Moreover, "a closer look . . . also reveals a too-great resolution of detail for an 1840s calotype" (Bennett 1987, 120–21). Other old-process pictures—including ambrotypes and even daguerreotypes—are also being counterfeited. *Caveat emptor* ("let the buyer beware") (Nickell 1994a, 51–53).

Although thus far we have been considering faked antique photos, it is important to recognize that modern ones can also be faked in a variety of ways. An entirely straightforward, unretouched picture may depict a scene that was staged in some way. Moreover, computer technology is becoming increasingly affordable and widely available, and it is capable of producing false images that are increasingly difficult to detect. (For an extensive discussion of these issues and strategies for detecting trickery, see my *Camera Clues* [1994a], especially chapters 6–8.)

The best advice comes from an expert in the field: "If something looks or even somehow 'smells' the slightest bit wrong, start asking questions. Provenance, technique, documentation, all these are legitimate subjects of enquiry of anyone offering works of art for sale" (Bennett 1987, 120–21). When the situation warrants it, seek expert advice.

Chapter 8

# A SECOND PHOTO OF EMILY DICKINSON

SPORADICALLY SINCE 1961, a controversy has flared over the "other" photograph of Emily Dickinson. Whereas history had seemed to bequeath only a single photograph of the poet—a daguerreotype of her at about seventeen years of age—a newly discovered portrait claims to depict her at about age twenty-nine (see figure 8.1). Many were persuaded that it was indeed Dickinson, and it was even reproduced as a frontispiece to volume two of Richard B. Sewall's *The Life of Emily Dickinson* (1974), although the caption left open the question of its authenticity. I was asked by Georgiana Strickland, editor of the Emily Dickinson International Society's *Bulletin,* to conduct an investigation (Nickell 1993b).

## Provenance

I began, of course, with the photograph itself. In contrast to the one-of-a-kind, mirror-image daguerreotype, the discovered photo was a *carte de visite* (a paper print made from a glass negative and pasted onto a small mount). On the back of the *carte de visite* in question was written "Emily Dickenson [*sic*] 1860." It had been purchased by bibliophile Herman Abromson from the 1961 mimeographed catalog of a Greenwich Village bookseller named Samuel Loveman. Unfortunately, Loveman (who died in 1976) had a dubious reputation. Many scholars and book dealers who had known him called him "a fraud and a forger" and avowed "his word was not to be trusted" (quoted in Langton 1984a, 1:11). William Bond (1982), director of the Houghton Library at Harvard, stated, "In addition to perfectly legitimate rare books and manuscripts, some of the things [Loveman sold] were certainly fraudulent. I remember in particular a

Figure 8.1. At left, the only acknowledged photograph of Emily Dickinson, taken in Amherst about 1847. At right, a questioned *carte de visite* labeled "Emily Dickenson [*sic*]." (Courtesy of *Emily Dickinson International Society Bulletin*)

number of books said to have come from Herman Melville's library with his annotations, in which the annotations were certainly forged."

Charles Hamilton, in his *Great Forgers and Famous Fakes* (1980, 198–99), wrote that Loveman "dabbled in forgery." For instance, he had obtained a supply of bookplates from the late Hart Crane (whom Loveman claimed had been his homosexual lover) and pasted them in books Crane would have been likely to own. Hamilton added, "Nearly every catalogue that Loveman issued was filled with fabulous 'bargains'—books signed by Melville, Mark Twain or Hawthorne—a whole galaxy of great authors, all priced at ten to twenty-five dollars each. The signatures were in pencil and were not, of course, genuine; but it was exciting to study his catalogue and pretend that such bargains really existed."

As it happens, the notation on the "Dickinson" *carte de visite* was in pencil; worse, it was in the distinctive, palsied, backhand script of Samuel Loveman. It was recognized as such by several of Loveman's acquaintances who were queried by mystery writer Jane Langton. She conducted extensive research on the photo (which she generously shared with me) as background for her suspense novel *Emily Dickinson Is Dead* (1984a). (See Nickell 1993b, 3n7.)

Loveman, however, had pretended that the signature was genuine. His catalog listing, alternately referring to the picture as a "daguerreo-type" and a "crad [*sic*] de Visite," described the notation as if it had already been there when Loveman acquired it. Observing that the last three digits of the 1860 date appear to have been erased from the mimeograph original, Langton (1984b, 8) noted, "It looked very fishy. Why did Loveman seem to pretend that someone else had written the inscription on the back? Why had he scrubbed out three digits from the date?" She wondered, "Had Loveman changed his mind about the date?" (1984b, 10). According to some of Loveman's acquaintances, his only known basis for identifying the portrait as Dickinson's was that he thought it resembled her and "had such a sensitive quality" (quoted in Langton 1984b, 10). A bookseller portrayed Loveman as someone who eschewed reference books and used his own impressions as the basis for his catalog claims (Langton 1984b, 14).

Unlike a daguerreotype of the poet's mother, Emily Norcross Dickinson, that was discovered among family photos (Nickell 1994a, 80–81), the questioned photograph has no provenance whatsoever. *Cartes de visite* were typically sold in batches of a dozen or more (Darrah 1981, 5–6), yet not one copy was found in the poet's effects after her death. Nor did family members have a copy; they had to resort to doctoring copies of the one known daguerreotype in an attempt to produce a more suitable, mature likeness for publication purposes (Bingham 1955, 519–20).

Indeed, in 1862, when Thomas Wentworth Higginson wrote to Dickinson and asked for a photograph, she replied: "Could you believe me—without? I had no portrait, now, but am small, like the Wren, and my Hair is bold, like the Chestnut Bur—and my eyes, like the Sherry in the Glass, that the Guest leaves—Would this do just as well?" She added, "It often alarms Father—He says Death might occur, and he has Molds of all the rest—but has no Mold of Me" (quoted in Leyda 1960, 2:63).

Whether Emily's self-description is compatible with the *carte de visite* is debatable, as are many other details. For example, as Sewall stated, "So far no technical reasons have been raised against its authenticity—except perhaps the fact that she's wearing earrings. . . . 'It doesn't seem like Emily Dickinson to be wearing earrings,' say some. But others say, 'Why shouldn't she have worn earrings?'" (quoted in DeNicola 1983, 124). Unlike the daguerreotype of her mother, which depicts her wearing a distinctive dove-and-flower brooch that was later found among the poet's effects, the jewelry worn by the person in the *carte* has no known connection with Emily Dickinson. The matching earrings and brooch are not among the family possessions at the Houghton Library at Harvard (Nickell 1993b, 2).

If Emily Dickinson had had a *carte de visite* picture taken in 1860, it probably would have been done by local Amherst photographer J. L. Lovell, who had bought out another photographer in 1856. Apparently, Lovell was the sole photographer in Amherst at the time. His *cartes,* however, invariably have his imprint on the back, whereas the "Emily Dickenson" *carte* bears no photographer's identification. Besides, if Lovell had taken such a photograph, Mabel Loomis Todd surely would have discovered that fact. She needed such a picture when she prepared Emily's letters for publication in 1893, and Lovell (who lived until 1903) was a close friend of hers (Langton 1984a, 1:20–22).

## A Likeness of Emily?

Although the lack of provenance and the other historical evidence weigh heavily against the photograph's authenticity, ultimately, the matter must be settled on the basis of the likeness itself. And there is a resemblance between the woman in the picture and the daguerreotype of the seventeen-year-old Emily Dickinson—otherwise, the equation would not have been made. But a mere resemblance between two people does not constitute proof of identity, and false photographic attributions are rife.

Early in her research, Langton received this cautionary response from John Lancaster, curator of Special Collections at Amherst College

Library: "You should know that we receive several inquiries each year asking us to pass judgment on pictures alleged to be of Emily Dickinson. . . . I have never seen one with any sort of useful provenance (including Abromson's), and visual comparisons are notoriously uncertain" (quoted in Langton 1984a, 2:6).

Likewise, William F. Stapp, curator of photography of the Smithsonian's National Portrait Gallery, responded: "It is difficult to reconcile the rather sensuous beauty of the woman in Mr. Abromson's carte de visite to the young woman depicted in the one authentic daguerreotype of Emily Dickinson. The piece, moreover, not only has no provenance, but it appears to be unique and completely undocumented. I have learned to be very suspicious of pieces like this, which essentially cannot be authenticated, and since it passed through the hands of a questionable dealer, there is an even greater likelihood that it is spurious" (quoted in Langton 1984a, 2:86–87).

Langton's research led her to query several doctors, who "differed on whether or not these two women are the same person." Also, superimposition of photographic transparencies by Tufts University medical photographer Kay Smathers showed some similarities in features but a marked difference in the breadth of the face (Langton 1984a, 1:iii).

## Forensic Analysis

In my estimation, the previous opinions offered in the case, though valuable, were insufficient. I therefore enlisted the services of nationally recognized forensic anthropologist Emily Craig, who readily agreed to assist in this important historical case. Craig was then on the staff of the Forensic Anthropology Center at the University of Tennessee–Knoxville. A medical illustrator as well as an anthropologist, she was featured on the CBS television series *48 Hours* in a May 13, 1992, program titled "Hard Evidence." There she demonstrated the technique of facial reconstruction on the skull of a murder victim whose body had been discovered in an advanced state of decomposition. Later she was on the forensic team that identified charred bodies in the wake of the Branch Davidian sect tragedy near Waco, Texas; she reconstructed the skull of cult leader David Koresh and proved that he had been killed by a bullet before the conflagration. She is the author of *Teasing Secrets from the Dead* (Craig 2004) and is currently the forensic anthropologist for the commonwealth of Kentucky.

Using photographic slides prepared from the two photographs, Craig employed an established forensic procedure that involves projecting the "known" image (the daguerreotype) onto a sheet of white paper and tracing the outlines of the features, then using another projector to superimpose the "questioned" image (the *carte de visite*) onto the first, adjusting the latter to achieve a best fit, and tracing its features. The projected images and the tracings are then compared and analyzed. The resulting file was designated case number 93–17 (Craig 1993).

Although Craig observed a few similarities (such as the vertical distance between the irises and the root of the nose, corresponding to the orbits of the eye and the anterior nasal spine), there were significant differences. One of these was a cleft chin in the portrait of Emily Dickinson that was absent from the woman in the *carte* photograph. This is a genetically determined feature that does not disappear with maturity (Enlow 1990). Other differences were the mid-philtrum distance (between the root of the nose and the upper lip) and the distance between the chin point and the root of the nose, the center of the right iris, and the chin-lip fold. In the last case, explained Craig (1993), "this distance variation can appear to be corrected with head tilt, but then the simultaneous superimposition of the eyes and the anterior nasal spine is eliminated." In addition, the root of the nose and corresponding anterior nasal spine failed to lie in the same vertical plane in the two portraits. There were other differences in the soft tissue contours, hairlines, and eyebrows, although they "may or may not be a direct result of anatomical variations in the underlying structure" (Craig 1993).

Noting that bones of the face are fully developed between ages fourteen and sixteen, and given the approximate age of Emily Dickinson when the daguerreotype was made, "there would not be any measurable modification in the bony structure of the face until advanced aging processes were evident." Therefore, according to Craig (1993), the differences in the location of the features between the two photographs "cannot be the result of age changes." She stated in conclusion (1993): "There is the possibility that a skull and face of one individual can fit all the facial features of another individual, and therefore superimposition is considered more of a value in exclusion. In case 93–17, all of the features cannot be simultaneously superimposed; therefore the evidence does NOT corroborate the hypothesis that the photographs are of the same individual."

The forensic analysis confirmed what had been suggested by the historical evidence. Apparently, Samuel Loveman simply came across the *carte de visite,* noted a passing resemblance to Emily Dickinson, took a pencil in hand, and gave the fantasy a semblance of reality.

## Chapter 9

# LIKENESSES OF LINCOLN

JUST AS AUTOGRAPHS and manuscripts of Abraham Lincoln (1809–1865) are much sought after, so are his photographs. Although some Lincoln *cartes de visite* were reproduced in quantity both before and after his assassination and are modestly priced, scarcer images are sought by serious collectors. Hope of finding such treasures is kept alive by discoveries such as the one at a Nashville garage sale, where a woman purchased what would prove to be the second-oldest known Lincoln photo. She sold the picture to Daniel Weinberg, owner of the Abraham Lincoln Book Shop in Chicago, who was able to trace it back to a previous owner. That man had been a caretaker of Lincoln's Springfield home into the 1890s, and his name was written on the photograph's case. The original picture had been taken in 1854 but had perished in 1871 in the great Chicago fire. However, it had been copied by a newspaper publisher, and based on image quality, Weinberg's photo appeared to be a genuine copy of the original. It was purchased by Illinois state historian Tom Schwartz for the Abraham Lincoln Presidential Library and Museum for $150,000 (Fitzsimmons 2006).

## Lincoln Fakes

Such discoveries inspire not only collectors but also unscrupulous dealers. One fake photo was a quarter-plate tintype copied from an 1863 print by Alexander Gardner. The tintype copies originally sold as novelties at Greenfield Village (the Henry Ford Museum in Dearborn, Michigan) and cost only a couple of dollars, but soon they began to appear at antique shops for more serious prices (Nickell 1994a, 50).

In one of my early photograph authentication cases, an antiquities dealer wanted to know whether two large Lincoln photos he had "on approval" were copies or originals. If the latter, he intended to invest a significant sum in purchasing them. Observing both a crease mark and the dark margins of a water stain in one of the photographs, I removed it from its frame and examined the back of the photographic paper. That paper was not creased or water-stained, proving that the photo was actually a copy of a print that had such damage. The other photo, I discovered, had an embossment in a lower corner. With the aid of a magnifier and oblique lighting (to intensify the shadows of the embossment), I learned that it was the mark of a particular New York studio. Subsequent library research revealed that that particular image had originally been made by Mathew Brady; therefore, that picture too was a copy (Nickell 1994a, 62).

In other cases, the photographs were genuine originals but the question was whether the subject was actually Lincoln or a look-alike. One such case involved a reputed deathbed portrait of Lincoln. The photographer who produced the image for the *carte de visite* had stood at the foot of the bed and literally looked up the bearded man's nose. Not surprisingly, this view was not available in any known photograph of Lincoln, making a comparison of facial features exceedingly difficult. I was, however, able to gain access to a Lincoln life mask in a museum and have it photographed from the requisite angle. Placing the mask photo beside an enlargement from the questioned photo made it easy to see that the features—the angle of the ear, shape of the nose, and so on—were entirely incompatible (Nickell 1994a, 89).

Another case featured a tintype that appeared to show Abraham Lincoln with another man posing before a waterfall (see figure 9.1). The tintype was by all indications an original and a mirror image of the scene (based on the buttoning of the men's coats). Enlargement of the face, which was only about two millimeters across in the tintype, failed to show sufficient detail for any meaningful analysis of facial features. So I tried another strategy that proved to be as effective as it was creative. First, I identified the scene (keeping in mind that the picture was reversed) as Minnehaha Falls near St. Paul, Minnesota (see figure 9.2).

Figure 9.1. Questioned tintype, thought to depict
Abraham Lincoln.

Second, I tracked Lincoln's activities from 1856 (when tintypes were invented) to 1865 (when he was assassinated), a period of nine years. For this purpose, I relied on a book-length timeline compiled by Earl Schenck Miers (1960) and appropriately titled *Lincoln Day by Day*. In brief, there was no period when Abraham Lincoln either was or reasonably could have been in the vicinity of Minnehaha Falls. Therefore, the image was merely that of another look-alike.

## The Kaplan "Lincoln"

As Illinois congressman-elect, Abraham Lincoln posed in 1846 for a daguerreotype portrait at the gallery of Springfield photographer N. H. Shepherd. It is Lincoln's earliest known photograph. However, in 1994

Figure 9.2. Photograph of Minnehaha Falls, identifying the scene in figure 9.1.

there surfaced two alleged earlier daguerreotypes of Lincoln: one in
the possession of Robert and Joan Hoffman that received considerable media attention (Pokorski 1995), and one acquired by New York
businessman Albert Kaplan that had supposedly been authenticated by
a French plastic surgeon, his report appearing in the *Journal of Forensic
Identification* (Frechette 1994).

There were defenders of both photographs, but there were even more
skeptics, and I was among them. Kaplan had contacted both me and
identification expert Alfred V. Iannarelli, with whom I have collabo-
rated on many cases. Subsequently, the two of us reported that—based
primarily on Iannarelli's comparison of the left ear in the questioned
photograph with that in the authentic 1846 Lincoln portrait—Kaplan's

photograph was definitely not that of Abraham Lincoln (Iannarelli 1994). Iannarelli and I thought we had settled the matter, so we were somewhat surprised to see the *Journal of Forensic Identification* article by Claude N. Frechette, M.D. The article gave the false impression that Frechette had been the only person consulted, but we knew that, in addition to us, Kaplan had received negative opinions from several other experts. Kaplan (1994) himself told me that he had obtained such opinions from a forensic anthropologist at the Smithsonian Institution and a forensic artist retired from the New York Police Department, among others.

As I told Kaplan, I would prefer the opinion of any forensic expert over that of a plastic surgeon; although the latter has expertise in facial features, he lacks training in identification. In fact, Frechette observed several differences between the Kaplan image and genuine Lincoln photographs but hastened to rationalize them. For instance, he admitted, "There is a blemish under the left commissure [corner of the mouth] that is not found in other Lincoln pictures," but he theorized that it "could be a 'cold sore' Lincoln had at the time the daguerreotype was made" (Frechette 1994, 422). He also stated, "There are some features in the Kaplan that seem, at first, not to coincide with features in known Lincoln images," one of which involved "the angle the ear lobe forms with the neck. The angle is very small in the Kaplan but more open in all other Lincoln pictures." Frechette attributed this to "differences in body weight" (1994, 423–24), even though this was only a supposition. He offered little support for his assertion that Lincoln "experienced one of his first dramatic weight losses in the early 1840s" (1994, 424), basing that statement on the fact that before his marriage, Lincoln suffered a period of depression and, according to the single source Frechette cited on the matter, a consequent "loss of appetite" (Clark 1921, 12–13). However, the supposed weight loss was not quantified, and there was certainly no proof that the earlier Lincoln had been as full-faced as the unidentified man in the Kaplan photo—a man who is unrecognizable as Lincoln. As he did elsewhere, Frechette employed circular reasoning.

"Another feature," conceded Frechette (1994, 424), "is that the chin in all of Lincoln's pictures shows a dimple while the chin in the Kaplan photo shows a cleft." He made no attempt to rationalize this difference and instead asserted another perceived similarity: "Of major importance . . . is that Lincoln's asymmetrical chin is perfectly matched [in asymmetry] by the chin in the Kaplan." In attempting to rationalize or gloss over dissimilarities between the real and questioned images, Frechette gave the impression that he had started with the answer and worked backward to the evidence. Frechette also seemed unaware that merely showing the correspondence of some facial features is insufficient for a positive identification because "there is the possibility that a skull and face of one individual can fit all the facial features of another individual" (Craig 1993).

Conversely, Frechette gave far too little emphasis to the facial feature with the greatest identification potential, saying simply that "Bertillon [the French identification pioneer] attached a great deal of importance to the structure of the ear," which "never changed during an individual's lifetime." He added that French police authorities "all agreed that the visible ear structure" of the man in the Kaplan daguerreotype was "identical to those in Lincoln photographs" (Frechette 1994, 426). He did not elaborate on this alleged—and crucial—match (which was entirely erroneous, in any event).

Because of the myriad problems with Frechette's report, I decided to thoroughly reinvestigate the Kaplan image, beginning with the historical evidence and including—in addition to Iannarelli's ear comparison—an analysis of facial features by a forensic anthropologist and an assessment by the leading authority on Lincoln's photographs. My findings were published in the *Journal of Forensic Identification* (Nickell 1996b), from which this discussion is adapted.

### Investigative Methodology

I began my investigation by looking at the historical evidence relating to the Kaplan image. Following Frechette's article in the *Journal of Forensic Identification* was another titled "Artifact Description of Kaplan Daguerreotype" by Grant B. Romer (1994), a conservator at the International Museum of Photography at George Eastman House in Rochester, New York. I reviewed Romer's findings in an attempt to provide a more precise date for the questioned Kaplan daguerreotype and to reassess its authenticity in that light.

I also addressed the matter of provenance. Genuine rare photographs often have a credible provenance, such as the daguerreotype of Emily Norcross Dickinson (mother of the poet) discovered among the Norcross family pictures (mentioned in chapter 8).

In addition, I contacted Lloyd Ostendorf, the noted Lincoln expert (see chapter 4), whose opinion on the Kaplan image had been solicited by Christie's auction house (Kaplan 1994). His opinion had also been sought by *National Geographic* magazine and others in the case of the Hoffman "Lincoln" daguerreotype, which Ostendorf had decisively debunked, observing that the facial features failed to match and that the pattern of blood vessels on the back of the questioned man's hand was unlike that in the Volk life casts of the president's hands made in the 1860s (Ostendorf 1994a; see also Pokorski 1995). In addition to those credentials, Ostendorf had been an illustrator and portrait painter since 1936, having rendered so many drawings and paintings of the sixteenth president that he was called the "Lincoln artist." He was also one of the foremost collectors of Lincoln photographs in the world, and his collection formed the nucleus of the book he coauthored, *Lincoln in Photographs: An Album of Every Known Pose* (Hamilton and Ostendorf 1963).

Further, I sought the expert opinion of Virginia Smith, an artist with a PhD in anthropology who had worked closely with Kentucky's medical examiner, reconstructing faces from human skulls and making identifications.

In addition, I studied the report of Alfred Iannarelli (1994), a distinguished identification expert with decades of experience in law enforcement, including as a criminal investigator with the U.S. Army Reserves. Iannarelli majored in criminology at the University of California–Berkeley, received a bachelor's degree in police science, and later obtained a law degree. Since 1949, he had studied ear identification extensively and had pioneered a system of classification allowing ear photographs to be filed systematically, as described in his comprehensive textbook *Ear Identification* (1989). Over the years, he has been involved in many important cases of identification, including some that remain confidential.

## Investigative Results and Discussion

Photographic expert Grant Romer determined that Kaplan's daguerreotype was in its original leather-covered wooden case and was in good condition. An inscription was stamped into the daguerreotype's silver-coated copper plate: "E. WHITE MAKER N.Y. SECOND QUALITY." Edgar White was a daguerreotypist and plate maker in New York from at least 1843. Romer (1994) concluded, "this daguerreotype is an entirely American product made prior to 1845. The style of case, plate housing, sitter's dress, and hair style suggest an earlier rather than later 1840's date." However, that time frame appears constrained by the fact that on December 14, 1844, White wrote, "we have commenced manufacturing plates." Romer provided no compelling evidence to indicate an earlier date for the Kaplan photo, and the late 1844 date would mean that the Kaplan daguerreotype had been made well *after* Lincoln's period of depression and presumed weight loss (a ten-month period during 1841 [Clark 1921]) and more than two years *after* his marriage. For Frechette's explanation of the full-faced Kaplan "Lincoln" to make sense, the photograph would have to have been made before January 1841, and that is untenable. Daguerreotypes were invented in France and announced to the public there in 1839 (Nickell 1994a, 6–7), whereas Lincoln was living in Springfield, Illinois, in the early 1840s. Thomas Schwartz, Illinois state historian and an expert on Lincoln, doubts that, during the infancy of photography, a daguerreotypist could have arrived in Springfield without his visit being heralded in the local newspapers. And there is no evidence of any daguerreotypist operating in Springfield prior to 1843. Schwartz said of the photo, "I don't find it convincing" (quoted in "Is It" 1994).

Regarding the provenance, all that is known is that the Kaplan image was purchased from a New York City gallery in 1977. That gives us at least two possible scenarios. Kaplan's scenario suggests that a daguerreotype plate, made by Edgar White at a date earlier than he is known to have made such plates, found its way to Springfield, Illinois, before any photographer is known to have worked there (or perhaps Lincoln traveled elsewhere to have his picture made), and then the photograph somehow ended up—quite coincidentally—back in New York City, where it was eventually discovered. The simpler, more likely scenario is that White's plate was used by him or another local New York photographer to take a picture of an unidentified young man in about 1845, and the resulting daguerreotype never left the city. Clearly, the historical evidence does not support Kaplan's notion. So it is not surprising that when he solicited the opinion of several Lincoln scholars, "they scoffed at the idea that it was Lincoln" (quoted in "Is It" 1994).

Such a scholar was Lloyd Ostendorf, who told me that he was positive the Kaplan daguerreotype did not depict Abraham Lincoln. He sent me a pair of sketches that illustrated the considerable differences between Kaplan's unidentified man and Lincoln. Rather than merely take measurements of features recorded on a flat surface, as Frechette had done, Ostendorf used his artistic depth perception (evident from the lights and shadows of Kaplan's daguerreotype), as well as additional visual information about depth imparted by the pose's being a three-quarter rather than frontal view, to project a profile of the unidentified man. He then presented this profile in a side-by-side comparison with a sketch drawn from an actual life mask of Lincoln (see figure 9.3). Ostendorf observed that the man in the Kaplan daguerreotype has a nose that is too pointed, lips that are too small, and an ear that is neither large enough nor sufficiently protruding. In addition, the man is pop-eyed and has both a receding chin and a weak jaw (Ostendorf 1994b). A measure of the accuracy of Ostendorf's work is that the recognizability of each man is retained, while the three-dimensional differences are heightened.

In addition, Ostendorf called attention to Lincoln's famous mole, which is missing from the right cheek of the Kaplan figure. Frechette (1994, 422) claimed to see "a faint circular shadow" at this location but failed to be convincing on this point. Ostendorf observed that the

Figure 9.3. Sketch by noted Lincoln artist and collector Lloyd Ostendorf, comparing the Kaplan "Lincoln" (which he first converted from a three-quarter to a profile view) with the real Lincoln. (Courtesy of Lloyd Ostendorf)

prominent mole "is always evident in Lincoln's photos." Citing both the Hoffman and the Kaplan daguerreotypes, Ostendorf (1994b) stated, "I stake my whole reputation as a Lincoln artist (since 1936) that these are not Lincoln!"

Further analysis involved forensic anthropology. Virginia Smith (1995) examined eight-by-ten prints of both the Kaplan and the 1846 Lincoln photographs (in her discussion, she referred to the 1846 Lincoln, as Frechette did, as "Meserve #1," after F. H. Meserve's [1944] system of cataloging Lincoln photos). She stated, "Although I agree with Frechette's use of the canon of vertical Golden Proportions and with his assertion that there are unavoidable 'errors in measurement' due to the nature of the samples, I am not convinced that the Kaplan portrait is, indeed, Lincoln." She explained that she had used Frechette's method of measuring the distances between the various features, including the level of the eyes (LC), base of the nose (LN), lips (ST), and position of the chin (ME). Here are her results:

| Measurement | Kaplan | Meserve #1 |
|---|---|---|
| LC to LN | 1 cm | 1.3 cm |
| LN to ST | 0.6 cm | 0.6 cm |
| ST to ME | 1 cm | 1.1 cm |

Smith stated:

> Allowing for differences in the size of the portraits with the Meserve portrait being larger than the Kaplan, one can still look for comparable proportions between reference points. Since LN to ST is the same in both portraits, the greater proportional differences between the Meserve #1 portrait and the Kaplan are clear. In effect, the Kaplan portrait shows much more balanced proportions with less elongation, especially from the level of the eyes (LC) to the position of the nose (LN). It is true that in the process of aging, the tip of the nose descends, but measurements were made from the base, not the tip of the nose.
>
> In addition, the longer chin, shown by the distance between the lip line (ST) and the edge of the chin (ME) in the Meserve portrait would have been far more visible if profile photos were available. The Kaplan subject had a more receding chin with a far sharper angle from the tip of the nose to the base of the chin than the more forward placed chin in the Meserve portrait.

Smith added:

> The thinner upper lip in the Meserve #1 portrait could be explained by the effects of aging. However, the Kaplan mouth

is less broad when the distance from the center of the mouth to the portraits' left outer edges of the mouth are compared. In the Kaplan portrait, a vertical line from either the center of the pupil of the eye or in the apex of the eyebrow's arch falls well outside the extent of the lip line. In the Meserve portrait, these two reference points are nearly in line vertically.

Further, even allowing for the neck tissue shown below the ear in the Kaplan portrait (as noted by Frechette's reference to Lincoln as a heavier person at the time the portrait was made), the ear lobe in the Meserve portrait is not just free hanging, as it is in the Kaplan portrait, but shows a far more projecting ear type. The Kaplan ear is much closer to the head. In the Meserve portrait, the face is tilted forward slightly, but the location of the ear, as most easily seen by comparing the distance between the tip of the lobe to the curved lower edge of the mandible, shows that this distance is more than twice as long in proportion in the Meserve portrait. I completely agree with Iannarelli's ear analysis pointing out the differences in the ears of both portraits.

Smith (1995) concluded: "I really did look for any possible way to think that the Kaplan portrait could be Lincoln. I just didn't find any evidence to support that thinking."

All three experts I consulted observed the obvious differences between the ears in the two photographs. Indeed, Iannarelli made a careful analysis of the ears in the Kaplan and Lincoln daguerreotypes—originally in 1978, and again, in more detail, in 1993. Comparing the Lincoln photograph to the Kaplan one, Iannarelli (1994) noted the following "points of characteristics and comparison":

1. Overall external ear is "medium set" compared to the "low set" ear [in the Kaplan photograph];
2. Lower portion of ear lobule is considered round compared to the oval shape ear lobule [in the Kaplan photograph];
3. The flesh line of the helix rim or border is less pronounced

than that of the Kaplan ear print. No evidence of a "Darwinian Enlargement" [i.e., a slight, blunt swelling of the helix rim, otherwise known as the helix border] in the above print;

4. Ear is NOT curved from the upper border of the ear proper to the lower point of the Lobule (Curvature is very obvious in the Kaplan ear print);

5. Slant of Antitragus is *horizontal.*

Iannarelli (1994) then compared the questioned Kaplan picture with the actual Lincoln portrait, reaching the following conclusions:

1. External ear is considered "low set" compared to the "medium set" ear [in the Lincoln photograph];

2. Lower portion of ear lobule is "oval" in shape compared to the round shape lobule [in the Lincoln photograph];

3. Helix Rim is more pronounced in the above individual's ear with evidence of a "Darwinian Enlargement";

4. A more obvious curvature of the outer ear proper than that of the ear [in the Lincoln photo];

5. Slant of Antitragus is *oblique.*

Summing up, Iannarelli (1994) stated: "My conclusion to the identification analysis relating to these two photographs remains the same today as the one I conducted . . . in June 1978." Having taken more time to examine the photographs, he was even "more assured" that the man in the Kaplan daguerreotype was not Lincoln. The differences in the anatomical configurations of the respective ears, he observed, "are quite obvious," as illustrated by the photographic enlargements.

My reinvestigation of the Kaplan "Lincoln" daguerreotype thus demonstrated that it does not depict Abraham Lincoln. The expert analyses found such significant differences between the two photographs as to clearly indicate two distinctly separate individuals. The ear evidence, in particular, refutes the claim that the Kaplan daguerreotype is a portrait of Abraham Lincoln.

# Chapter 10

# ASSASSIN OR LOOK-ALIKE

Do photographs and videotapes of the assassin of President John F. Kennedy really depict ex-marine Lee Harvey Oswald, as the public has been led to believe? Or do they actually show a look-alike, a professional whose job it was to kill the president of the United States?

The allegations are fantastic. They were advanced in 1977 by retired British solicitor Michael Eddowes in his book *The Oswald File* (see figure 10.1). He wrote that he would "endeavor to prove beyond reasonable doubt" the following claims: first, that Soviet premier Nikita Khrushchev gave the order for the Soviet Secret Police to assassinate President Kennedy; second, that "the real . . . Lee Harvey Oswald" did not return from the USSR (where he had defected in 1959) but rather a KGB assassin "entered the United States in the guise of Oswald" in 1962 and carried out the order; and finally, that "to avoid the possibility of World War III," the U.S. government undertook a massive cover-up (Eddowes 1977, 1–2).

Needless to say, such an astonishing resemblance between two unrelated people would be incredibly rare. It is true that twice, in 1896 and 1904, a Londoner named Adolph Beck was mistakenly identified as swindler William Thomas, and only the subsequent correct identification of Thomas kept Beck from having to serve out a second prison term. However, it is also true that their similarity extended only to a general resemblance and their walrus mustaches. And in the most famous instance of "unrelated" look-alikes—the 1903 case of Will and William West, whose astonishing similarity, even as to name, helped advance the use of fingerprinting in the United States—we now know the rest of the story. As shown by one of my early investigations (Nickell

Figure 10.1. Michael Eddowes's *The Oswald File* advanced a conspiracy theory involving an alleged double of Lee Harvey Oswald.

1980), genetic evidence from ear patterns and fingerprints, as well as documentary evidence, convincingly demonstrated that they were actually identical twins.

The evidence cited by Eddowes was extremely weak. Beyond innuendo and conspiracy mongering, he offered little more than some discrepancies in height and scars between Oswald's Marine Corps service files and post-1962 official records. Though conceding that the "two" men's fingerprints matched, he advanced the notion that "the KGB had substituted a forged print card in the FBI fingerprint files, the forgery substituting the impostor's prints in place of the ex-Marine's prints" (Eddowes 1977, 139). That is a classic conspiracy-theory tactic: claiming that the very evidence that refutes the conspiracy has been altered by the conspirators.

I have no data on the sale of Eddowes's book, but it received mixed reviews. *Publisher's Weekly* (August 1, 1977) observed that it "demanded attention," while *Library Journal* (November 15, 1977) disparaged the "paranoid conspiracy scenario" and concluded: "Geared to exploit the widespread interest in the assassination, this shoddy book is not recommended." Nevertheless, Eddowes continued to make headlines. "Oswald's Widow Says Briton's Theory Wrong," read an Associated Press article of August 17, 1980. Marina Oswald Porter said that, by agreeing to Eddowes's request for an exhumation of the body, "I called his bluff." Oswald's brother Robert sued to halt the exhumation on the grounds that Eddowes's motives were merely to promote his book for personal gain. The tabloid *Globe* rang in with a headline proclaiming "Oswald Is Alive" (1980). The article was accompanied by a photo of a dapper Eddowes—decked out in a hat and a three-piece suit—resting on one knee while pointing to Oswald's grave marker with his cane.

In late 1980, after discussing the issue with Robert Oswald by telephone, I launched an identification project, with three goals: (1) to make a positive identification of the person arrested as Lee Harvey Oswald, shot to death by Jack Ruby, and buried in Oswald's grave; (2) to make the identification without recourse to records that could theoretically have been switched (such as fingerprints, dental records, or medical files); and (3) to accomplish this without exhumation, which would require breaking into the concrete burial vault and intensifying the anguish of the Oswald family.

In the course of my investigation, I studied Eddowes's book as well as Robert Oswald's *Lee: A Portrait of Lee Harvey Oswald by His Brother* (1967), plus the Warren Commission report (formally, the *Report of the President's Commission on the Assassination of President John F. Kennedy*, headed by Supreme Court Justice Earl Warren), the report of the House Select Committee on Assassinations, and many other books, articles, and textbooks. I also consulted with a distinguished identification expert.

## Background: Forensic Identification

As far back as the ancient Egyptians, descriptions of wanted criminals have been employed. The first scientific attempt to identify felons began in 1860, when a Belgian prison warden named Stevens began recording the measurements of convicts' heads, feet, body length, and the like. This imperfect method was abandoned, but by 1882, French anthropologist Alphonse Bertillon had developed an elaborate system involving sitting and standing height, length of the outstretched arms, length and breadth of the head, and length of the right ear. Bertillon supplemented his *bertillonage* with additional data, such as scars and other markings and eye color, plus full-face and profile photographs. Although fingerprinting eventually replaced this cumbersome system, Bertillon's descriptive *portrait parle* (or "word picture") component and "mug shots" remain in use.

Fingerprints are the mainstay of identification. However, in some cases when there are too few ridge characteristics to make a positive fingerprint identification, the pattern of tiny pores along the ridges is employed (a method known as poroscopy). Like fingerprints, the patterns of the palms and the soles of the feet may prove valuable. And because no two things in nature are precisely identical, various other methods of identification have served on occasion, including lip impressions, bite marks, and dental X-rays, to name only a few. Criminals who thought they were being clever by wearing gloves have occasionally been convicted when it was demonstrated that the gloves left weave or other patterns identical to latent imprints at the scene of the crime (Nickell and Fischer 1999, 7–9, 112–36, 148–50).

Quite often, when attempting to make an identification, several factors that are suggestive but not conclusive must be weighed together. Consider, for example, a case that occurred in 1949 (before DNA testing). It involved comparing the description of a missing man with that of a badly decomposed corpse recovered from a river and lacking a head, hands, and feet. The estimated age, height, and weight of the victim were consistent with that of the missing man. So were remnants of dark trousers, certain scars, and evidence of a heart condition. Ultraviolet light revealed the initials A. H. S. on the deceased's wallet. The missing man's initials were A. H. S. L., but on a clinic card, he had used only the first three letters. The body was identified as that of the missing man.

Figure 10.2. According to Eddowes, the "real" Oswald (left) was in the U.S. Marines, but an "impostor" (right) sent by the KGB assassinated President Kennedy in Dallas and was subsequently arrested. (from official photographs reproduced by Eddowes)

## The Oswald Identification

In the Oswald case, I resolved to make the identification from photographs (see figure 10.2), since the authenticity of the two sets—those of Oswald and those of the Dallas assassin—were not questioned and were not susceptible to accusations of having been switched, unlike fingerprints and dental records. I was able to rely on ear identification (discussed in the previous chapter), which is based on principles common to other methods of identification.

In the case of the Dallas assassin—the man arrested for assassinating President Kennedy—there was a considerable amount of data, some of which, as Eddowes observed, was conflicting. For instance, the autopsy report of the Dallas assassin recorded his height as five feet nine inches, whereas Lee Harvey Oswald's U.S. Marine Corps (USMC) records gave his height as seventy-one inches (five feet eleven). Eddowes emphasized this discrepancy. However, a photo of Oswald in his USMC "Miscellaneous Information and Index" record, where his height was recorded as sixty-eight inches (five feet eight), placed him in front of a height chart, where he just reached the five-nine mark. At this time, Oswald was apparently five foot eight but appeared an inch taller in the photo because he was standing slightly away from the chart and thus closer to the camera.

Eddowes cited the Marine Corps records as evidence of inconsistency with the autopsy report, but the opposite conclusion could also be drawn. The evidence suggested that the mature Oswald had stood five feet nine, but perhaps out of vanity, he claimed to be taller and his word was accepted by those not having a yardstick handy. Moreover, Eddowes (1977, 41–43) himself mentioned that Oswald wore thick-heeled boots, which could add two inches to a man's height. Also, Eddowes knew of a discrepancy between the descriptions of two journalists who had interviewed Oswald in Russia. One described him as five foot nine with brown eyes, and the other as five foot eleven with blue eyes. Eddowes (1977, 17) conceded, "Although it would appear that they were interviewing two different men, it was, of course, the same man."

Other apparent discrepancies concerned Oswald's scars, notably a mastoidectomy scar behind his left ear that was recorded in the USMC records but not in the autopsy report. But the pathologists who conducted the postmortem were not looking for such a scar (not having the USMC records at the time for comparison), and it might have been hidden in the hair. Also, having been made when Oswald was just six years old, it might have grown faint over time. Certain other scars noted in the postmortem report (discussed in some detail in Nickell 1992b, 40–41) were quite similar to those of Oswald. It must be concluded that although there were some explainable omissions of scars on the autopsy report (including one that was not in the USMC records either, because it had not yet occurred), those mentioned were consistent with those of Lee Harvey Oswald.

Apart from these understandable discrepancies in height and scars, Eddowes offered little else to support his "double" theory. He tried to convince readers that the famous "backyard" photos of Oswald holding a rifle and a communist newspaper had been tampered with. In fact, some publications had retouched the photos prior to their publication, the Warren Commission learned; however, expert examination determined that the actual photographs were not montages, as Eddowes (1977, 117–19) had asserted (see House 1979, 6:138–215).

In contrast to Eddowes's view, there was much positive identification data. First, there was the fact that the fingerprints of the "two" men matched. Eddowes (1977, 137) stated: "There is no easy way to traverse the fingerprint evidence. If the facts that speak for an imposture were not so compelling, it would be logical to accept the evidence of the fingerprints at face value and to accept the Commission's findings—that the assassin was the former Marine, Lee Harvey Oswald." But the facts were surely not so compelling and certainly did not go "beyond reasonable doubt," as Eddowes had promised.

Moreover, the blood type of the Dallas assassin, noted on the original autopsy report, matched that in Oswald's USMC record—both were type A. Although that alone could not determine positive identification, it was certainly noteworthy.

Then there was the evidence from the next of kin. For about a month after Oswald's return to the United States, he and his wife Marina lived with his brother Robert and his family. Lee Harvey Oswald also saw his mother during that time, and the couple subsequently lived with her for two weeks until Lee and Marina secured their own apartment. During that brief but intense period of intimate contact, it was clear that Robert Oswald and his mother knew beyond any doubt that the man subsequently arrested and then killed in Dallas was Lee Harvey Oswald. For the record, Robert, his mother, and Marina each had a conversation with Oswald while he was in custody after the assassination, and following Oswald's death at Parkland Hospital, Robert viewed his body there (Oswald 1967, 152). At the graveside at Rose Hill Cemetery on November 25, 1963, the coffin was opened and the body was viewed by the family. Robert stated that he took "a last, long look at my brother's face" (Oswald 1967, 164).

In addition, there was considerable handwriting evidence. Numerous samples of writing by Oswald and by the Dallas assassin were compared by experts who subsequently testified before the Warren Commission. The various writings were positively identified by both an FBI expert and a Treasury Department examiner as originating from the same individual. The House committee enlisted a team of independent document examiners, each of whom concluded that documents from the period were "all in the handwriting of the same person" (House 1979, 8:247).

The committee also convened a panel of photographic experts and forensic anthropologists to determine whether there was any photographic evidence of an Oswald impostor. The panel examined photographs of Oswald "ranging in time from his Marine Corps enlistment to his arrest in Dallas after the assassination." One analysis was "based on 15 indices derived from 16 measurements of the head and face." For comparison, photographs were included of Oswald's fellow employee, Billy Lovelady, who bore a "strong physical resemblance to Oswald" and who had been "a source of controversy and confusion regarding the 'man in the doorway' photograph." The Lovelady photographs were intended to provide "a convenient control or yardstick to measure the variation observed in the facial indices derived from the Oswald photographs." The analytical indices for Lovelady (the closest Oswald "double" connected with the case) were quite different from those of the other photos. The experts concluded: "There are no biological inconsistencies in the Oswald photographs examined that would support the theory that a second person, or double, was involved." They added: "In addition to the analysis of facial indices described above, other facial features were compared. For example, in the three profile views, the angle of the nasal bridge in relation to the face was 37° in all three cases and the angle between the nasal septum and the facial plane varied by less than 1°. *The ears are relatively distinctive in shape and are strikingly similar in all photographs where they can be examined*" (House 1979, 6:273–81; emphasis added).

The reference to the "strikingly similar" ears was significant and paved the way for my own approach to the identification question. As discussed in chapters 7 and 9, ear identification is a technique with great potential for identifying persons in photographs. In their *Modern Criminal Investigation,* Soderman and O'Connell (1952, 97) stated, "The ears constitute the most characteristic part of the body next to the patterns of the friction ridges. They remain unaltered from birth until death. In cases where an arrested person has to be identified by photograph they play a deciding role." For example:

> An interesting case in which the ears were used for identification purposes was that of the false Grand Duchess Anastasia of Russia. Some years after World War I a woman, after an attempt at suicide in Berlin, Germany, declared herself to be the daughter of the murdered Czar Nicholas. She said she had escaped the execution of the Czar's family in Ekaterinburg, Siberia, had lost her memory as the result of a blow on the head, and after many adventures had finally come to Berlin. She had a superficial similarity to the real Anastasia, but Professor Bischoff, the head of the Scientific Police Institute at Lausanne, Switzerland, established her non-identity by means of the ears—by comparing profile photographs of the impostor and of the real Anastasia.

As noted in previous chapters, Alfred V. Iannarelli is the world's foremost expert in the specialized field of ear identification, and I proposed my plan to identify the Dallas assassin to him. He wrote in reply on October 1, 1980: "I totally agree with your suggestions." In fact, he had previously made a similar suggestion in "a letter to Jerry Pittman, Eddowes' attorney of record in Dallas. . . . To this day I have neither heard from Pittman nor Eddowes." He offered, "If you would like to go forward with it [the investigation of identity] I will give you all the support I can since your proposals were well taken."

Iannarelli studied a variety of photos alleged to be those of Oswald, particularly the photographs in the report of the House Select Committee on Assassinations and in the Warren Report. Subsequently,

Iannarelli sent me a copy of a letter he had addressed to the Honorable
Louis Stokes, chairman of the House committee, in which he explained
that he had "made a thorough study of the anatomical structure" of the
ears of the marine Oswald and of the subject arrested in Dallas and
identified by fingerprints as Oswald. Iannarelli concluded "that the
flesh lines of the Helix Rim, Lobule, Antihelix, Antitragus and Concha"
[structures of the external ear] were "identical" in both. He added: "My
total interest in this case is to set the record straight that there is no
doubt that the individual arrested, photographed, and identified as Lee
Harvey Oswald by the Dallas Police Dept. on November 23, 1963, for the
investigation of President Kennedy's murder is indeed, the deceased, Mr.
Lee Harvey Oswald" (Iannarelli 1980).

## Denouement

Our report was ignored at the time, although I subsequently published
a version of it (Nickell 1992b, 35–52). In 1981 Oswald's body was disin-
terred and autopsied by a team of distinguished pathologists. Hopefully,
few were surprised when it was revealed that the assassin was in fact Lee
Harvey Oswald. The identification was based on dental records as well
as on the defect of the left mastoid process (the bony prominence behind
the ear), which was consistent with Oswald's mastoidectomy (Norton
1984).

This conclusive identification should put to rest one of the most
troubling questions of our time. Of course, questions about the assassination persist, and conspiracy theories abound. But evidence once
believed to indicate two assassins—Oswald firing from the rear, from a
sixth-floor window of the Texas School Book Depository, and another
gunman shooting from the front, from the area known as the "grassy
knoll"—has been discredited. That evidence included the sound recording that supposedly registered an extra shot from the grassy knoll, the
motion-picture frames of the Zapruder film that showed Kennedy's
head snapping backward in a manner supposedly indicating a frontal
shot, and the sarcastically dubbed "super-bullet theory" (that one of the

bullets that struck Kennedy also wounded Governor John Connally yet remained relatively intact). (For a discussion, see sources cited in Nickell 1992b, 50–52; Posner 1994.)

An excellent summary of the years of speculation was provided by Jacob Cohen. In an articled titled "Conspiracy Fever," he stated (1975, 34–35):

> One would think that such tension would welcome the relief of decisive resolution. And if ever a question of fact has been resolved it is this one. Late in 1966, the Kennedy family relinquished the autopsy materials to the National Archives, placing strict restrictions on access to them. In February 1968, a panel of four prominent physicians, three forensic pathologists, and a radiologist, each nominated by a prominent person outside of government, was convened by Attorney General Ramsey Clark to review that material and the panel unanimously confirmed every conclusion of the autopsy including the location of the back wound and the evidence of its passage to the throat. They found evidence of no other wounds except those which could have been caused by a gunman above and behind the President.

Concluded Cohen (1975, 41):

> The public . . . never judges issues on their merits—having neither the time, inclination, opportunity, nor ability—but rather forms its conclusions from the sound and the style of the debate and its brute sense of the plausible. When the Gallup poll finds, as it has consistently since late 1966, that two-thirds and more of the American public doubt the essential conclusions of the Warren Commission, that only means that many people have heard an ill-mannered debate raging and concluded that such passionate and apparently well-informed dissent must signify something. After all, where there is smoke there is fire. But the

smoke in this case is only the smoke of verbal battle, a green, chemically produced mist not at all like the black billows which arise from real flames. What is alarming is that the public seems incapable of detecting the difference because its sense of the plausible has come to include incredible charges of government wrong-doing.

Perhaps time will heal the nation's wounds.

*Chapter 11*

# FROM THE ALBUM

THE FOREGOING CASES illustrate some important methodologies for investigating questionable photographic images. Here are three more cases from my files, involving the identity card photo of an alleged Nazi war criminal, the photograph of a humble Civil War soldier, and a sensational film supposedly proving extraterrestrial visitations.

## Nazi Identification Card

Among my most significant cases was that of accused Nazi death-camp guard John Demjanjuk, which is treated at length in my *Unsolved History* (2005, 37–50). The question of the authenticity of an SS identification card photo (see figure 11.1) was a life-or-death one when I was brought into the case. Demjanjuk had been sentenced to be executed in Israel, having been convicted of being the notorious "Ivan the Terrible" at the Treblinka concentration camp. Demjanjuk's family wanted me to review the evidence against him, with a view toward supporting his claim of innocence (Nickell 1994a, 90).

Although I actually found further evidence of Demjanjuk's guilt, he was acquitted in 1993 by the Israeli Supreme Court as a result of newly discovered evidence. Statements by former Treblinka death-camp guards had been discovered, wherein each man—interrogated by the Soviet KGB and convicted of war crimes—claimed that Ivan the Terrible was not Demjanjuk but one Ivan Marchenko. Yet even this evidence proved less credible than it first appeared. In 2000 I was visited by two agents from the U.S. Office of Special Investigations (OSI), with whom I shared my files. I gave testimony in an affidavit as part of a new trial in the United States not for Demjanjuk's war crimes but to revoke his

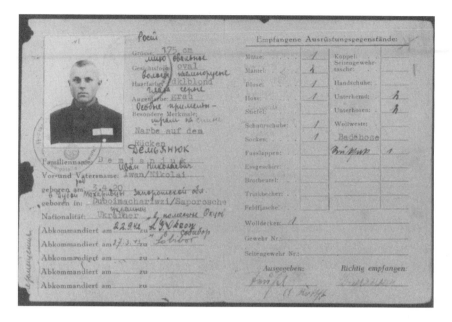

Figure 11.1. Nazi SS training camp identification card bears an incriminating photograph and the name of Ivan (now John) Demjanjuk.

citizenship for having lied about his Nazi past upon entering the country (Nickell 2005, 49–50).

The unrefuted evidence against Demjanjuk remained powerful. It included his positive identification by a fellow guard at the Sobibor death camp and documentary evidence placing him as a guard at two other camps (though not at Treblinka). Demjanjuk also admitted to having an SS tattoo removed, with no credible explanation of why he had such a tattoo in the first place (Nickell 2005, 39). The most incriminating evidence, however, was an SS identification card bearing his apparent photo and signature. But was the card authentic?

In 1987 I assembled a team of experts to compare the questioned photo with known photographs of Demjanjuk (e.g., from a 1947 driver's license) using a variety of approaches (see figure 11.2). Forensic analyst John F. Fischer applied a superimposition technique; forensic anthropologist Virginia Smith found similar skull structures, including a similarly enlarged right orbit; and Alfred V. Iannarelli concluded that

Figure 11.2. The photograph from the SS identification card (left) matches that from a 1947 driver's license (right) issued to Demjanjuk, although his face has become less muscular and his hairline has receded over the years.

the ears in the questioned and known photos matched. The questioned photograph was also determined to lack any signs of alteration. Our forensic review supported the previous detailed study conducted for the Israeli prosecution using measurements of eleven facial landmarks (Nickell 1994a, 90–96).

Other evidence supported the matching photographs: the signatures on the card were authentic, the information thereon was corroborated by other documents, and the card precisely matched genuine SS identity cards. Even if Demjanjuk had not been one of the various death-camp guards known as "Ivan" at Treblinka, he had certainly been one at Sobibor—a fact established by an authenticated photograph on an authenticated document (Nickell 2005, 39–48).

## From a Family Album

Questions of identity come from the ranks of the nonfamous as well as the famous and the infamous. This is illustrated by the interesting case

Figure 11.3. This Civil War photograph provided clues that ultimately
confirmed it to be a portrait of Milo
Welton. (Courtesy of Professor
Oscar W. Dillon Jr.)

of a Pennsylvania Union army soldier named Milo Welton, who died in
a military hospital in Washington, D.C., in 1862. A photograph identified as depicting Welton (see figure 11.3) had been handed down in his
family, and such traditions must be given due weight, especially when
there is no motive to deceive. However, doubts were eventually raised
by the man's uniform: he appeared to be an officer, whereas Welton had
supposedly never been more than a private. Perhaps, his descendants
thought, the picture was of his son, John Alexander Welton, who had
been promoted to lieutenant. The man in the picture is bearded, and
according to family tradition, John Welton had grown a beard to cover
the scar from a wound received in battle. "The picture is most likely
John," concluded a note accompanying the picture when it was entrusted
to me for study (Nickell 1994a, 81–82).

The picture was obviously a copy of a paper portrait that had a
crack or tear in it, and that image (as revealed by a magnifier) had been
a crayon enlargement (discussed in chapter 7). It had apparently been

copied from a direct-positive type of photograph—an ambrotype or, more likely, a tintype—since the image was obviously reversed (note that the jacket is buttoned backward and that the *K* on the hat is reversed).

I consulted Tom Fugate, an expert in military dress and curator of the Kentucky Military History Museum in Frankfort, Kentucky. He immediately identified the uniform as being not that of an officer but the regulation-issue dress or parade uniform of an enlisted man, complete with shoulder scales and a Hardee-pattern dress hat (turned up on the soldier's right, if the picture were not a mirror image). According to Fugate, the hat's crossed-swords insignia indicated a cavalry unit, and obviously, the soldier was in Company K (Nickell 1994a, 82).

It was now possible to compare this information with the military records of Milo and John Welton. (Such records can be obtained by completing NATF Form 80, available from the General Reference Branch, NNRG, National Archives and Records Administration, 8th and Pennsylvania Avenue NW, Washington, DC 20408.) They showed that both Milo Welton and his son John A. had served in Company K, Fourth Pennsylvania Cavalry. The man in the picture appeared to be closer to Milo's age of forty-three (in 1862) than John's age of nineteen to twenty-two (from 1862 to his death of a gunshot wound in 1865). Also, the eyes of the soldier in the photograph were very light, consistent with the description of Milo's eyes in his military record as "gray" but not with John's recorded eye color as "brown" and "dark" (Nickell 1994a, 82). Based on this preponderance of corroborative evidence, the identity of the soldier as Milo Welton was confirmed.

## "Alien Autopsy" Film

It surfaced in 1995 as part of a controversial "documentary" that aired on the Fox television network. The film purportedly depicts the post-mortem examination of an extraterrestrial who had died in a UFO crash at Roswell, New Mexico, in 1947 (see figure 11.4).

Skeptics like myself, and even many flying-saucer enthusiasts, quickly branded the affair a hoax. Among numerous observations, they noted that the film bore a bogus, nonmilitary code mark; that the inju-

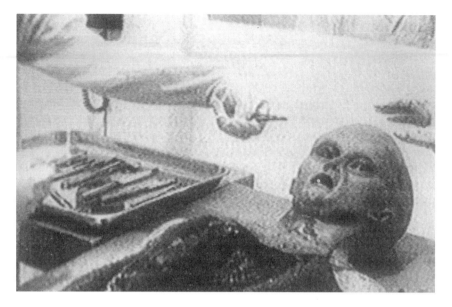

Figure 11.4. Scene from *Alien Autopsy* television program purports to show the post-mortem of an extraterrestrial from the Roswell UFO crash. (Courtesy of *Skeptical Inquirer* magazine)

ries sustained by the extraterrestrial were inconsistent with an air crash; and that the person performing the autopsy held the scissors like a tailor rather than like a pathologist (the latter would place his middle or ring finger in the bottom of the scissors hole and use his forefinger to steady the blades). In my original article (Nickell 1995, 18), I quoted several experts. Houston pathologist Ed Uthman faulted the film for lacking what he aptly termed "technical verisimilitude." Cyril Wecht, former president of the National Association of Forensic Pathologists, described the viscera in terms that could apply to supermarket meat scraps: "I cannot relate these structures to abdominal context." Nationally known pathologist Dominick Demaio was even more succinct: "I would say it's a lot of bull."

Although the film had supposedly been authenticated by Kodak, only the leader tape and a single frame had been submitted for examination, not the entire footage. In fact, a Kodak spokesman told the *Sunday Times* of London: "There is no way I could authenticate this. I saw an image on the print. Sure it could be old film, but it doesn't mean it is what the aliens were filmed on" (quoted in Nickell 1995, 18). Hollywood special-effects expert Trey Stokes (whose film credits include *The Blob, Batman Returns,* and *Tales from the Crypt*) observed that the alien corpse behaved like a dummy, seeming lightweight and "rubbery" and moving unnaturally when handled (Stokes 1995).

More than a decade later, a Manchester sculptor and special-effects creator, John Humphreys, admitted that the Roswell alien was his handiwork and had been destroyed after the film was shot. He made the revelation just as a new movie, *Alien Autopsy,* was being released, a film for which he had re-created the original creature. Released in April 2006, it told the story of the making of the 1995 hoax autopsy film, with a pair of British television celebrities playing the original producers, Ray Santilli and Gary Shoefield. Santilli now claims that the 1995 film was a re-creation of genuine footage that was damaged when its container was opened after forty-eight years (Horne 2006). It is hard to imagine anyone believing him.

As Humphreys told the BBC, "Funnily enough, I used exactly the same process as before. You start with the stills from the film, blow them up as large as you can. Then you make an aluminum armature, which you cover in clay, and then add all the detail." The clay model was used to produce a mold that yielded a latex cast. The body cavities were filled, Humphreys admitted, with chicken entrails, sheep brains, and the like, purchased from a meat market near the north London flat in which the film was shot (Horne 2006).

Are Humphreys's claims credible? Indeed, he is a graduate of the Royal Academy and a special-effects model maker whose credits include *Max Headroom* and *Doctor Who.* His re-creations are so good that his ability to have made the originals is unquestioned. In addition, examples of his work displayed on his Web site (Humphreys 2006) are stylistically consistent with the hoaxed aliens. Humphreys also admitted that he actually played the role of the pathologist in the original autopsy film; his identity was concealed by a contamination suit.

The alien autopsy hoax represented the culmination of several years' worth of rumors, urban legends, and outright deceptions purporting to prove that saucer wreckage and the remains of its humanoid occupants were stored at a secret facility—the (nonexistent) "Hangar 18" at Wright Patterson Air Force Base—and that the small corpses were autopsied at that or some other site. The film will be remembered as a classic of the genre.

The truth about the "Roswell incident"—that the crashed device was a secret U.S. spy balloon, part of Project Mogul, which was attempting to monitor emissions from anticipated Soviet nuclear tests—continues to be obscured by hoaxers, conspiracy cranks, and hustlers.

# Part III

## OTHER ARTIFACTS

*Chapter 12*

# AUTHENTICATING ARTWORKS AND OTHER ARTIFACTS

ALL PRODUCTS OF human workmanship are called *artifacts*. They include documents and photographs (already discussed) as well as a bewildering variety of other items both prehistoric (such as Stone Age tools) and historic (such as millstones or spinning wheels). All provide tangible links with the past and can help fill in the gaps in humankind's knowledge. Observed one writer (Mills 1973, 6–7):

> History, the total story of mankind, comes to life for us when we can see and study the treasures man has left behind in his journey through time. The word "treasure" usually evokes images of jewels and gold and silver plate set with precious stones, or ancient chests bursting with coins, pearls or uncut diamonds. Yet the smallest finds uncovered on an archaeological dig—a single stone weapon, some shreds of food left in a tomb a thousand years ago, or the hub and broken spokes of an ancient wheel—all of little intrinsic value—may be treasures, too. Treasures of the mind, that is, for each could be a link to man's past, leading to the discovery of new and unexpected wealth of understanding human history.

Of course, this applies only if the artifacts are authentic.

## Questioned Artifacts

In contrast to genuine relics of the past, spurious artifacts are not merely non-treasures. They are actually anti-treasures because they are capable of distorting the historical picture and thus are analogous to a

Figure 12.1. This sculpture (top) is not a forgery but a cast made from the original. X-rays revealed armatures that made no sense sculpturally and were not connected. This indicates that they came *after* the molding of the plaster (to strengthen it). (Exhibit, Buffalo State University)

sociopath's act of vandalism. At the very least, they can divert scholars' attention from more profitable study (see figure 12.1).

Consider, for instance, the case of the notorious Kensington Stone. In 1898, on his farm near Kensington, Minnesota, Olof Ohman claimed to have unearthed a curious stone entwined in the roots of an aged tree. Bearing what proved to be a runic inscription (runes are medieval Scandinavian letters), the 200-pound slab of graywacke became the subject of protracted controversy. If genuine, the inscription—telling of a fourteenth-century Viking penetration of the North American interior—would require the rewriting of American prehistory, specifically that of pre-Columbian exploration. Translated, the inscription read: "Eight Goths and twenty-two Norwegians upon an exploring journey from Vinland to the west. We had camped by two skerries [rocky islets] one day's journey north from this stone. We were fishing one day; when we returned home [we] found ten men red with blood and dead. A.V.M.

166

[*Ave Virgo Maria* (Hail, Virgin Mary)] save [us] from evil. [We] have ten men by the sea to look after our vessel fourteen [or forty-one] days' travel from this island. Year 1362."

Although Norwegian American writer Hjalmar Holand spent much of his life attempting to authenticate the Kensington Stone, scholars demonstrated that the alleged fourteenth-century Scandinavian dialect contained countless anachronisms. Indeed, the writing was a thousand years out of style. Finally in 1976, Walter and Anna Josephine Gran reported that their father, John, had confessed his involvement in the hoax. He, together with Ohman and schoolteacher Sven Fogelblad (who was knowledgeable about runes), had carved the bogus inscription as a prank to show up some of the more learned members of their community (MacDougall 1958, 109–11).

False artifacts include religious relics that proliferated during the Middle Ages—items such as Moses' rod and Joseph's "coat of many colors." There are also nonartifact relics, such as vials of Jesus' blood, skulls of the three Wise Men, and so on. (Although I decided to limit this book to artifacts, nonartifact items can also be faked—fossils, for example. Ironically, such fakes may themselves be artifacts. In any case, the basic principles of authentication apply to them as well.)

Alleged relics of Jesus (and those associated with him) dominated. It was said that there were enough fragments of the cross from Jesus' crucifixion to fill a ship's cargo hold. At least four churches claimed to have the single lance that had pierced Jesus' side. And there were some forty "genuine" shrouds, including the notorious Holy Shroud of Turin. The latter is especially instructive. It lacks any provenance before the mid-fourteenth century, at which time a bishop claimed that the artist who had made it confessed. In addition, it has been shown conclusively to have been rendered with vermilion and red ocher pigments and has been carbon-dated to the time of the reported confession. (For a fuller discussion of all these fakes, see my *Relics of the Christ* [2007].)

The advent of the Renaissance, the revival of learning following the medieval period, awakened an interest in the acquisition of artifacts: old coins, ancient statuary and other objets d'art, arms and armor, manuscript books, and similar rarities. Public and private collections grew, and from the latter, fine art museums developed (Mills 1973, 118–23). Forgers followed close behind, and their nefarious activities have continued unabated. For example, in 1931 a British authority stated, "One does not require an expert, but an actuary, to tell the collector of English furniture that, in one year, more is shipped to America than could have been made in the whole eighteenth century" (Cescinsky 1931, 1). More recently, another writer (Hamblin 1970, 130–31) pointed out:

Most of the "antiquities" which eager Italian policemen confiscate today are fakes. In February 1968, Rome police broke up what they said was an international ring that had dealt in clandestine antiquities for more than ten years. In an abandoned lime kiln just a few miles outside of Rome they found a cache of the ring's goods: more than two hundred pieces of Etruscan and Greek pottery, Roman carved heads, jewelry, vases, bronze statues, ancient coins. Some of the treasure was already boxed for shipment abroad. Officials studied it all carefully and pronounced some ten to thirty percent of it genuine and valuable; the rest of the hundreds of pieces were fakes. Police estimated that gullible buyers in Belgium, Switzerland, Germany and the United States had been deceived through the years by this one ring of dealers and shippers.

Some appreciation for what is required of a good forger can be garnered from the modus operandi of Italian forger Alfredo Fioravanti and his friends, three members of the Riccardi family. They produced terra-cotta statues of Etruscan warriors that—for forty years—fooled experts at New York City's Metropolitan Museum of Art (Hamblin 1970, 141–42):

To make the Etruscan figures they worked slowly from catalogue illustrations of Etruscan ware in Italian and foreign museums. They were careful never to excite suspicion by copying a known statue exactly. They always adapted slightly or changed size and proportions. They used the same native clay that the ancient Etruscans had used, and they modeled their figures from the feet up, as the Etruscans had done. When they began making really big pieces, however, they had a problem. Their ovens, designed for firing pottery only, were small, only about four feet high. The Etruscans had had gigantic ovens which could take life-size figures. There was only one solution for Fioravanti and the Riccardis: they would have to break their big statues before firing them, and then fire them in pieces.

The range of specialization in artifact fakery is impressive: prehistoric stone implements, Old Masters' paintings, antique sculptures, Etruscan pottery, ancient coins, bronze tablets, Spanish armor, Stradivarius violins, antique furniture, Tiffany glass, folk samplers, and pre-Columbian figures. In many cases, honest reproductions are simply converted to forgeries by amateurs who remove telltale imprints and artificially age the pieces (Nickell 2005, 72).

## Detecting Fakes

Just as the production of forged artifacts can require specialized knowledge, so can their detection. According to a British expert in antique furniture:

To explain the tools of the various periods and the evidence of their use is impossible in a book. Such knowledge can only be acquired in the workshop. Yet it must be obvious that tools, which were utterly unknown in the eighteenth century or earlier, cannot have been used on the furniture of that period, and if one finds indications of the circular saw, for instance, it must be evidence of modern origin. Conversely, one would hardly look for signs of the adze—the tool of the primitive carpenter—in the furniture of Georgian days. Side by side with this acquaintance of tools goes the knowledge of woods. There are nearly thirty different kinds of mahogany at the present day, and more than half that number of walnut. There is English oak of at least two kinds, oak from Riga, Holland, France, Germany, Italy, Austria, America and even Japan. Even with English oak, at the present day, the timber is not that from the age-old trees such as was used in the sixteenth and seventeenth centuries; these have been cut down long ago. (Cescinsky 1931, 14)

Yet the need for detailed knowledge does not mean that only specialists can function as historical investigators. It merely means that—at an appropriate stage in the investigation of a questioned artifact—a specialist *may* need to be consulted.

The antique detective's first step is simply to recognize when an artifact may be questionable. For example, the presence of worm channels—rather than mere bored holes—on the surface of a piece of antique furniture is prima facie evidence of spuriousness. It indicates that the piece was made from worm-eaten wood, with the furrows being exposed by the subsequent workmanship, such as by planing (Cescinsky 1931, 107).

In important cases, the matter should be passed on to an expert. Many excellent experts are as close as the nearest bookshelf. One is Harold L. Peterson, chief curator of the National Park Service, who is responsible for more than 200 museums and 64 historical buildings. In his *How Do You Know It's Old?* (1975), Peterson discusses how to distinguish signs of age in wood (e.g., shrinkage, wear, discoloration, tool marks, fasteners, worm holes), metals (e.g., oxidation, patina), and other materials such as glass, pottery, porcelain, ivory, horn, and stone, which show fewer apparent signs of age but may exhibit evidence of wear, manufacturing technique, and style that provide useful clues.

Another expert consulted by antique dealers and collectors is Mark Chervenka. His *Antique Trader™ Guide to Fakes & Reproductions* (2003) features 1,036 photographs of fakes and originals shown side by side to help expose forgeries and reproductions.

And then there is Anne Gilbert, whose excellent *How to Be an Antiques Detective* (1978) features the "Sherlock Holmes approach to solving antiques mysteries." This involves researching the subject, using a magnifying glass, checking for clues, applying the process of elimination, and making deductions—steps all well illustrated in photos and case studies by the savvy Gilbert.

In the introduction, I mentioned four major factors to be considered in the authentication of questioned artifacts: provenance, content (or elements of style), material composition, and scientific analysis. The last may prove decisive in certain instances.

## Scientific Tests

Scientific analysis is indispensable to the investigator. Quite often it can be a deciding factor in resolving some important historical question, as suggested in previous chapters.

Microchemical analyses are useful not only in questioned document cases but also to determine which pigments and binding media were used in paintings, among other things (Mills 1973; Fleming 1980, 37). (See figure 12.2.)

Emission spectroscopy can be used to analyze materials when a tiny amount can be spared. The sample is heated to the glowing point, and the light is passed through the prism in a spectroscope so that its distinctive spectrum can be identified. In this manner, an "ancient bronze" piece was shown to be almost pure zinc, a metal that was unavailable to the Romans who supposedly made it (O'Hara 1973, 719–23; Mills 1973, 24, 29).

Nondestructive tests are employed when not even a tiny sample can be sacrificed, as in the case of a rare metal coin or a precious porcelain artifact. For example, electron beam analysis (capable of examining microscopic areas) was used to test the tiny pieces of glass making up a three-quarter-inch Roman mosaic plaque. And X-ray fluorescence spectroscopy, which indicates surface composition, has been employed to distinguish between imported and native cobalt in the blue glazes of Chinese pottery (Mills 1973, 29–31).

An example of the importance of ordinary X-ray photography was given in the introduction—the case of the ostensibly fifteenth-

Figure 12.2. Renowned microanalyst Walter C. McCrone discovered paint pigments on the Shroud of Turin. His motto was "Think Small." (Photograph by Joseph Barabe, copyright McCrone Scientific Photography)

century triptych constructed with modern hardware. The radiograph also showed that underneath the painting and gilding was wood that had been worm-eaten *before* those materials were applied. X-rays of paintings can reveal creative changes made by the artist in the course of his or her work that would probably not be done by a mere copyist. Occasionally, X-rays reveal an entire painting lurking under the surface. Beneath a sixteenth-century *Adoration of the Maji*, for instance, was a *Holy Family* by the same artist, Jacob Jordaens. And underneath an "El Greco" was an old painting over which the modern forgery had been done (Mills 1973, 25, 31–34, 85).

Infrared photography—used with dramatic success to read age-darkened portions of the Dead Sea Scrolls—has many traditional applications. Museum curators employ it to detect restoration on

Figure 12.3. X-ray fluorescence is a nondestructive test. Here, a Civil War minié ball shows the characteristic profile for lead, a small amount of tin, and surface iron from dirt—all consistent with genuineness. (Exhibit, Buffalo State University)

tapestries and to reveal designs on pottery and other artifacts that may have become invisible to the naked eye (*Applied* 1972, 36–38, 52). Other nondestructive tests include ultraviolet radiation, X-ray diffraction analysis (used to identify crystalline compounds), laser light (which may reveal traces not detected by ultraviolet or infrared light), and X-ray fluorescence (see figure 12.3) (Mills 1973, 28–29; Fischer and Nickell 1984, 26–27).

Scientific techniques to determine the age of an artifact include radiocarbon dating of organic materials, thermoluminescence (particularly important in dating pottery), and various other methods (Mills 1973, 39–45). The presence of certain materials used in the making of an artifact (such as machine-made nails, celluloid, or paint pigments) can also assist in age determination.

Some of these analytical techniques were applied to a group of "lost" paintings bearing the signature of Dutch master Jan Vermeer (1632–1675). The result was scientific proof that they were actually fakes rendered by forger Han van Meegeren (mentioned briefly in the introduction). The story began with van Meegeren's arrest in Amsterdam in 1945 on a charge of "collaboration with the enemy." Within weeks, the jailed painter was claiming that the *Christ and the Adulteress* he had sold to Nazi leader Hermann Göring was his own work—not a national treasure; he had merely signed Vermeer's name to it. To silence skeptics, who believed that a mediocre artist was lying to avoid punishment for treason, van Meegeren produced yet another "Vermeer," *The Young Christ,* while behind bars (Bianconi 1967, 101).

Eventually, it was learned that van Meegeren had also forged works by some of Vermeer's contemporaries: Pieter de Hooch, Frans Hals, and others. He had used old canvases, mixed paint from natural pigments (including the true ultramarine that had been a Vermeer favorite), and developed effective artificial aging techniques. (He used a mixture of phenol and formaldehyde to harden his paint to resemble that which was three centuries old. He was even able to simulate the *craquelure* associated with age.) Rather than copy known works, however, van Meegeren created new paintings. According to one commentator (Mills 1973, 76–77):

> With great skill he had cunningly imitated the style of Vermeer and had painted works that the experts might be expected to think would turn up one day. Besides being a master of techniques, the wily Van Meegeren was also a student of art history. He knew that most of the Dutch painters of Vermeer's time had painted at least some New Testament scenes. But if Vermeer had followed the trend of his time, his biblical paintings had either been lost or destroyed—with the exception of one early work. Yet the art experts hoped more might be discovered. Indeed, Van Meegeren "discovered" them for the world of art, and, by providing what the experts were ready to accept, diverted suspicion. Was he to be tried for the signatures or the paintings? It was an

interesting legal question, and, in fact, he was eventually tried for both.

Belatedly, scientists reexamined the paintings. Whereas prior study had been comparatively superficial—consisting of the identification of some pigments and tests of paints for their resistance to certain solvents—the paintings were now subjected to a panoply of analyses. Further microchemical, microscopic, radiographic, spectroscopic, and other tests were carried out. As a result, traces of formaldehyde and phenol were detected, and the presence of cobalt blue, a pigment not known until 1802, was discovered. Residue of black ink was even found in the cracks of the varnish, where it had been placed to simulate the grime of centuries.

Van Meegeren thus revenged himself on the very critics who had dismissed his early paintings. He received a relatively light sentence of one year's imprisonment but died of a heart attack a month later. His legacy remains, however, providing a lesson for today's historical detectives and authentication experts on the value of thorough scientific examination (Bianconi 1967, 100–102; Mills 1973, 75–83; MacDougall 1958, 87).

Whenever a significant artifact is questioned, the historical detective must devise an investigative strategy capable of resolving the issue. He or she may make (or commission) an investigation of provenance, a stylistic study, a detailed examination of workmanship, scientific tests of materials, or other appropriate analyses. The following chapters present case studies illustrating such methodologies.

# Chapter 13

# LOST ICON FOUND

THIS INTRIGUING LITTLE case came my way in 1982, but its story began in World War II with a fire-damaged religious icon that had reportedly been taken from Poland (see figure 13.1). The man who owned it wished to return it to that country through Pope John Paul II. But when questions were raised about its origins, my forensic colleague John F. Fischer and I took the case.

The owner, George Chesney of Orlando, Florida, told this story of the icon's provenance, writing in 1979 to the apostolic delegation in Washington, D.C.:

> This may sound a bit fictitious, but [it] goes back to 1941 when the Russians sacked the Cathedral at Gdynia and most of the interior was destroyed by fire and many of the priceless objects either looted or destroyed.
>
> But among those saved was an "Icon" which was passed onto me to bring back to the U.S. for repairs.
>
> The man involved with this object was also connected with the Underground and a few years later removed from that country for his safety. He went to another country where he died. His wife and family were allowed to leave Poland but in the passing years [I] lost contact with them.

Chesney was taken aback by this response from the apostolate: "According to diocesan authorities in Danzica (aka Gdansk), there must be some misunderstanding. Gdynia is a relatively new city. It has no cathedral. None of its churches have had antique icons. The Russians had

176

Figure 13.1. Fire-damaged religious icon (with ornate covering in place) was scarcely recognizable but held an intriguing story. (Photograph by John F. Fischer)

not yet occupied the area by 1941. The icon to which you refer would have had to be taken by the Germans and not the Russians" (Jadot 1979).

Chesney (1982) told us that he might have gotten the date wrong, and he had intended no real distinction between "cathedral" and "church." It was indeed the Russian occupation to which he referred, and he had taken possession of this icon in Gdynia in about 1948 or 1949. Chesney was unsure how to proceed, but he finally resolved to accede to the apostolic delegation's request for "a photograph of the work in order to facilitate the identification of its place of origin" (Jadot 1979). At Chesney's behest, Fischer and I agreed to photograph the icon and to examine and describe it more fully in the hope of solving the growing mystery.

## The Origin of Icons

The icon proved to be a traditional one. Icons (from the Greek *eikon*, for "image") are common to the Eastern Orthodox Church (with Greek,

177

Russian, and other adherents) but much less so the Roman Catholic Church. The supposed origin of icons is interesting. From about 723 to 842, certain iconoclasts (Greek "image breakers") interpreted the biblical commandment against "graven images" literally. According to art historian H. W. Janson (1963, 177):

> During the Iconoclastic Controversy, one of the chief arguments in favor of sacred images was the claim that Christ Himself had permitted St. Luke to paint his portrait, and that other portraits of Christ or of the Virgin had miraculously appeared on earth by divine fiat. These original, "true" sacred images were supposedly the source of the later, man-made ones. Such pictures or icons, had developed in early Christian times out of Graeco-Roman portrait panels. . . . Little is known about their origins, for examples antedating the Iconoclastic Controversy are extremely scarce.

Traditionally, icons were painted on varnished wood panels and over time acquired a dark patina from candle smoke. Typically, icons have a tooled metal covering with cutout areas revealing the important image areas (usually the face and hands) of the painting. Called a *riza,* such a protective covering was added by the fourteenth century in Russia, influenced by the Greeks (Kondakov 1927, 37).

In the first half of the nineteenth century, when they began to be collected by art lovers, icons started to proliferate. According to Anne Gilbert (1983):

> In the small villages of Russia icon painting became a peasant craft. Many icons were cheaply made to be covered with metallic covers; only the exposed faces, hands and feet required hand painting. As the demand for icons continued to increase, factories were opened to meet the demand. The white metal covering many of the factory-made works often were decorated with fake gems and Cyrillic words.

## The Examination

Our examination of Chesney's mystery icon took place over two days and consisted of visual inspection, light microscopic study, infrared and ultraviolet examination, and limited microchemical analyses. Photographic techniques—including side-light and diffuse-light photography—were also employed. In addition to conducting historical research on antique icons, we consulted an expert who translated the inscriptions on the metal coverings.

The panel on which the icon was painted measured about 172 mm wide by 222 mm long by 16 mm thick (approximately 6¾ by 8¾ by ⅝ inches). It was made of two pieces: a main portion plus an additional strip of wood about 16 mm wide running the entire length. At either side, along the edge, were some small pieces of cardboard ranging from 1 to 5 mm thick, obviously used to accommodate the slightly out-of-square panel so that the covering would fit more closely. (The icon's brass covering was removed by Chesney for our examination, and the separate halo had already been detached. The nails affixing it had broken free of their solder and were missing.) The panel was covered on all edges and on the back by a single piece of red velvet from which most of the pile had been worn away. It was discolored and showed evidence of staining by some liquid—possibly only water stains.

We detected scratched numerals—"34"—on each of the three pieces: on the front panel in the upper right corner, on the uppermost edge (on the right) of the covering, and on the reverse of the halo at three o'clock. We speculated that this might have been done to mark the pieces for identification while being worked on separately so they could be reassembled. (We considered this somewhat more likely than the explanation that the marking was for inventory recording, since it would be unnecessary to disassemble the piece for this purpose.)

The painted image corresponded to that of the covering. We noted that the face and hands had been rendered in detailed fashion, whereas the portions unexposed when the cover was in place had been done in a comparatively sketchy fashion. This suggested that the panel had

179

been prepared expressly with the intention of its being covered. This probability was supported by the fact that only the figure had been varnished; the varnish coat extended irregularly beyond the figure without covering the full front of the panel. These observations were consistent with the previously quoted comments about the proliferation of nineteenth-century Russian icons.

The icon had been stained or varnished prior to painting, and limited microchemical tests indicated the use of iron-earth pigments (e.g., red ocher or burnt sienna) in the red-brown hues making up most of the figure and the background and a copper-based pigment in the green of the tunic. (More extensive testing seemed neither mandated nor cost-effective.) Examination under long-wave ultraviolet light detected no obvious signs of earlier restoration (Fischer and Nickell 1983). (However, such signs were revealed in another icon in Chesney's possession, which he acknowledged having professionally cleaned and restored.)

The story about the icon having been salvaged from a burned church gained credence from the painting's appearance. The picture had been rather severely damaged by checking and cracking, with the cracks showing wide separation. Those portions exposed when the cover was in place showed the greatest damage. In fact, in strong light, the image was practically unrecognizable, but Chesney thought it portrayed the Virgin Mary. Under different lighting, however, the effect of the damage was minimized, and the portrait image was revealed more clearly. In his forensic laboratory, Fischer used diffuse lighting and viewed the icon from an oblique angle and through a red filter. The best results were obtained by infrared photography (see figure 13.2). Indeed, the image was revealed sufficiently to see that it was not the Virgin Mary but Jesus in a portrayal known as "Christ Pantocrator" (see, for example, Taylor 1979, 19). The recovery of the original appearance was actually good enough that it could serve as the model for artistic restoration.

Embossed writing on the metal cover required translation, so we consulted Professor Boris Sorokin from the Department of Slavic and Oriental Languages at the University of Kentucky in Lexington. From a photograph, Sorokin (1983) identified the inscription as Cyrillic and

Figure 13.2. Infrared photograph of the icon restores the image and assists in solving the mystery. (Photograph by John F. Fischer)

therefore not Polish. He told us that the writing was Russian and that the words on the bottom of the metal cover read "Lord Pantocrator" (essentially, as we had expected). The embossed text of the open Bible read: "A new Commandment I give you: 'Love one another'" (a quotation from the New Testament, John 13:34). Sorokin, who was familiar with Russian icons, believed that this one was no older than the nineteenth century.

## The Verdict

In contrast to the story told to its owner—murky and filled with hints of intrigue—the icon had not been taken from a Catholic cathedral or church in Gdynia, Poland, in 1941. If it was connected with the later Russian occupation of that city, it was more likely brought there by an Orthodox soldier, since it was of Russian manufacture. Its small size, skimpy painting, and other elements suggested no great antiquity, and it probably dated from the latter nineteenth century. In brief, the icon was authentic, but the story told to its owner was not—a tale possibly garbled by processes best understood by folklorists.

181

*Chapter 14*

# JEFFERSON DAVIS'S MUSKET

IN 1995 I WAS commissioned by a historical society to investigate the authenticity of an antique firearm that purportedly belonged to Jefferson Davis (see figure 14.1), president of the Confederate States of America (CSA). What were the true facts about this potentially rare piece of Americana? And how did they fit into the context of historical firearms—questioned and otherwise?

## Historical Firearms

Firearms represent a highly specialized—and popular—field of collecting. Interest in them ranges from early blunderbusses (short guns with flared muzzles) and muskets (long-barreled guns that lack rifling) to long rifles (including those termed Pennsylvania or Kentucky rifles). Firearms used during the American Civil War are of particular interest. So are ones from the 1880s onward that bear such important names as Sharps, Winchester, Springfield, and Remington. Among valuable pistols and revolvers are those made by Colt, as well as derringers, dueling pistols, and other specialty types (Jenkins 1963, 372–73; Miller and Miller 1988, 156–69).

According to Harold L. Peterson (1975, 113–15), fakery in firearms can include engraving decorations on plain originals and welding extra pieces of barrel onto standard Colt single-action revolvers to make them appear to be long-barreled "Buntline" variants, which are rare and valuable. Moreover, "some few firearms such as Patterson and Walker Colt revolvers and Confederate revolvers have been made completely from scratch or altered from other less expensive pistols because of their great value." But, Peterson (1975, 115), explained:

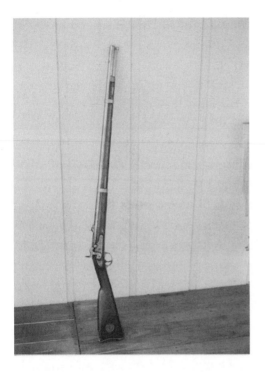

Figure 14.1. Antique firearm thought to have belonged to Jefferson Davis. (Courtesy of Odell Walker)

The most common type of fakery . . . involves the adding of famous names—either makers or owners, or sometimes the name of an historic ship. The most spectacular of this sort of forgery involves obliterating British marks on a pocket or dueling pistol and replacing it with the name of an American maker. Some skillful fakers try to hide the evidence of the lost metal caused when grinding out the original marks by inlaying a gold plate to bear the new name. American makers seldom ever did this, in fact, and if they did, it was only on the highest quality pistols. . . . Grinding out engraved marks entails the removal of less metal than stamped marks, but even then you can usually detect the activity through changes in patination, the accidental removal of parts of original engraved decoration or follow lines around the border of the lockplate. The new marks normally give themselves away also by stylistic errors, by interrupting the patination or by the cleanness of their cuts when examined under magnification.

Firearms reputed to belong to famous and infamous personages may attract as much emotional investment as they do hard currency. As a result, they proliferate like saints' relics. One Alabama scholar observed that "there are in existence about 200 pistols of which each owner believes he has the one that killed Abraham Lincoln" (MacDougall 1958, 165). Clearly, at least 199 of these must be spurious.

Many years ago, I had occasion to investigate a couple of alleged Daniel Boone rifles in Kentucky historical collections. One was owned by the Kentucky Historical Society. Its stock was carved with "D.B." and "BOoNs bESt FREN," along with a pictorial of a tomahawk-bearing Indian plus fifteen notches—"for Indians shot," according to the seller, "Professor" Gilbert Walden. Of its provenance, he stated in part, "For a long time it was hidden away in an old closet until found" (quoted in Nickell 2005, 81). In addition to the suspect provenance, the carvings were clearly fraudulent. For example, the frontiersman invariably spelled his name "Boone," and the custom of notching a gun originated out west during the later era of Buffalo Bill. Moreover, according to an expert in American long rifles, John Bivins of the Museum of Early Southern Decorative Arts in Winston-Salem, North Carolina, "It could not have been made earlier than the year of Boone's death" (based on details of the gun stock and iron mounts). "For that matter," he added, "I don't believe Boone would have so wretchedly defaced the stock of a rifle in such a manner" (quoted in Nickell 2005, 83).

The other "Boone" rifle I investigated was in the collection of the Kentucky Military History Museum, where it was kept in storage, presumably because it was such an obvious fake. Its provenance was unknown beyond the fact that it had been donated by a Florida man in 1979. Thus, the sole "proof" that it had belonged to the famous Kentuckian consisted of its inscription. On the right-hand side of the stock was carved: "D. Boon. CILLED. BIG / PanTHER. This GUn. I

WAS 13. YEAR. OLD. / in. BUCKS CO. PA." An inscription on the other side had an altered date. In addition to that suspicious detail were the obvious spurious elements of the misspelled name and the word "cilled" (for Boone's "kiled"). A series of notches on the stock was another phony element (Nickell 2005, 74–89).

There are also some uninscribed rifles that supposedly belonged to Boone, including one in the Tennessee State Museum in Nashville. Its provenance is known from 1852, at which time it was presented to the Tennessee Historical Society by Dr. J. G. M. Ramsey, a longtime president of the society. It is a French musket of a type supplied to American Revolutionary War soldiers and therefore, according to the museum's curator, "could have been used by Daniel Boone," although the museum "has no information as to the basis for their belief" (Baker 1974).

Of related interest, there are several inscribed powder horns and other items that supposedly belonged to the wilderness explorer, both inscribed and not. They include a watch (totally lacking in provenance) and a reputed walnut beam from Daniel Boone's cabin in Mason, Missouri, suspected of coming from an old railroad tie (Nickell 2005, 84–85).

As these examples show, a firearm or other artifact may be genuine or counterfeited, or it may be entirely authentic except for an inscription that allegedly ties it to a historical figure.

## Background on Jefferson Davis

Jefferson Davis (1808–1889) was a central figure in the War Between the States. Born in Kentucky, he was a West Point graduate and became a U.S. Army soldier, then a Mississippi cotton planter. He served in the U.S. Senate (1847–1851) and as secretary of war (1853–1857); from 1857, he served in the Senate again and was a leader of the southern Democrats. Davis defended what he termed "humane slavery," and in 1860 he issued a declaration that advocated the South's secession from the United States. He subsequently became president of the CSA, assuming strong political leadership though frequently disagreeing with military policy. His temperamental and self-righteous personality were among the impediments to broad unification of the southern states (*Webster's* 1997, 318).

After the defeat of the Confederacy in 1865, Davis was captured in Georgia and imprisoned at Fort Monroe, Virginia. After two years he was released on bail, and charges against him were dropped following the general amnesty declared by President Andrew Johnson on Christmas Day 1868. Davis, however, never regained his American citizenship. He sought convalescence in Canada and then in England, but he eventually settled on a small Mississippi estate given to him by a friend. He was alternately condemned and celebrated (*Collier's Encyclopedia* 1983, s.v. "Jefferson Davis"). Out of the latter impulse, he might have been presented with a gun in honor of his service as the only president of the CSA.

## The Investigation

Owned by the Lyon County, Kentucky, Historical Society (whose president, Odell Walker, commissioned my investigation), the Jefferson Davis firearm was ostensibly a presentation gun. That is, it had presumably been given to Davis as a gift, because a medallion bearing his name was embedded in the stock (see figure 14.2).

Prior to my involvement in the matter, the "Jefferson Davis" gun was examined by professional appraiser and firearms expert Turner E. Kirkland of Dixie Gun Works Inc., Union City, Tennessee. He authenticated the item as a genuine "Fayetteville two-banded .58 caliber brass-mounted Confederate musket." The date "1863" was stamped into the lock plate, along with "CSA" and "FAYETTEVILLE" (see figure 14.3). Kirkland cited evidence that the musket has been rather poorly treated and had a replacement ramrod. Also, he described a cast-brass medallion (see figure 14.4) inset into the right-hand side of the buttstock as "of great importance," but he was unable to identify the "large tower" depicted on the medallion. Kirkland (1994) concluded that the rifle had a "standard" value of $6,000 to $7,500 plus an "unestimated intrinsic

Figure 14.2. Detail of musket showing Jefferson Davis medallion embedded in the stock. (Courtesy of Odell Walker)

value" of about $500 to $1,000 more because of the interest occasioned by the medallion. If the rifle could be authenticated as Jefferson Davis's, he concluded, it would be valued at $30,000 to $80,000.

### Provenance

Since the musket itself was certainly authentic, the question left to be resolved was, had it belonged to the president of the Confederacy? To answer that question, I naturally began with the matter of provenance.

According to Odell Walker (1995), the late Mr. Lee S. Jones, a corporate tax attorney, had purchased the gun from an auction house in Louisville, Kentucky, some years ago, saying, "I was not about to allow one of those Texans to take that Jefferson Davis Rifle to Texas." Reported Walker: "In our backward search, we are told that the auction house is no longer in business and the owner is now retired to Florida. We are still tracking, but information is hard to come by."

Figure 14.3. Musket's lock plate has a place, "FAYETTEVILLE," and a date, "1863," stamped into the metal. (Photograph by Odell Walker)

Such a lack of provenance was disappointing. Nevertheless, as one professional art dealer observed, "Failure to record does not necessarily indicate any deception; rather one might consider it like a missing piece of a complicated puzzle" (David 1981, 67). Another significant piece of the puzzle remained, of course—the medallion—and it would prove crucial.

### The Medallion

I consulted expert Charles E. Walsh of Antique and Modern Firearms Inc. in Lexington, Kentucky, who stated that there was a long tradition of decorating American firearms with inset coins and similar artifacts. Walsh (1995) noted that some staining of the wood around the medallion (see figure 14.4) was a typical heat-radiation stain, indicating that the gun had probably been placed over a fireplace for some time.

I sought to identify the medallion's imagery. Using a computerized library card catalog and employing the keywords "Confederate" and "symbol," I located the book *Confederate Monuments: Enduring Symbols of the South and the War Between the States.* Therein I located

Figure 14.4. Medallion "to Jefferson Davis President of the Confederate States of America" held the key to the mystery. (Photograph by Odell Walker)

a photograph proving that the tower on the medallion was in fact the Jefferson Davis Monument in Richmond, Virginia (Widener 1982, 281). My identification was subsequently confirmed by the editor of the Jefferson Davis Papers at Rice University, Lynda Crist (1995). The memorial's cornerstone had been laid in 1896 (Crist 1995), and the completed monument had been dedicated June 3, 1907 (Widener 1982, 281). This was long after Davis's death in 1889, and it seemed self-evident that the medallion—the sole piece of evidence supposedly connecting the rifle to Davis—could not have been incorporated into the rifle during his lifetime. Indeed, the curator of the Museum of the Confederacy in Richmond, Robert F. Hancock (1995), told me: "As you suggested, the medallion was struck to commemorate the unveiling of the Davis monument in Richmond. However, there is little documentation on this medallion and sources do not indicate how many were struck." He added, "Its introduction onto the stock of the rifle may have been a fraudulent attempt to make the piece more valuable, or, on the other hand, honestly commemorate the occasion."

In any case, the medallion did not authenticate the gun as Jefferson Davis's but actually detracted from that possibility. That the musket had been rather poorly treated and that its ramrod had been replaced were independent indicators that the gun had not been presented as a gift. The motive of the person who cobbled together gun, ramrod, and medallion cannot be determined, but the result was to create, in effect, a forgery.

## Chapter 15

# DEBRIS FROM THE *TITANIC*

AT THE TIME, it was "the greatest marine disaster in history" (Marshall 1912, 1). When the 46,328-ton cruise ship *Titanic* sank in the North Atlantic on April 15, 1912, there were more than 2,200 people on board. Only about 700 were rescued. Many of the recovered bodies were buried in cemeteries in Halifax, Nova Scotia (which I visited in August 1998 to give a talk to the Canadian Society of Forensic Science). (See figure 15.1.) Some debris were also recovered, dubbed "floating relics" (Lynch 1992, 178). In 1998 I was commissioned to examine three artifacts bearing labels identifying them as part of that wreckage. Had they really come from the ill-fated ship?

The first was a piece of shaped, partially painted wood (see figure 15.2). On the front of it, printed in ink, were these words: "Part of a panel picked up by cable Str 'Minia' from wreckage of Str 'Titanic.'—Lost Apl 15, 1912.—Lat 41.° 42'—Long 49° 20'—1635 perished." It measured about 15.5 cm long by 7.2 cm wide by 2.4 cm deep (approximately 6 by 3 by 1 inches). The second was a smaller block of wood (see figure 15.3) measuring about 8.15 cm long by 5.8 cm wide by 4.3 cm deep (approximately 3 by 2 by 1½ inches). On the front painted surface was printed in ink: "Part of Door Picked up by Cable Str. Minia. From wreckage of—Str Titanic—Lost Apl 15, 1912. Lat. 41° 42' Long. 49° 20'—1635 perished." The third was a metal nut and bolt (see figure 15.4) to which was tied a paper tag bearing a handwritten label: "Bolt from Companionway Picked up by Cable Str Minia from wreckage of Str Titanic Lost Apl 15 1912. 1635 perished, Lat 41° 42' Long 49° 20'." It measured about 7.3 cm (close to 3 inches) long, with the head being 2.7 cm (nearly 1 inch) in diameter.

Figure 15.1. Cemetery in Halifax, Nova Scotia, where many victims of the 1912 *Titanic* tragedy were buried.

The artifacts were owned by Mike Brackin of Manchester, Connecticut, who commissioned my investigation. I examined the artifacts in reflected and oblique light, both macroscopically and stereomicroscopically. I also inspected them by infrared and ultraviolet light and subjected them to certain microchemical and other tests. I was assisted in my historical investigation by *Titanic* researcher Timothy Binga.

## Provenance

Brackin (1998) had purchased the items in 1991 "with a group of artifacts of various Boston area ships." He acknowledged, "The items have no provenance—I purchased them at an antique show; the seller did not even recognize that they were of any significance. He did not provide any information as to their origin."

Although it is desirable to know the provenance of any valued artifact, a missing provenance in the case of a souvenir item is not prima facie suspicious. According to one expert, "Provenance can be impor-

Figure 15.2. Piece of a wood panel from the *Titanic*.

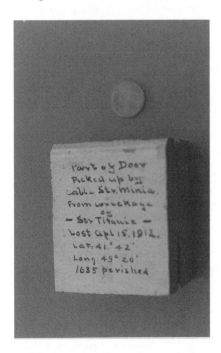

Figure 15.3. Portion of a door.

Figure 15.4. Bolt from a companionway.

tant, but it can never be impeachable—externals must always be inferior to a thorough examination" of the items in question (Davids 1978, 281).

The three artifacts were reportedly accompanied by two labeled segments of transatlantic telegraph cable dated 1912. These cable segments were linked to the *Titanic* artifacts by similar tags and writing; they were also logically related because the *Titanic* artifacts had reportedly been among wreckage recovered by the cable steamer *Minia.* Cable steamers were especially active during the period in question. Submarine telegraphy and the laying of cable systems grew rapidly from the latter part of the nineteenth century, with twenty-one cables spanning the Atlantic Ocean by 1928 (*Encyclopaedia Britannica* 1960, s.v. "Telegraph").

The *Minia* was indeed a cable steamer and actually participated in recovering bodies and wreckage from the *Titanic.* One well-known artifact from the doomed steamer was a segment of a carved oak newel post from one of the *Titanic's* first-class staircases. Illustrated in the book *Titanic: An Illustrated History* (Lynch 1992, 179), it is acknowledged to have been salvaged by the *Minia.*

The *Minia* arrived at the wreckage site on Friday, April 25, relieving the *Mackay-Bennett,* which took 190 bodies to Halifax after burying 116 at sea. The *Minia* scoured the area for bodies, which had been scattered up to 130 miles from the site by wind and bad weather. However, only 17 additional bodies were picked up during a week of searching. Two other ships followed but recovered only a single victim, and the effort was abandoned, although a few more decomposed bodies were sighted by passing steamers.

A letter written by the *Minia's* wireless assistant, Francis Dyke, to his mother concluded that the *Titanic* "must have blown up when she sank" (actually, it broke in half), "as we have picked up pieces of the grand staircase & most of the wreckage is from *below* deck" (Eaton and Haas 1995, 234). Other recovered items included one of the hundreds of deck chairs that floated to the surface after the wreck; it is now at the Maritime Museum of the Atlantic in Halifax, Nova Scotia (see figure 15.5). Another was a carved piece of oak paneling from the first-class lounge entrance (Lynch 1992, 178–79).

Figure 15.5. "Floating relics" from the disaster were also recovered, including a deck chair. The author lounges in a replica of it at the Maritime Museum of the Atlantic in Halifax, Nova Scotia. (Photograph by Ruth Whitehead)

A minister on board another search ship, the *Montmagny,* stated that on Friday, May 10, "The morning was not far advanced before we began to see a succession of drifting wreckage. Once the ship was stopped, an oak newel post [was] picked up. A bedstead was seen, also hats, polished and white painted woods, and a great square of probably forty feet dimensions, which may have been part of the ill-famed steamer's deck" (Eaton and Haas 1995, 234).

Although the three artifacts in question lacked provenance, there was evidence (from the accompanying pieces of cable) consistent with their having been collected by someone connected with the cable steamer *Minia*. That, plus the fact that the *Minia* was known to have picked up *Titanic* debris, made a credible historical context for the artifacts.

## The Wooden Artifacts

The two wooden artifacts, labeled as part of a panel and part of a door, had obviously been sawed into their present shapes. This had probably been done partly to make them presentable as relics as well as to divide up larger pieces. The person doing the writing referred to larger entities—a panel, a door, and, in the case of the bolt, a companionway—indicating that the pieces had been taken from clearly recognizable structures.

Both wooden pieces were of tongue-and-groove construction. Their reddish brown color, straight grain, density, and other properties identified the wood as a variety of mahogany—a hardwood popularly used for panels and cabinetry. (For wood identification, see Aidan Walker's *Identifying Wood* [1997].) It has been termed "the foremost cabinet wood in the world" and has been used for shipbuilding as well (*Encyclopaedia Britannica* 1960, s.v. "Mahogany"). Mahogany was used for panels and other woodwork in the *Titanic* (Lynch 1992, 83).

The door piece (see figure 15.3) had three screw holes, one of them bisected when the item had been sawed to its present size. The evenly spaced thread imprints indicated a machine-made screw. The array of three holes was typical of a pattern used for a hinge, consistent with the piece being cut from a door.

The panel piece (see figure 15.2) exhibited both "stuck" (shaped on the solid frame) and "planted" (fastened in position) molding (*Encyclopaedia Britannica* 1960, s.v. "Joinery"). The molding appeared to be consistent with published photographs of paneling in the *Titanic* staterooms. The single piece of planted molding had been removed, leaving an exposed nail. (The owner stated that he had removed the piece to keep for his personal collection.) The old nail was of wire manufacture and was a "finishing" nail type. Made of plain ferrous metal rather than galvanized or aluminum composition, it was heavily rusted, even though it had not been exposed along its length until its recent removal. The rust was consistent with exposure to salt water, although other conditions could have caused it.

To the left of the inscription was a mark that, under magnification, appeared to have resulted from a rusty nail being glued to the surface. It may have been affixed at a later date, since the lines of text are effectively centered in the overall space. In other words, the text seemed to have been penned prior to the nail being mounted.

Visual inspection of the panel showed a coat of primer and a single finish coat of paint. No evidence of repainting was observed. The white paint seemed consistent with black-and-white photos of the interior of *Titanic* staterooms. It responded strongly to a chemical spot test for lead. It had yellowed with age, which is typical of old white lead paint subjected to indoor exposure, especially in the dark (Gettens and Stout 1966, 174–76).

At one place, affecting the beginning of the last two lines of text, the paint on the panel had been damaged. Inspection indicated that the damage had occurred after the surface of the paint was dry but before the film had dried through and through. The damage consisted of a slippage of the paint, pushing it into a "bunched" configuration. The ink writing had definitely been penned over (and therefore after) this damage. This finding was consistent with applied force (as from a wrecked ship) while the paint was relatively new. There was other paint damage in the form of flaking, consistent with the brittleness of age.

## The Bolt

The label attached to the bolt (see figure 15.4)—stating that the item came from the *Titanic*'s companionway (a stairway between decks)—

explains the fact that it was salvaged at all, since, obviously, bolts cannot float. The bolt's coming from a larger piece of wreckage would also be consistent with the common practice of dividing up artifacts as a means of multiplying the number of souvenirs (other examples of this practice I have encountered involved religious saints' relics, a tiny block of wood from a beam in Independence Hall, and a little square of wallpaper from the house where President Lincoln died). That possibility was supported by the two accompanying pieces of transatlantic cable that were similarly prepared (both having wire-whipped ends to prevent unraveling) and that had labels in the same handwriting and the same line-for-line wording (apparent even though half of one label was missing).

The bolt was made of ferrous metal, as indicated by its attraction to a magnet and traces of obvious rust. It had not rusted extensively because it had been coated with aluminum paint. Made from aluminum metal powder, this type of paint existed since the middle of the nineteenth century but did not become readily available commercially until about 1896 (Gettens and Stout 1966, 92).

## The Paper Tag

The tag affixed to the bolt was made of layered paper with a hole punched in one end. The hole was surrounded by a reinforcing ring of paper on both sides. The ring on one side was imprinted with "DENNISON'S E/E MANILA" (see figure 15.6). The tag had been broken in two places and inexpertly repaired with a piece of gummed transparent tape torn by a serrated cutter from a common dispenser. The tag had been further stressed at the breaks so that the end piece was barely attached and could not be expected to remain so with much additional handling. A piece of one reinforcer had been broken off.

I examined the tag under ultraviolet light, which failed to show any optical brighteners. These had been used in paper only since World War II, and their presence—which would have been indicated by UV fluorescence—would have revealed a more recent manufacture.

The Dennison printing was done rather poorly in what appeared to be printer's ink. The fibrous paper seemed consistent with its "Manila"

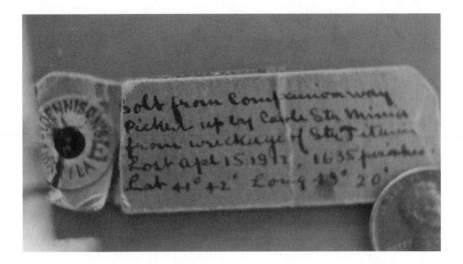

Figure 15.6. Detail of the tag attached to the bolt (see figure 15.4) provides manufacturer's markings for identification and dating.

imprint, indicating manila hemp. The attaching string was equally fibrous, being a coarse variety evidently dyed black. The term *manila paper* dates back to at least 1873, according to the authoritative *Oxford English Dictionary*. Founded in 1844, the Dennison Manufacturing Company (now part of Avery Dennison Corporation) had been making manila tags since 1893. And the specific "E" or "Manila Quality" type of "Dennison's Patent Shipping Tags"—billed as the "cheapest tag of equal strength on the market"—had been featured on page 8 in an 1896–1897 Dennison salesmen's catalog. (A photocopy of the catalog page was supplied by Irene Woodbury of the Avery Dennison Law Department, Framingham, Massachusetts.) This information about the tag was important, since the writing on the tag could be no older than the tag itself. The tag's commercial availability by 1896 made it a credible writing material for a 1912 artifact, whereas a much later date of manufacture would have raised doubts. In fact, a very similar tag—a "DENNISON E/C MANILA"—had been used for cabin baggage tags on the Cunard Line's SS *Carpathia,* the ship that rescued the *Titanic* survivors (see Lynch 1992, 160).

I considered the possibility that someone could have recently discovered a supply of such old but unused Dennison tags and utilized them to counterfeit labels for the bolt and the pieces of telegraph cable. That was unlikely, however. Old paper tends to become absorbent with age, and ink writing placed on aged paper becomes suspiciously "feathered" in appearance. That had clearly not happened with the tags in question.

## Ink, Pen, and Handwriting

I analyzed the ink for all three artifacts. It proved to be an iron-gallotannate variety to which a provisional blue colorant (probably indigo) had been added—an appropriate ink for the period in question. In reflected light, the ink was brown, especially where it was less dense—a property consistent with iron-gall ink that has aged. Stereomicroscopic examination of the ink on the panels showed that it was in a rather thick film, attributable to the nonabsorption of the painted surface, and that the ink exhibited fine cracks, consistent with genuine age. None of the writing showed any evidence of artificial aging (such as by heat or chemical application).

The writing on the paper tag exhibited the hairline upstrokes and shaded (heavy) downstrokes of writing done with a split-nib pen. Nib tracks (showing as scratches under the ink), which were revealed by stereomicroscopic examination under oblique lighting, indicated a steel pen. A dip pen, rather than a fountain pen, was indicated by variations in the density of the ink. (The script moved from dark to light to dark again as the pen was dipped.) The same pen was probably used for all writings, even though the beginnings and endings of the strokes were a bit more rounded in the printing on the painted wood than on the paper tag. That could be attributed to the ink pooling on the nonabsorptive paint. The steel dip pen was common in the second half of the nineteenth century and the first half of the twentieth, making its use entirely consistent with the period in question.

The handwriting on the label attached to the bolt had features in common with various writing styles that preceded 1912. These included print (rather than cursive) forms of the capital *S* and the small *y* (with its loopless tail)—features that, with the lack of a forward slant, suggested a carryover from the faddish "vertical writing" taught in schools from 1890 to 1900. Also, the ending *t,* with its lack of a separate crossbar, was consistent with the Palmer style of penmanship that began to be taught in about 1880. These and other handwriting characteristics were consistent with someone writing in the post-Spencerian period (the distinctive Spencerian style having dominated from about 1865 to 1890). The handwriting exhibited natural "shading" and had been executed confidently and smoothly by a writer familiar with such a pen and reasonably practiced in producing such script with it.

## Writing Content

I studied the text of the writings penned on the two pieces of wood and on the paper shipping tag to learn whether there were any anachronisms in language or factual errors that might be revealing. All referred to "Cable Str. 'Minia'" (although only the panel piece had the name *Minia* in quotation marks, and only the door piece had the period after "Str"). The reference to the *Minia* as a "cable steamer" was correct. The term was in use in 1912, as shown by a letter to White Star authorities from the parents of crewman Herbert Jupe. They noted that the body of their "Precious Boy," which was "on the Ill Fatted [*sic*] Titanic has been recovered and Buried at Sea by the Cable Steamer 'Mackay-Bennett'" (Lynch 1992, 174). The descriptor "cable steamer" was so common that it was often abbreviated "c.s." (as in a bill submitted to White Star Line by the Commercial Cable Company for the "Charter of c.s. 'Mackay-Bennet'"). (See Eaton and Haas 1995, 242.)

Also correct was the labels' reference to the "Str Titanic." Technically, the British ship was not an "HMS" (His Majesty's Ship) but an "RMS" (Royal Mail Steamer), as noted, for example, on the *Titanic*'s menu cards (see Lynch 1992, 55). It was referred to as "S.S. 'Titanic'" (that is, steamship) in the announcement for the memorial service for the victims, held April 21, 1912 (see Lynch 1992, 176). The ship's bow merely read "TITANIC." It was also referred to as a "steamer" on the ticket for its launching at Belfast, May 31, 1911. It read: "Launch of White Star Royal Mail Triple-Screw Steamer 'TITANIC.'" Ads for the White Star Line also called its ships "steamers." The *Titanic* was specifically referred to as a "steamer" in contemporary accounts of the disaster, such as the *Virginian-Pilot* newspaper of April 17, 1912 (see *Front Page* 1985).

The labels' consistent reference to "Lat 41° 42' Long 49° 20'" suggested that the precise location of each piece had not been noted; rather, an approximate latitude and longitude had been applied to all three artifacts. That seemed appropriate, since there would be no reason to note the exact location of each piece of wreckage as it was found. Bodies were another matter, and so the *Minia* reported (in a message relayed from Halifax on May 1) that it had "found body TW King pursers assistant Lat 41.30 long 48.15 being forty five miles east of that found yesterday showing how widely scattered and difficult to find. . . . Icebergs numerous as far South as 40.30 in 48.30 [*sic*]" (see Eaton and Haas 1995, 243).

The labels' reference to the *Titanic*'s being "Lost"—that is, having sunk, not having gone missing—is consistent with contemporary usage. For instance, the memorial-service notice referred to the "S.S. 'Titanic,' Lost off Newfoundland Banks, on the night of April 14th, 1912" (Lynch 1992, 176). The date on the notice was actually in error. The *Titanic* struck the iceberg on the fourteenth but did not go down until the early morning of the fifteenth. The correct date, "Died April 15, 1912," appears on the headstones of the victims buried in Halifax cemeteries. The date on the three artifact labels was also correct.

The labels did contain an error, however: the notation that "1635 perished." The actual figure was more than 100 fewer. However, the 1,635 figure was cited in an early book, *Sinking of the Titanic and Great Sea Disasters* (Marshall 1912). Therefore, the error was not problematic and could indicate that the labeling had been done not long after the event.

Taken together, the various details—the historical context, the association with other artifacts, the composition and signs of age, and the consistency of the writing materials with the time period indicated—provided credible testimony that the artifacts were what they purported to be: relics of wreckage from the 1912 *Titanic* disaster, picked up by the cable steamer *Minia* and labeled in a manner that gave them the impress of time.

*Chapter 16*

# OFF THE SHELF

THE LIST OF potentially questioned artifacts is endless, ranging from an antique abacus to a Zulu shield. Here is a miscellany of other cases from my files, each instructive in its own way.

## Civil War Artifacts

Collecting Civil War memorabilia began during the war itself, when soldiers—like those in every war—retained small mementos of places and events. During the 1880s and 1890s, poor southerners did a brisk business in selling—and sometimes counterfeiting—relics of the war. Logs containing embedded artillery shells from the battlefield at Chickamauga were among the fakes cleverly produced by a Tennessee farmer. In modern times, X-rays of such a log displayed by the Museum of Connecticut History revealed that the shells had not been fired into a tree that then grew around them, as purported. Instead, the log had been carved to permit the shells to be inserted. Apparently, no one had considered the fact that artillery shells probably would have splintered a tree (Zeller 2002).

In addition to fake documents and photographs, there are ubiquitous bogus Civil War artifacts—or "artifakes," as writer Bob Zeller (2002) dubbed them—that pollute the collectibles market. Many began as reproductions, intended for use by reenactors or as souvenirs for tourists to buy. The list is long: coins and currency, slave tags, belt buckles, uniform buttons, wood canteens, glass bottles, newspapers, cutlery, plates, and so on. Although a few responsible manufacturers deliberately add details to distinguish their simulations from authentic artifacts, most do not. In any case, modern markings can be removed and the items "aged" for sale to collectors.

Many articles are deliberately counterfeited, and even the most knowledgeable dealers get fooled. According to Mike O'Donnell, coauthor (with J. Duncan Campbell) of *American Military Belt Plates:*

> The best fakers are better than the experts. There are a few people who have been doing this for 20 years and are incredibly good. They can cast Confederate plates just the way they did back then. They were made from a mixture of brass and copper that you don't see today, so they'll melt down brass Confederate Sabots from artillery shells—the ground is full of that stuff—and make the fake buckles with real 19th-century metal. (quoted in Zeller 2002, 43)

Some deliberately faked artifacts are what are referred to as "fantasy fakes"—that is, items that never existed. "Kentucky slave tags" are one example. There were genuine slave tags, but they came from Charleston and Charleston Neck, South Carolina, having been issued there as evidence of tax payment. One British company not only produced a number of fantasy fakes—including "Memorial to Lincoln" belt plates, Tiffany Western Union belt plates, and Overland Wells Fargo and Co. horse harness brass plates—but also published a book that authenticated its own counterfeits (Zeller 2002, 47).

Still other artifakes are part genuine, part bogus. One common approach is to enhance an authentic item, such as by engraving a famous military figure's name on a presentation sword or by adding a counterfeit guard and hilt to a real sword blade. Or the faker may "marry" two genuine items—the military discharge papers of one soldier and a photograph of another, unknown one—to make them more valuable as a pair than as single items (Zeller 2002, 43, 47).

Other "Civil War" artifacts may be inauthentic without having been faked at all; they may be merely misidentified. For example, a schoolteacher brought me a large bullet-shaped object that had been found in a Kentucky creek. He wanted to know if it was a Civil War artillery projectile. I took possession of it for study.

I thought the object's covering of heavy brass foil made it extremely unlikely to be a projectile, but I decided to query an expert. I eventually located M. E. Mason Jr. of Richmond, Virginia, a collector and appraiser of Civil War arms, ammunition, and artifacts. I sent him detailed measurements and close-up photographs. He concluded not only that the unidentified object failed to match any known Civil War projectile but also that its proportions would have rendered it ballistically unstable—that is, it would not have flown straight (Mason 1984).

## Rare Money

Money—both counterfeited and reproduced, both currency and coins—is the root of evil in the world of collectibles. "Coins have been faked from antiquity," according to Harold L. Peterson (1975, 98), "usually with the intent to use them as currency rather than for the later collector. In fact, "some of the ancient forgeries have more value today than the coins they attempted to simulate" (since the counterfeits are rare in comparison). For that reason, "though modern fakes are just fakes, period counterfeits are artifacts" (Zeller 2002, 44).

Numismatics (from the Latin *numisma,* for "coin") is the term for the study of coins and medals, but it is sometimes extended to related fields (Doering 1980, 66–79). Serious numismatists specialize in coins of various countries or periods, such as ancient Greece, Rome, China, or medieval Europe. Other interesting areas of specialization include coins referred to in the Bible, wartime coins, or even wooden nickels (and such related items as tokens, banknotes, stock certificates, and so on). One numismatist amassed an impressive collection of John F. Kennedy coins and medals. (For an introduction to various numismatic fields, see Doering 1980, 80–99; *Encyclopaedia Britannica* 1960, s.v. "Numismatics.")

Confederate States of America (CSA) currency is quite collectible, and I am reminded of one visit I made to an antique mall. A dealer had wandered away from his booth while I was looking at his batch of CSA bills. When he returned, he asked, "What are you doing?" as he saw me sorting them into two piles. "I'm separating the genuine from the fake,"

I replied. He leaned forward. "How can you tell?" he asked with some urgency. I explained a couple of the signs of reproductions: the phony "parchment" paper (which is utterly ridiculous for currency) and, under magnification, the presence of a modern halftone screen pattern. I also showed him that real Confederate bills had been individually signed in ink that browned with age; therefore, signatures in jet-black printing ink were a dead giveaway. The gentleman was pleased with his newfound knowledge, despite my caution that it was insufficient to detect the more clever fakes.

In the case of U.S. coins, one factor that may increase their value is the mint mark: *C* for Charlotte, North Carolina, where only gold coins were minted, 1838–1861; *CC* for Carson City, Nevada, 1870–1893; *D* for Dahlonega, Georgia, 1838–1861, for a gold coin, or for Denver, Colorado, 1906–present; for other coins, *O* for New Orleans, Louisiana, 1861–1909, and *P* for Philadelphia, Pennsylvania, 1793–present, although many Philadelphia-minted coins lack an identifying mark (Jenkins 1963, 392).

The significance of mint marks helped launch the career of master forger Mark Hofmann. At age fourteen, he was collecting antique coins and had also developed an interest in electroplating. Using a simple procedure, Hofmann was able to change the mint mark on one coin from a *C* to a *D*, thus transforming it from worthless to rare. Hofmann showed the coin to a Salt Lake City coin dealer, who in turn sent it to the U.S. Treasury Department, where, reportedly, it was declared genuine (Worrall 2002, 77).

Guidebooks, such as *Warman's U.S. Coins & Currency Field Guide* (Berman 2006), help collectors identify and value their items, as well as point out many known counterfeits. A specialized text in this regard is *The Official Guide to Detecting Altered & Counterfeit U.S. Coins & Currency* (Hudgeons 1981). Peterson (1975, 98) provides a succinct introduction to detecting fake coins:

> During the course of history coins have been both cast and struck, and the connoisseur should know which technique would be proper for the coin he is examining. He should also know the

proper metal, and the quality of the metal. Most modern fakes of coins are casts, and these can be detected by examining the surface under magnification to pick up the tiny bubbles and pits that typify a casting as well as the loss of detail and crispness that must result when a cast is made from another coin. False patination is another clue, and you should make sure that if a portion of the design is blurred from wear, the entire surface is smooth as it should be from the constant rubbing that produced the wear. Sometimes you can detect facets on the edge from careless filing of mold seams. Once in a great while you may encounter a fake coin made from a new die. This usually happens only in the case of very rare and expensive pieces. In such cases the first thing to do is to check the suspected coin against an original to see if there are any aberrations in workmanship or design. Then look for wear and other signs of use as well as patination. An apparently mint uncirculated pine tree shilling or a Bermuda hog penny or any other such early rarity should give a prospective buyer "pause with cause."

Although I am far from a coin expert, I have solved a few questioned coin cases. For instance, in the spring of 1995, one of my students at the University of Kentucky brought me a coin his father had found. Was it valuable? The case demonstrated that even a novice can succeed by following a cardinal rule of authentication: carefully examine the artifact in the event an unexpected clue might turn up. In this case, I found that the questioned item—an ostensible Continental Congress 1776 coin (Breen 1988, 110–12) bore on its obverse the tiny imprinted word "copy" (see figures 16.1 and 16.2). Case closed.

Because I write a historical column for my hometown newspaper (the Licking Valley Courier, published in West Liberty, Kentucky), editor Earl Kinner Jr. directed another coin mystery to me. Local businessman Paul Ison had acquired a $5 gold piece that was supposedly a 1795 U.S. half eagle. Such a coin—if genuine—could be worth hundreds of thousands of dollars, surely making it the most valuable coin in the

Figure 16.1. Questioned Continental Congress coin of 1776 represented an easy case. (Photograph by Tom Mulvaney)

Figure 16.2. Stamped word "copy" reveals the coin to be a fake. (Photograph by Tom Mulvaney)

region. Even though the coin had been defaced by a hole drilled through it, probably so that it could be worn on a thong or chain, it could still be quite valuable due to its rarity. And, of course, it would always be worth its weight in gold.

But was it an authentic gold half eagle, an old counterfeit, or a modern reproduction? Paul was not sure: some evidence argued for authenticity, some against it. I agreed to look into the matter, hoping to at least get an interesting column out of it, and Paul promptly sent the coin to me. He informed me that he had obtained the coin from a man in Wolfe County, who said he had traded a twelve-gauge shotgun for it.

The 1795 date was important because it was the first year the half eagle had been minted. Designed by chief engraver Robert Scot, it was the first gold coin struck by the U.S. Mint. It depicted Liberty wearing a cap and facing right. On the reverse was the national bird, the eagle. The coin featured a reeded edge, a weight of 17.50 grams, and a diameter of 33 mm. Its composition was 0.9167 gold, 0.0833 silver and copper (see Yeoman 2005; Hudgeons 2005).

While examining Paul's coin, I noticed that its diameter, about 37.5 mm, was larger than that of the half eagle. This suggested that it was a reproduction (a counterfeit, intended to deceive, would be the correct size). Colleague Ed Buckner, a former coin dealer, looked at it and commented that the coin's color lacked the appearance of genuine gold, confirming my impression. He added that the details of the reeding (the knurling on a coin's edge) were less sharp than they should be. He thought the coin was probably a reproduction.

Another colleague, Andrew Skolnick, suggested a simple but definitive scientific test: measuring the coin's specific gravity. Also known as relative density, the specific gravity is the ratio of the object's weight to that of an equal volume of water. This is based on Archimedes' principle, a law of physics attributed to the Greek mathematician who lived from about 287 to 212 B.C. The king of Syria wanted to know if his gold crown was genuine or if the goldsmith had adulterated it with silver. Archimedes supposedly came up with his principle when he stepped into the public bath and observed that his body caused the water level to rise. Legend says that in his delight he ran home naked, exclaiming, "Eureka! Eureka!" ("I have found it!").

Andrew resolved to take an Archimedean approach to Paul's coin mystery. Using a triple-beam balance, he weighed the coin (21.04 grams), then weighed it again suspended in water (18.65 grams, a difference of 2.39 grams). He performed the necessary calculation (21.04 divided by 2.39), yielding a specific gravity of 8.80. Considering the approximate specific gravities of the metals in question—gold, 19.2; silver, 11; brass, 8–9—that of the questioned coin was consistent with that of brass and not even close to that of gold.

However, if the coin was indeed brass, shouldn't it have become tarnished? Paul had tested the coin by immersing it for a time in acetic acid (white vinegar), which corrodes brass but not gold. There had been no effect. However, the coin appeared to have a clear protective coating (possibly lacquer). Microscopic observation showed that inside the drilled hole were distinctive green traces that I suspected were verdigris (a greenish coating that forms on copper and copper alloys such as brass and bronze).

The evidence therefore confirmed the earlier suspicions that the coin was a reproduction. The good news was that its owner has a nifty conversation piece and that it served as an example of how to creatively attack a problem. (I published the story in my column "Historical Sketches" on May 4, 2006.)

## Stradivarius Violin

They evoke strains of beautiful music, romantic legend, and even intrigue and crime. Although Stradivarius violins are essentially priceless, buyers, sellers, and insurance companies must, of necessity, put prices on them. For instance, a Stradivarius was stolen from the estate of violinist Erica Morini, who died in 1995, at age ninety-one, in her New York apartment overlooking Central Park. Rewards of more than $100,000 were offered for the return of the treasure, which was valued at $4 million ("Reward" 1995).

The celebrated violins—along with violas, cellos, guitars, and other stringed instruments—were produced by the family workshops of Italian Antonio Stradivari (1644–1737), *Stradivarius* being the Latin form of the name. Born in Crimona, he studied with Nicolo Amati (1596–1684) and went on to become acknowledged as the greatest violin maker of all time.

Stradivari's secret, some say, was the wood. Others insist it was the varnish, a preparation that had some beneficial effect on the vibrating wood. Legend holds that Stradivari's special formula was a closely guarded family secret—before it disappeared. Stated Morley Safer (1995) on CBS's *60 Minutes*:

> The last direct descendant to have it was one Giacomo Stradivari,
> a great-great-grandson. To all requests for it, he would reply this
> way: "You ask something impossible of me. I have not entrusted

even my wife and daughters with this secret. I would never disclose to anyone the contents of this precious recipe." It turns out Giacomo was a bit of a scoundrel. He'd been trying to get an English dealer to give him one of his ancestor's violins in exchange for that precious recipe. The recipe turned out to be a useless concoction Giacomo himself had invented, and he never got his Strad. Great-great-grandpa, it seems, took the actual formula to his grave.

Stradivari crafted some 1,200 violins, of which only about half remain. Ernest N. Doring (1945) traced all the known examples for his book *How Many Strads?* and concluded that all had been accounted for. Nevertheless, according to antique experts Ralph and Terry Kovel (1973, 293): "There is always a chance that Doring made a mistake, but this is very doubtful. There is also a slim chance that several rumors about Strads being stolen during World War II are true." As they explain, "Supposedly, a famous German musician owned an authenticated Strad that vanished during the war. A G.I. might have picked it up."

Violin dealer and restorer Charles Beare is even more hopeful. He says: "There must be a dozen sitting somewhere. I mean, these old Italian palaces are full of things that haven't been dusted since the 18th century, some of them. And, you know I wouldn't—it wouldn't surprise me at all if there was one hidden in Italy somewhere" (Safer 1995).

In any event, rumors and legends regarding the violins have often surfaced. One woman told *Antiques Roadshow* (March 1, 1997) that her "Stradivarius" had been passed down in her family and was a model supposedly named for Stradivari's second wife, Faciebat Anno. The violin's label indeed bore the words *Faciebat Anno,* but they are Latin for "made in the year of"! Her violin was a reproduction.

Connoisseurs of stringed masterpieces are usually able to distinguish the various schools of violins and their makers based on the instruments themselves. Laypersons, in contrast, must often rely on the label as a guide, and the practice of deceptive labeling of violins can be traced to the time of Amati (Doring 1945, 330). Countless violins have been bought on the basis of counterfeited labels—and perhaps an engaging tale to go with them (Kovel and Kovel 1973, 293):

> Many farmers living in the northern part of the United States and Canada have carefully guarded the valued Stradivarius violin that has been passed down through the family. Question each family and you will learn the same story. From about 1880 until the first part of the twentieth century, a hungry peddler sold his treasured violin because of a desperate need for money. It was labeled "Antonius Stradivarius Cremonensis Faciebat Anno 1734," so of course it must be true.

As I was to learn, in the most obvious of the faked labels, each digit of the date—for example, "1716" or "1722"—was printed in type, whereas in a genuine Strad, the final numeral or numerals were penned by hand. From a batch of labels printed in 1666, with the final 6 left blank, the violin maker filled in the last digit each year, then began to alter the date as necessary: during the 1670s, the second 6 was erased and the last two numbers were written in; in the 1680s, a small circle was added above the lower one of the 6 to make an 8; and in the 1690s, the top of the 6 was erased and a downward stroke was added to create a 9. During 1698 a new date setup was employed that, in obvious anticipation of the changing century, had only the numeral 1 printed. In about 1729, another, final change was made (Doring 1945, 331, illustration 332).

In February 1995 I was asked to look at an old violin owned by Kentucky resident Wayne Yeager, who told me what he knew of it. It had belonged to his great-uncle Charles Brecht, who died in the late 1970s. Brecht had received it as a gift from an elderly nun from Holy Cross in Latonia, Kentucky, around 1910. The nun—or possibly her aunt, who had given it to her (the details of the story were a bit garbled)—had brought the violin from Germany. When the nun stopped giving lessons because of her age and failing eyesight, she decided to present the violin to her favorite pupil—Brecht. The nun had told him the violin was a Stradivarius, "and he had no reason to doubt a nun!" stated Yeager

(1995). "Apparently," according to Yeager (1995), Brecht "was not aware that the label was even in the violin, because when I showed it to him, he pressed on his glasses and seemed astonished." A violin repairman who had put on a new bridge and strings had told Yeager it was probably not authentic, noting that the maker's name was misspelled "STRADIUARIUS." However, Yeager had since learned that some of the genuine labels were written that way, which is indeed the case.

In investigating the Yeager violin, I not only researched the life and work of Antonio Stradivari but also sought out other violins bearing the famous maker's name (see figures 16.3 and 16.4). In addition, I consulted two experts. One was Paul Evans Holbrook of the University of Kentucky's King Library Press, which helps keep alive the art of printing from hand-set type (see figure 16.5). He carefully studied the label using a magnifier and flexible light (see figure 16.6). All but four letters (the *An* of "Antonius," the second *a* of "Stradivarius," and the first *a* of "Faciebat"), he concluded, "appear to be of a late-nineteenth century type-face called 'Bold Face Condensed,' produced by the American Type Foundery at their Dickinson Type Foundery Branch" (as shown in a standard reference work *Desk Book of Printing Types* 1898, 192–93). He observed, "The other four letters are a different type face, probably accidentally mixed into the case from which the type compositor was setting type for the label" (Holbrook [1995]).

The second expert I consulted was Lexington, Kentucky, violin maker J. B. Miller, whose father and grandfather had been old-fashioned fiddlers. Born in 1902, the elderly craftsman began making violins at age twenty-four and had crafted approximately fifty. Miller (1995) examined the "Stradivarius" and noted that the wood was coarse-grained. The fingerboard, he observed, was only stained black, whereas that of a genuine Stradivarius would have been ebony. Everywhere, Miller told me, corners had been cut. The instrument was of "false construction" (made with an economy of separate pieces) and had been put together in an assembly-line process. Miller said that most such violins had been made in the nineteenth century in a German town where one family made one piece, another family a different one, and so on; then someone

Figure 16.3. Fake "Stradivarius" violins are far more common than the real variety. This one was found in an antique store.

Figure 16.4. This photograph accompanied another heirloom fake violin found in an antique shop.

Figure 16.5. Printing craftsman Paul Evans Holbrook is an expert in old printing type, such as that on Stradivarius labels.

Figure 16.6. Holbrook uses a flexible light and magnifier to examine the "Stradivarius" label in question.

would gather up the parts and take them to a central place for assembly and finishing (Miller 1995).

Indeed, forged or reproduction violins were made as late as 1930 in Germany, notably in Metten, Bavaria, and in Markneukirchen and Klingenthal, Saxony. Others were produced in Mirexoud, France, and in Gaslitz and Schonback, Czechoslovakia. Each town produced thousands of the instruments, some selling for just 50 cents (Kovel and Kovel 1973, 294). Such violins, imported "direct from Europe," appeared in old mail-order catalogs. For example, the *Sears Roebuck & Co. Catalog No. 110* (1900, 252–53) featured "A Genuine Stradivarius Model" for $2.50; better-quality ones, costing up to $9.60, even boasted a "genuine ebony fingerboard and tailpiece." There were few indications the violins were knockoffs, except that the $7.85 model was described as having "reddish brown varnish beautifully shaded in imitation of an old violin." Another model was advertised as a "Copy of a Genuine Amati for $7.75."

As all the evidence clearly proved, the questioned "Stradivarius" was merely a nineteenth-century reproduction. It had come from Germany—just as its limited provenance had indicated—not from Italy, and certainly not from the seventeenth or eighteenth century.

# REFERENCES

Anderson, Warren. 2001. E-mail to George Scott, April 20.

*Applied Infrared Photography.* 1972. Rochester, N.Y.: Eastman Kodak.

Baker, William C. 1974. Letter to William Barrow Floyd, May 9. Cited in Nickell 2005, 84.

Baym, Nina. 2004. The case for Hanna Vincent. In Gates and Robbins 2004, 315–31.

Beamis, Joan M., and William E. Pullen. N.d. [ca. 1870]. *Background of a Bandit: The Ancestry of Jessie James,* 2nd ed. N.p.: privately printed.

Begg, Paul, Martin Fido, and Keith Skinner. 1994. *The Jack the Ripper A–Z,* rev. ed. London: Headline Book Publishing.

Benjamin, Mary A. 1986. *Autographs: A Key to Collecting,* rev. ed. New York: Dover. (Orig. pub. 1963.)

Bennett, Stuart. 1987. *How to Buy Photographs.* Oxford: Phaidon-Christie's.

Berman, Allen G. 2006. *Warman's U.S. Coins & Currency Field Guide.* Iola, Wis.: Krause Publications.

Bianconi, Piero. 1967. Fake Vermeers and the van Meegeren "affair." In *The Complete Paintings of Vermeer,* 100–102. New York: Harry N. Abrams.

Bingham, Millicent Todd. 1955. *Emily Dickinson's Home.* New York: Harper & Brothers.

Blodgett, Richard. 1979. *Photographs: A Collector's Guide.* New York: Ballantine Books.

Bond, William. 1982. Letter to Jane Langton, March 29. Quoted in Langton 1984a, 18.

Bovée, Courtland L., and John V. Thill. 1989. *Business Communication Today,* 2nd ed. New York: Random House.

Brackin, Mike. 1998. Letter to Joe Nickell, March 24.

Breen, Walter. 1988. *Walter Breen's Complete Encyclopedia of U.S. and Colonial Coins.* New York: Doubleday.

Briquet, Charles-Moise. 1907. *Les filigrantes. Dictionnaire historique des marques du papier des leur apparition vers 1282 jusqu'en 1600.* Reprint, Amsterdam: Paper Pub. Soc., 1968.

Brown, Katherine L., and Robin J. H. Clark. 2002. Analysis of pigmentary materials on the Vinland map and Tartar relation by Raman microprobe spectroscopy. *Analytical Chemistry* 74 (15): 3658–61.

Brown, Stanley W. 1992. Letter to Jerome Meckier, September 21.

Cahill, T. A., et al. 1987. The Vinland map revisited: New compositional evidence of its inks and parchment. *Analytical Chemistry* 59:829–33.

Cahoon, Herbert, Thomas V. Lange, and Charles Ryskamp. 1977. *American Literary Autographs from Washington Irving to Henry James.* New York: Dover.

Cescinsky, Herbert. 1931. *The Gentle Art of Faking Furniture.* Reprint, New York: Dover, 1967.

Chervenka, Mark. 2003. *Antique Trader™ Guide to Fakes & Reproductions.* Iola, Wis.: Krause Publications.

Chesney, George. 1979. Letter to Jean Jadot, June 29. Cited in Fischer and Nickell 1983.

———. 1982. Personal communication to John F. Fischer and Joe Nickell, May 27.

Chittenden, M. 1994. Scrap dealer confesses he faked Jack the Ripper diary. *Sunday Times* (London), July 3.

Chittenden, M., and C. Lloyd. 1993. Fake! The detective work that revealed the truth about Jack the Ripper's "diary." *Sunday Times* (London), September 19, 6–7.

Churchill, W. A. 1935. *Watermarks in Paper in Holland, England, France, etc. in the XVII and XVIII Centuries.* Amsterdam: M. Hertzberger.

Clark, L. P. 1921. Unconscious motives underlying the personalities of great statesmen and their relationship to epoch-making events. *Psychoanalytical Review* 8 (1): 12–13.

Cohen, Jacob. 1975. Conspiracy fever. *Commentary,* October, 33–42.

*Collier's Encyclopedia.* 1983. New York: P. F. Collier.

Computer upholds Billy the Kid legend. 1990. *Lexington Herald Leader,* March 4.

Cornwell, Patricia. 2002. *Portrait of a Killer: Jack the Ripper—Case Closed.* New York: G. P. Putnam's Sons.

Cowan, C. Wesley. 1995. *Historic Americana Auction* [catalog]. Terrace Park, Ohio: privately printed.

Cowell, Alan. 2006. Book buried in Irish bog is called a major find. *New York Times,* July 27.

Crafts, Hannah. 2002. *The Bondwoman's Narrative.* Edited by Henry Louis Gates Jr. New York: Warner Books.

Craig, Emily. 1993. Report to Joe Nickell; forensic anthropology case no. 93–17, July 26.

———. 2004. *Teasing Secrets from the Dead: My Investigations at America's Most Infamous Crime Scenes.* New York: Three Rivers Press.

Crist, Lynda. 1995. Letter with enclosures to Joe Nickell, March 1.

Darrah, William C. 1981. *Cartes de Visite in Nineteenth Century Photography.* Gettysburg, Pa.: W. C. Darrah.

David, Carl. 1981. *Collecting and Care of Fine Art.* New York: Crown.

Davids, Roy L. 1978. English literary autographs. In *Autographs and Manuscripts: A Collector's Manual.* Edited by Edmund Berkeley Jr. New York: Scribner's.

Deas, Michael J. 1989. *The Portraits and Daguerreotypes of Edgar Allan Poe.* Charlottesville: University Press of Virginia.

DeNicola, Dan. 1983. Is it really you, Emily Dickinson? *Yankee Magazine,* November, 123–25, 216–19.

De Santis, Sylvia. 1993. Letter (as head librarian of Monson Free Library and Reading Room Association, Monson, Mass.) to Joe Nickell, March 3.

*A Desk Book of Printing Types.* 1898. Boston: American Type Founders Company.

Doering, Henry, ed. 1980. *Book of Buffs, Masters, Mavens and Uncommon Experts.* Englewood Cliffs, N.J.: World Almanac Publications (Prentice-Hall).

Donahue, D. J., J. S. Olin, and G. Harbottle. 2002. Determination of the radiocarbon age of parchment of the Vinland map. *Radiocarbon* 44 (1): 45–52.

Doring, Ernest N. 1945. *How Many Strads?* Chicago: William Lewis & Son.

Driscoll, Emily. 1951. Letter to Dorothy Porter, September 27. Copy from Henry Louis Gates Jr. Cited in Nickell 2002, 283–315.

Eaton, John P., and Charles A. Haas. 1995. *Titanic: Triumph and Tragedy,* 2nd ed. New York: W. W. Norton.

Eddowes, Michael. 1977. *The Oswald File.* New York: Clarkson N. Potter.

Elliott, Stephen K. 2002. To whom it may concern letter of December 17. Copy provided by George E. Scott.

———. 2003. Billy the Kid . . . a forgery? Says who? Fax from "Silver Lady" (Stephen K. Elliott), November 18. Copy provided by George E. Scott.

*Encyclopaedia Britannica.* 1960. Chicago: Encyclopaedia Britannica.

Enlow, D. H. 1990. *Facial Growth.* Philadelphia: W. B. Saunders. Cited in Craig 1993.

Epstein, Gideon. 1987. Testimony at the Israeli trial of Nazi war criminal John Demjanjuk, May 5 and 11. Transcript pp. 5720–23. Cited in Nickell 1990, 190.

Evans, Stewart P., and Keith Skinner. 2001. *Jack the Ripper—Case Closed.* New York: G. P. Putnam's Sons.

Fido, Martin. N.d. Report on "Jack the Ripper" diary. Prepared for English publisher, Smith Gryphon (copy obtained from Warner Books).

———. 1993. *The Crimes, Detection and Death of Jack the Ripper.* New York: Barnes & Noble.

———. 2001. Foreword to Evans and Skinner 2001, vii–x.

Fields, Joseph E. 1984. Confused identities. In Taylor 1984, 34–37.

Fischer, John F., and Joe Nickell. 1983. An examination of two icons. Report, May 20.

———. 1984. Laser light: Space-age forensics. *Law Enforcement Technology,* September, 26–27.

Fitzsimmons, Emma Graves. 2006. Photo shows the "raw" Abe Lincoln. *Buffalo News,* December 11.

Fleming, Stuart. 1980. Detecting art forgeries. *Physics Today,* April, 34–39.

Flynn, Katherine E. 2004. Jane Johnson found! But is she "Hannah Crafts"? The search for the author of *The Bondwoman's Narrative.* In Gates and Robbins 2004, 371–405.

Found: A legendary city that history forgot. 1995. *U.S. News & World Report,* December 4.

4,500-year-old family tomb of Governor found in Egypt. 1998. *Buffalo News,* March 8.

Frechette, C. N. 1994. A new Lincoln image: Report on an unusual study. *Journal of Forensic Identification* 44, no. 4 (July–August): 410–29.

*Front Page: Major Events of the 20th Century Selected by the Associated Press.* 1985. New York: Gallery Books.

Gascoigne, Bamber. 1988. *How to Identify Prints: A Complete Guide to Manual and Mechanical Processes from Woodcut to Ink Jet.* New York: Thames & Hudson.

Gates, Henry Louis, Jr. 2002a. Introduction to Crafts 2002, ix–lxxiv.

———. 2002b. A note on Craft's literary influences. In Crafts 2002, 331–32.

———. 2002c. Testimony of Jane Johnson. Appendix B of Crafts 2002, 319–20.

Gates, Henry Louis, Jr., and Hollis Robbins, eds. 2004. *In Search of Hannah Crafts: Critical Essays on* The Bondwoman's Narrative. New York: BasicCivitas Books.

Geitner, Paul. 1999. Draft of Eichmann memoir discovered. *Buffalo News,* August 13.

Gettens, Rutherford J., and George L. Stout. 1966. *Painting Materials: A Short Encyclopedia.* New York: Dover.

Gilbert, Anne. 1978. *How to Be an Antiques Detective.* New York: Grossett & Dunlap.

———. 1983. Be on the lookout for fake icons. *Orlando Sentinel,* January 8.

Gravell, Thomas L., and George Miller. 1979. *A Catalog of American Watermarks, 1690–1835.* New York: Garland.

———. 1983. *A Catalogue of Foreign Watermarks Found on Paper Used in America 1700–1835.* New York: Garland.

Grossberg, David. 2007. Joe Nickell, autograph detective. *Autograph Collector,* April–May, 78–80.

Hamblin, Dora Jane. 1970. *Pots and Robbers.* New York: Simon & Schuster.

Hamilton, Charles. 1978. *The Book of Autographs.* New York: Simon & Schuster.

————. 1979. *The Signature of America: A Fresh Look at Famous Handwriting.* New York: Harper & Row.

————. 1980. *Great Forgers and Famous Fakes: The Manuscript Forgers of America and How They Duped the Experts.* New York: Crown.

————. 1983. *American Autographs,* 2 vols. Norman: University of Oklahoma Press.

————. 1989. Letter report to Joe Nickell, November 3.

————. 1996. *The Signature of America.* New York: Harper & Row.

Hamilton, Charles, and Lloyd Ostendorf. 1963. *Lincoln in Photographs: An Album of Every Known Pose.* Norman: University of Oklahoma Press.

Hancock, Robert F. 1995. Letter to Joe Nickell, March 10.

Harris, Melvin. 1994. Telephone conversations with Joe Nickell, n.d.

Harrison, Shirley, ed. 1993. *The Diary of Jack the Ripper: The Discovery, the Investigation, the Debate.* New York: Hyperion.

Hilton, Ordway. 1982. *Scientific Examination of Questioned Documents,* rev. ed. Amsterdam: Elsevier.

Hoefnagel, Dick. 1986. An early hint of *Great Expectations. Dickensian* 82 (summer): 82–84.

Holbrook, Paul Evans. [1995]. Report to Joe Nickell, n.d.

Horne, Marc. 2006. Max Headroom creator made Roswell alien. *Sunday Times,* April 25.

House Select Committee on Assassinations. 1979. *Investigation of the Assassination of President John F. Kennedy: Appendix to Hearings Before the Select Committee on Assassinations.* Washington, D.C.: Government Printing Office.

Hudgeons, Marc. 1981. *The Official Guide to Detecting Altered & Counterfeit U.S. Coins & Currency,* 7th ed. Orlando, Fla.: House of Collectibles.

————. 2005. *The Official 2006 Blackbook Price Guide to United States Coins,* 44th ed. New York: Random House Reference.

Humphreys, John. 2006. Official Web site: http://www.john-humphreys.com/index.html (accessed April 18).

Iannarelli, Alfred V. 1980. Letter to Hon. Louis Stokes, Chairman, House Select Committee on Assassinations, December 5.

————. 1989. *Ear Identification.* Rev. ed. of *The Iannarelli System of Ear Identification.* Fremont, Calif.: Paramount.

————. 1994. Letter report to A. Kaplan, March 19.

Is it honestly Abe? 1994. *Rochester (N.Y.) Times-Union,* July 15.

Jackson, Radway. 1991. *The Visual Index of Artists' Signatures and Monograms.* London: Cromwell Editions.

Jadot, Jean. 1979. Letter to George Chesney, November 17. Cited in Fischer and Nickell 1983.

Janson, H. W. 1963. *History of Art*. Englewood Cliffs, N.J.: Prentice-Hall.

Jenkins, Dorothy H. 1963. *A Fortune in the Junk Pile*. New York: Crown Publishers.

Kaplan, A. 1994. Personal communication to Joe Nickell, March 1.

Kilian, Michael. 1999. *Titanic's* locator finds two sunken Phoenician vessels. *Chicago Tribune,* June 24.

Kirkland, Turner E. 1994. Notarized appraisal report to Lyon County Historical Society, October 17.

Kondakov, Nikodim Pavlovich. 1927. *The Russian Icon*. Translated by Ellis H. Minns. Oxford: Clarendon.

Kovel, Ralph, and Terry Kovel. 1973. *Know Your Antiques: How to Recognize and Evaluate Any Antique—Large or Small—Like an Expert*. New York: Crown Publishers.

Kuranz, R. L. 1986. Technique for transferring ink from a written line to a thin layer chromatography sheet. *Journal of Forensic Sciences* 31 (2): 655–57.

Langton, Jane. 1984a. *Emily Dickinson Is Dead*. New York: St. Martin's Press.

———. 1984b. Emily Dickinson's appearance and likenesses with special consideration of the Abromson photograph. Typescript, 4 vols.

Lay, Loretta. 1994. Note to Joe Nickell (from Grey House Books, London), February 8.

Leeman, Sue. 2001. Expert says "lost" score is Mozart's. *Buffalo News,* March 16.

Leyda, Jay. 1960. *The Years and Hours of Emily Dickinson,* 2 vols. New Haven, Conn.: Yale University Press.

Linder, Seth, Caroline Morris, and Keith Skinner. 2003. *Ripper Diary: The Inside Story*. Stroud, England: Sutton Publishing.

Lofaro, Michael A. 1978. *The Life and Adventures of Daniel Boone*. Lexington: University Press of Kentucky.

Lombardo, Daniel. 1986. *Tales of Amherst*. Amherst, Mass.: Jones Library.

Longsworth, Polly. 1990. *The World of Emily Dickinson*. New York: W. W. Norton.

Lynch, Don. 1992. Titanic: *An Illustrated History*. New York: Hyperion.

Lyter, Albert H., III. 2003. Report of laboratory examination (Federal Forensic Associates, Raleigh, N.C.), May 29.

MacDougall, Curtis D. 1958. *Hoaxes*. New York: Dover.

MacLean, David G. 1992. Fake Civil War tintypes discovered at antique mall. *Antique Week,* November 16.

Marshall, Logan, ed. 1912. *Sinking of the* Titanic *and Great Sea Disasters*. Philadelphia: John C. Winston. Reprinted as *Sinking of the* Titanic. Halifax, Nova Scotia: Nimbus, 1998.

Mary Shelley's lost children's story found in Italian palazzo. 1998. *Manuscript Society News* 19, no. 1 (winter): 23–24.

Mason, M. E., Jr. 1984. Letter to Joe Nickell, April 2.

McCrone, W. C. 1974. Chemical analytical study of the Vinland map. Report to Yale University Library, New Haven, Conn.

———. 1992. Letter to David Warren, January 17.

McNeil, R. J. 1994. Scanning Auger microscopy for dating of manuscript inks. *Advances in Chemistry Series,* no. 205, chap. 13, 255–69.

Mearns, David C., and Lloyd A. Dunlap. 1963. *Long Remembered.* Washington, D.C.: Library of Congress.

Meckier, Jerome. 1992. Dickens, *Great Expectations,* and the Dartmouth College notes. *Papers on Language and Literature* 28:111–32.

Meserve, F. H. 1944. *The Photographs of Abraham Lincoln,* 1st ed. New York: Harcourt, Brace.

Miers, Earl Schenck. 1960. *Lincoln Day by Day.* Reprint, Dayton, Ohio: Morningside, 1991.

Miller, J. B. 1995. Interview by Joe Nickell, March 31.

Miller, Judith, and Martin Miller. 1988. *Miller's Pocket Antiques Fact File.* New York: Viking.

Mills, John FitzMaurice. 1973. *Treasure Keepers.* Garden City, N.Y.: Doubleday.

Naifeh, Steven, and Gregory White Smith. 1988. *The Mormon Murders: A True Story of Greed, Forgery, Deceit, and Death.* New York: Weidenfeld & Nicolson.

Nickell, Joe. 1980. The two "Will Wests": A new verdict. *Journal of Police Science and Administration* 8, no. 4 (December): 406–13.

———. 1989. Dartmouth's Dickensian notes: An investigative report. Prepared for Jerome Meckier, December 11. Cited in Meckier 1992.

———. 1990. *Pen, Ink, & Evidence: A Study of Writing and Writing Materials for the Penman, Collector and Document Detective.* Lexington: University Press of Kentucky.

———. 1991. Erasures and corrections in historic documents: An overview. Paper presented to the 49th Annual Conference of the American Society of Questioned Document Examiners, Lake Buena Vista, Fla., August 3–8.

———. 1992a. A brief history of graphology (chap. 2) and Handwriting: Identification science and graphological analysis contrasted (chap. 4). In *The Write Stuff: Evaluations of Graphology.* Edited by Barry L. Beyerstein and Dale F. Beyerstein, 23–29, 42–52. Buffalo, N.Y.: Prometheus Books.

———. 1992b. Assassin's double. In *Mysterious Realms: Probing Paranormal, Historical, and Forensic Enigmas.* With John F. Fischer. Buffalo, N.Y.: Prometheus Books. (Chapter 10 was adapted from this source.)

———. 1993a. The alleged diary of "Jack the Ripper": A summary assessment of its provenance, internal evidence, and physical composition. Prepared for Kenneth W. Rendell, August 29. (Chapter 2 is adapted in part from this source.)

——. 1993b. A likeness of Emily? The investigation of a questioned photograph. *Emily Dickinson International Society Bulletin* 5, no. 2 (November–December): 1–3, 15. (Chapter 8 was adapted from this source.)

——. 1993c. Stationers' crests: A catalog of more than 200 embossed paper marks 1835–1901. *Manuscripts* 45, no. 3 (summer): 199–216.

——. 1994a. *Camera Clues: A Handbook for Photographic Investigation.* Lexington: University Press of Kentucky.

——. 1994b. Examination of several questioned historical documents. Report to Steve Barnett, May 8.

——. 1994c. A likeness of an old mill. In *Elijah Craig and His Paper Mill,* by Ann Bolton Bevins et al., 21–26. Georgetown, Ky.: Georgetown and Scott County Museum.

——. 1995. "Alien Autopsy" hoax. *Skeptical Inquirer* 19, no. 6 (November–December): 17–19.

——. 1996a. *Detecting Forgery: Forensic Investigation of Documents.* Lexington: University Press of Kentucky.

——. 1996b. Kaplan "Lincoln" photograph: Dissenting opinions. *Journal of Forensic Identification* 46, no. 6 (November–December): 702–14. (Chapter 9 is adapted from this source.)

——. 1997. The "Jack the Ripper diary." *International Journal of Forensic Document Examiners* 3, no. 1 (January–March): 59–63. (Chapter 2 is adapted in part from this source.)

——. 1998. *Inquest on the Shroud of Turin: Latest Scientific Findings.* Amherst, N.Y.: Prometheus Books.

——. 2001. *Real-Life X-Files: Investigating the Paranormal.* Lexington, Ky.: University Press of Kentucky.

——. 2002. Authentication report (June 12, 2001) publ. as Appendix A to Crafts 2002, 283–315.

——. 2003a. *Pen, Ink, & Evidence: A Study of Writing and Writing Materials for the Penman, Collector and Document Detective.* Reprint, New Castle, Del.: Oak Knoll Books.

——. 2003b. The strange case of Pat the Ripper. *Skeptical Inquirer* 27, no. 2 (March–April): 55–58.

——. 2004. Searching for Hannah Crafts. In Gates and Robbins 2004, 406–16.

——. 2005. *Unsolved History: Investigating Mysteries of the Past.* Lexington: University Press of Kentucky.

——. 2006a. The case of the missing edition. *CEA Critic* 68, nos. 1–2 (fall–winter): 111–16.

——. 2006b. Postmortem on "Alien Autopsy." *Skeptical Briefs* 16, no. 2 (June): 5–6.

——. 2007. *Relics of the Christ.* Lexington: University Press of Kentucky.

Nickell, Joe, and John F. Fischer. 1999. *Crime Science: Methods of Forensic Detection.* Lexington: University Press of Kentucky.

Norton, Linda E. 1984. The exhumation and identification of Lee Harvey Oswald. *Journal of Forensic Sciences* 29, no. 1 (January): 19–38.

O'Hara, Charles E. 1973. *Fundamentals of Criminal Investigation,* 3rd ed. Springfield, Ill.: Charles C. Thomas.

Osborn, Albert S. 1978. *Questioned Documents,* 2nd ed. Montclair, N.J.: Patterson Smith. (Orig. pub. 1929.)

Ostendorf, Lloyd. 1994a. An open letter from Lloyd Ostendorf. *Lincoln Ledger* 3, no. 1 (May): 10–11.

———. 1994b. Personal communication to Joe Nickell, December 27.

Oswald, Robert L. 1967. *Lee: A Portrait of Lee Harvey Oswald by His Brother.* New York: Coward-McCann.

Oswald is alive. 1980. *Globe,* October 21.

Owens, Maureen Casey. 1993. Report to Kenneth W. Rendell, August 30.

Palmquist, Peter E., ed. 1991. *Photographers: A Sourcebook for Historical Research.* Brownsville, Calif.: Carl Mautz Publishing.

Penry, Jacques. 1971. *Looking at Faces and Remembering Them: A Guide to Facial Identification.* London: Elek Books.

Peterson, Harold L. 1975. *How Do You Know It's Old?* New York: Charles Scribner's Sons.

Pokorski, Doug. 1995. Negative results: Vein comparison shows photo not of young Lincoln. *State Journal-Register* (Springfield, Ill.), January 15.

Posner, Gerald L. 1994. *Case Closed: Lee Harvey Oswald and the Assassination of JFK.* New York: Anchor Books.

Rawlins, Ray. 1970. *Four Hundred Years of British Autographs.* London: Dent.

———. 1977. *The Guinness Book of World Autographs.* Enfield, Middlesex, England: Guinness Superlatives.

Reed, Stephen R. 2001. Letter (as mayor of Harrisburg, Pa.) to George E. Scott, October 4.

Rendell, Kenneth. 1978. The detection of forgeries. In *Autographs and Manuscripts: A Collector's Manual.* Edited by Edmund Berkeley Jr., 73–91. New York: Scribner's.

———. 1993. Report on the diary of Jack the Ripper. Reprinted in Harrison 1993, 305–12.

———. 1994. *Forging History: The Detection of Fake Letters and Documents.* Norman: University of Oklahoma Press.

———. 2001. Letter report to Laurence Kirshbaum, April 26.

Reward is offered for $4 million violin. 1995. *Buffalo News,* November 3.

Ribadeneira, Diego. 1998. Ancient texts shine new light on Taoism: Find is likened to Dead Sea Scrolls. *Boston Globe,* reprinted in *Arizona Republic,* May 30.

Romer, Grant B. 1994. Artifact description of Kaplan daguerreotype. *Journal of Forensic Identification* 44 (4): 430–36.

Ruane, Michael E. 1996. Smithsonian acquires long-lost photo of noted abolitionist. *Buffalo News,* December 20.

Rubinfine, Joseph. 1993. Letter to Joe Nickell, July 6.

Russia to display what it says is a fragment of Hitler's skull. 2000. *Buffalo News,* April 24.

Safer, Morley. 1995. Stradivari. *60 Minutes,* CBS television, April 9.

A scandal in America, part 2. 1988. *Book Collector* 37 (spring): 12–18.

Schmemann, Serge. 1997. Dead Sea Scroll gives up its secret. *New York Times,* reprinted in *Arizona Republic,* August 2.

Scott, George E. 2002. Authenticating William H. Bonney's letters, correspondence, Pat Garrett's and J. W. Bell's handwritings. *BTKOG [Billy the Kid Outlaw Gang] Gazette,* March. Photocopy provided by Scott.

———. 2004a. Letter to Joe Nickell, February 15.

———. 2004b. Letter to Joe Nickell, June 11.

*Sears, Roebuck & Co. Catalog No. 110.* 1900. Chicago: Sears, Roebuck.

Sewall, Richard B. 1974. *The Life of Emily Dickinson.* New York: Farrar, Straus and Giroux.

Shurr, William H. 1983. *The Marriage of Emily Dickinson.* Lexington: University Press of Kentucky.

Sillitoe, Linda, and Allen Roberts. 1988. *Salamander: The Story of the Mormon Forgery Murders.* Salt Lake City, Utah: Signature Books.

Smith, Robert. 1993a. Interview by Joe Nickell, Chicago, August 21.

———. 1993b. Rebuttal (following report of Kenneth W. Rendell). In Harrison 1993, 313–17.

Smith, Virginia. 1995. Report to Joe Nickell, January 3.

Soderman, Henry, and John J. O'Connell. 1952. *Modern Criminal Investigation.* New York: Funk & Wagnalls.

Sorokin, Boris. 1983. Personal communication to Joe Nickell, March 9.

Stokes, Trey. 1995. Personal communication, August 29–31.

*The Story of the Typewriter, 1873–1923.* 1923. Herkimer, N.Y.: Herkimer County Historical Society.

Streitfeld, D. 1993. "Diary" of Jack the Ripper canceled as hoax. *Washington Post,* September 8.

Taylor, John. 1979. *Icon Painting.* New York: Mayflower Books.

Taylor, John M. 1968. *From the White House Inkwell: American Presidential Autographs.* Rutland, Vt.: Charles E. Tuttle.

Taylor, Priscilla S., ed. 1984. *Manuscripts: The First Twenty Years.* Westport, Conn.: Greenwood Press.

Thomas, Robert McG. 1996. Charles Hamilton Jr., 82, an expert on handwriting [obituary]. *New York Times,* December 13.

Thornton, John J., and Edward F. Rhodes. 1986. Brief history of questioned document examination. *Identification News,* January 7.

Throckmorton, George J. 1988. A forensic analysis of twenty-one Hofmann documents. In Sillitoe and Roberts 1988, 531–52.

Tillotson, Kathleen. 1987. *Great Expectations* and the Dartmouth College notes. *Dickensian* 82 (spring): 17–18.

Triplett, Frank (with Mrs. Jesse James and Mrs. Zerelda Samuel). 1882. *The Life, Times and Treacherous Death of Jesse James.* St. Louis: n.p.

Unknown Goya canvas discovered. 1996. *Buffalo News,* March 9.

Utley, Robert M. 1989. *Billy the Kid: A Short and Violent Life.* Lincoln: University of Nebraska Press.

Vrzalik, Larry F., and Michael Minor. 1991. *From the President's Pen: An Illustrated Guide to Presidential Autographs.* Austin, Tex.: State House Press.

Waldon, Ann. 1983. *True or False? Amazing Art Forgeries.* New York: Hastings House.

Walker, Aidan. 1997. *Identifying Wood.* Edison, N.J.: Chartwell Books.

Walker, Odell. 1995. Letter to Joe Nickell, January 16.

Walsh, Charles E. 1995. Interview by Joe Nickell, May 18.

Warren, David. 1990–1991. Has Lincoln's final draft of Gettysburg Address been found? *Lincoln Legacy* 4, nos. 3 and 4 (fall 1990, winter 1991): 1–18.

Webber, Tammy. 1999. Ancient works of Archimedes to be restored and studied. *Buffalo News,* November 6.

*Webster's New Universal Encyclopedia.* 1997. New York: Barnes & Noble.

Widener, Ralph W. 1982. *Confederate Monuments: Enduring Symbols of the South and the War Between the States.* Washington, D.C.: Andromeda Associates.

Wills, David. 1863. Letter to A. Lincoln, November 23. Original in Library of Congress. Cited in Warren 1990–1991, 10.

Wilson, Colin. 1989. *Clues! A History of Forensic Detection.* N.p.: Warner Books.

Wolff, Camille, ed. 1995. *Who Was Jack the Ripper? A Collection of Present-Day Theories and Observations.* London: Grey House Books.

Worrall, Simon. 2002. *The Poet and the Murderer: A True Story of Literary Crime and the Art of Forgery.* New York: Dutton.

Yeager, Wayne. 1995. Letter to Joe Nickell, February 28.

Yeoman, R. S. 2005. *The Official Red Book, A Guide Book of United States Coins,* 59th ed. Edited by Kenneth Bressett. Atlanta: Whitman Publishing.

Zeller, Bob. 2002. Artifakes. *Civil War Times,* October, 42–47.

# INDEX

*Italic* page numbers refer to illustrations